terra australis 44

Terra Australis reports the results of archaeological and related research within the south and east of Asia, though mainly Australia, New Guinea and island Melanesia — lands that remained terra australis incognita to generations of prehistorians. Its subject is the settlement of the diverse environments in this isolated quarter of the globe by peoples who have maintained their discrete and traditional ways of life into the recent recorded or remembered past and at times into the observable present.

List of volumes in Terra Australis

terra australis 44

An Archaeology of Early Christianity in Vanuatu

Kastom and Religious Change on
Tanna and Erromango, 1839–1920

James L. Flexner

Australian
National
University

PRESS

ANU PRESS

Published by ANU Press
The Australian National University
Acton ACT 2601 Australia
Email: anupress@anu.edu.au
This title is also available online at press.anu.edu.au

National Library of Australia Cataloguing-in-Publication entry

Creator:	Flexner, James Lindsey, author.
Title:	An archaeology of early Christianity in Vanuatu : kastom and religious change on Tanna and Erromango 1839 - 1920 / James L. Flexner.
ISBN:	9781760460747 (paperback) 9781760460754 (ebook)
Series:	Terra Australis ; 44.
Subjects:	Archaeology and religion--Vanuatu. Christian antiquities--Vanuatu. Tanna Island (Vanuatu)--Church history--19th century. Eromanga (Vanuatu)--Church history--19th century.
Dewey Number:	200.99595

Cover design and layout by ANU Press. Cover photograph by James L. Flexner.

Contents

Smol Toktok

Long 1839, John Williams ibin fol daon long Dillon's Bay long Erromango. Ded blong hem wetem James Harris ibin jenjim histri blong New Hebrides big wan. Afta samting ia, taem blong ol fes misnari we oli bin kam long ol aelans blong saot ibin stat. Ol misnari ibin kam long New Hebrides, mo fulup man mo woman ibin kam insaed long jioj. Be hemi long taem we ol man oli faetim jioj olsem. Sam man ibin mixim jioj wetem kastom olsem. Histri blong jioj long 1800s i olsem.

Blong tingbaot histri blong jioj long Vanuatu, hemi gud blong tingbaot sam difren tingting. Igat ol difren staels blong histri blong bifo. Sam histri istap insaed ol buks, sam we oli bin raetem long 1800s. Be igat wan difren kaen blong histri we istap insaed long graon. Buk ia, hemi wan buk blong 'akiologi'. Akiologi hemi wan saens blong save sam niu wes blong save wanem ibin hapin long histri, we i yusim ol difren samting we istap long graon.

Blong save wanem ibin hapin long histri blong ol misnari blong Presbyterian Jioj long 1800s mo earli 1900s, yu save ridim sam samting long ol buks blong olgeta. Be olsem, yu save lukim akiologi blong olgeta blong save wan difren we blong save wanem ibin hapin evri de. Akiologi i kivim yu janis we yu save luk long graon, mo yu save lukim wan samting we ol man oli no bin raetim long ol buks. Istap long graon nomo. Akiologi i yusim doti blong bifo blong save wanem nao ibin hapin bifo.

Buk ia, hemi wan histri blong wan projek blong five ias we Vanuatu Kaljoral Senta (VKS) wetem Dr James Flexner we i wok long saed blong akiologi blong Australian Nasonal University (ANU) i bin mekem tugeta. Oli bin wok long Erromango mo Tanna. Oli bin lukaotem ol olfala ples blong ol misnaris mo man ples long 1800s. Oli bin lukim long sam kastom mo tabu saets olsem blong save wanem ol bilif blong ol man ples bifo ol misnari ibin kam long New Hebrides. Oli bin dig long graon long faev haos blong misnari (tu long Tanna, mo tri long Erromango), mo oli bin dig long wan kastom vilej blong bifo long Tanna. Afta, oli bin kaontim evri smol pis blong ol samting blong bifo we oli bin katimaot long graon. Naoia, ol samting we oli bin faenem, istap long VKS long Port Vila. Narfala pat blong projek, hemi wan studi blong ol museum long Scotland, Canada, mo Australia mo sam narfala ples we ikat sam samting blong New Hebrides.

Wan diskovri blong projek, hemi blong talem ol waes we ol samting we hemi 'material', hemi bin mek wan impotan wok long histri blong taem we ol man mo woman blong New Hebrides, oli bin kam insaed long jioj. Ol misnari, ibin talem stori blong Gospel long ol man mo woman, be oli bin askim olgeta blong jenjim kalja blong olgeta olsem. Oli sud jenjim ol bilifs blong kastom. Be olsem, oli mas jenjim ol nambas mo gras sket wetem kaliko mo aelan dres. Oli sud jenjim ol waes blong bildim haos, plantim katin, mo mekem kaekae. Be sipos yu luk long histri ia, sam samting ino bin jenj nating. Ol man ples long Vanuatu tidae istap kontinu wetem ol stael blong haos mo kaekae blong olgeta. Sam samting blong kastom istap yet long laef blong ol aelans.

Las wan, we hemi impotan big wan, ol man ples long Tanna mo Erromango, oli bin holem taet long kastom even long taem we fulup samting ibin jenj long aelan blong olgeta. Fulup man ibin ko long jioj, be ol man mo woman istap kipim sam samting blong kastom, olsem ol danis, bilif, tabu ston, mo ol narfala samting we hemi wan pat blong kastom. Bigfala tingting blong projek i olsem: Christianity ino bin kaekae kastom. Kastom ibin kaekae Christianity, mo kastom istap strong yet long Vanuatu tidae. Christianity, hemi bin kam wan pis blong kastom blong planti man mo woman long Vanutau.

Preface

For the reader who hasn't skipped directly to the 'meat' of the argument in this book, I would like to offer a brief caveat about what I know about Vanuatu. The idea is to outline my own 'historicity' (Ballard 2014) within a long-term field research project that is now coming to an end. What consisted of many months of time mapping, walking, discussing, excavating, collecting, analysing, but also inhabiting, sharing meals, laughing, sleeping in and around the ruins of mission stations in Vanuatu will be presented as a *fait accompli*, an 'objective' analysis of archaeological data.

In the pages that follow, I will make assertions about Melanesian people, *kastom*, and indigenous practices. Since excessive reflexivity can become tedious and even distracting in a technical monograph like this one, I want to make this clear at the outset so I don't have to revisit it throughout: I am not Melanesian. My assertions are not based on an authority derived from identity. They are based on my observations from time spent living with Melanesian people in villages on Tanna and Erromango, and respectfully asking many questions, as well as my knowledge of the archaeological record of the places where I've worked. Of course my experiences of living in Vanuatu shape my interpretations of the past on these islands. The daily pattern of archaeological fieldwork (carefully digging through layers of sediment, sieving for finds, mapping, drawing, photographing, noting; the variable rhythms of excitement at finding something new, extreme tedium at finding the same old stuff, or worse, nothing) was matched with the daily patterns of village life (eating yams, drinking kava, speaking Bislama, playing football, sleeping under a thatched roof). At the same time, I have made all possible efforts not to romanticise or unduly project such patterns into the past uncritically. Much of what I am able to say is thanks to the many Melanesian people listed in the Acknowledgements.

Claims to knowledge about Melanesia are also based on a century or more of ethnological observations, first by the missionaries who are one of the foci of this book (e.g. Gray 1892; Inglis 1854; Watt 1895), and later by professional ethnographers of various sorts (Bonnemaison 1994; Guiart 1956; Humphreys 1926; Lindstrom 1990). What follows are not meant to be incontestable, final statements about Tannese and Erromangan *kastom*. This probably wouldn't be possible anyway, and others have noted the ways that knowledge in these islands is contested in various fields, particularly on Tanna (Adams 1987; Lindstrom 1982). I want to make very clear that I am not claiming to have a full insider's knowledge of the cultures discussed in this book, especially in the contemporary context. Ni-Vanuatu reading this book can and should be able to contradict my ideas and interpretations. Likely they will.

Likewise, I will be presenting some ideas about Western people, and particularly the Scottish and Scots-derived missionaries who settled on Erromango and Tanna from the 1850s onwards. Ironically, I can count Scotland among the places of my ancestors, from both sides of my family. But it is just one place in Europe among many that my ancestors came from before emigrating to North America. Thus I don't feel any special ability to comment on British identities from an 'emic' perspective, particularly 'Scottishness'. I don't own a kilt, nor can I play the bagpipes. I do enjoy Single Malt Whisky, and my Scottish middle name (Lindsey) is occasionally materialised in a tie or scarf received from my parents at the holidays. But this is not the basis of my interpretations about missionaries' relationships to British 'civilisation' or Scottishness. Here again, I draw on some of the deeply insightful writings about European culture in social theory (for example, Foucault 1988; Gilbert 2004; Poovey 1995; Weber 2002[1905]). Likewise, Scottishness has its own rich literature, particularly Scotland as seen from the Lower Provinces of British North America from which so many of the missionaries in the southern New Hebrides originated (e.g. Symonds 2003; Vance 2005, 2011).

What I do have an authoritative sense of are the archaeological data that are presented in this work. If I had to pick a tribe that I represent, it is *archaeologists*. Like other tribes, we don't all agree all the time on the best ways to do our work, in theory, method, or in working with local communities. What follows represents a first attempt to work through some of the big and small questions that arise when studying the historical archaeology of religious change in a Melanesian society, and the historical archaeology of the missionaries who were agents of that change.

Note that I leave the question of religious truth ('Big T Truth', as it was called in my Catholic High School religion classes) to the side in this analysis. Whether God exists, descended to Earth in human form, was crucified and returned to heaven to forgive us our sins is not really a hypothesis that could be tested with this material. Certainly for the missionaries who I write about, these truths were above questioning. The truths of Christian faith led them to travel to the ends of the Earth. Many died trying to bring this knowledge to other people. Christian belief is also true for the descendants of the early Melanesian converts who are equally part of the story. In that context, the truths of Christianity exist alongside the *kastom* truths of magic stones, *tabu* places, and stories that are equally part of the Melanesian cosmos.

The question of belief becomes a thorny one for anthropologists, as our acceptance of local realities in the fields where we do our research sometimes appears to be at odds with the rational, secular humanist project that many of us see ourselves as working at. If we start from a premise of accepting cultural beliefs and experiences as real for the people doing the believing and experiencing ('cultural relativism'), where do we place ourselves in relation to that premise? Are there limits to the extent to which we can place different epistemologies (scientific; Christian; Melanesian) on equal footings? What happens when these epistemologies overlap, as they must for many people (Barker 2012)? In this book, I follow from Fowles' (2013) analysis of this dilemma in attempting to understand Melanesian *kastom* and its relationship with Christianity as it emerged in the 19th century on its own terms (see Chapter 1). The goal is to explain what certain beliefs do or did in terms of patterns of human behaviours, social structure, and cultural evolution. The story is told from the perspective above all of the materials from the era of early Christianity in the New Hebrides. If this book provides a small amount of progress in explaining the evolution of religious beliefs in colonial societies, then it has done its job.

A Note on Place Names

A note on the use of Vanuatu and New Hebrides: New Hebrides is a colonial name, given to the islands by Cook in 1774 (Beaglehole, ed. 1969), while Vanuatu is the name of an independent nation established in 1980. They refer to the same group of islands, and as such will be used somewhat interchangeably here. I will use New Hebrides when discussing colonial-era phenomena, and Vanuatu to refer to the land in abstract, as well as contemporary places and people (ni-Vanuatu).

There are other cases where European names overlie indigenous ones, a result of a palimpsest of toponymy derived from explorers, traders, missionaries, and contemporary political landscapes (see Jolly 2009). In general, I try to follow the names that would have been used in the missionary period, making reference to local toponymy where possible. For example, the village called 'Williams Bay' by Erromangan people today after the first martyr missionary was only named as such after a 2009 reconciliation ceremony. Before that it was Dillon's Bay, named after a sandalwood trader, and the area has for much longer been referred to as Umpongkor. I generally use Dillon's Bay, but may use the indigenous toponym to refer to the broader Melanesian landscape in which European settlement was embedded.

Acknowledgements

Even though my name is the only one on the cover of this book, as with so many archaeological projects there is a cast of hundreds that deserve my sincere thanks for making this work possible. I am honoured to have worked with so many worthy collaborators whose tireless efforts support so many projects like this one. So for all who were a part of this work, I say *tangyu tumas, kombolongi tama, tanak asori*, thank you!

I must thank the main funders and institutions that supported this research. Initial funding for the project came from Lenfest Grants from Washington and Lee University in 2011 and 2012 when I was visiting lecturer in Sociology and Anthropology. The main financial support for the research was an Australian Research Council DECRA fellowship (DE130101703) hosted in the School of Archaeology and Anthropology at The Australian National University (ANU), my base from 2013–2015. The Vanuatu Cultural Centre (Vanuatu Kaljoral Senta/VKS) provided support for my work in Vanuatu. I am especially thankful for the work done through the regional VKS office on Tanna, and the network of *filwokas* on Tanna and Erromango.

It is with a great deal of pleasure that I thank the many individuals who have helped me along the way, professionally and otherwise. Through a suggestion from Jack Golson, Matthew Spriggs offered me the initial invitation to start a project on mission archaeology in Vanuatu as a postdoctoral endeavour. Spriggs is a valued mentor, collaborator, and colleague whose continuing collaboration in Vanuatu research is heartily appreciated. Stuart Bedford has likewise been a valued collaborator and source of ideas and knowledge about Vanuatu archaeology. Martin Jones taught me everything I needed to know about buildings archaeology, and I owe him a great deal of thanks for the richness of the work on the Lenakel Church.

At the VKS, I want to thank my colleagues in the archaeology department: Richard Shing, Iarowai Philp, McKerras Numa, and particularly Edson Willie. Credit for the shell analysis of this project goes entirely to Edson, who also contributed to fieldwork on Tanna. I also want to thank the Director of the VKS for arranging my permit. Special thanks to Henline Mala, who works tirelessly to help visitors arrange visas and other bureaucratic necessities. Kaitip Kami organised export permits for artefact analyses carried out in Canberra. In the National Archives of Vanuatu, I want to thank Anne Naupa and Agustin Tevi for facilitating access to mission lands records. Francis Hickey has been great for a yarn and a shell of kava on many occasions. At the TAFEA Kaljoral Senta (TKS) on Tanna, I offer my sincere thanks to Jacob Kapere, who helped organise my fieldwork and has generally helped the project along. Jimmy Takaronga Kuautonga was very supportive and helpful, particularly in setting up public lectures at the TKS. Thanks to Jean Pascal Wahe Kuren, particularly for his technical knowhow. Joel Iau collaborated with our fieldwork at Waisisi and generally offered a friendly face on Tanna.

Special thanks go to many people on Erromango and Tanna. They make this project possible, and the overall project is dedicated to those communities where fieldwork took place. I name as many people who helped with the project as I can here, though I'm sure I have missed some. I offer my apologies to anyone who was left off the list. To the communities at Dillon's Bay, Cook's Bay, and Port Narvin on Erromango, *kombolongi tama!* Jerry Taki, whose tireless work as a VKS *filwoka* made my work on that island possible, deserves very special thanks. It is to Jerry that I owe any ability to talk about Erromangan *kastom* (though I take all the blame where I missed or misinterpreted things). Thanks also to the other Erromango *filwokas*, Malon Lovo who helped with our work at Dillon's Bay, and Annie Lui who worked with us at Potnuma. At Dillon's Bay,

I thank the following people who helped with the project as excavators, knowledge keepers, and hosts: Thomas Poki ('*jif blong problems*'), Manuel Naling, Harrison Netai, Dick Mete, Sempet Naritantop, Oliver Nombuat, Georges Niura, Malon Narvu, Gibson Uswo, William Natngo, Charlie Usau, Jon Umbkoin, Joseph Navoi, and Pastor Robi White. At Port Narvin, thanks go to Peter Nowai, Simon Melkum, Erick Melkum, Solomon Potnilo, Esron Melkum, Stanley Simo, James Netai, Charlie Nampil, and Jean-Pierre Livu. Thanks to Anna Naupa for support and interest via the Erromango Cultural Association.

On Tanna, a general thank you goes to the communities of Lenakel, Port Resolution, Kwamera, Kwaraka, and Waisisi. In Lenakel, I must thank Peter Marshall, who was instrumental in welcoming me to the community and helping to launch this project, as well as to Evelyn who was our chief cook, Thomas who helped with early survey work, and Brownie who offered comic relief when needed. Iavis Nikiatu was also a great supporter of the project, and special thanks go to Elizabeth. We enjoyed many good meals at Joy Beach Café! Shem Noukout and Natato Philip were also involved closely with the site survey in Lenakel. In Port Resolution thanks go to George Turiak, Harry Iabatu, Pastor Isak Fai, Samson Kwanbikin, John Turu, and David Karawi. Werry, Monique, and the staff of the Port Resolution Yacht Club provided great lodging, food, and company. Fieldwork in Kwamera and Kwaraka was facilitated by chief Samson Ieru, who has been integral to some of the really important discoveries from the area. Initial survey in Kwamera included Joseph Narkahau, Larin Pop, Steven Saba, Yati Kwanange, Andre Saba, Pamu Isak, and Daniel Kamisak. Robert Steven and family hosted us for two of our field seasons in Kwamera. Fieldwork thanks to Andrew Yoko, Uli Silas, Daniel Nirwa, Dick Samson Ieru, Kumei, Andrew Ieru, Nahi, and Richard Kapuku, Johnson Saba, Lilien Saba, Narko Samson. Many others joined the work for a day or two here and there. Chiefs Joe Hauia and Mosman both helped with fieldwork, and organised other aspects of our work. Special thanks to Rehab, Nringa, and the mamas who provided our room and board. Alexon K. showed us around Itapua. In Waisisi, our fieldwork team was joined by Obed Butal, Thomson Laiwaka, Diksen, Moses Lamai, Kahi, Tausikatua, and Yakoli. These and other community members on Tanna and Erromango contributed so much to this project, and I am eternally grateful for their hospitality, welcome, and generosity. I consider myself extraordinarily lucky to collaborate with these remarkable communities.

I have many people to thank from museums and archives, who facilitated research for those portions of the project. I am humbled by the work of library, museum, and archive staff as keepers of knowledge. In roughly geographical order (from closer to further away from Canberra), my thanks go to Kylie Moloney from the Pacific Manuscripts Bureau; staff of the State Library of New South Wales; Robin Torrence, Yvonne Carillo-Huffman, Logan Metcalf, and Kirk Huffman at the Australian Museum (and I note that my work at the Australian Museum is supported by a Leo Fleischmann Fellowship for 2015–2016); Chantal Knowles and Nick Hadnutt at the Queensland Museum; staff of the State Library of Queensland; Fuli Pereira, Kolokesa U Māhina-Tuai, Tessa Smallwood, and Shaun Higgins at the Auckland War Memorial Museum; Jo Birks, Stephen Innes and William Hamill at the Western Pacific Archives in Auckland; Moira White and Jamie Metzger at the Otago Museum; Yvonne Wilkie and Mychael Tymons at the Knox Archives of the Presbyterian Church of Aotearoa-New Zealand; staff of the Hocken Library; Arthur Smith, Ken Lister, and Molly Minnick at the Royal Ontario Museum; Bob Anger of the Archives of the Presbyterian Church in Canada; Barbara Lawson at the Redpath Museum; Peter Larocque and colleagues at the New Brunswick Museum; Roger Lewis at the Nova Scotia Museum; Gabriele Weiss at the Weltmuseum; Eve Haddow, Ross Irving, Margaret Wilson, and Antje Denner of the National Museum of Scotland; staff of the National Library of Scotland; Patricia Allan from Museums Glasgow; Sally-Anne Coupar and Lizzie O'Neill from the Hunterian Museum; and Neil Curtis and Louise Wilkie at University of Aberdeen Museums.

At ANU, I would like to offer my personal thanks to the staff of the School of Archaeology and Anthropology, especially the office staff for their patience and support. Special thanks to Matiu Prebble, Jack Fenner, Dougald O'Reilly, Phil Piper, Duncan Wright, Cate Freiman, Ash Lenton, Carly Schuster, Chris Ballard, Bronwen Douglas, Matt Tomlinson, Margaret Jolly, Latu Latai, Antje Lubcke, Mathieu Leclerc, Ben Shaw, Bec Jones, Rose Whitau, Tim Maloney, Eve Haddow, Michelle Richards, Joakim Goldhahn, and Sally May (from whose kitchen table I wrote much of this book while housesitting), among many others who have shared thoughts, stories, food, drink, and fellowship throughout my time working on this project. I would also like to thank colleagues from other institutions who have been supportive and helpful in various ways, including Monty Lindstrom (who provided helpful comments on an early draft of Chapter 3), Howard Van Trease, Patrick Kirch, Frédérique Valentin, Angela Middleton, Ian Smith, Mark McCoy, Mara Mulrooney, Guillaume Molle, Christophe Sand, Peter White, Colleen Morgan, Andrew Roddick, Jillian Swift, Tsim Schneider, Lee Panich, Janice Adamson, Penny Crook, and Martin Gibbs. Special thanks to Phil Evans who took time to do the timber identification for the Lenakel Church. A huge thank you to the student volunteers who spent time in the field: Andrew Lorey (who also transcribed the Gray diary quoted in Chapter 4), Craig Shapiro, Rob Williams (who spotted the adze blade fragments among the stones in Anuikaraka), and Helen Alderson. Thanks to Andrew Ball for his work on the ceramic assemblage from Imua.

Finally, to my family and close friends I offer my deepest thanks for their interest and support over the course of my career. My parents particularly were there as I was starting down this path, and I hope everyone can begin to see where my work has taken me after these years of travelling all over the world. Thanks to all the friends who offered a couch to sleep on as I was travelling to or from the field. Dogs Otter and Bunyip have been great research companions (mostly), and our long walks in Virginia and Australia have helped me work through some of the tougher problems I explore in this text. Thanks buddies, even if you can't read this. Last but definitely not least, I offer my sincere appreciation to my wife, Karen, who has been a source of commendable patience and inspiration for almost the entire duration of the project, who has dealt with my long absences for fieldwork, moved to the other side of the world on my account, and put up with my piles of books and field notes being all over our house as I prepared the manuscript of this book. I dedicate this book to you, my love.

I would like to thank Sally Brockwell, Ursula Frederick, Katie Hayne, and Emily Tinker for their work copyediting and typesetting this volume. As always, while I have many people to thank for their role in supporting my work, any errors or lacunae are the author's responsibility.

List of Figures

List of Tables

Theories, Methods, and Materials

> Thus fell JOHN WILLIAMS – 'the Apostle of Polynesia' – a man who had won the most splendid reputation perhaps of any missionary since the days of the great Apostle of the Gentiles … died a martyr on that ever memorable day, NOVEMBER TWENTIETH, 1839 … and now in glory shines as the stars for ever and ever (Gordon, ed. 1863: 101).

The death of John Williams and James Harris on the beach at Dillon's Bay, Erromango, in 1839 (see Chapter 2) was a pivotal moment in the history of the New Hebrides (now Vanuatu). This event crystallised the reputation of indigenous Melanesians as hostile and inherently dangerous. The New Hebrides were characterised as a place of fear, black magic, and cannibalism (e.g. American Sunday School Union 1844; Copeland 1878). At the same time, this moment provided a rallying point for missionaries determined to 'bring light to dark isles' in the region. Thus began a century or so of mission labour in the New Hebrides, resulting in the widespread conversion of Melanesian people to Christianity (indigenous ni-Vanuatu identified as 86 per cent Christian in the most recent census; Vanuatu National Statistics Office 2009: 25).

It is an archaeological truism that many phenomena treated as historical events are in fact better understood as moments within long-term cultural *processes*. The work of Christian conversion in the New Hebrides is no exception. Conversion was part of a long-term process of accommodation, adaptation, and appropriation of European things and beliefs by Melanesian people. The process was shaped by Melanesian people in ways that allowed for a great deal of flexibility in responses to the emergence of modernity and colonialism in their islands. Religious change in these islands was not simply a result of the efforts of European missionaries, but also of the indigenous Melanesians who converted, often assisting the mission endeavour as teachers (see Miller 1978). Equally a part of this story are those people who resisted the spread of mission influence, as well as those who sought to avoid contact altogether, holding tight to *kastom* (referring to a variety of indigenous traditional beliefs and practices).

This book demonstrates that the social process of religious change in the southern New Hebrides had an inherently material basis. The focus will be the islands of Tanna and Erromango, though reference will be made to the neighbouring islands of Aneityum, Futuna, and Aniwa (Figure 1.1), especially with regards to museum collections from this period (see Chapter 5). Broad regional or inter-site patterns are relevant for explaining the overall process of conversion, while local or intra-site variability reflects the importance of rooting interpretations to specific places where conversion happened.

The Presbyterian missionaries who established the earliest permanent footholds and largest groups of converts in these islands saw spiritual conversion and transformation of the material conditions of everyday life as inherently intertwined. It was not enough for indigenous Melanesian people to learn to pray, read the Scriptures, and attend church under missionary instruction. They were also expected, to greater or lesser extents depending on the missionary, to alter their agricultural practices (towards a monocropping system that would have been more legible in capitalist terms); their habits of dress (not just to cover more skin than was customary, but also to set aside indigenous materials in favour of imported European ones); and their daily rhythms of labour, devotion, and domestic life (particularly to closer approximate expected gender roles; see Jolly and Macintyre, eds 1989; Choi and Jolly, eds 2014). Further, native converts were expected to cast off all signs of 'idolatry' and other dangerous anachronisms that could interfere with the process of true conversion (see Keane 2007).

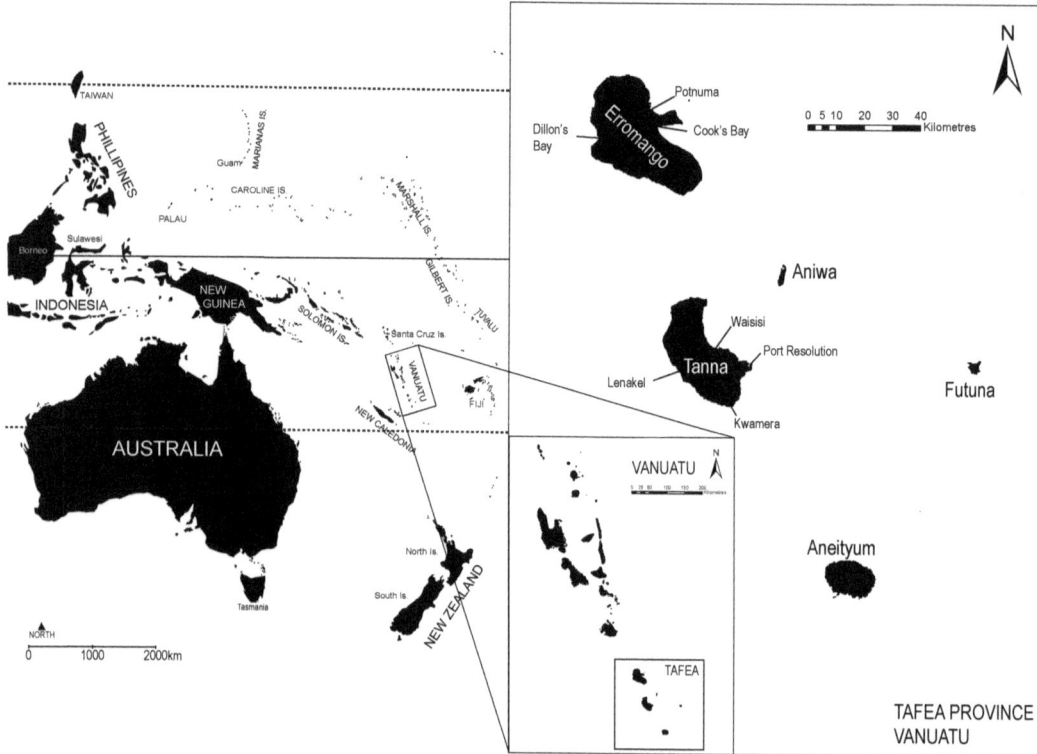

Figure 1.1 Map of southern Vanuatu, including islands and communities mentioned in the text.
Source: James Flexner

The resident Presbyterian missionaries in the New Hebrides were meant to model these changes for Melanesian people, with mission houses and missionary family life providing the civilised exemplar to which Melanesian people should aspire (though the extent to which missionaries expected native people to achieve civilisation was debatable; see Lydon 2009: 154–155). At the same time, this was not a one-sided exchange. Missionaries and their accompanying family members were deeply dependent on local and non-local resources for their survival. In the remote islands of the New Hebrides, local resources became necessary for the long-term survival of missionary families. This included material things, particularly food staples and building materials, but also the less tangible social networks of indigenous people who might be convinced to convert. Without Melanesian 'heathens', the missionary had no reason to travel to these islands. Conversion was more than a simple individual decision. Wider networks of people, places, and objects are implicated in the conversion process (Keane 2007; see also Latour 2005).

Besides simple reliance on indigenous people, missionaries themselves became localised, partaking of an increasingly Melanesian set of social and material references, especially in the later decades of the 19th century when longer-term missions were established. This was part of the wider process of indigenising Christianity in the New Hebrides (Flexner and Spriggs 2015). Mission houses, once showcases of civilisation, became increasingly filled with indigenous things.

Further, missionary collection of Melanesian 'curiosities' greatly amplified the social networks of such objects, eventually resulting in their dispersal to urban centres throughout Europe and European settler societies. Fascination with the exotic was not simply about Melanesian interest in the 'advanced' industrial material culture of Europeans. The 'primitive' things of Melanesians held an allure of their own (Thomas 1991).

Conversion had a material basis because individual or group decisions to adopt Christianity in the New Hebrides were not simply a matter of internal spiritual awakening. They resulted from a network of linked things, people, social relationships, and material encounters. To examine any one individual's decision to convert is to pull on a web of social obligations, gifting relationships, ecological variables, historical trajectories, and supernatural beliefs, all mediated through things of various sorts. This is what is meant by the idea that Christian conversion had a material basis: you can't separate the 'religious' nature of conversion from the wider social networks in which conversions took place, and these networks by necessity include objects. As Fowles (2013) suggests, any attempt to separate 'religious change' from 'culture change' more broadly is part of a modernist ideological framework in which 'purified' forms of social institutions (politics, economics, religion) are properly ordered when they do not mix. Ironically, attempts at purification if anything intensify the proliferation of hybrid or mixed categories (see also Latour 1993). Religious change *is* culture change, and vice versa.

Networks composed of missionaries and Melanesian converts, non-converts, backsliders, and uncontacted communities included the objects that Melanesians made, and those that missionaries brought with them. Archaeologists increasingly recognise that objects themselves should be included as agents within such human networks (e.g. Byrne et al. 2011; see also Latour 1987). To the networks of people and objects should be added the primary importance of place in Melanesian social networks (Rodman 1992). Places simultaneously contain the things (people and objects) of social networks, and are themselves things within the social network. In the analysis below, the importance of place (or in Bislama, Vanuatu pidgin, *ples*) will become clear in the ways that local people remember and engage with the locations where the work of conversion happened (see also Flexner 2014c). Mission sites, rather than being part of foreign, colonial '*waet man*' (white man) history, are integrated into the pantheon of traditional *kastom* sites, just as Christianity is integrated into what it means to be ni-Vanuatu today (see also Flexner and Spriggs 2015).

How and Why Did People Convert?

The history of the Presbyterian missions in the New Hebrides is not a story of 'triumph of the Gospels' as one later missionary account suggests in its title (Paton 1903). The one early missionary who had great success was John Geddie, who settled on the island of Aneityum in 1848 (Patterson 1882). As a memorial pulpit in his main station at Anelcauhat reads, 'When he arrived there were no Christians, and when he departed, there were no heathen'. Yet even Geddie's success involved a long-term process of material exchange, local demographic collapse, and gradual integration of the church into local social networks (Spriggs 1985, 2007). On the islands of Tanna and Erromango, where this study is focused, missionary progress was much slower. Attempts at starting missions on both islands repeatedly failed over the course of the 1840s through the 1860s. The first long-term stations were only established in the 1870s, and even then it was decades before the numbers of converts began to outnumber those who held onto traditional religious practices.

In other cases, there were mass conversions, as on Aniwa where John G. Paton not only survived on the *tabu* ground of the sea snake god, but also dug a freshwater well. This convinced the local chief of the potency of the foreign god, and where the chief converted, so did his followers (Paton 1907 Vol. 2: 130–196). So it appears that people in the southern New Hebrides held out against converting for a certain amount of time, and then converted; sometimes more slowly and gradually, as happened generally on Tanna and Erromango, or sometimes very rapidly, as happened on Aniwa. As we develop an account of the material networks that drove the conversion process, we have to start by asking: *why did people choose to convert at all?* What was it about the new religion of the missionaries that led people to change what they were doing eventually when, at first, people simply ignored, drove off, or even killed the would-be agents of change?

In attacking this problem, there is a related, and fundamental problem that needs to be addressed first. The name of that problem is 'religion', at least as the term is typically used in modern secular scholarship as well as popular rhetoric. In his account of the archaeology of Southwestern North American Pueblo 'doings', Fowles (2013) provides a compelling critique of the ways that scholars have tended to analyse religion as a human social institution. In orthodox models, modern subjects separate religion from other realms of behaviour (particularly political and economic behaviours). In analysing pre-modern societies and subjects, religion increasingly becomes blurred with the appropriately purified, and in modern societies separate institutions of politics and economics. In reality, however, there is immense overlap with other categories, and the secularisation narrative is a 'just-so' story that masks the complexity of both 'traditional' and 'modern' religious life and practice (Fowles 2013: 1–37). The tendency of 'religion' to blend with other aspects of life, from subsistence to chiefly politics, likewise holds true for the New Hebrides. The indigenous term *kastom* (Bislama, 'custom') is probably more appropriate to discussing local experiences of religious change. The introduction of Christianity did not change this, as the foreign faith was simply integrated into *kastom*.

If religion permeates all aspects of pre-modern societies, then what is the analytical use of religion if it can't be purified from other realms? Situations of colonial religious conversion highlight the instability of these kinds of categories. Historical archaeology shows the ways that religious conversion was part of a broader process of 'culture change' in the colonial era, particularly in North America (e.g. Arendt 2010; Lightfoot 2005; Panich and Schneider, eds 2014) and Australasia (e.g. Lydon 2009; Middleton 2008; Morrison et al. 2015). The emerging perspective eschews any simple transition of religious beliefs from 'indigenous' to 'introduced', as aspects of traditional belief and practice are always included as the spiritual realm is transformed. Likewise, there is no situation in which religion changes separately from other realms such as politics or economics. Christian conversion is inevitably accompanied by transformations in everyday life including aspects that leave material traces, such as dress, food, and domestic architecture. I recognise these 'hybrid' (*sensu* Latour 1993) realities, both in terms of the overlapping of cultural categories and the lack of a stable 'purity' of transformation in those categories. However, I frame the argument here in terms of a focus on 'religious change', specifically in terms of the umbrella term of *kastom* that I see as central to Melanesian identities, practices, and beliefs spanning the pre-Christian era through the present and into the future. In *kastom*, the supernatural cannot be separated from the everyday and mundane, so any changes in *kastom* are by necessity 'religious' changes.

As Keane (2007: 85) points out, one of the major problems missionaries can encounter when doing the work of conversion is determining what native practices are harmless 'traditions' and thus acceptable to be kept, and what are dangerous fetishisms or idolatries that need to be rooted out. It will be seen that in Melanesian *kastom*, it was nearly impossible for missionaries to separate out the religious practices that needed to be eliminated from the broader realm of traditional practice. This led missionaries to adopt a variety of strategies, from integration of customary beliefs into Christian practice, to attempts to violently crack down on native practices (the latter approach almost always failed spectacularly). In fact, crackdowns if anything solidified *kastom* as a resilient aspect of indigeneity in the colonial era. For example, the so-called 'Tanna Law' enforced by early 20th-century Presbyterian missionaries and their converts outlawed traditional kava drinking, dancing, and other practices. This repression of *kastom* resulted in widespread abandonment of church practices, a resurgence of traditional beliefs, and the emergence of the new John Frum 'cargo cult' on the island (see Bonnemaison 1994: 201–219; Lindstrom 1993).

Yet *kastom* could be remarkably flexible, employed and enacted in a variety of settings incorporating the political, economic, and religious, for different purposes in different places and different historical moments (Jolly 1994; Lindstrom 1982). Attempts to separate religion from *kastom* are doomed to failure because such categorical divisions do not exist within *kastom*. As Fowles (2013: 102) notes, Pueblo people distinguish not between sacred and secular, but 'between the sacred and the sacred'. While indigenous people in Vanuatu recognise a category of 'church' (*jioj*) in the present, within *kastom* engagements with the sacred, including Christian beliefs, are generally integrated into everyday life and habits.

Melanesian people had their own reasons for engaging with Christianity, or not. It is of course difficult to speak to the motivations of any particular person or group in the past, especially when writing across the boundaries of tradition and culture. Not growing up with *kastom*, I am still something of a neophyte, so my ideas on the topic must be taken with a grain of salt against possible alternative interpretations by people in the Melanesian communities where I worked on this project (see Preface). What I can speak to authoritatively is the archaeological evidence that speaks to the materiality (or materialisation; Bell and Geismar 2009) of conversion processes. Regardless of any individual reason (or rationalisation) for converting, and how specifically people integrated Christianity into beliefs and rhetoric about *kastom*, the archaeological evidence indicates that the process involved transformations of material things.

To say that conversion was a material process is not an end-point to the discussion. It offers a challenge to interpret why people in southern Vanuatu chose to indigenise Christianity. A number of alternatives present themselves, which will be explored in the chapters to follow. One possibility that has been offered for eventual widespread conversion is a demographic shift (Bedford, *pers. comm.*). Massive population declines following European contacts in Oceania are well established, and southern Vanuatu was no exception to this pattern (Adams 1984; Humphreys 1926; McArthur 1981; Speiser 1922; Spriggs 2007). So one possible argument is that as populations were severely decimated, people moved to coastal areas, and people whose villages had essentially been wiped out aggregated around the mission stations. Having seen most of their friends and relatives perish within a few generations, people were less resistant to the possibilities offered by the new religion of the missionaries.

Another possibility would be that the new economic opportunities offered by the mission drew people in at least initially. Fascination with European goods and the ability to engage with new trading networks led people to begin interacting with missionaries, eventually resulting in their integration into communities of Christian converts. This possibility has been suggested at the Te Puna Mission in New Zealand (Middleton 2006), though it is clear that Maori were interested in trade on their terms, including trading for things that were generally discouraged by the Church Missionary Society (CMS), such as alcohol and firearms. These two possibilities, demographic change and economic opportunity, are driven largely by external phenomena (introduced diseases and foreign trade goods).

While such factors certainly had a role to play in driving the conversion process, we also have to consider what internal factors may have shaped religious change on Erromango and Tanna. One of the clear patterns in mission historiography is that without the consent of local chiefs, missionaries had no chance of settling or surviving in Melanesian communities. So why would a chief allow a missionary to settle in his territory? The trading hypothesis offered above is an obvious answer, though it actually appears to be only a small part of the story, especially when weighed against archaeological evidence for European trade goods in native settlements (Chapter 3; Flexner et al. 2016c). Perhaps more valuable were the advantages chiefs gained over other local chiefs. The prestige of having foreign visitors in one's territory may have made missionary settlement appear worthwhile for some chiefs, especially if that settlement was assumed by Melanesians to be temporary in nature. It also appears that some chiefs sought to use missionaries to support their side or assist in brokering peace during conflicts over land and chiefly titles.

Finally, by the end of the 19th century, mission presence may have been seen as a buffer against a colonial regime that was by turns neglectful and deeply abusive of the indigenous population. This is somewhat ironic, as on Tanna in the 1860s John G. Paton, one of the unsuccessful missionaries on that island, caused several villages in the Port Resolution area to be bombarded by the British Navy in retaliation for the missionaries being driven away, an event known as the '*Curaçoa* affair' (Adams 1984: 150–167). By the time the Anglo-French 'Condominium' was established in 1906, missionaries could offer some protection by formalising land claims for indigenous communities (of course only for those who had converted), and mediating with government forces. This is one of many tensions in the missionaries' position in Melanesian society, however, as they were both forces for the incursion of state power (Flexner 2014b), and one of the early options for indigenous people hoping to deflect or resist that power.

Ultimately, conversion was a complex process shaped by multiple causal factors. All of the above were important to the indigenisation of Christianity in the southern New Hebrides. One final point about the economic basis for conversion: just as conversion could hardly be considered a 'triumph of the gospels', it was also not simply a result of Melanesians becoming good capitalists through an interest in consumer goods. Melanesians are well known for having a 'partible' view of material culture (Gosden 2004; Strathern 1990). They did not divide things and people into separate categories (nor really did or do Europeans, including Presbyterian missionaries, but that is another point to be raised later). Thus interest in foreign things was not based on their 'value' from a capitalist perspective. Rather, things were valued for the networks in which they were enmeshed. Missionary objects were fascinating for their connections to foreign people, places, ancestors, and spirits. They provided an opportunity for Melanesians to amplify the social-material networks of which they were a part.

Why Archaeology?

That conversion was a material process is abundantly evident in the mission houses, church buildings, and assemblages of artefacts found in archaeological sites on Tanna and Erromango (Chapters 2–4). That the process inflected the material culture of both sides, European and Melanesian, is evident in the relatively small number of indigenous artefacts found on mission sites, and more dramatically in the large assemblages of native things found in Western museum collections (Chapter 5). Because material things were so important to the conversion process in the New Hebrides, archaeology provides the most analytically powerful toolkit for understanding the theoretical problems outlined above.

The approach used here is archaeological in two senses. First, it is concerned with the emergence of present patterns by searching for their origins or roots in the relatively deep past (Sahlins 2004: 43; see also Olivier 2011). Second, the basis for arguing about the how and why of conversion on Erromango and Tanna is based primarily on the archaeological record, which is then informed by documentary evidence, rather than the other way around. The archaeological record includes the expected array of old buildings, stone ruins, stratified deposits, and artefacts. Oral traditions and documentary evidence are also understood archaeologically (see Beaudry, ed. 1988; Beck and Somerville 2005; David et al. 2012). Oral histories can be systematically mapped onto the landscape in the same way as stone terraces or scatters of potsherds. By the same logic, 'natural' features such as stones or trees related to *kastom* stories are an important part of the record of mapped archaeological sites (see Flexner 2014c).

There is an abundant written record for the Presbyterian New Hebrides missions, including primary sources such as missionary correspondence, land records, and published biographical works (e.g. Gordon, ed. 1863; Gunn 1914; Paton 1903; Paton 1907; Patterson 1864, 1882; Watt 1896). These works not only have to do with the work of conversion, but often include some of the earliest detailed ethnographic observations of the New Hebrides (Gray 1892; Inglis 1854; Robertson 1902; Turner 1861). While missionary descriptions of *kastom* must be taken with a grain of salt, they also contain significant grains of truth. These accounts are extremely important for understanding New Hebrides cultures in the 19th century. Missionary ethnographies must be read critically, but they can provide valuable information both about traditional cultures and the prejudices and worldviews of the missionaries themselves (Douglas 2001). Published missionary works are supplemented with other documentary evidence such as drawings, photograph albums, and magic lantern slides. There are valuable historical accounts of mission history in the New Hebrides that rely primarily on such documents that inform my scholarship (e.g. Adams 1984, 1998; Lubcke 2009; Miller 1978, 1981). Documents such as missionary correspondence provide a record of what people thought or said they were doing, but they are simultaneously 'things' in the sense that certain documents could be used to act on the world (as with land records), or to tell stories about exotic people and places (as with photograph albums).

These documentary and oral historical things are just as much a part of the archaeological record. There are more prosaic reasons for relying on an archaeological approach to better understand the conversion process on Tanna and Erromango. Colonialism was an inherently material process, in which people, domesticated and commensal organisms, objects, and ideas encircled the globe. As they moved around, these things formed new networks, at times transcending or even dissolving or hybridising cultural differences, at others creating marked resistance movements that threw such differences into starker relief. Much that happened as part of this process was simply never written down, or what was written reflected the cultural values and biases of those doing the writing as much as anything else.

Historical archaeologists have long asserted the importance of materials-based approaches to literate societies (Andrén 1998). The history of the discipline in many ways follows the broader trajectory of archaeology from antiquarian concerns (Harrington 1955), to 'processual' functionalist accounts of past societies (South 1978), structuralist approaches concerned with identifying meaning in the archaeological record (Deetz 1996), and more 'post-processual' approaches concerned with identifying conflict, resistance, and power in colonial interactions (Hall 2000). Colonialism has become one of the main concerns of modern historical archaeology, in Anglophone literature largely focused on encounters and interactions between Europeans and indigenous peoples throughout the world over the last five centuries (e.g. Cusick, ed. 1998; Gosden 2004; Kirch 1992; Lawrence and Davies 2011; Lightfoot 2005; Murray, ed. 2004; Mills 2002; Rubertone 2000; Silliman 2005).

One of the major problems that has arisen from historical archaeologies of colonialism is the issue of indigenous resistance to European colonial incursions. Recently, scholarship has converged on the issue of persistence and continuity in indigenous practices, including in part a sustained critique of issues of authenticity as they pertain to native communities (Flexner 2014a; Lydon and Burns 2010; Panich 2013; Silliman 2009). At the same time, there is an ample literature on the creativity of indigenous peoples in response to colonialism, particularly emphasising the 'hybrid' forms that emerged from indigenous appropriation, adaptation, imitation, or remixing of foreign things (e.g. Card, ed. 2013; Harrison 2006; Torrence and Clarke, eds 2000). As Silliman (2014) notes, probably the best approaches to hybridity follow the idea that the 'pure' categories (such as native/introduced) don't really exist in practice. What we are in fact observing is the proliferation of hybrids that emerges from the act of creating categories (Latour 1993; see also Flexner 2014a).

It is easily acknowledged that indigenous people did not disappear, despite 19th-century predictions to the contrary. That indigenous practices survived, adapted, and transformed through five centuries of colonial violence is indisputable from the available archaeological evidence, not to mention the resilient indigenous communities that continue to survive in the contemporary world. The questions that remain are highly relevant but contentious: What does it mean to be indigenous (or not)? Who gets to make authoritative statements about indigeneity? Is it enough to simply assert that the world's native peoples 'have history' or 'have agency'?

These are not problems that will be easily solved by scratching away at the dirt and using broken bits and pieces from past lives to determine degrees of change and continuity in the archaeological record, tied up as it is with living peoples' identities, lives, politics, and so on. On the other hand, archaeologists absolutely can contribute important evidence to these discussions since often the important data points in the colonial period cannot be gleaned from the written record alone. Assertions about 'invented' traditions or 'inauthentic' claims to indigenous rights for political or economic reasons can be thoroughly undermined in the face of the material traces of native resilience and adaptation during the colonial period.

While it is not a major point in this book, the authenticity question relates to colonial processes of religious change. Westerners may consider conversion to Christianity as an element of inauthenticity in indigenous cultures. At the same time, experience of the mission setting by one's ancestors in some indigenous communities can be an integral component to claims of authenticity (as is sometimes true for Aboriginal Australians, McNiven and Russell 2005: 226–227; see also Lydon and Burns 2010). Questions of indigenous authenticity tend to be most marked in European settler societies (United States, Canada, Australia, New Zealand), where the settler population has to deal with the uncomfortable reality of a dispossessed population of colonised people who often continue to survive as the poorest inhabitants of the lands from which they were often illegally and violently removed. An ideology of *terra nullius*, in which the indigenous population never 'really' owned the land, and disappeared anyway, provides the ideological prop for maintaining such a status quo (e.g. Gosden 2004: 114–152).

Archaeologies of Christian missions have important implications for this discussion. If it was in the process of becoming Christian that indigenous people lost their authentic religion, among other practices, this should be visible in the archaeological record. Yet what historical archaeologists find repeatedly is the integration and subsumption of Christian missions and missionaries into indigenous landscapes and communities, not the other way around (e.g. Ash et al. 2010; Middleton 2003; Panich and Schneider, eds 2014). In the Bay of Islands, New Zealand, missionaries at Hohi and later Te Puna were reliant on Maori interest in exchange relationships for their acceptance into the community. Further, the presentation of Maori children for education on the mission was used as a way to draw missionaries and the European goods they could access into Maori networks of reciprocal social obligations. Producing Christian Maori was a secondary outcome of that process (Middleton 2003, 2006, 2008; Smith 2014; Smith et al. 2012, 2014).

Missions in Aboriginal Australia tended to be more centralised and institutional, at least physically (Middleton 2010; Sutton 2003; for a critique of this see Morrison et al. 2015: 98–99). However, these missions were no less shaped by the indigenous landscapes where they were set, a pattern visible throughout Aboriginal Australia and Australasia more broadly (Lydon and Ash

2010). Aboriginal people were drawn to missions for complex reasons, having to do with new opportunities for trade, expanding social networks, dispute resolution, and escape from settler violence on the colonial frontier (e.g. Lydon 2009; Morrison et al. 2015: 100–101). What is clear from both Australia and New Zealand is that to enter the mission was by no means to abandon one's indigeneity (see also Lydon and Burns 2010; McNiven and Russell 2005).

In Vanuatu, questions of authenticity do not arise in the same ways, since the majority of people are indigenous Melanesians, who have largely retained land rights and ownership (though there is a complicated history to this; Van Trease 1987). However, the significant fact is that Christian conversion in no way undermines the extent to which ni-Vanuatu can be considered indigenous. Rather, Christianity and *kastom* do and did go hand-in-hand for Melanesian people who converted, and their descendants who largely continue to practice Christianity today (Flexner and Spriggs 2015). This project is a result of indigenous interest in Christian archaeological sites on Tanna and Erromango, which are not seen as separate from any other category of *kastom* places. There is no reason to assume that the indigenous relationship to Christianity would be any different in the European settler societies. The either/or Christian/Native division represents yet another artificial binary that masks a more complex hybrid reality.

In addition to questions of indigeneity, archaeologies of colonialism necessitate an exploration of the identities of the colonisers. European Christianity involved a set of embodied material practices that had to be enacted every day by its practitioners, especially in colonial settings where such practices were thrown into relief against those of non-Europeans or non-Christians (e.g. Chenoweth 2009, 2012). Missionaries would have identified primarily as European (British, and particularly Scottish), even if they were born in one of the settler societies. While the majority of missionaries came from what is now Canada, the area was in the 19th century the Lower Provinces of British North America. Scottishness may have been a significant component of people's identities (a pattern visible in the present, though the history of this is complicated; Vance 2005, 2011). In entering the mission field, to what extent did missionaries hold on to their European-derived identities? What aspects of the mission encounter changed their habits and worldviews, and what aspects of continuity in material practice are visible? In such an analysis, the object is to offer the same treatment to Melanesians and missionaries. In the case of Europeans, the authenticity of their identities is rarely questioned, and the goal here is not to say necessarily that the missionaries became anything else (the identity and political issues at stake would be different anyway). Rather, I am interested in the possibility of applying the same metrics of continuity and change to the colonisers that were traditionally used in studying the colonised (e.g. Ramenofsky 1998). Archaeology provides the best means to understand this dynamic.

Outline of Mission History in the Southern New Hebrides

A brief summary of the history of Presbyterian missions on Tanna and Erromango is provided to give readers a basic temporal framework and cast of characters for the archaeological analyses that follow. More specific, detailed accounts drawn from the documentary sources left behind by particular missionaries will be given in the relevant chapters to follow. The London Missionary Society (LMS) was the earliest organisation active in the southern New Hebrides. Mission history in the New Hebrides began on a tragic note with the death of John Williams and James Harris at Dillon's Bay on 20 November 1839. The importance of this event for shaping the history of Christianity in the New Hebrides cannot be understated, especially when considering the long-term patterns of resistance, conversion, and guilt as experienced by people on Erromango (Chapter 2; see also Mayer et al. 2013). On this same trip, Williams established colonies of Samoan teachers, themselves recent converts to Christianity, on Aneityum and Tanna (Liuaʻana 1996). Many of these died no less tragic, but less widely acknowledged martyrs' deaths on these islands.

Following from Williams and Harris, there was basically sustained missionary contact with the southern New Hebrides over the ensuing century (Table 1.1). The LMS continued to send Polynesian teachers in the early 1840s (Liuaʻana 1996). There was also a short-lived mission station on Tanna, inhabited by the LMS missionaries Turner and Nisbet in 1842, though this was abandoned after less than one year. While the LMS would remain somewhat active in the New Hebrides, the Presbyterian Church became the main Protestant missionary supporter in the New Hebrides (Miller 1978), alongside the Anglican Melanesian Mission, which was active in the northern and eastern islands of the group (Armstrong 1900; Hilliard 1978).

Table 1.1 European missionaries on Tanna and Erromango, 1839–1920.

Island	Missionary Name	Year(s)	Place
Erromango	John Williams	1839	Dillon's Bay (1 day)
Erromango	George and Ellen Gordon	1857–1861	Dillon's Bay
Erromango	Hugh and Christina Robertson	1872–1904	Dillon's Bay
Erromango	James Gordon	1864–1872	Dillon's Bay/Potnuma (post-1868)
Tanna	John Williams	1839	Port Resolution (1 day)
Tanna	Turner and Nisbet	1842	Port Resolution (7 months)
Tanna	Thomas Neilson	1868–1882	Port Resolution
Tanna	Joseph Copeland	1858–1862	Port Resolution
Tanna	John G. Paton	1858–1862 [1903]	Port Resolution, Kwamera [later Aniwa]
Tanna	John and Mary Matheson	1858–1862	Kwamera
Tanna	William and Agnes Watt	1869–1894	Kwamera
Tanna	Frank Paton	1896–1902	Lenakel
Tanna	John C. Nicholson	1903–1917	Lenakel
Tanna	William and Elizabeth Gray	1882–1894	Waisisi

The first significant long-term mission settlement in the New Hebrides was established on Aneityum in 1848 by Rev. John Geddie, with the support of the Presbyterian Church of the Lower Provinces of British North America (now the Presbyterian Church of Canada). Geddie was a resident missionary on Aneityum for over four decades, and his was without question the most successful early mission in the New Hebrides, in the sense that he was able to achieve widespread local conversion to Christianity during a long tenure on the island (Patterson 1882). The mission station at Anelcauhat boasted a large stone masonry house and church (Jones 2013), and remained the main stronghold for the Prebyterian Church in the New Hebrides until the 1890s. During his time working on the island, Geddie not only converted a significant percentage of the population, he could also claim to have planted 'a school in every district' of the island, providing the Aneityum Mission with the strongest early network of mission stations and native teachers (Spriggs 1985). Arguably, Geddie's success stemmed largely from his willingness to learn Aneityumese language and *kastom*, and to adapt mission practice appropriately (see Flexner and Spriggs in press). As suggested above, the notion of missionary 'success' should be tempered against the more hybrid realities of religious and cultural change in the Melanesian context.

In the middle of the 1850s, the Presbyterian Church sought to expand upon its success on Aneityum, establishing George and Ellen Gordon as missionaries on Erromango in 1857 (Gordon, ed. 1863), and Reverends John G. Paton, John Matheson, and Samuel Johnston with their wives on Tanna in 1858 (Paton 1907 Vol. 1; Patterson 1864). The Canadian Church continued to be the main source of missionaries and support for these missions, though Paton was from Scotland. These were to be relatively short-lived endeavours. By 1860, Johnston was dead of malaria and the Tanna Mission had to be temporarily abandoned because of increasingly hostile local communities. After a brief resettlement in 1861, the Tanna Mission was completely abandoned in February 1862 as the Mathesons and Paton were unable to successfully re-establish footholds on the island (Adams 1984: 144–145; see also Chapter 3). On Erromango in 1861, George and Ellen Gordon were killed at Dillon's Bay by warriors from a neighbouring village. George's brother James Gordon followed on Erromango, arriving at Dillon's Bay in 1865. By 1868, James Gordon had resettled to Potnuma, near the large village of Port Narvin on the east side of the island. In 1872, James would also die a martyr's death at the hands of local people (Robertson 1902; see also Chapter 2).

Early missionary work did not follow an easy road to conversion. These short-lived missions did have some factors in common. Missionaries generally had a poor understanding of local customs, had to learn local languages from scratch, and often suffered because of their lack of knowledge. Paton and colleagues were chased off Tanna because the mission had inadvertently placed itself in the middle of a local land dispute. James Gordon may have been killed for serving poisonous fish at a local feast. The 1850s–1870s on Tanna and Erromango could be considered an 'adaptive' period, when missionaries were still learning how to survive in the island environment (Birmingham and Jeans 1983). That said, later missionaries would credit the struggles of these earlier missionaries to win converts during this period with their ultimate successes.

The missionaries' fortunes would change by the early 1870s. This period saw the establishment of long-term missions, with the Watts at south Tanna (Watt 1896) and the Robertsons at Dillon's Bay (Robertson 1902). Both families would stay through the turn of the century, successfully converting large numbers of local people. Further, the archaeological record shows that during this period missionaries began to invest in larger, more elaborate, more permanent infrastructure in their settlements. In 1882, Rev. William Gray, an Australian missionary, joined the Watts on Tanna, settling at Waisisi.

During this time the mission also expanded to the Polynesian Outliers of Futuna and Aniwa (Capell 1958). Rev. William Gunn, a Scot and medical missionary for the group, would establish his primary settlement on Futuna in 1883 (Gunn 1914). John G. Paton returned to the New Hebrides after his failure on Tanna, eventually being sent by the Church to Aniwa (Paton 1907). The story of Paton's success on Aniwa is relevant to a pattern in missionary settlement in indigenous landscapes. As often happened, Paton was allowed by the Aniwans to settle in a poisoned, *tabu* area inhabited by the local sea snake deity. After Paton not only survived in this spiritually dangerous place, but successfully dug a freshwater well, he achieved a mass conversion of the populace on Aniwa. This episode is notable in that missionary successes could come about because of resilience and survival in spiritually dangerous places. In other cases, as will be seen, missionary illnesses or deaths may also have been attributed to the inability of their deity to protect them from local spirits, inhibiting the conversion process.

By the 1890s, the Presbyterian Church had permanent mission stations established on Tanna and Erromango, and had expanded into the central and northern islands of the New Hebrides. This expansion was matched by an expansion of connections between the mission stations and global networks of consumer materials. In the west Tanna Mission, established at Lenakel by John G. Paton's son Frank in 1896 (Paton 1903), the initial station looked much like newly established stations elsewhere: limited infrastructure and buildings primarily of local materials. However, within two decades, the Lenakel Mission would expand to include a large prefabricated church manufactured as a kit in Sydney, a large hospital, and 'model village' of native converts (Chapter 4; Flexner et al. 2015). The west Tanna Mission, then, represents an ultimate stage in mission endeavours in the New Hebrides, which was bolstered by the ability to draw widely on the global networks of industrialised Europe and European settler societies. Buoyed by an increasing sense of triumph, the missionaries overreached, attempting on Tanna to eliminate traditional ceremonies, dancing, and kava drinking completely. The result was a backlash in which the missions and model villages were largely abandoned, people retreated to *kastom*, and rumours of a new 'cargo cult' began to spread, especially in the southeastern part of the island (Bonnemaison 1994: 226; see also Guiart 1956: 163; Lindstrom 1993).

Presbyterians were not the only missionaries in the New Hebrides. The Presbyterian Church worked closely with the Anglican Melanesian Mission (Armstrong 1900; Hilliard 1978), sharing resources, particularly mission ships, and amicably dividing geographic responsibilities, with the Anglicans proselytising to the islands in the north and east, and the Presbyterians to the south and west (Miller 1978: 142–146). In contrast, the Protestant missionaries were deeply distrustful of, even antagonistic towards, the Catholic Church and its missionaries, though they were not really active in the New Hebrides until after 1885 (Miller 1978: 139–141). The Presbyterians not only distrusted Roman Catholics for their loyalty to the Pope, but probably worse, they were closely aligned with the French, who were seen as competing with British imperial ambitions in the region. By the early 1900s, various other evangelical sects began working in the New Hebrides, notably the Church of Jesus Christ of Latter Day Saints (LDS, or Mormon Church), and the Seventh Day Adventists (Bonnemaison 1994: 67–80).

Today, it can be said that Vanuatu is, for the most part, a Christian society. That said, Christianity did not replace *kastom*, rather it was simply incorporated into Melanesian tradition in Vanuatu, as happened throughout the region (see Taylor 2010; Tomlinson and McDougall, eds 2012). What follows is an archaeological account of the process of conversion over the first eight or nine decades of mission work in the New Hebrides. The 'success' of Christianity should not be taken as a foregone conclusion. Throughout the history of conversion local people resisted missionary settlement, missions failed more or less catastrophically, apparently sincere converts defected, and missionaries perished as a result of their efforts. In many cases, communities did not convert, and today there remains a significant population of non-Christians in Vanuatu who still maintain the beliefs of their ancestors, or have developed new ones in response to colonialism, such as the John Frum 'cargo cult' of Tanna (Lindstrom 1993).

Neither can we say that the work of conversion was a completed project. Throughout the archaeology of early Christianity in the New Hebrides, we find evidence of what missionaries would have seen as dangerous mixing of heathen and Christian religious beliefs and practices. Indeed, many of the more divisive debates that took place within the Church during the missionary era revolved around the question of which Melanesian practices could be kept, and which had to be eliminated among convert communities (see also Keane 2007). In many cases, it has been argued that apparent converts simply hung the trappings of Christianity on extant beliefs and practices (e.g. Bonnemaison 1994: 211). Archaeology has an important role to play in illuminating how this situation came to be. As I will conclude, the discoveries of this project hold important implications for how the question of religious change in Vanuatu might be considered in centuries to come.

Archaeological Methodology

Mission archaeology projects in Oceania have generally focused on a single mission station, which is then sometimes tied into a wider landscape (e.g. Dalley and Memmott 2010; Ireland 2010; Lydon 2009; Middleton 2008; Smith et al. 2012). One of the innovations of this project was that archaeological survey covered multiple sites, allowing for documentation of variability across time and space (Flexner 2013; see also Ash et al. 2010; Morrison et al. 2010), as well as presumably cultural variability (the research area covers four different language areas). Work was spread out among seven mission landscapes on two islands: Port Narvin, Cook's Bay, and Dillon's Bay on Erromango; Lenakel, Waisisi, Port Resolution, and Kwamera on Tanna (Figure 1.1). In many of these landscapes, there are multiple mission sites. For example, both Kwamera and Dillon's Bay have an early mission abandoned in the 1860s, and a later, longer-duration mission spanning the period from the 1870s to the early 1900s.

While mission sites were the focus, one of the goals of research was to situate the missions in terms of the indigenous landscapes in which they were embedded (Appendix A). A corollary to this involved recording local social memories, both of mission sites and older sites associated with *kastom* stories. In some cases, as in the villages at Kwaraka and Anuikaraka on south Tanna (Chapter 3; Flexner et al. 2016c), the *kastom* sites were immediately recognisable as archaeological, with the landscape consisting of stone mounds, walls, and enclosures. In other cases, interpretation of archaeological features such as rock art sites on east Erromango could be augmented with local oral traditions. Landscape features that would be considered 'natural', such as trees and stones, were documented where they were associated with particular social memories. These 'memory places' represented the largest category of features documented in archaeological survey (Table 1.2). Where a group of memory places were linked to a common story, the resulting assemblage is referred to as an 'event landscape'. Event landscapes offered a useful way of capturing the local sense of 'historicities' (Ballard 2014) regarding both mission-related and indigenous happenings in the recent past (Flexner 2014c). As I've noted elsewhere, 'Event landscapes are places where social memory is both constructed and performed as people follow in the footsteps of historical characters, spirits of the ancestors, or supernatural beings' (Flexner 2014c: 8).

Recording of indigenous perspectives of history as written on the landscape augmented the more traditional archaeological techniques that formed the bulk of fieldwork for this project. A few technical details about field methods should be noted when interpreting the data in the following chapters. Initial surveys documented site locations, architectural forms, surface artefacts, and other relevant details in and around mission sites. Mission houses were identified early on in the project as significant places of contact and interaction between missionaries and Melanesians (Flexner 2013: 16–20). A program of test excavations covering areas ranging in size from 1m x 1m to 4m x 4m was carried out at five of the mission houses (George Gordon House and Robertson House at Dillon's Bay; James Gordon House at Potnuma; Matheson House/Imua at Kwamera; Watt House at Kwamera), and at the native villages Kwaraka and Anuikaraka. Excavations were carried out stratigraphically, following natural layers where possible, and all sediments were sieved using 0.5cm mesh. Sediment samples were taken at each of the excavated sites, and all samples and artefacts are curated at the Vanuatu National Museum in Port Vila.

Recovered artefacts were analysed in detail by material class, and the results were entered into a relational database. These objects and their spatial contexts provide critical data about the everyday interactions with things that shaped the conversion process in the New Hebrides Presbyterian missions. In addition to the excavated material, which was almost entirely European (or European-derived, as in the case of locally produced lime mortar), a survey of museum assemblages was carried out at museums in Australia, New Zealand, Canada, and Europe. These materials provide a sample of artefacts from the other side of mission exchanges, things that were given to missionaries within the context of ongoing conversion and indigenisation of Christianity.

Table 1.2 Types of landscape features recorded during archaeological survey.

Feature Type	Cook's Bay, Erromango	Dillon's Bay, Erromango	Eastern Erromango	Kwamera, Tanna	Kwaraka, Tanna	Lenakel, Tanna	Port Narvin, Erromango	Port Resolution, Tanna	Potnuma, Erromango	Waisisi, Tanna	Grand Total
Burial Ground										1	1
Cave			1				1				2
Church		1		1		2		2	1	1	8
Hospital						5					5
House		1				1					2
Land Marker										1	1
Memorial		1		2		2		4	1	1	11
Memory Place		7	4	1	2		1	2	1	3	21
Mission House	1	2		1		1		2	1	1	9
Mission Infrastructure		4		1		2		3		2	12
Nakamal					1			1		3	5
Native Village					2						2
Other						1					1
Petroglyph Site			1				2				3
School						1					1
Tabu Site		3	3		2					5	10
Grand Total	1	16	9	6	7	15	4	14	4	18	94

Outline of the Book

This book is primarily divided by place. The chapters on each of the islands where the project took place will involve a discussion of *kastom* as it likely appeared in the decades leading up to the arrival of the missionaries, based on missionary accounts, early ethnographies, and contemporary social memories. Of course these interpretations of *kastom* are limited by the source material, and so should be read with an understanding that alternate perspectives are possible and indeed reasonable, particularly among ni-Vanuatu. One chapter will focus on analysing and interpreting fieldwork data from Erromango (Chapter 2). Fieldwork data from Tanna is divided into two chapters, covering earlier and later periods of mission life on the island (Chapters 3 and 4). Discussions will include detailed outlines of event landscapes, survey results, and stratigraphic excavations. In discussing the excavations, I avoid artificially dividing the 'finds' from excavated 'sites' (Lucas 2001: 75). Discussions of artefact assemblages will take place alongside the narrative about places where the objects were found, with some comparative discussion as warranted, and more general synthesis in the concluding chapter.

After outlining some of the relevant details of *kastom* on Erromango, Chapter 2 deals head-on with the event landscapes that record the deaths of early missionaries on the island. These dramatic events were sedimented into local places through social memories, and have shaped Erromangan experiences through the present, even to the point where 21st-century Erromangans have held reconciliation ceremonies with the descendants of martyred missionaries (Mayer et al. 2013; Naupa, ed. 2011: 90–102). The primary goal of archaeological research on Erromango's colonial period is to move away from the rhetoric of the 'martyr isle', and to begin to understand the patterns of everyday life that shaped the history of interaction with outsiders on the island. If missionaries died on the island, these were events that account for a miniscule percentage of the actual span of time covered between when John Williams and James Harris were killed in 1839, and the Robertsons left after a long missionary career on the island in the early 1900s. Landscape archaeology on the island shows some of the ways that the missionary settlement reflects the changing relationships between outsiders and Erromangans, while the recovered artefacts provide data reflecting the material interactions that took place on the island.

Chapters 3 and 4 focus on Tanna. While Tanna did not see the dramatic and widely publicised martyrdoms of Erromango, the mission likewise saw early challenges, catastrophic failures, and eventually the establishment of long-term stations and fairly widespread conversion. Here, too, excavations of mission house sites provide an illuminating picture of life in the mission, and interactions with the Melanesian community over a period covering nine decades. In the Kwamera area of south Tanna, we get some of the most useful insights into everyday life in the native villages around the mission sites at Kwaraka and Anuikaraka, settlements occupied for a time period predating missionary arrival through the post-WWII era, after which the Presbyterian missionaries had mostly departed the southern New Hebrides. Significantly, occupation overlaps with the mission houses at Imua and Kwamera, just 2km away. At the coastal stations on east (Waisisi) and west (Lenakel) Tanna, we see a later period of mission history where missionaries were increasingly able to draw on global capitalism to acquire materials for their work (Chapter 4). Lenakel represents the last major Presbyterian Mission station established on Tanna, a massive infrastructural investment pulling on truly global resources, a far cry from the initial beachheads established on these islands a half-century earlier.

If fieldwork on Tanna and Erromango tells us about the material that was brought to the islands, museum assemblages can tell us about the things that travelled from the islands, collected by missionaries as 'curiosities' during their tenure in the New Hebrides. Missionary collections will be the focus of Chapter 5. Collections both augment what is found archaeologically, as they often contain indigenous material culture unlikely to survive locally on archaeological sites, and provide valuable data about indigenous agency in the curiosities trade (Flexner 2016b). These objects (wooden clubs, barkcloth, bows and arrows, grass skirts) blur the line between ethnographic and archaeological material, being contemporaneous with the earthenware, nails, and shells excavated on mission sites. They are just as much artefacts as the fragments found in the ground. Just as stratigraphic location provides a context for excavated material, the museum collections provide a context for understanding the social lives of missionary collected objects in the Western world.

Finally, Chapter 6 provides a synthetic overview of the big ideas that these materials speak to. Questions of identity, materiality, and religious change arise when studying the process of Christian conversion in the New Hebrides from an archaeological standpoint. Things writ large, from individual ceramic dishes to houses, to places marked on the landscape either physically or in social memory, all played a role in the indigenisation of Christianity on Tanna and Erromango. One of the major points here is that the category of 'religion' could not be separated from *kastom*. If *kastom* is taken as an all-encompassing category for social life in Melanesia, a 'total social fact' (Mauss 1990 [1954]), then it follows that Christianity as a new kind of engagement with the supernatural, a new ideology, and a new way of engaging with everyday life, would simply be subsumed into and adapted to fit *kastom*, rather than the other way around. It is almost certainly not what the Protestant missionaries would have intended (Keane 2007). But, it provides a remarkable case study of the ability of indigenous people to take things from the colonial world and make them their own as they adapted to life in an age of colonialism.

It might be said that the outline of theory and method presented above overstates the case. Because material things are deemed important, I will present an analysis of materials relating to Christian conversion, and then conclude that objects mattered in the New Hebrides missions. But this would be to miss the point of such an analysis. Physicists studying the universe believe physics is fundamental to understanding its origins and the way it works, so they use the methods and theories of physics to answer their questions. As archaeologists, we should not be shy about asserting the primacy of archaeological approaches when addressing archaeological questions. The point isn't simply to assert that 'things matter', but to try to use a specific case study to understand *why* they matter, *how* they inflected patterns of everyday life in situations of contact and colonialism. Of course, many complementary approaches to this topic would be possible. Besides the historical studies mentioned above, the question of how and why Melanesians converted to Christianity could be beneficially addressed from the perspectives of sociology, psychology, ecology or evolutionary biology. Each approach has its benefits and limitations. The chapters that follow represent an initial account of systematic archaeological study of mission sites on Tanna and Erromango and the material processes at work that shaped the experience of religious conversion both among Presbyterian missionaries, and among the Melanesian communities in which they settled. This material is essential for understanding the 19th-century Melanesian universe of the southern New Hebrides.

2

Erromango: Archaeology and the Martyr Isle

Erromango is the fourth-largest island in Vanuatu, and the largest in the southern TAFEA province, with a surface area of 855km² (Figure 1.1; TAFEA is an acronym consisting of the first letters of the five islands in the province: Tanna, Aniwa, Futuna, Erromango, Aneityum). The island has a high volcanic plateau that has formed over the last 5.5 million years, with most of the volcanic activity occurring within the early Pleistocene period and continuing until the end of the Pleistocene. The volcanic cones that formed Traitor's Head on the east coast of the island are the most recent formations. The coasts are characterised by uplifted limestone reef terraces, especially in the northern and western areas of the island (Colley and Ash 1971).

The early archaeological sequence of Erromango is better understood than on the other TAFEA islands. Initial human settlement of Erromango is well attested by the presence of Lapita pottery, which is the marker of initial colonisation in the western islands of Remote Oceania (Green 1991). The sites of Ponamla and Ifo are the primary Lapita sites on Erromango, dating to roughly 2800BP (Bedford 2006: 32–39) (Figure 2.1). The Ponamla site is notable for the presence of possible 2,700-year-old stone structures (Spriggs 1999). Within a few centuries of settlement, there is a notable change in ceramic decoration style to incised and fingernail-impressed wares, as well as red-slipped and plain ceramics. Ceramic technology disappears from Erromango by about 2000BP. After this point, archaeological material culture consists of distinctive stone and shell artefacts, both tools and objects of personal adornment (Bedford 2006). Rock art sites are widespread on Erromango, with a prevalent tradition of black linear paintings and drawings (Wilson 1999, 2002).

First European contact on Erromango occurred during Cook's second expedition in 1774. This was a very brief encounter. Cook went ashore at a place he called Polenia Bay, now Port Narvin (a European orthography of 'Potnarvin', literally 'sandy place'). After handing out some 'trinkets' and receiving some food and fresh water, Cook determined to return to the main ship. At this point, the local people attempted to try to keep Cook and the ship's boat on shore. In the ensuing scuffle, Cook ordered his men to fire and it appears that four Erromangans died in the attack. Cook and his men returned to the ships while local people continued to fire arrows and throw stones as they retreated (Beaglehole, ed. 1969: 477–480). After this, the ships weighed anchor and headed south for Tanna (see Chapter 3). The main legacy of this encounter is the name Erromango from Cook's hearing local people saying, 'armae n'go', 'good food' when offering yams. The original name for the island was Nelokompne (Huffman 1996: 129), though I will use the more common name Erromango here.

It would be another 50 years before Europeans would return to Erromango in earnest. The discovery of sandalwood, a valuable trade item, in the area known locally as Umpongkor, now called Dillon's Bay, in 1828 attracted the first traders to the island (Shineberg 1967: 16–28). In a single decade, one trader removed 1,600 tons of sandalwood from the island, with a gross value of £64,000, a monumental sum for that time. Within 50 years, Erromango's uplands were largely deforested and sandalwood almost entirely wiped out. By one estimate, £175,000 worth of sandalwood (over £19,000,000 in 2016 estimated equivalent currency; Morley 2016) was removed from Erromango (Robertson 1902: 34, map insert). As we will see, tensions between Erromangan people and sandalwood traders would have some impacts on the missionary experience.

With sandalwood largely exhausted, traders in the New Hebrides sought other sources of profit. Particularly important on Erromango was the labour, or 'Blackbirding' trade (Docker 1970; Palmer 1871; Shineberg 1999), which resulted in hundreds of young Erromangan men travelling to Queensland and Fiji, primarily to work on sugarcane plantations. Some would not return. Missionaries were vehement in their descriptions of the negative impacts of the labour trade (e.g. Kay, ed. 1872), though these accounts should be tempered against the fact that they were watching potential converts disappear from the islands. Many Erromangans and others likely boarded labour vessels voluntarily, though there was some trickery, kidnapping, and abuse during the Blackbirding era (Moore 1992). The labour trade combined with epidemic diseases to decimate the Erromangan population. By one estimate, the mid-19th-century population of about 5,000 (possibly 7,000; Gordon, ed. 1863: 134), which may already have been down because of earlier contacts, was reduced to a low of about 600 inhabitants in 1967 (Colley and Ash 1971: 2–3). One of the early ethnographers on the island believed that population decline was to some extent responsible for loss of cultural traditions and general 'despondency' or 'apathy' on Erromango (Humphreys 1926: 123, 129, 133, 148; see also Speiser 1922).

Today, Erromango remains sparsely populated, but the 'despondency' asserted as relating to cultural traditions was certainly overstated. Erromangan people continue to have a keen interest in cultural traditions and arts, many of which are currently undergoing something of a renaissance (Carillo-Huffman et al. 2013; Christidis et al. 2009; Huffman 1996; Lawson 2001; Naupa, ed. 2011).

Kastom on Erromango

What was life like on Erromango in the decades leading up to European, and particularly missionary, arrival on the island? To understand this, we can turn to a variety of sources, including early missionary accounts (Robertson 1902) and ethnographies (Humphreys 1926). Both of these sources come with their own kinds of biases, and must be read critically (Douglas 2001). On the other hand, they also represent early recordings of traditions not currently practiced or largely transformed. It is worth 'triangulating' the common observations from various sources that may reflect some aspects of cultural reality. What follows is an account of Erromangan *kastom* that is by necessity incomplete, fragmented, and non-authoritative. It is a preliminary attempt to organise this information in a way that may explain patterns relevant to the historical archaeology of missionary encounters that follows. Future research, and particularly the observations of Erromangan scholars (e.g. Naupa, ed. 2011) can and should refine these observations. This basic outline offers a starting point for the broad patterns and 'deep structures' that may have shaped Erromangan experiences through the colonial era.

Traditionally, Erromango was divided into six districts (Figure 2.1). The districts were called *lo* (canoe), and consisted of collections of villages, though an early ethnographic account indicates that tribal organisation was not strictly geographic in nature (Humphreys 1926: 128). There were six or seven languages on the island originally, though only three are spoken today, and the primary language, Syé, is quickly absorbing the remaining speakers of the other two. Language boundaries and district boundaries did not overlap precisely across the island.

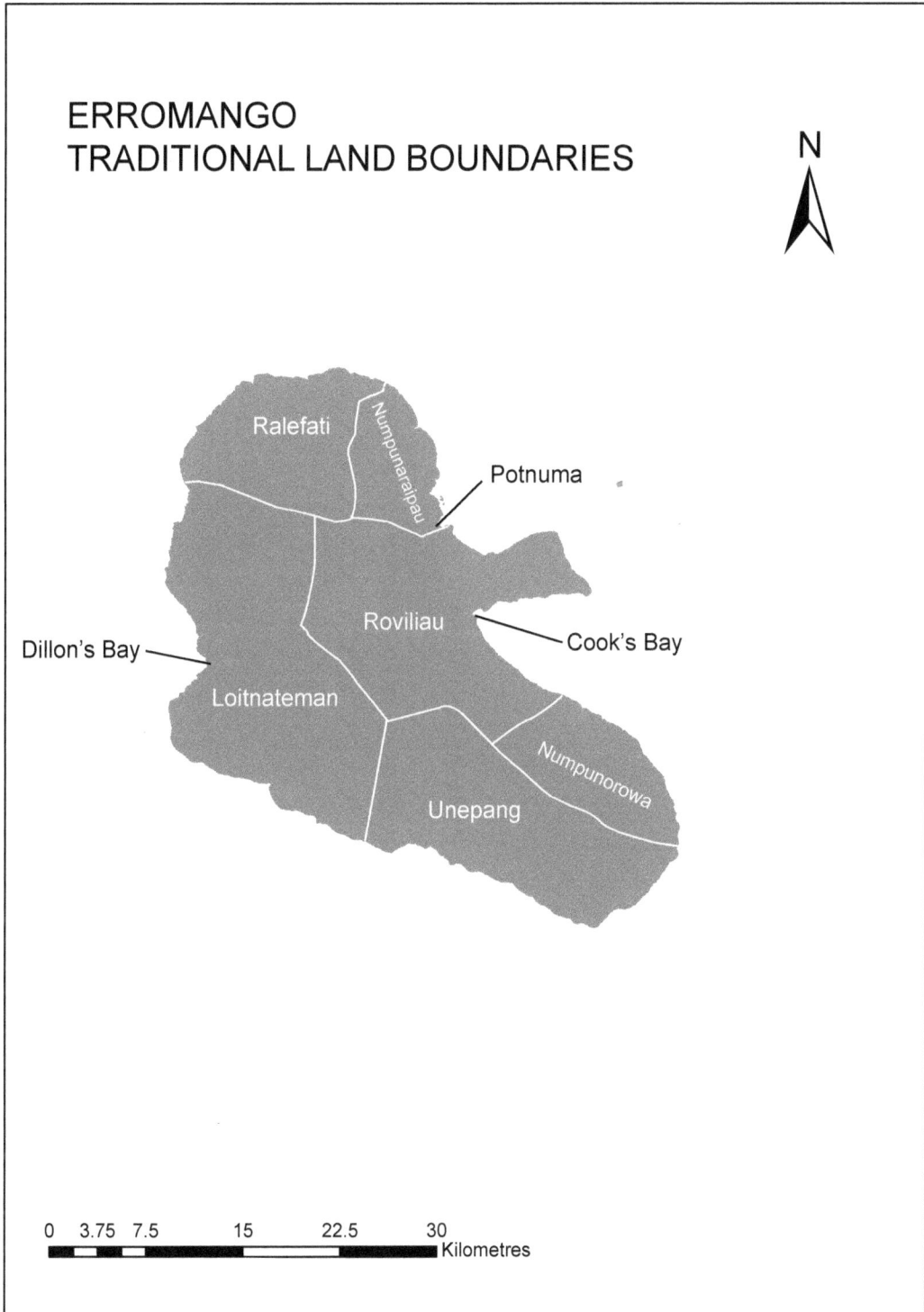

Figure 2.1 Map of *lo* (districts) on Erromango, and sites mentioned in text. Note that division boundaries are approximate only and meant to be for general reference.

Source: James Flexner

Chiefs were called *Fan lo*, and women of the chiefly class referred to as *Nasimnalan*. Each village had a *Fan lo*, and there was a higher-ranking *Fan lo* in charge of each district. Commoners were referred to as *Taui natimono*. Chiefly women were required to marry men from the *Fan lo* class, but in some cases, male chiefs could marry women of the commoner class, particularly as

Fan lo were allowed multiple wives. Chiefly titles were hereditary rather than achieved, passed primarily through the male lineage, though chiefs could also nominate an appropriately ranked successor as they neared the end of their lives (Humphreys 1926: 128–134; Spriggs and Wickler 1989: 83–85).

Erromangan subsistence used the typical suite of Oceanic crops, including yams, taro, banana, coconuts, various fruits and 'island cabbages', as well as marine resources (Figure 2.2). While the garden soils of the west coast were less productive overall, each *lo* offered enough resources for surplus agricultural production in normal years. Early observers recorded 26 varieties of yams, 17 of taro, 13 of banana, as well as a great variety of other crops. Food was either roasted in the coals of an open fire, or prepared in earth ovens. Dishes included roasted tubers, fish, and pigs, and various sorts of starchy puddings, including *neoki*, which was made with yam or papaya, coconut, and prawns. People ate fruit or small amounts of roasted vegetables or fish during the day, with the main meal taking place in the evenings (Humphreys 1926: 138–140; Robertson 1902: 376–381). Pigs were raised on the island, but were used primarily in feasting.

Figure 2.2 A traditional Erromangan garden.
Source: James Flexner

The main type of feast on Erromango was the *nisekar* (Humphreys 1926: 180–182; Naupa, ed. 2011: 30–32; Robertson 1902: 390–391). These feasts, presented by one village to another through the *Fan lo*, often began with a sham fight, followed by an exchange of gifts, and feasting could last for several days. Often a feast presented by one village would be reciprocated by the other, sometimes almost immediately. A large ceremonial structure, called the *nevsem*, was often constructed to display agricultural produce at *nisekar* and other events, such as a chief's funeral. The feasts and *nevsem* have been interpreted both as a means of keeping the peace on the island (Naupa, ed. 2011: 24–26) and as a means of competition among rival chiefs (Spriggs and Wickler 1989: 84–85). There is no reason to take these as mutually exclusive proposals, as competitive feasting provided an alternative to competition through warfare, though it has been suggested that feasting and fighting were carried out in alternate seasons (Humphreys 1926: 181).

Another significant structure in Erromangan life was the *Siman lo*, a large ceremonial house structure inhabited by young and unmarried men (Figure 2.3). It was a shared sleeping and eating house, but also served a number of important social functions. The *Siman lo* was a symbolically dense, important meeting place where the *Fan lo* would meet to make community decisions. It was also the place where men would meet in the evenings to drink kava, the intoxicating beverage made from the root of the *Piper methysticum* plant (or there may have been a separate, but nearby kava house of similar form; Humphreys 1926: 156–158, 178; Naupa, ed. 2011: 26–30). A mid-19th-century *Siman lo* was measured as 100 ft (30m) long, 20 ft (7m) wide, and 25 ft (8m) high (Robertson 1902: 375). Erromangan people made a variety of objects out of wood, plant materials, bark, shell, and stone, which will be described at greater length in Chapter 5. Star-headed carved wooden clubs (*telugohmti*), stone money (*navela*), barkcloth (*nemasitse*) and cowrie shells (*numpuri*) were important ceremonial and exchange items. The subsistence system and chiefly system provided the structure for everyday life on Erromango in the centuries surrounding the arrival of missionaries and other Europeans.

Figure 2.3 *Siman lo* (men's house) at Dillon's Bay, Erromango.
Source: James Flexner

Missionaries who arrived in Erromango settled on an island with already rich supernatural beliefs, legends, and stories, many of which have been lost because of demographic and religious change on the island. Others have survived through the present, and in early texts. Erromangans believed in a creator being, *Nobu*, who made the island, the first people, the *navela* (stone money), and in some stories the surrounding islands, but was generally not otherwise involved in the world after that. Much more important supernatural beings consisted of ghosts and spirits (*natemas*). Ghosts of deceased ancestors were thought to roam the island at night, and if encountered, could cause illness, bad fortune, or even death, and were to be propitiated with offerings of food (Humphreys 1926: 165–167; Robertson 1902: 389).

There were powerful practitioners of magic on Erromango, called *Tavuwa*. *Tavuwa* were capable of both beneficial and detrimental magic. The beneficial kinds involved calling the rains and causing crops to grow. The same kinds of magic could be used to call cyclones or damaging storms and damaging crops to limit growth for reasons both apparently bad (attacking a rival district) and good (reducing crop waste, though it should be noted that this reasoning is probably a bit tenuous, as excess crops could always be used to raise more pigs for feasting). Perhaps equally influential was the ability of *Tavuwa* to cause illness or death. The method is remarkably similar to that used on Tanna (see Chapter 3), where something that had come into contact with a man's body, especially food waste such as banana peels or sugarcane mast, was tied in a bundle with a magic stone (*natemas evai*) with malicious power. In fact, it has been suggested that the magic stones themselves as well as these practices came originally from Tanna. Missionaries and early ethnographers suggest all deaths were believed to be caused by *natemas* or *Tavuwa* (Humphreys 1926: 167–170; Robertson 1902: 400–402), though of course such an observation should be read as partly reflecting European biases about native superstitions.

Erromango is known to have had strong connections with neighbouring islands Tanna and Aniwa. Besides the *natemas evai*, which indeed could originally have been brought to Erromango from Tanna, there were more regular material exchanges. Black manganese and red ochre, used as pigment, clubs, bows and arrows, and brides were exchanged with neighbouring islands. In return, Erromango received pigs, kava, and shell valuables (Spriggs and Wickler 1989: 84). Thus when missionaries arrived on Erromango in 1839, they landed on an island that already had a rich cosmology and human social ecology. They also were not the first Europeans to visit the island, and this may be partly responsible for the tragic shape of mission history on Erromango.

The First Martyrs: John Williams and James Harris

The basic events surrounding the deaths of John Williams and James Harris at Dillon's Bay on 20 November 1839 are generally well agreed upon. Williams was a London Missionary Society missionary who had success on Samoa, the Cook Islands, and Tahiti, having worked in Polynesia since 1817. Harris, a young man who had travelled to the South Seas for health reasons, was working as his secretary. With a contingent of recent Samoan converts who had volunteered to expand the mission field westward, Williams and Harris travelled to the New Hebrides in the mission brig *Camden* to attempt to establish new mission stations. They arrived on Tanna on 18 November, dropped a few Samoan teachers off at Port Resolution, and then went on to Erromango. On the morning of the 20th, Williams and Harris landed on the beach at Dillon's Bay in the hopes of meeting a chief. Despite the reluctance of local people, Williams and Harris insisted on travelling inland. Subsequently they were chased and attacked by local warriors, and both men died trying to escape back to the mission ship (see Gordon, ed. 1863: 99–101; Robertson 1902: 47–56).

News of Williams' and Harris' deaths travelled fairly quickly, solidifying the impression among Europeans that Erromango, and the New Hebrides more generally, were dangerous islands ruled by black magic and death (American Sunday School Union 1844; Copeland 1878). Ironically, this reputation if anything seemed to further encourage potential missionaries hoping to 'bring light to dark isles'. A week after this event, the HMS *Favourite* arrived and collected the bones of Williams and Harris (note that the bodies had allegedly been butchered and cooked, so bones rather than bodies were offered). Williams' body was returned to Samoa, and is currently buried on the foreshore in Apia (Figure 2.4).

Figure 2.4 Marker of John Williams' grave, Apia, Samoa.
Source: James Flexner

The European version of these events is missing several key plot points. H.A. Robertson, a later missionary, was able to ascertain from talking to several eyewitnesses that the reasons for the attack stemmed partly from outrages committed by previous white visitors, one of whom 'had stolen a chief's daughter' (Robertson 1902: 56). Local people today remember that two sons of a local chief had been shot during a feast just before Williams' and Harris' arrival. It is possible that this was the feast relating to the circumcision ritual (Humphreys 1926: 177–179). It would have been an unimaginable insult to mar such an event with a violent act. Regardless, it is clear that the people at Umpongkor (Dillon's Bay) had good reason to be wary of the intentions of the foreigners. It was suggested locally that after these events, Erromangans decided to block any European settlement on their island.

The deaths of Williams and Harris had deep reverberations in the Erromangan as well as European communities. The 'event landscape' relating to Williams' and Harris' deaths is remembered to this day (Flexner 2014c: 8–11), encapsulated in place on the west Erromangan coast. Walking through the landscape, Erromangan people can point to the places and material traces that relate to 20 November 1839. At the time of Williams and Harris' arrival, there was a *nisekar* happening at a place in the uplands called Nokiyangouwi, where a *nevsem* had been erected. Auwi-Auwi, the chief who was hosting the *nisekar*, decreed that the visitors were to be welcomed so long as they remained on the beach (points 1 and 3 in Figure 2.5). Despite warnings by local people (who did not speak English just as Williams did not speak Erromangan), Williams and Harris insisted on proceeding inland, and the events proceeded as recorded above.

From here, the event landscape again picks up some of the threads not present in the documentary accounts (Figure 2.5). As the crew of the *Camden* retreated, the bodies of Williams and Harris were dragged up the river. Where some drops of Williams' blood fell, red-leafed *lompot* (*Cordyline fruticosa*; Bislama *nangare*) plants sprouted, and the same kinds of plants still grow on the spot today (point 4 in Figure 2.5). Williams' body was placed on a large stone, and cupules were pecked to mark the location of his head, feet, and hands (point 6 in Figure 2.5; Robertson (1902: 58) suggests local people believed the missionary was short and stout). From there, the bodies of Williams and Harris were taken to the river, where they were divided among local chiefs, and taken away to be ritually eaten (point 7 in Figure 2.5). Or, as Robertson (1902: 58) recounts, the bodies were taken to a village about three miles inland to be exchanged for pigs. There is some question in local reckoning about whether Williams and Harris were cannibalised. Several studies suggest that scepticism is a reasonable stance when presented with such cases (Arens 1980; Barker et al., eds 1998; Goldman, ed. 1999; Obeyesekere 2005). We should simultaneously be careful to take the equally erroneous revisionist stance that suggests cannibalism *never* happened in the past in Melanesia. One way to find out for certain would be to examine the bones of John Williams for evidence of butchery or cooking, though obviously this would be a politically and socially complicated process involving many stakeholders.

Regardless of whether it involved cannibalism or not, John Williams' death had a major impact on Erromangan consciousness. Erromangan people's guilt was so intense that in 2009 a reconciliation ceremony was held at Dillon's Bay with descendants of John Williams and descendants of those responsible for his death (Mayer et al. 2013; Naupa, ed. 2011: 92–108). It was believed that Erromango had been 'cursed' by the death of John Williams, and it was necessary to make amends before the population of the island could grow to its pre-colonial level. The name of Dillon's Bay was changed officially to Williams Bay (though Dillon's Bay remains in common use outside of west Erromango, and was used historically so will be used elsewhere here).

Erromango remained largely without resident missionaries in the years immediately following this event. A few Samoan teachers were present on the island in 1840, dropped off by the *Camden*, but they had little success and had to be essentially rescued from the island in 1841 (Liua'ana 1996: 60–63). In 1848, the Canadian missionary John Geddie established the first successful mission to the New Hebrides on Aneityum. A little over a decade later, George Gordon and his wife Ellen Powell Gordon landed at Dillon's Bay, becoming the first resident European missionaries on 'the martyr isle'.

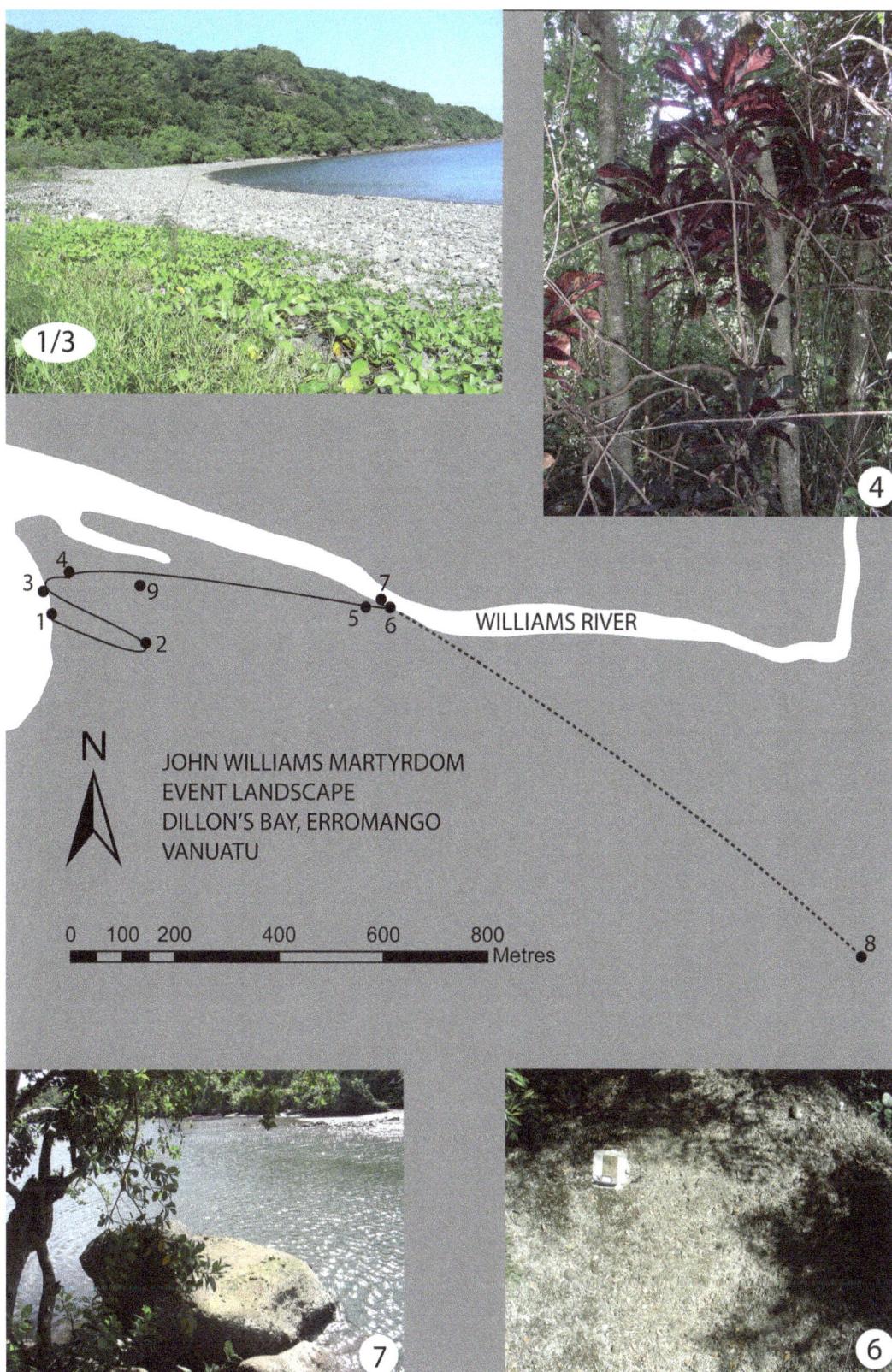

Figure 2.5 Event landscape covering the death of John Williams and James Harris (see text for explanation of features).

Source: James Flexner

George and Ellen Gordon at Dillon's Bay

George Gordon grew up on Prince Edward Island in the Lower Provinces of British North America. Gordon's grandfather had emigrated from Scotland after serving in the British Army during the American Revolution and later in India. George Gordon served as a city missionary in Halifax before volunteering for the foreign mission and being appointed to the New Hebrides, for which he departed in 1855. On his way to the mission field, he met Ellen Powell in London and they were married before departing together for the South Seas. The couple settled at Dillon's Bay in June 1857 (Gordon, ed. 1863).

The Gordons' mission work progressed slowly but steadily. They were supported by Samoan teachers who were resident on the island. Early victories included the conversion of the young Erromangans Yomot and Usuo, who became important supporters of the church. The Gordons lived at Dillon's Bay for slightly less than four years. During this time they won some native converts, and their work is credited with the long-term success of the Presbyterian Mission on Erromango (Robertson 1902: 66–71). They are best remembered as Erromango's second martyrs, but their final moments were only a tiny fraction of the time the Gordons spent at Dillon's Bay.

There is some documentation of the Gordons' lives on the island, which mostly revolved around learning language and customs and attempting to convince Erromangan people to convert (Gordon, ed. 1863: 132–184). However, we know little of the form of everyday life for the missionaries. Further, if conversion work was a process of material entanglement as much as transformation of spiritual belief, we must look to the spaces where such interactions took place. For this, we turn to the archaeological record, which has proven to be an invaluable primary source of interaction for understanding mission life in Oceania (e.g. Lydon 2009; Middleton 2008; Smith et al. 2012, 2014).

The Gordons built their house high on a cliff overlooking the Williams River, and fairly far from the main population centre in the river valley. This was apparently to escape the 'bad air' and miasmas that caused tropical illnesses, particularly malaria (Gordon, ed. 1863: 199–200). Indigenous settlement in the river valley was said to be sparse, with depopulation resulting largely from violent contacts with sandalwood traders and introduced diseases (Gordon, ed. 1863: 137). As is the case on Tanna and elsewhere in Vanuatu, the inland areas of Erromango were likely much more densely populated during the past than they are today. Coastal aggregation of settlement took place later, partly as a result of missionary and other colonial activities.

We excavated a single test-pit at a site near the Williams River called Undam, where a local villager had found a few sherds of red-slipped pottery, probably made around 2,000 years ago (Bedford 2006: 158). The unit yielded an assemblage of shells, fire-cracked rock, and charcoal typical for the later prehistoric sequence of Erromango. While the pre-European assemblage seems poor in material compared to the mission sites discussed below, it should be noted that most of the objects used by the people who lived along the Williams River would have been made of organic materials unlikely to preserve archaeologically (Chapter 5). A 19th-century map of the area of Dillon's Bay south of the Williams River shows a high density of indigenous place names around where the Gordons settled (Vanuatu National Archives Land Record 46 S.I. 3), indicating the rich cultural landscape within which the missionaries lived.

G. Gordon House Domestic Space and Stratigraphy

The remains of George and Ellen Gordon's house (referred to as the G. Gordon House below, Figure 2.6) today consist of a long, low wall running perpendicular to the line of the cliff. The site was cleared of vegetation some time in the 1990s and, during this time, the Erromangan people who did the clearing built a small memorial circle of stones at the northern part of the site.

Like so many missionary sites, G. Gordon House has been incorporated into the local pantheon of customary sacred places (Flexner and Spriggs 2015), and is periodically visited as such. Apparently some of the surface artefacts were removed and thrown over the cliff during cleaning of the site, or taken as souvenirs by local people. It is also likely that the Gordons dumped their rubbish over the cliff, though reconnaissance of the area below the house has yet to locate any midden deposit.

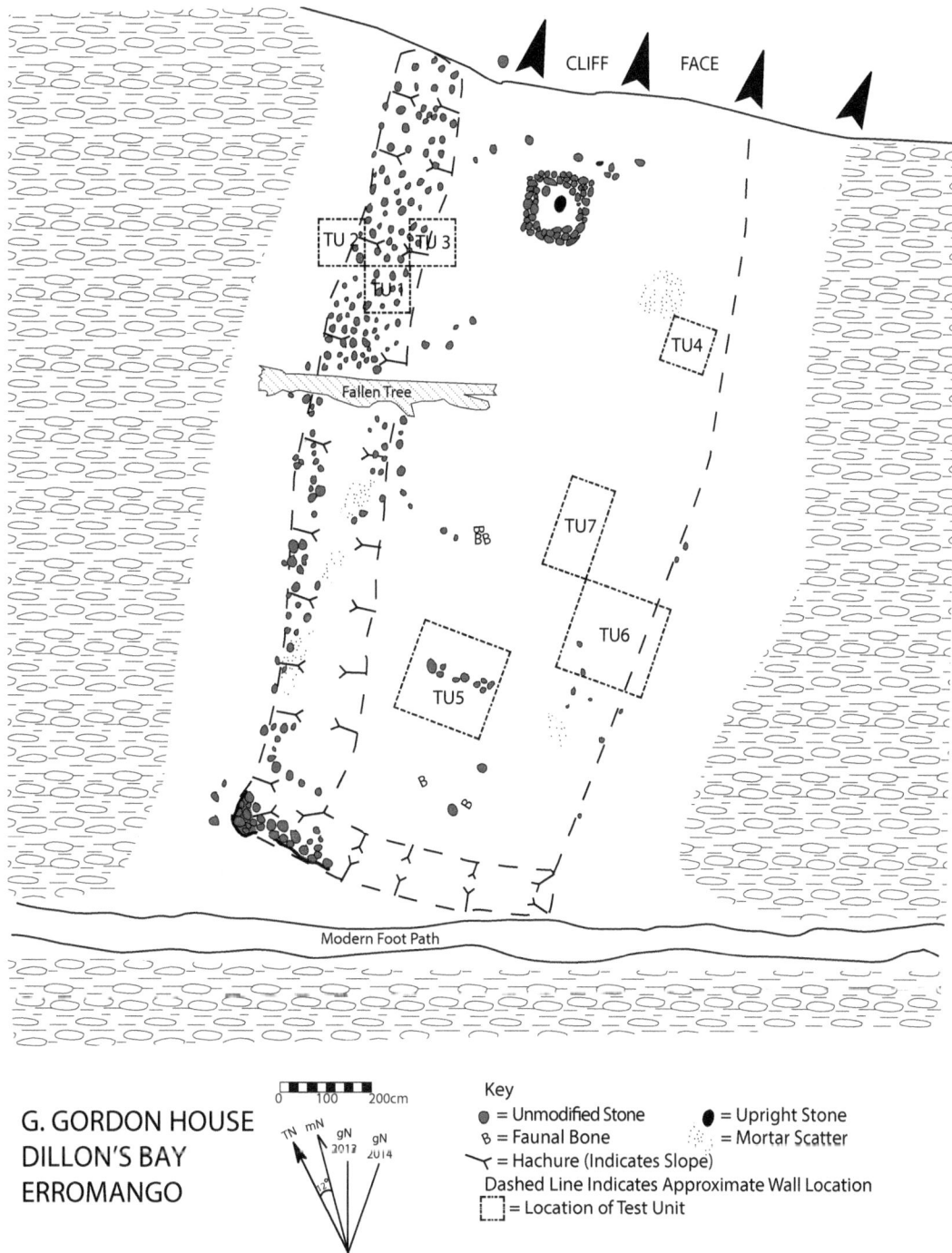

Figure 2.6 Plan of G. Gordon House.
Source: James Flexner

To better understand the arrangement of domestic space, and to obtain a sample of material culture from G. Gordon House, we excavated a series of test pits ranging from 1x1m to 2x2m in size around the site (see Appendix B for a list of excavation contexts). The excavated area totals 14m². Across the site, we revealed a single, shallow occupation layer with artefacts dating to the middle of the 19th century. All of the pre-1870s mission houses display this kind of pattern, as they were generally inhabited briefly (less than five years), and abandoned suddenly. Some of the recovered artefacts were likely deposited in the course of everyday life, while others remain from the abandonment deposit as the house was left to decay following the Gordons' deaths in 1861.

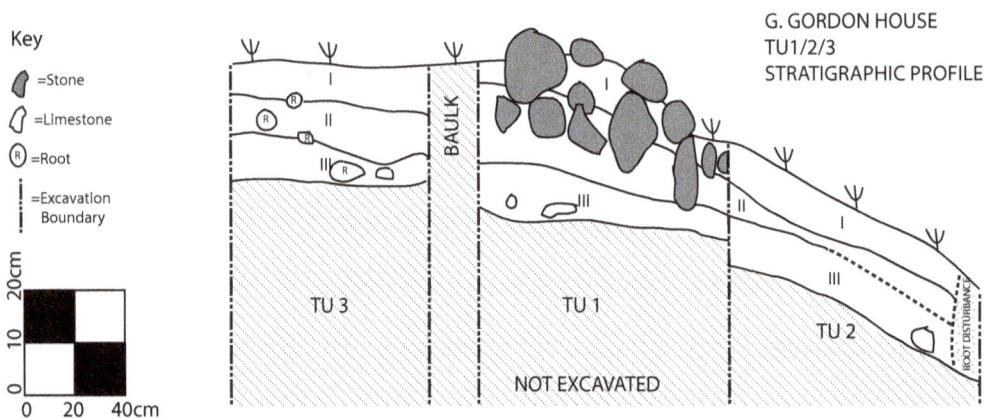

Figure 2.7 Closing plan photograph and stratigraphic profile of TU1/2/3, G. Gordon House. Note that the vertical scale of the profile drawing has been distorted to make the layering clearer.

Source: James Flexner

Three test units (TU1/2/3) were excavated across the northern part of the wall feature that forms the western boundary of G. Gordon House. The stratigraphic sequence from these units consists of sediment accumulated from slope wash during the time after the site was abandoned, with few artefacts found, overlying the main occupation layer, and a red clay subsoil with high percentages of limestone inclusions from the underlying uplifted Pleistocene-age reef (Figure 2.7). Excavations revealed that this stone wall was likely unmortared, and was probably built as a stone retaining wall to maintain a level terrace for the Gordons' house.

Elsewhere on the site the accumulated sediment is not present, owing to the absence of stone wall features. A unit excavated in the northeastern area of the site (TU4) revealed very shallow deposits and relatively low artefact density, suggesting this area was part of the yard or garden. Significantly, there was no window glass, or indeed glass of any kind in TU4, and relatively few nails, though the quantity of lime mortar was comparable to the other units. The southern and eastern limits of the house are defined by a linear stone feature that was centred in TU5 (see Figure 2.6), and a diffuse linear stone feature uncovered running north–south in TU6 (visible in the north and south profiles; see Figure 2.8). We did not uncover any intact walls or other architectural features. This indicates that G. Gordon House was constructed quickly and with relatively minimal labour input, which is typical of the early New Hebrides mission structures. However, the presence of lime mortar throughout the site and the stone alignments suggests a modest stone footing for the house walls.

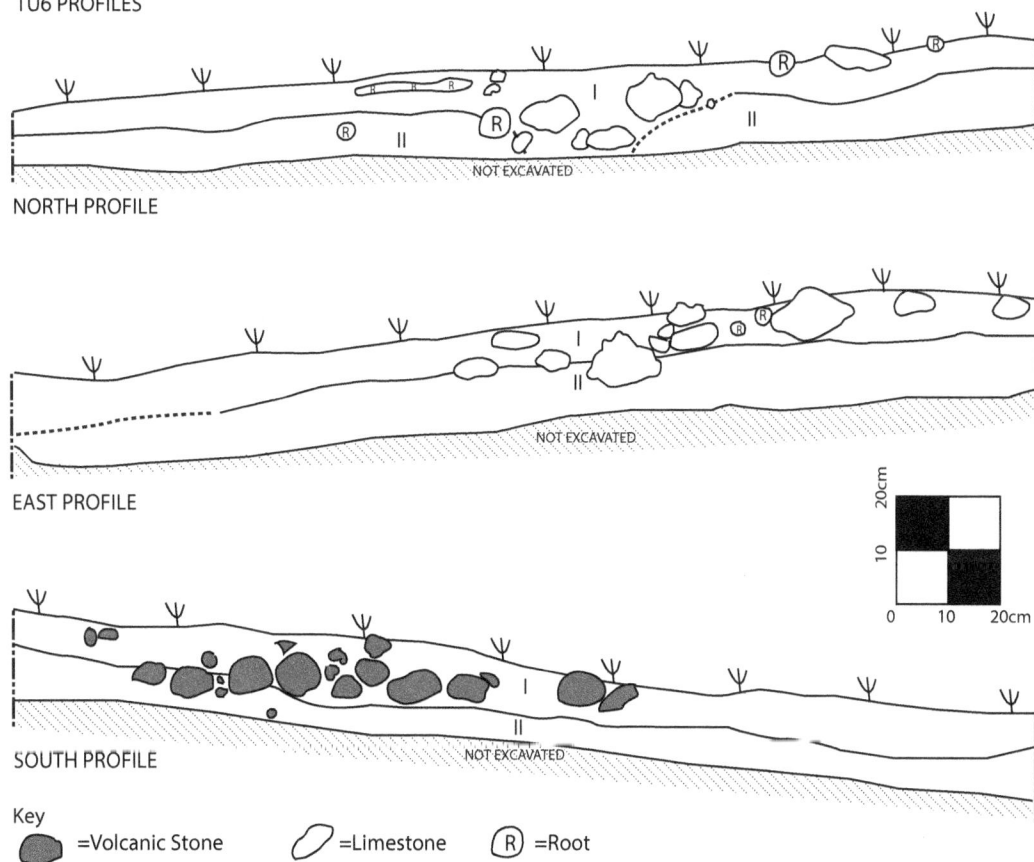

Figure 2.8 Stratigraphic profiles, TU6, G. Gordon House.

Source: James Flexner

G. GORDON HOUSE
TU5 PROFILES

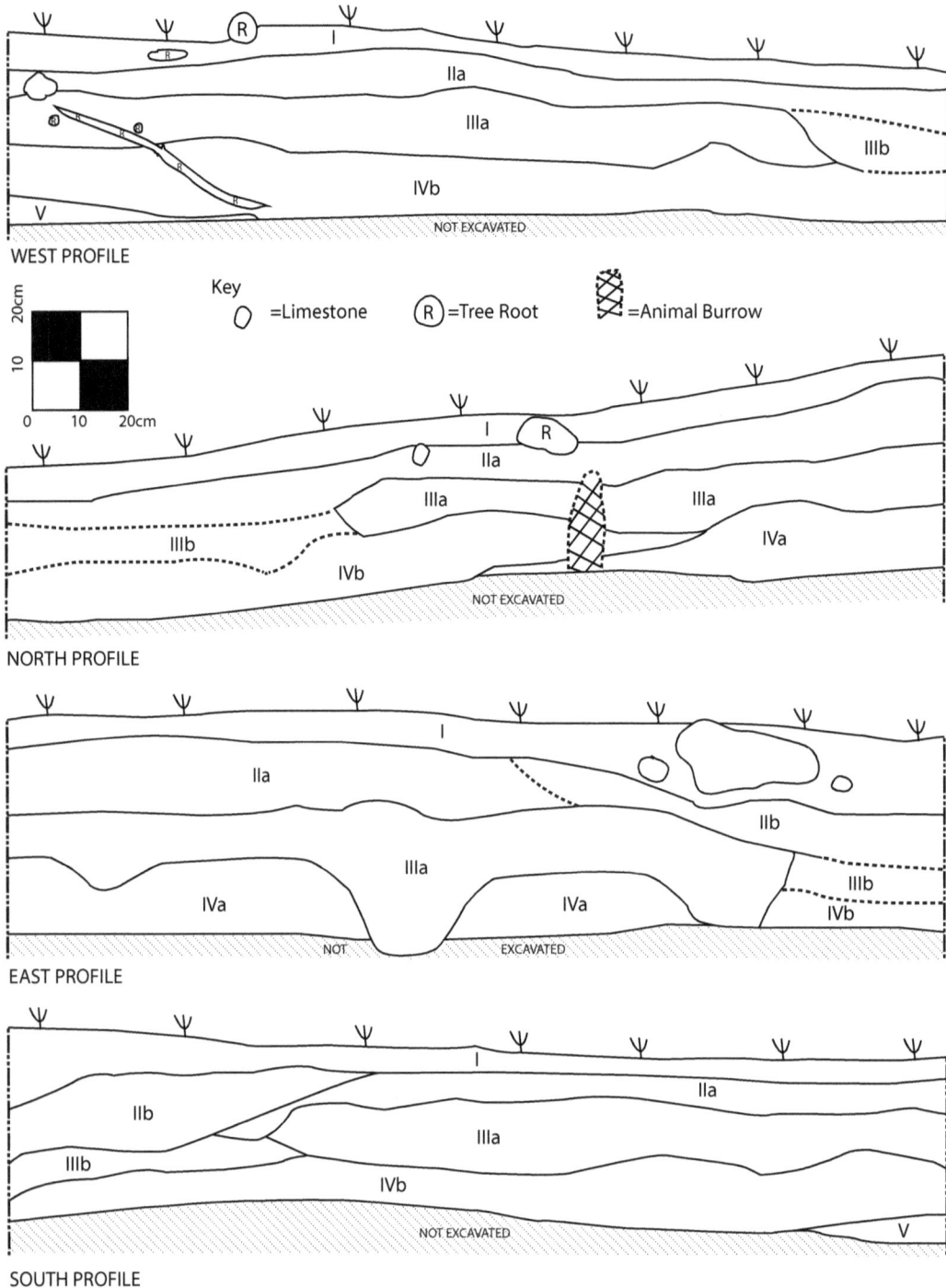

WEST PROFILE

Key   ○ =Limestone   Ⓡ =Tree Root   ▨ =Animal Burrow

NORTH PROFILE

EAST PROFILE

SOUTH PROFILE

Figure 2.9 Stratigraphic profiles, TU5, G. Gordon House.
Source: James Flexner

To the north of TU6, the deposits again become very shallow and artefact densities decrease, as was evident in TU7. The overall impression is of a site that was briefly occupied and left a relatively light impact on the environment, just as the Gordons made a light but apparently significant impact on the religious landscape of Erromango. In TU5, the occupation deposit overlay not red clay subsoil as elsewhere in the site, but a transition to mottled soil containing charcoal and a small amount of 19th-century material. Excavation revealed cross-bedded deposits that went down to roughly 30cm below the ground surface, where they overlay the red clay subsoil found elsewhere on the site (Figure 2.9). A few mortar fragments and some charcoal came from this sediment. These deposits are interpreted as possible infilling of this area of the site to create the level terrace on which the Gordons built their house. Thus while the building itself does not appear to represent a major labour investment, the Gordons did apparently spend some time shaping the space upon which the house was built. It is quite likely that they engaged local labourers in doing so (Gordon, ed. 1863: 136–137).

G. Gordon House Artefact Assemblage

A total of 1,651 artefacts were recovered from G. Gordon House, which had the lowest find density of any of the mission houses excavated on Tanna and Erromango (see Appendix C for an overview of recovered finds). The assemblage consists primarily of architectural materials. Lime mortar fragments (3.7kg were recovered across the site) represent a European material type that was produced locally by burning coral and shells, almost certainly with help of indigenous labour. At least 67 per cent of the nails recovered were hand-wrought, with most of the remaining nails too corroded to identify. Seven of these nails appear to have been intentionally bent into hooks and loops to hang clothes or household items, or to run a rope through. Two round wire nails were found, but likely relate to more recent activities around the site as they came from surface deposits.

Window glass occurred in relatively small amounts at G. Gordon House. Just 45g of window glass were recovered, and no excavation unit contained more than 20g. This suggests the house had few windows, which is significant as again it appears that the house was built as simply as possible. Imported materials like window glass would have been an expensive, difficult to transport luxury, and it is likely that most of the openings of G. Gordon House would have been covered with wooden shutters instead. That said, the house was one of the first on Erromango to have window glass of any kind, which may have made it something of a source of curiosity for local people.

The rest of the domestic assemblage consists primarily of small amounts of olive bottle and colourless vessel glass, and refined earthenware ceramics. The olive glass bottle is a nearly ubiquitous object of 19th-century domestic sites, associated generally with alcohol consumption, though also re-used for many other purposes. Notably, G. Gordon House yielded the highest quantity of olive bottle shards of any of the excavated mission houses (though even then not a huge quantity at 120g from 14m^2 of excavation units). This suggests that the Gordons at Dillon's Bay may have consumed more alcohol than their fellow missionaries. It has been suggested that alcohol consumption was one of many class markers viewed negatively in the CMS missions in New Zealand (Middleton 2007). It is not clear whether the same was true of the Presbyterian missions in the New Hebrides. Further, glass bottles were likely kept as water storage containers after their original contents were consumed, especially considering the remoteness of the Gordons from regular capitalist trade networks.

A very small number (N=37) of ceramic sherds were recovered at G. Gordon House. They are primarily the type called 'Whiteware', which was a hard-bodied refined earthenware produced from 1820 to the present, though many of the sherds show the 'bluing' suggesting a transitional form from the earlier 'Pearlware' (see Majewski and O'Brien 1987). The decorated refined earthenware sherds, of which there were 11, are all decorated with blue transfer-printed designs. Identifiable motifs are of the 'Oriental' type, including bamboo, Chinese-style bridges, and pagodas (Figure 2.10). The 'Chinoiserie' and 'Willow' patterns that exemplify the Oriental style are extremely common on mission sites elsewhere in Oceania, and were generally popular worldwide during this period (Lydon 2009: 141–143; Middleton 2008: 202–209; Smith et al. 2012: 58–67, 2014: 30–40). Intriguingly, the only sherd of Chinese porcelain recovered from a mission site on Tanna or Erromango came from G. Gordon House.

Figure 2.10 Decorated ceramics, including transfer-printed whitewares and Chinese porcelain (second from right on bottom row).

Source: James Flexner

One each of clay tobacco pipe bowl and pipe stem fragments were recovered at the house. Ceramic pipes and tobacco were extremely important trade items in the mission setting, as objects valued by Melanesian people but seen by missionaries as less problematic when compared with even more valuable alcohol or firearms. Four slate pencil fragments were recovered. Literacy was a massively important technology, especially for the Calvinist-derived Presbyterians for whom reading scripture was an absolutely necessary Christian practice (see Keane 2007). Their low density at G. Gordon House suggests the Gordons were only beginning to invest time and material in this practice, and they struggled with convincing local people to attend, or allow others to attend lessons (Gordon, ed. 1863: 142).

One of the recovered slate pencil fragments was modified, and local people indicated the form was likely that of a large 'needle' used in the manufacture of *numplat* or grass skirts (see Lawson 2001). In addition, we recovered two sea urchin spine abraders at the site. Other sea urchin spine and coral fragments are likely also intentional manuports considering the distance from the site to the sea. A fine-grained basalt flake and a core uncovered during excavations around the stone retaining wall are likely also markers of indigenous craft and labour around the Gordons' house (see also Gordon, ed. 1863: 136–137). While small in number, these artefacts are important reminders of the early material entanglements between missionaries and Melanesians. Such objects likely wound up in the G. Gordon house deposits as indigenous people helped with house building activities, or began visiting, trading, and engaging with the missionaries.

In addition, the Gordons would have been almost entirely reliant on local people for their food. Faunal preservation at the site was poor, suggesting acidic soils. Only 25 shell fragments were recovered, but significant food taxa were identified, including Arcidae, Conidae, *Nerita* sp., *Turbo* sp., and *Tridacna* sp. No mammal remains were found aside from a few cattle bones on the surface, which probably post-date habitation of the site. Likely the vast majority of protein for the Gordons came from local marine resources. Likewise, small amounts of flour or rice were probably dietary supplements to the staple yams, taro, and local fruits and vegetables.

G. Gordon House is the earliest mission site on Tanna and Erromango. It represents the initial foothold on the furthest frontier of global Christianity in the late 1850s. Unsurprisingly, then, the site has a relatively small archaeological footprint. The household deposits are shallow, and the artefact density relatively diffuse compared with the other sites. There are some valuable but fleeting hints at interactions with local people. While the overall amount of imported material at the site is small, it does contain a few objects that would have been particularly valued, such as the Chinese porcelain vessel. Limited investment in the physical mission house may also relate to the fact the George Gordon spent much of his time itinerating, visiting other areas of Erromango as he gauged possible interest in missionary presence among various communities (Gordon, ed. 1863: 138–139). Perhaps if he had found a more willing community than the one at Dillon's Bay, the Gordons would have moved to another place, in which case there might have been some sense that the house was to be temporary anyway.

The Second Martyrdom

The Gordons' work on Erromango was cut short abruptly on 20 May 1861. A group of warriors from Bungkil and Unepang to the south came to the mission house asking for Mr Gordon. They claimed there was a sick man and they wanted his help treating him. Gordon accompanied the men, who ambushed him on the road, killing the missionary as he attempted to flee. The men then returned to the mission house and killed Mrs Gordon in turn. After their deaths, the house was abandoned and the Erromangan converts fled the island for Aneityum, fearing they too would be the targets of violence (Gordon, ed. 1863: 182–183; Robertson 1902: 73–77).

Like the earlier martyrdom, the Gordons' deaths left an 'event landscape' (Flexner 2014c) that cements the social memory of this moment in place (Figure 2.11). Walking on the trail towards Bongkil, there is a boulder outcrop with a slight discoloration (point 2 in Figure 2.11). This is said to be George Gordon's 'bloody footprint', and significantly, it's thought to be a reference to Matthew 16:18: 'on this rock I will build my church'. Thus Gordon in his moment of death is thought to have made a statement of the future of the church on Erromango (see also Robertson 1902: 126). Further south, there is a natural stone basin that collects rainwater, where the warriors who killed the Gordons are said to have washed their weapons while returning home (point 3 in Figure 2.11).

Figure 2.11 Event landscape covering the deaths of George and Ellen Gordon (point 1: G. Gordon Mission house; point 4: 'guard's house', apparently belonging to a native guard meant to protect the house; point 5: Vedavil Stream, the nearest water source; see text for explanation of features 2 and 3).

Source: James Flexner

Unlike Williams and Harris, the Gordons had a relatively long residence on Erromango, learned enough of the language and *kastom* of the island to survive, and had even managed to win a few converts. So why were they suddenly attacked and killed? The answer to this question is something of a refrain in the story of early missions on Erromango and Tanna (see Adams 1984: 64–65). Before the attack, there had been a number of destructive tropical storms, and more significantly repeated outbreaks of introduced disease, mostly measles, some of them extremely severe. The native population was dying in unprecedented numbers, which coincided with the arrival of Europeans, and the missionaries were especially close with local populations. George Gordon was even believed to have poisoned an Erromangan chief when he visited the dying man to administer medicine (Gordon, ed. 1863: 184–203).

As mentioned above, there was no natural cause of death in Erromangan *kastom*. It was the work of *Tavuwa*, powerful sorcerers. When missionaries arrived, and people began dying in a way they never had before, the association was more than most people could overlook. The cosmology of the missionaries did not help their case. Germ theory was still decades from being invented, let alone gaining acceptance in European communities. For the missionaries, disease was caused by bad air or humoural imbalances, but whether people got sick, lived, or died was completely in God's hands. In expressing this to Erromangan people, the missionaries cast themselves as a new kind of *Tavuwa*, with God as another, more dangerous *natemas* (spirit) than had existed on the island before. When disaster struck, it was only natural that some Erromangan people blamed the missionaries and acted to protect their island.

Figure 2.12 Burned bottle glass shards from G. Gordon House.
Source: James Flexner

There is a final archaeological legacy of this story. Of 256 glass artefacts recovered from the site, 68 per cent (N=175) showed evidence of burning (Figure 2.12), as do a few of the ceramic artefacts. When James Gordon visited the site a few years after his brother's death, he found the house was no longer standing (Robertson 1902: 126). The burned artefacts indicate that the G. Gordon House may have been burned shortly after the Gordons were killed. Perhaps this was meant to cleanse the site of any missionary *natemas* that may have remained. Yet the event still remained heavy on the hearts of Erromangans, and in 2012 another reconciliation ceremony was held, this time with Gordon family descendants.

James Gordon at Potnuma

George's brother James would follow to the New Hebrides, settling on Erromango in 1864 (Robertson 1902: 124–130). In the first part of James Gordon's tenure on Erromango, he focused on the western side of the island. Land records indicate that he purchased large tracts on behalf of the Presbyterian Church at Dillon's Bay and Bongkil from the trader Andrew Henry in 1865 (Vanuatu National Archives Land Record 33 S.I. 10, 34 S.I. 2). Gordon sought to continue his brother's work, protecting converts and looking for new areas with good potential as mission stations, not only on Erromango, but also further north, particularly on Espiritu Santo (Robertson 1902: 135, 141–142).

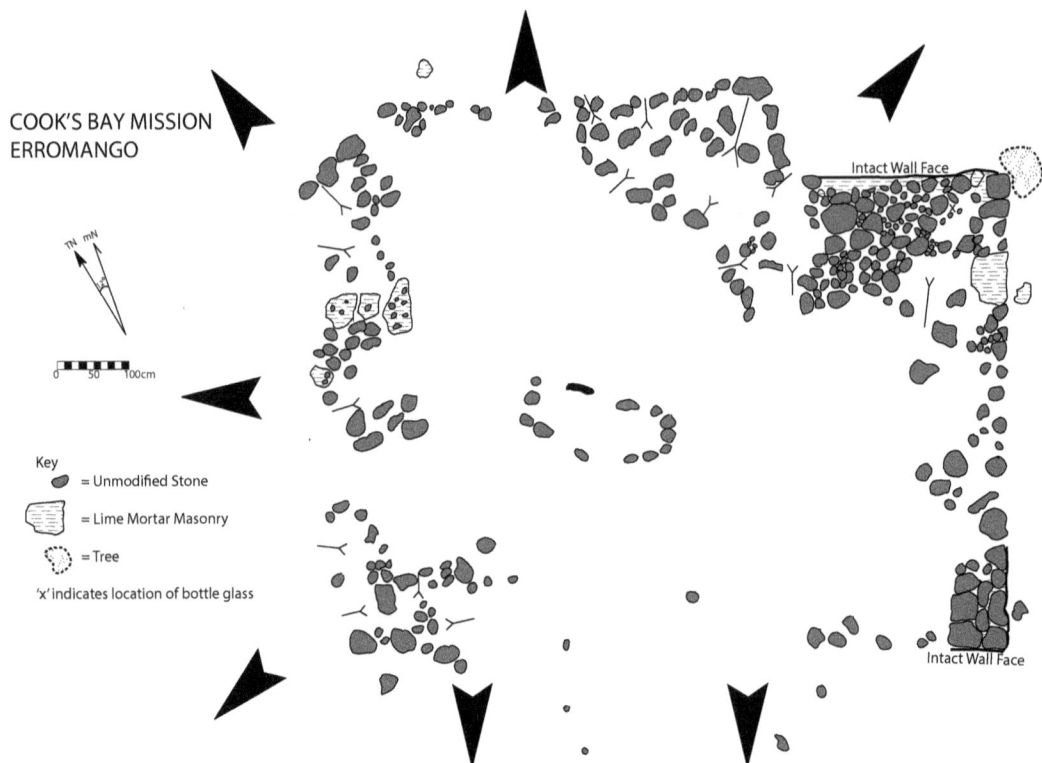

Figure 2.13 Mission building, Cook's Bay.
Source: James Flexner

Another Canadian missionary couple, James Macnair and his wife, joined James Gordon in 1867. Macnair helped to expand the mission field on Erromango, establishing a station at Cook's Bay, specifically near the harbour at a place called Unōva. Lifu Nokilian sold the land to Macnair. The young chief Potnilo was instrumental in the establishment of this settlement according to local traditions. While it wasn't a major focus of mission activity, a small church with stone footings was built at Unōva (Figure 2.13). A stone-lined grave in the center of the church is said to hold the remains of Narainabuo, the first male convert from Cook's Bay, along with those of Neri, the first female convert. Macnair died of illness, probably malaria, in 1870. His wife left the New Hebrides and later married George Turner, an important LMS missionary in Samoa (Robertson 1902: 132–135).

When Macnair settled on the island, James Gordon shifted his focus and primary mission station to the more populous eastern side in 1868, settling at Potnuma, just north of the large village in Port Narvin (Robertson 1902: 134). Potnilo, who may have been the district *Fan lo* of Roviliau considering the extent of his influence, was also key to allowing Gordon to settle at Potnuma. Novolu and Netai were likewise early allies of the mission cause. However, the fact that Gordon settled on the border between the *lo* of Roviliau and Numpunaraipau may have made his situation a somewhat precarious one. James Gordon became the last martyr missionary of Erromango in 1872. Here we focus once more on the patterns of everyday life around the mission house and in the surrounding Melanesian communities rather than the final moments and their ongoing presence in the landscape, though these will also be discussed below.

Around Potnuma

Before turning to the mission house itself, there are a few significant features in the surrounding area (Figure 2.14). Rock art is an important feature of the archaeological landscapes on Erromango (Wilson 1999, 2002). In the area between Port Narvin and Potnuma, there are several major rock art sites, including a cave site called Netngonavon with painted motifs, and two coastal sites with petroglyph fields pecked into volcanic rock outcrops, Malap and Bomtal. Motifs from these sites were initially recorded by Wilson (2002: 24–25), and the petroglyph fields were more completely mapped for this project (Flexner 2013: 21, 2014c: 12).

Malap displays classic motifs of 'contact' rock art (Figure 2.15). These include European sailing ships, bottles, an axe, and what appear to be muskets (they might also be stylised fish). The documented petroglyphs also include a single serif letter 'T'. The petroglyphs continue below the current low tide line, suggesting that the sea level may be rising on this side of Erromango. Alongside the introduced motifs are stone cupules, which were used as a counting device, and pecked circles, which were male and female symbols. Bomtal is primarily a cupule site, though a possible sailing ship is present (Figure 2.16). Significantly, the site is associated with a local oral tradition about Sou Sou, an early Christian convert who apparently defended his faith with a club (each cupule is said to represent a battle he fought; Flexner 2014c: 11–12).

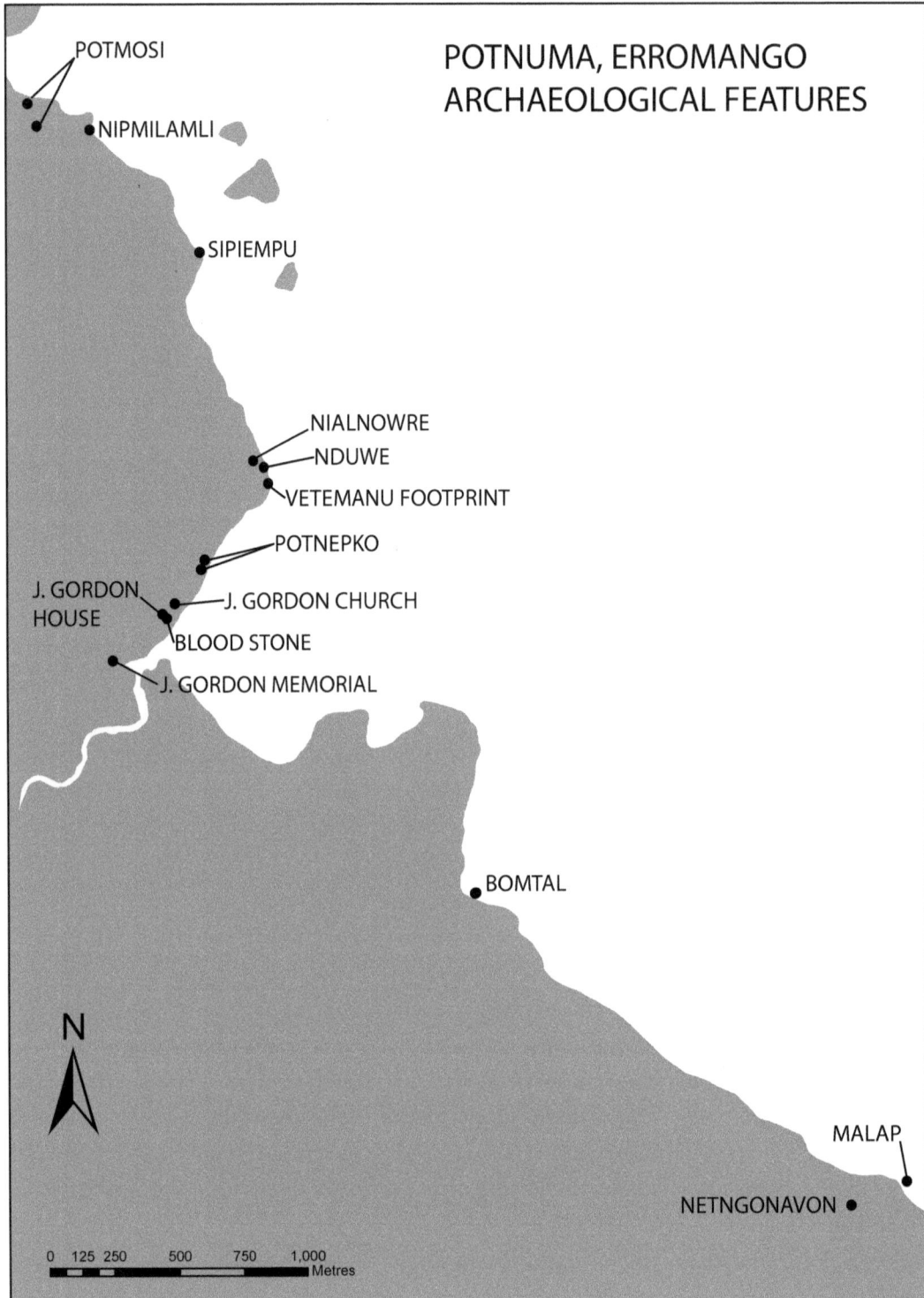

Figure 2.14 Archaeological features in and around Potnuma.
Source: James Flexner

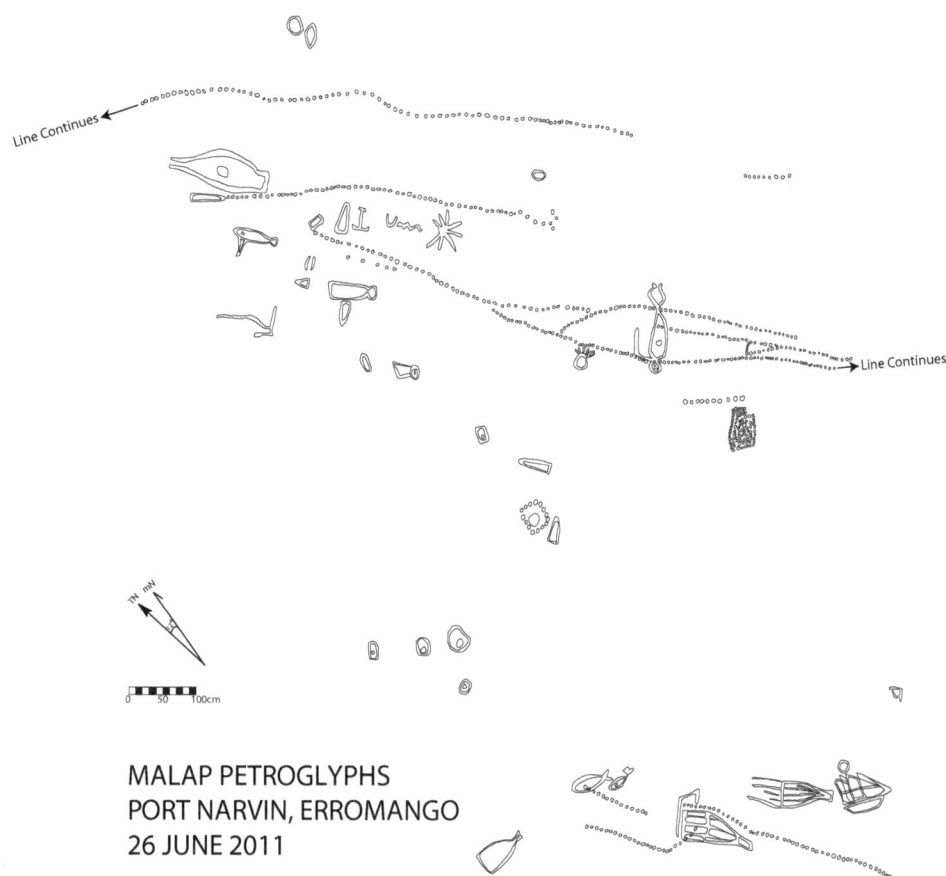

MALAP PETROGLYPHS
PORT NARVIN, ERROMANGO
26 JUNE 2011

Figure 2.15 Petroglyphs at Malap.
Source: James Flexner

These sites have been interpreted as reflections of 'social upheaval' during the contact era: '[K]een resistance to social transformation may have prompted a resurgence in the production of traditional symbols, as a way of maintaining a former social order. Acceptance of incoming ideas, in contrast, may have seen the incorporation of new motifs into the rock-art record' (Wilson 2002: 140). Not surprisingly, what is apparent is not an either/or tendency towards purely traditional and purely introduced motifs, but overlap and blending of the two. Traditional patterns of cupules and concentric ovoids form the structure within which European things are placed.

In the other direction, to the north of Potnuma, there are several *kastom* sites that were recorded during archaeological survey of the area (Figure 2.14). At the boundary between the two *lo*, at a place called Potnepko, lie two natural tubes in the uplifted limestone that were used as places to dispose of the dead. The inland tube was used specifically for sacrificial victims and to 'block' travel on the road along the coast (presumably during times of war, because of fears about *natemas*). Further along is a stone with natural impressions said to be the footsteps of Vetemanu, a 'giant' who was killed and his head sent to Goat Island (a small islet off Traitor's Head). A rock with numerous egg-shaped ground cupules called Nduwe is said to have been used to increase the rate at which chickens laid eggs (a classic case of 'sympathetic magic'; Frazer 1922: 14–62). Finally, there is a small rockshelter with a stone wall enclosure in the front said to be where Nialnowre, the first woman to keep pigs, lived at Ntue. This landscape of storied places would also have likely been densely inhabited, though the population had decreased dramatically by the time James Gordon arrived at Potnuma.

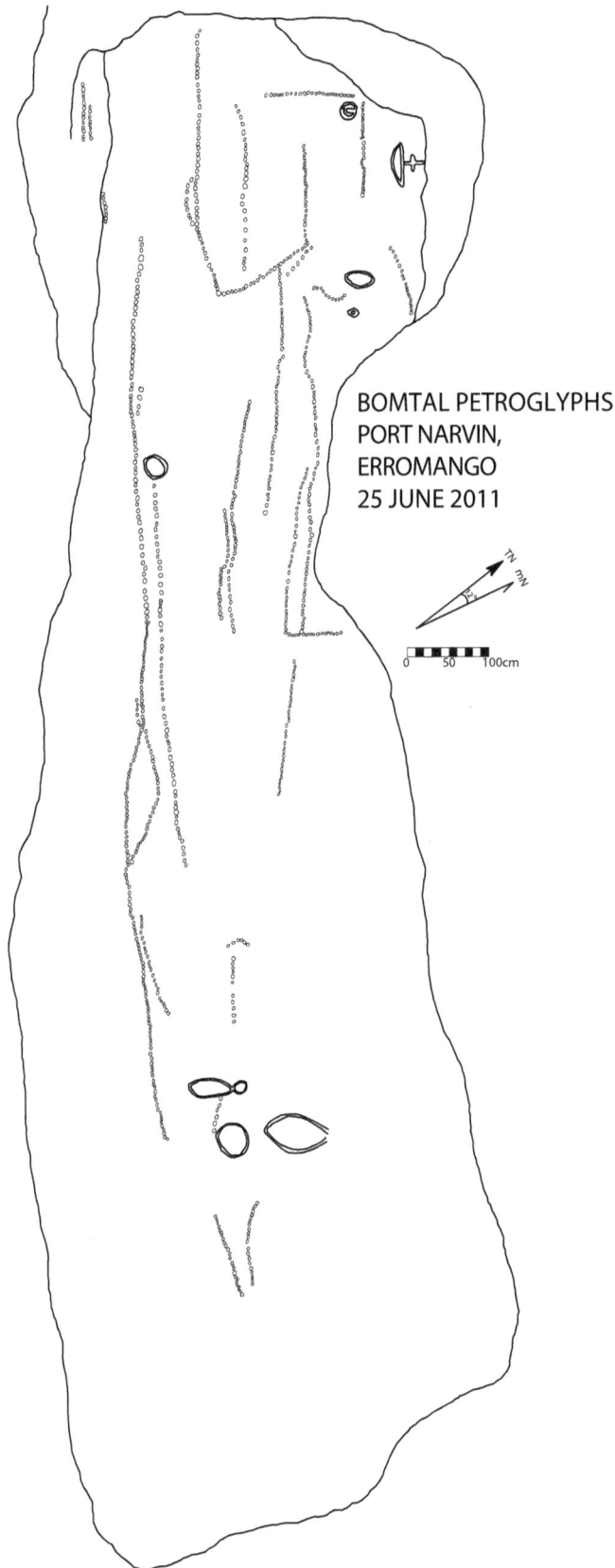

BOMTAL PETROGLYPHS
PORT NARVIN,
ERROMANGO
25 JUNE 2011

Figure 2.16 Petroglyphs at Bomtal associated with oral traditions about Sou Sou.

Source: James Flexner

J. Gordon House Domestic Space and Stratigraphy

When James Gordon chose to relocate to the east coast of Erromango, there is some evidence that he was becoming increasingly withdrawn from the main hierarchy of the Presbyterian Church (Church of the Lower Provinces of British North America 1869–1871). He built a compound consisting of a two-storey mission house and a mission church, both of which had substantial limestone footings and walls. Of the church, the walls on the eastern side, which was where the sanctuary was located, are particularly well-preserved (Figure 2.17). The lime mortar is a European material, but produced locally. Construction of mission buildings almost certainly involved significant inputs of local labour, which would have been organised by the local chiefs.

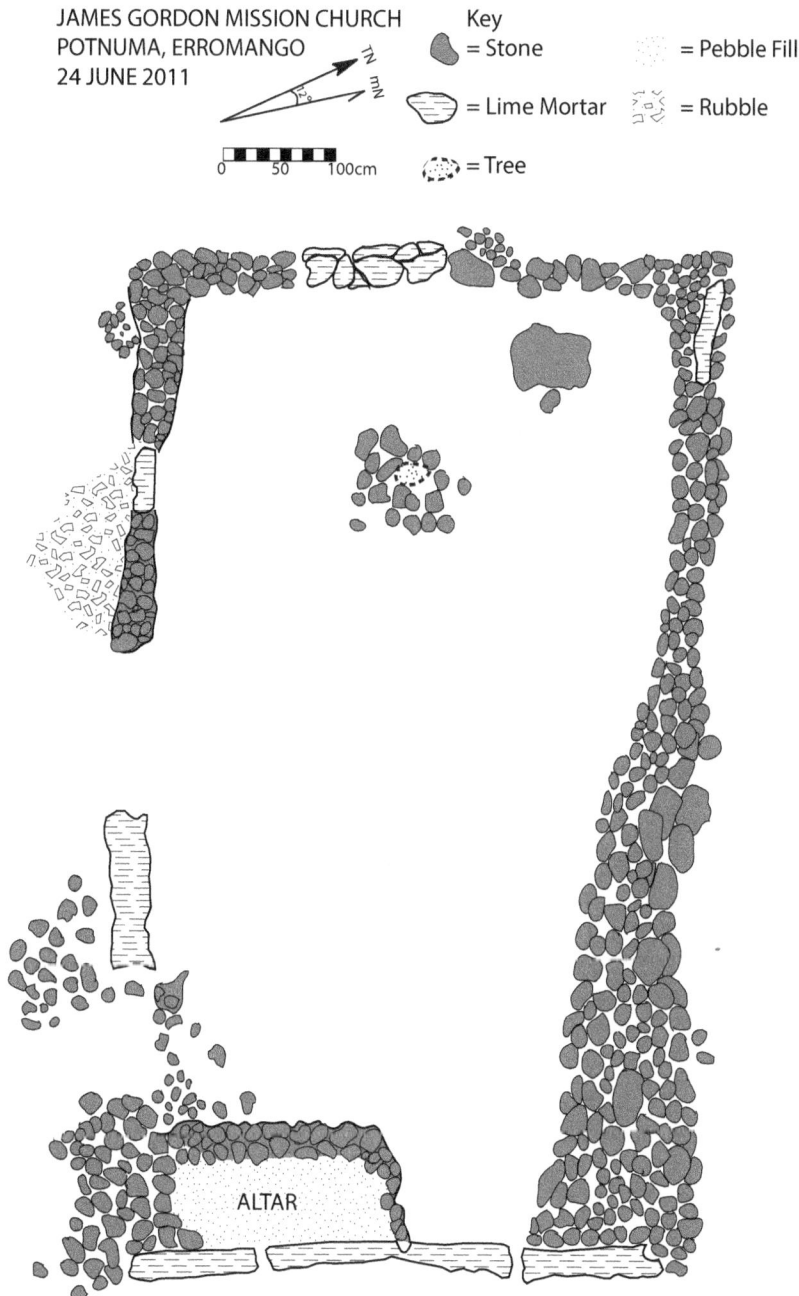

Figure 2.17 Plan map of James Gordon's church at Potnuma.
Source: James Flexner

The mission house (called J. Gordon House below) had lower footings of lime mortar and probably a timber upper storey (Figure 2.18). There was a scattering of surface artefacts at the site, primarily refined earthenware dishes but also some glass (Figure 2.19). Three test units ranging in size from 1x1m to 2x2m were excavated around the site. The excavations revealed the extent of the house, which is estimated as covering an area of 10x5m (32x16ft). The remains of the lime mortar walls are mere stumps, but the openings in the front of the feature suggest the front (sea-facing) wall contained a central front door with two windows to either side.

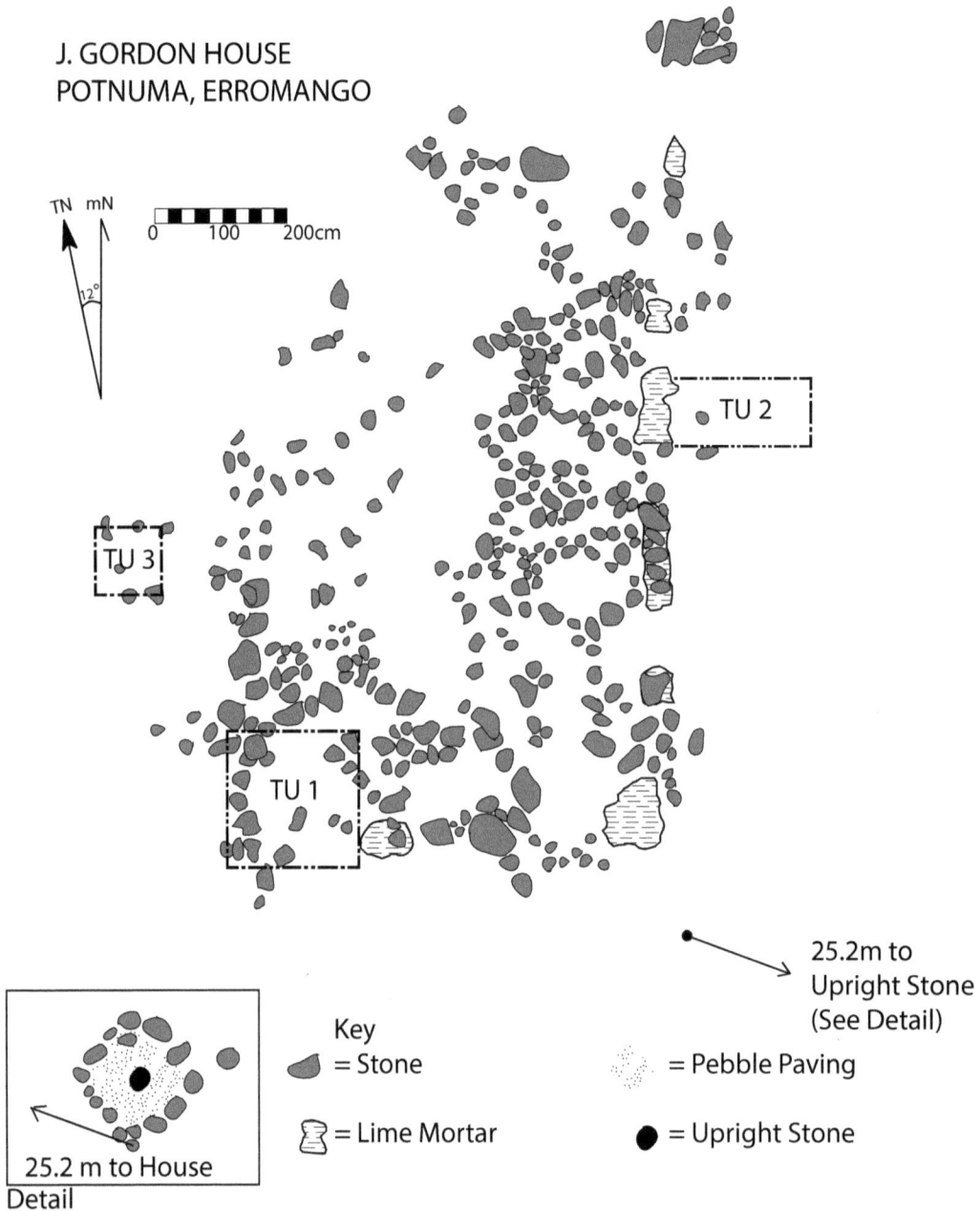

Figure 2.18 Plan of J. Gordon House.

Source: James Flexner

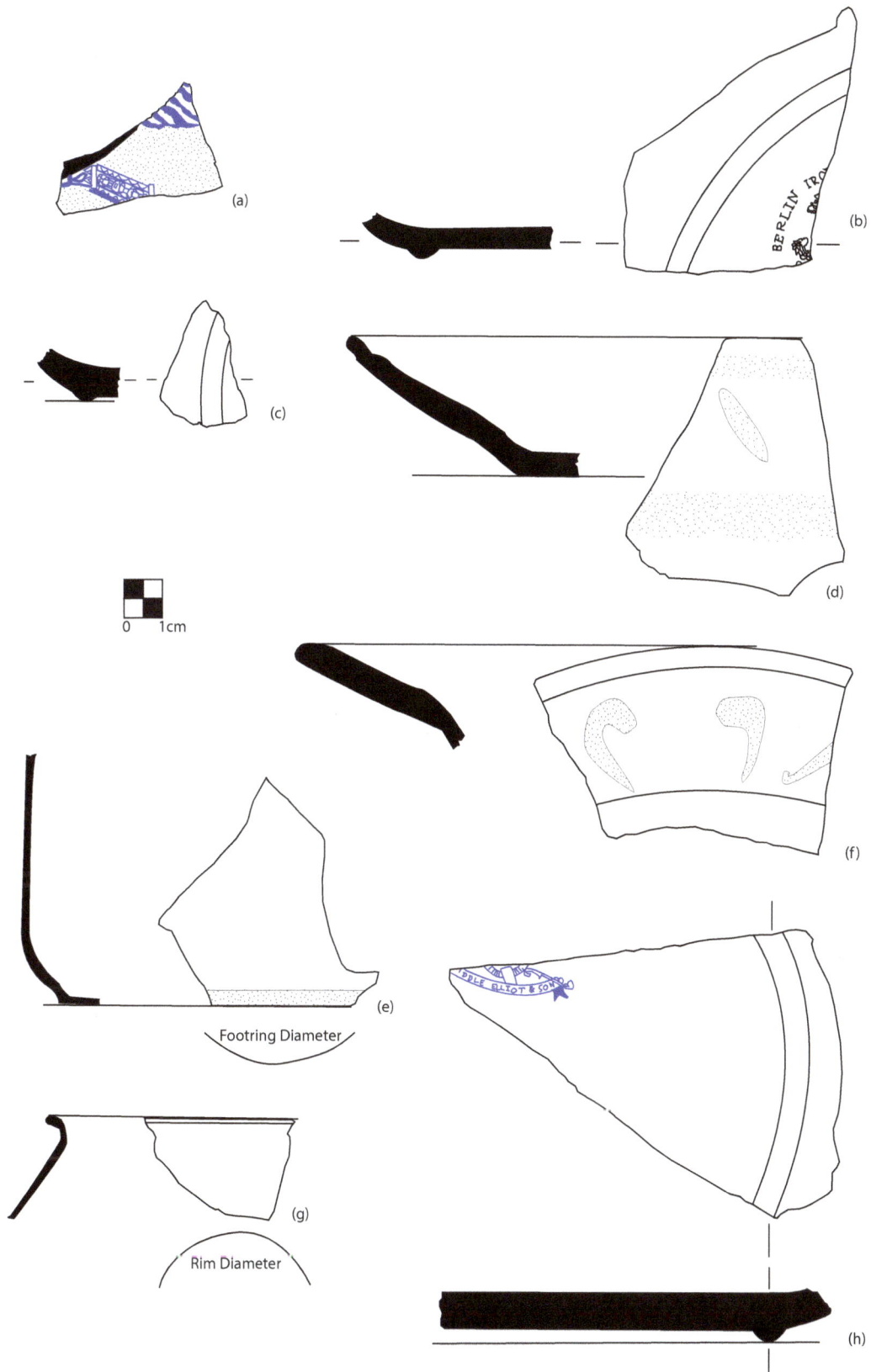

Figure 2.19 Surface artefacts from J. Gordon House.

Source: James Flexner

Three test units covering a total of 7m² were excavated at J. Gordon House. Stratigraphy across the site is uniform, with a single, shallow layer containing the majority of the artefacts. There is a large population of burrowing crabs on the site, and their burrows have caused a great deal of vertical displacement of materials. In the front of the house, TU2 showed that the lime mortar footings rested directly on the clay soil of the site (Figure 2.20). TU1 was located directly along the southern part of the western wall of the house. This unit showed the shallow stratigraphy, and contained refuse possibly disposed through the rear of the house (Figure 2.21). Further west, TU3 was located in the shallow midden deposit. In each case, a single, slightly darker layer containing materials from the short habitation of the site overlay the natural brown clay of the coastal flat.

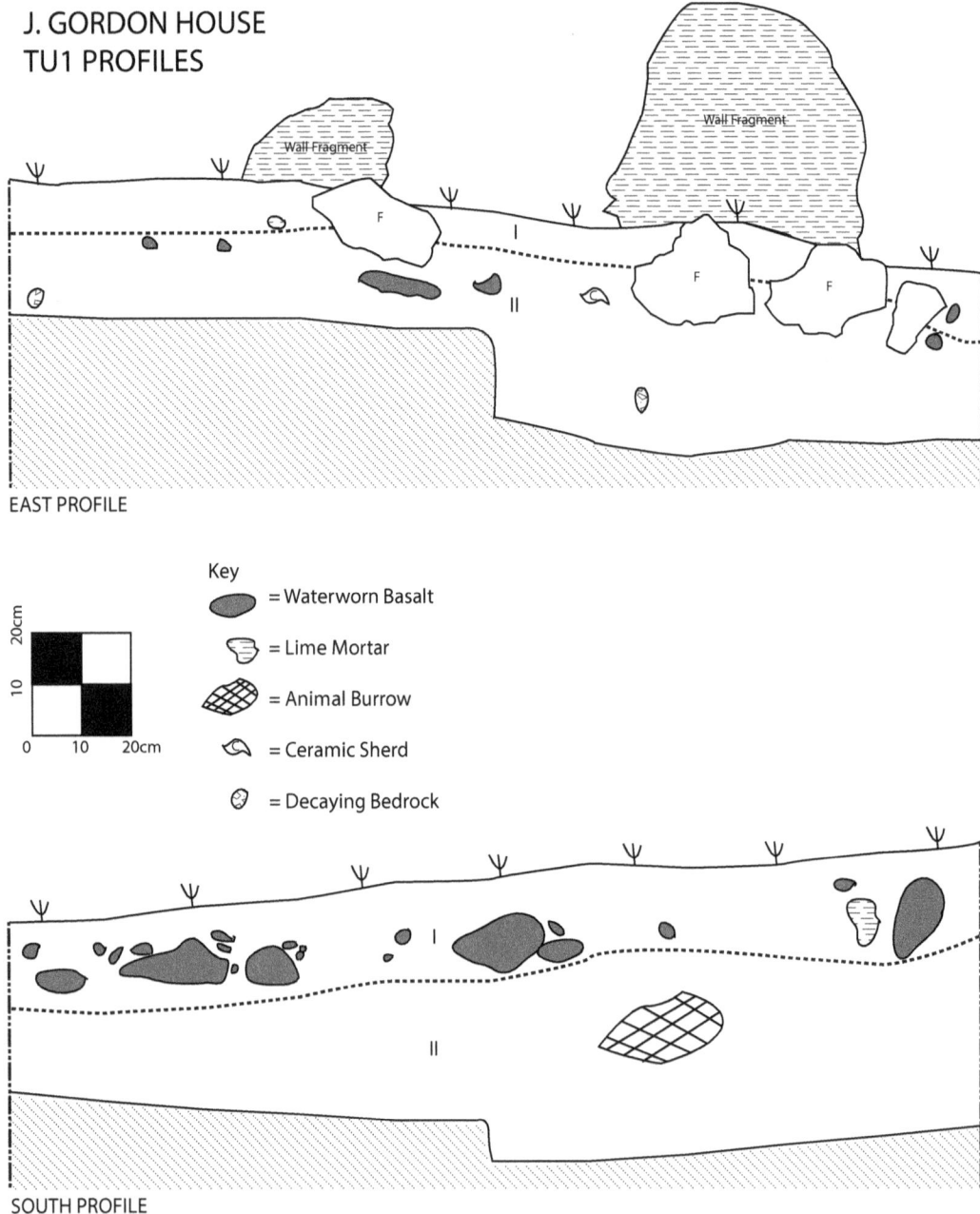

Figure 2.20 Stratigraphic profiles, TU1, J. Gordon House.
Source: James Flexner

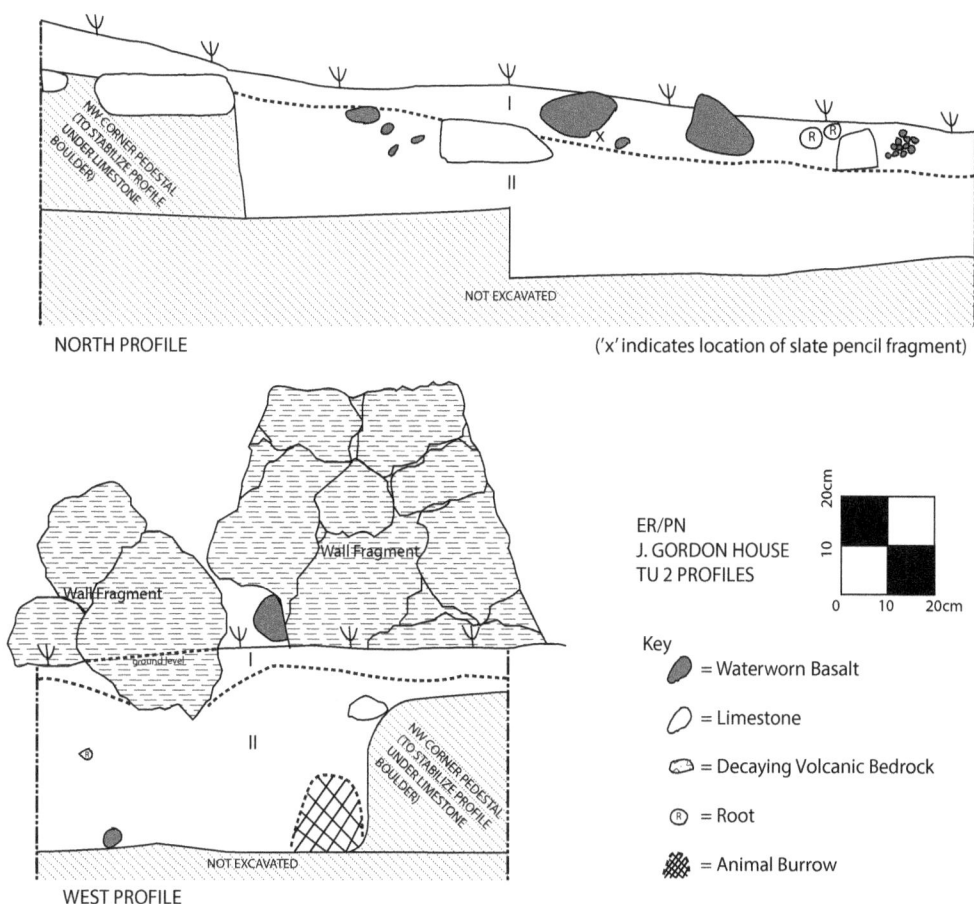

Figure 2.21 Stratigraphic profiles, TU2, J. Gordon House.
Source: James Flexner

J. Gordon House Artefact Assemblage

Artefact density at J. Gordon House was roughly double that of G. Gordon house at Dillon's Bay (N=1753 from 7m^2 vs N=1651 for 14m^2). The assemblage was also a much richer one, carrying a wider variety of imported material culture. As the Erromango Mission was better established and more secure, more materials were brought in by the Presbyterian Church. Erromangans may have read the increasing material affluence of the mission in positive terms. This was not just a matter of increased trading opportunities, but also a means of expanding prestige in Melanesian terms, as chiefly converts had access to a material world not so easily available for rival *Fan lo* who avoided the mission.

Despite the surface evidence for mortared stone architecture, the amount of lime mortar at J. Gordon House was quite small compared to other Erromango sites (1.3kg versus 3.7kg at G. Gordon House). Possibly this relates to preservation conditions at the site. The compact clay soils and rainy environment, combined with ongoing bioturbation means that softer materials, like mortar, are less likely to survive. Other architectural materials were abundant. Hand-wrought nails were still the most common identifiable type (N=70, or 53 per cent of the total nail count), but there were a few machine-made cut (N=5) and round wire (N=15) nails as well. Window glass was abundant on the site, with a total of 265.7g recovered, the largest amount from any of the Erromango Mission houses. A few shards of window glass (N=5) had linear or cruciform discolourations etched into the glass, which may be evidence for screens that have since disintegrated (Figure 2.22a, b, c).

DIAGNOSTIC GLASS ARTEFACTS
JAMES GORDON HOUSE

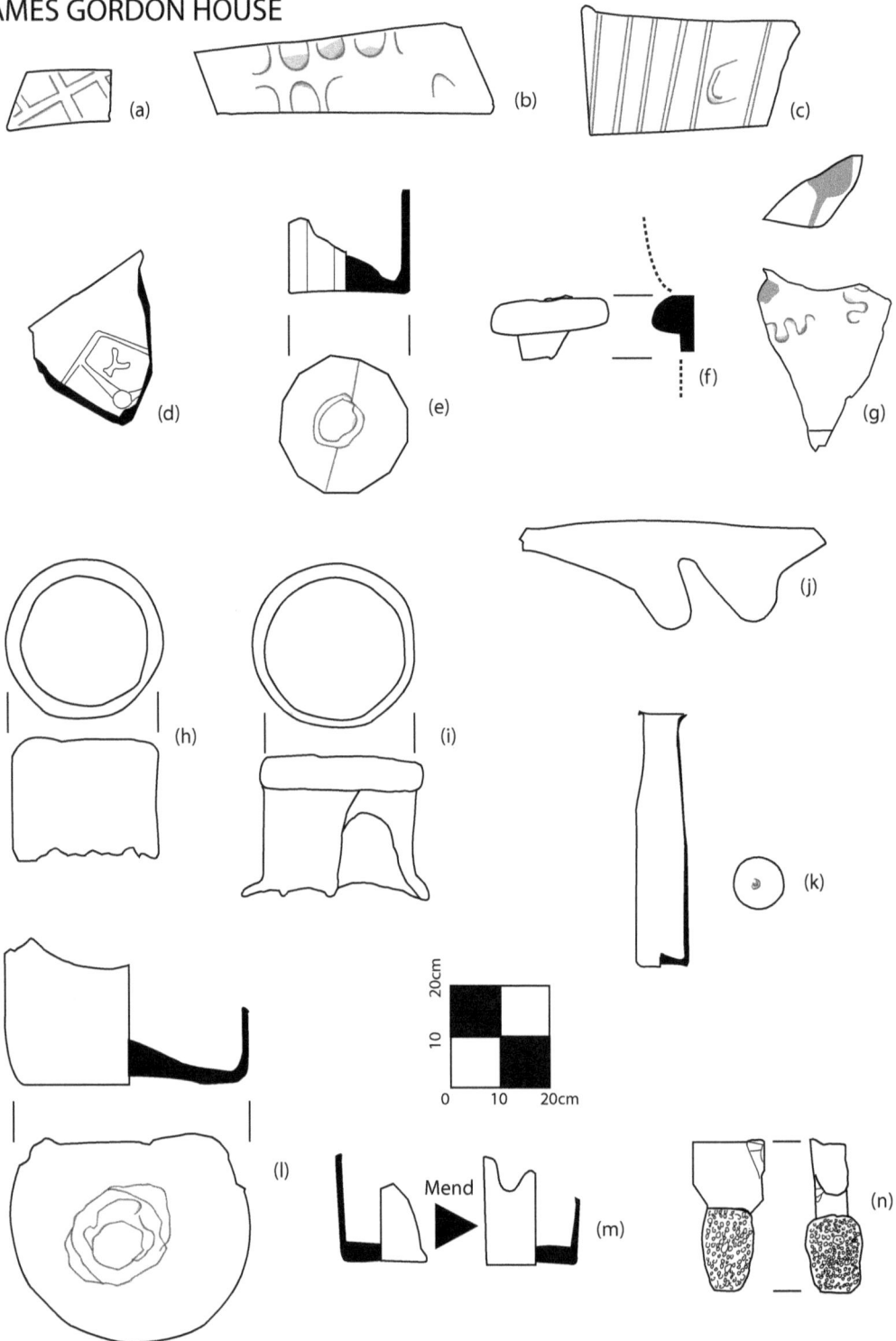

Figure 2.22 Glass artefacts from J. Gordon House.
Source: James Flexner

J. Gordon House yielded a number of other glass finds. Perhaps most remarkable were 45 shards of hand-blown colourless glass vials, as well as one complete example (Figure 2.22k). These vials likely came as part of a medical kit. Also of note is a frosted glass stopper (Figure 2.22n), which probably came from a perfume bottle. Colourless drinking glass fragments (Figure 2.22f, g) included etched stemware fragments that may have had a vine motif, probably indicating alcohol consumption. However, there was relatively little olive glass, at just over half the density found at G. Gordon House (34.6g from 7m² versus 120.2g from 14m²). This suggests that James Gordon may have primarily consumed alcohol as part of European social rituals when hosting white visitors.

Refined earthenware ceramics also relate to European dining rituals. The most common type found at J. Gordon House was Berlin Swirl Ironstone (Figure 2.19, 2.23), produced by Liddle Elliot & Son in Staffordshire around 1864 (Dieringer and Dieringer 2001: 66). Berlin Swirl was sent to Australasia in large quantities when commercial markets were disrupted by the American Civil War (Brooks 2005: 57–60). There was a single sherd of a transfer-printed vessel with an Oriental motif on the surface. The other transfer-printed vessel (Figure 2.24) was identified as 'Minerva' pattern, which was produced by Podmore, Walker & Co., an English Staffordshire pottery, between 1834 and 1859 (Godden 1991: 501; Williams and Weber 1978: 72). The pattern featured the Roman goddess of wisdom seated alongside classical urns in the centre, with urns and columns in cartouches around the rim. Another moulded refined earthenware plate with grape vine motifs around the rim is likely a 'cheese plate' form, with a radiating ribbed surface to allow the oil of a cheese to drip down. These kinds of plates would have been important for Victorian dining rituals. The Minerva plate specifically may have served a further purpose as a storytelling object when describing deeper European traditions to local people.

The site yielded one sherd from a vessel bearing a currently unidentified transfer pattern signified by a patent mark. There were also sherds from a porcelain measuring cup. This object reflects the increasing standardisation of everyday life in the industrial era, a pattern that apparently extended all the way to the remote corners of the New Hebrides. The final ceramic vessel identified at the site is represented by 11 sherds of a red-slipped coarse earthenware recovered from TU2. Indigenous ceramic production ceased on Erromango around 2000BP (Bedford 2006: 158). There is evidence that on his last trip to Espiritu Santo Island in 1869 James Gordon was trading for curiosities, using the Erromangan convert Novolu as an indigenous middleman to get better prices (Robertson 1902: 141). It is reasonable, then, to interpret this object as a souvenir collected by Gordon on one of his trips north. Petrographic analysis of the red-slipped vessel indicates not Santo, but Ambae, a neighbouring island some 400km north of Potnuma (Dickinson 2014).

Evidence for more local interactions with Melanesian people were less clear in the artefact assemblage from J. Gordon House, which lacks the coral or sea urchin spines common on other sites. We recovered 17 slate pencil fragments from TU1 and TU2 (Figure 2.25). These objects ranged in diameter from 0.46cm to 0.58cm. Pencils from the two different test units in which they were found have different diameters, further bolstering the argument that teaching occurred throughout the domestic space at Potnuma over time. The pencils were grey to dark grey in colour. The fragments are generally quite small, averaging just 1.7g each. It is quite likely that most of these fragments were broken by Erromangan students in the process of learning to write, including both unintentional breakage and regular sharpening as the pencil tips dulled from repeated use. Slate pencils were crucial technological implements for mission work, as literacy was one of the necessary disciplines required of Christian converts.

CERAMIC MARKS
JAMES GORDON HOUSE

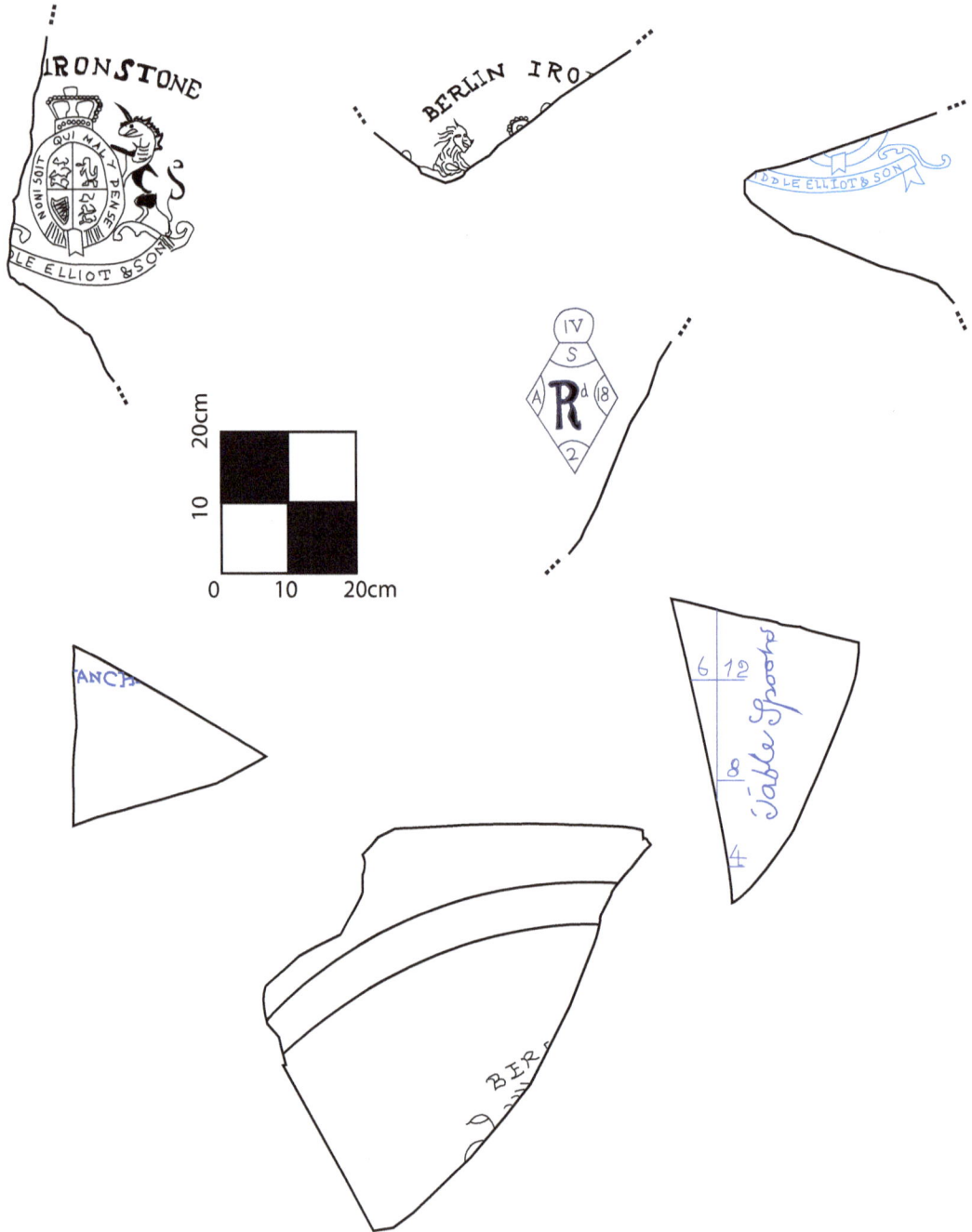

Figure 2.23 Ceramic manufacturers' marks and other markings, J. Gordon House.

Source: James Flexner

Figure 2.24 'Minerva' transfer-pattern ceramics, J. Gordon House.
Source: James Flexner

Figure 2.25 Slate pencil fragments, J. Gordon House.
Source: James Flexner

The faunal assemblage at J. Gordon House probably suffers from poor preservation conditions. Of the shell remains recovered, the primary taxa were *Turbo* sp. and *Nerita* sp. As elsewhere on Erromango, James Gordon would likely have relied on local fish and shellfish as his primary protein source at Potnuma. The ceramic dishes noted above also likely held yams or bananas more often than rice or bread. The only mammal remains found at J. Gordon House consist of a single, isolated human molar recovered in TU1 (PN34). This is interpreted as possible evidence of historical dentistry work, though whether the molar is Gordon's or a Melanesian convert's is a matter for future research to discover. Certainly missionaries regularly used their medical 'expertise' as a way of engaging with local people, though the state of medical practice was fairly primitive before formally trained medical missionaries began arriving in the 1880s (Miller 1986: 16–25).

Erromango's Final Martyr

Despite his considerable success in winning converts, and greater access to imported things, James Gordon became the last missionary to suffer a martyr's fate on Erromango (ironically, he published a biography of his brother and sister-in-law called *The Last Martyrs of Eromanga* shortly before departing Canada). On 7 March 1872, Gordon was ambushed in his house by Nerimpau and Naré, men from a nearby village. As noted above, the Cook's Bay people were much more sympathetic to the mission cause, so Gordon's presence at Potnuma for nearly four years was always a threatened one, as noted after the fact by Yomot, one of Gordon's supporters. The event set off a series of revenge killings, following in some ways existing patterns in Erromangan warfare. Notably, the killer Nerimpau was tracked and killed (Robertson 1902: 156–163). He was beheaded, and his body hung from a tree that still stands today (Figure 2.26). The tree is still *tabu*, considered to be poisoned because of Nerimpau's evil deeds and not to be touched.

Figure 2.26 *Tabu* tree where Nerimpau's body was hung.
Source: James Flexner

Missionary accounts suggest that the motivation for the killing was simply hatred of missionaries and the mission cause. However, local social memories suggest that Gordon had accidentally brought poisonous reef fish to a local feast, and that he was killed for causing illness among the local population (another possible example of a missionary being identified as a dangerous sorcerer). It was also apparently rumoured that Gordon was keeping a large amount of gold in the house, a tantalising hint at an early version of later beliefs that associated capitalist wealth also with foreign sorcery or magic (e.g. Lindstrom 1993; Taylor 2016).

Erromangan people marked James Gordon's death in several ways. Gordon died in the front of his house. An upright stone was later erected to mark the spot where his blood had apparently run, over 25m away towards the sea. To the southwest, local people also constructed a memorial grave enclosure of lime mortar and stone (Figure 2.27). Significantly, this monument takes the form of a sea turtle. Turtles were both male symbols in Erromangan cosmology, and known for making long sea voyages. The head of the turtle faces towards the northwest, which is in the general direction of the Presbyterian homeland in Scotland, and Gordon's homeland in Canada's Maritime Provinces. The rectangular concrete slab over the grave marker, which appears to be a later addition, integrates a headstone flanked with a brown glass jar and green glass bottle, and a ceramic water filter with the mark '[A]ND SONS PATENT LIMESTONE FILTER', which was probably salvaged from J. Gordon House and repurposed as a flower urn for the memorial. This resting place shows that missionaries had begun to be integrated into Melanesian societies. The objects are foreign, but the overall form of the memorial uses distinctively local references. The process is one of Melanesians integrating European people, things, and religious beliefs into their world, rather than the other way around.

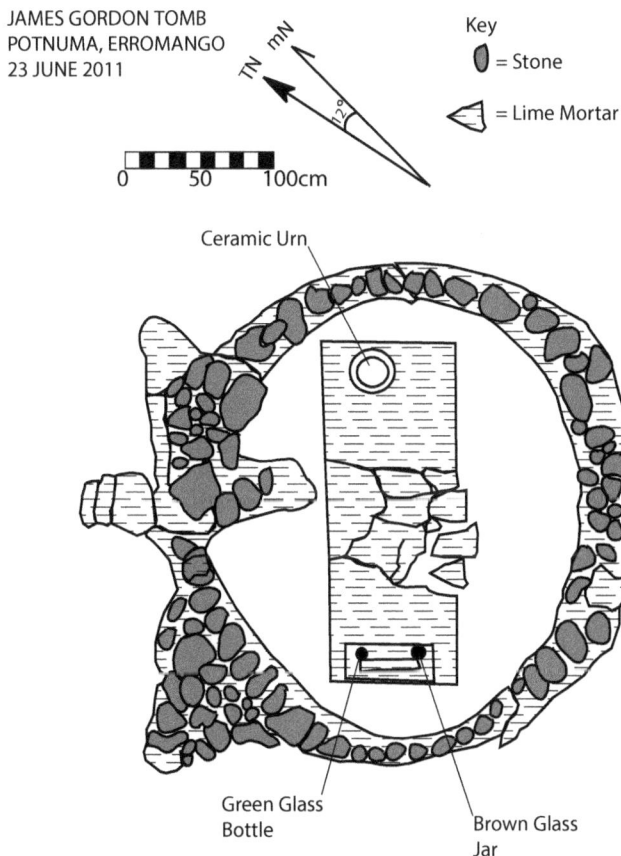

Figure 2.27 Sea turtle-shaped memorial to James Gordon, Potnuma.
Source: James Flexner

The Robertsons at Dillon's Bay

Hugh Angus Robertson and his wife Christina settled at Dillon's Bay mere weeks after James Gordon had been killed on the other side of the island. Robertson was another Nova Scotian missionary, who had initially sailed with James Gordon to the New Hebrides on the *Dayspring* in 1863, arriving in the islands in 1864. Like James Harris before him, Robertson was travelling for health reasons as warm climate and fresh air were thought to improve the constitution (Robertson would have infinitely more luck than Harris in the New Hebrides). Inspired by what he saw on Aneityum, Robertson determined to study to be a missionary when he returned to Nova Scotia. He was ordained and licensed, and returned to take up the assignment on Erromango in 1872 (Robertson 1902).

Upon arriving in Dillon's Bay, the Robertsons set about resuming mission work in the area, having some reason to be optimistic despite James Gordon's recent death. However, the situation on the island was far from stable. The Robertsons would themselves narrowly escape possible attacks on several occasions (Robertson 1902: 195–196, 315–318). The Robertsons lived on Erromango for over four decades, and managed to convert large portions of the population. The archaeology of their mission station reflects material processes of labour and settlement patterns that were instrumental to that apparent success.

The Robertson Mission

Unlike previous missionaries on Erromango, the Robertsons built their mission in the middle of the indigenous village at Dillon's Bay. Their house became a major attraction for parties of Erromangan visitors almost immediately. In January 1873, the house was blown down in a hurricane, an event that would have been interpreted in terms of supernatural causes. Indeed, Robertson notes that he was warned to keep doors closed for fear of attack particularly after the storm. Robertson embarked immediately on a project of rebuilding the house, which he describes as 62x28ft (19x9m) with a 6ft (2m) veranda. The house had wooden walls, plastered on the interior, and a thatched roof. Yomot, an early friend of the mission, 'worked splendidly' on the construction of the house (Robertson 1902: 193–208).

The archaeological remains of the mission house (called Robertson House below) consist of the large stone and mortar foundation (Figure 2.28). Excavation of the area immediately in front of the front step (TU1) revealed a foundation measuring 140cm from top to bottom (Figure 2.29), which is extremely deep for a single-storey house, even on the sandy soil by the coast in Dillon's Bay. In fact, it appears that Robertson engaged local people for major construction projects of all kinds, building a storehouse for his materials, and eventually a large timber church, called the Martyr's Memorial Church, in 1880. This was a prefabricated timber church built from a kit from Australia, the first in the New Hebrides (Robertson 1902: 321–326). Around these buildings, Robertson had native labourers drag boulders from the beaches of Dillon's Bay to construct a series of stone walls outlining the paths around the village (Figure 2.30).

Robertson's ability to call on large labour parties is not simply a reflection of the increasing power of the mission on Erromango in the later part of the 19th century. Rather, Robertson's organisation of labour parties may have been a causal factor in his long-term ability to continue mission work and win converts. The fact that Robertson had local people working for him while managing to avoid illness and death that might have been wished upon him by the *Tavuwa* would have offered a powerful sign about the efficacy of his spiritual prowess, and that of his *natemas*, Iesu, the Christian God.

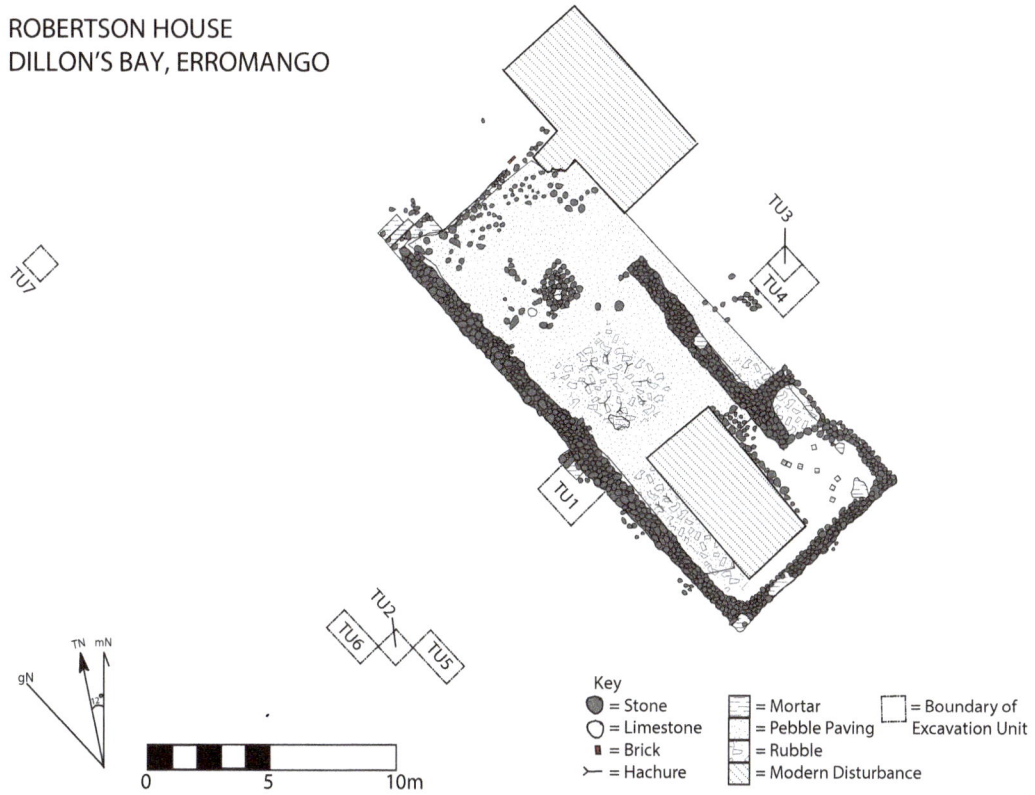

Figure 2.28 Plan of Robertson House, Dillon's Bay.

Source: James Flexner

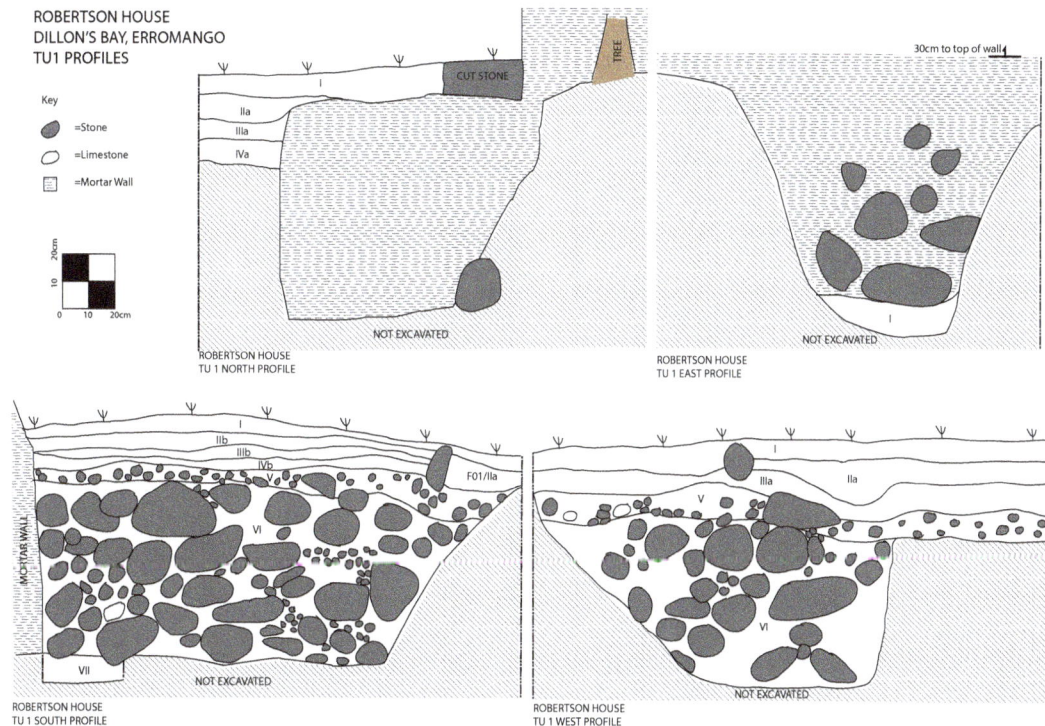

Figure 2.29 Stratigraphic profiles, TU1, Robertson House.

Source: James Flexner

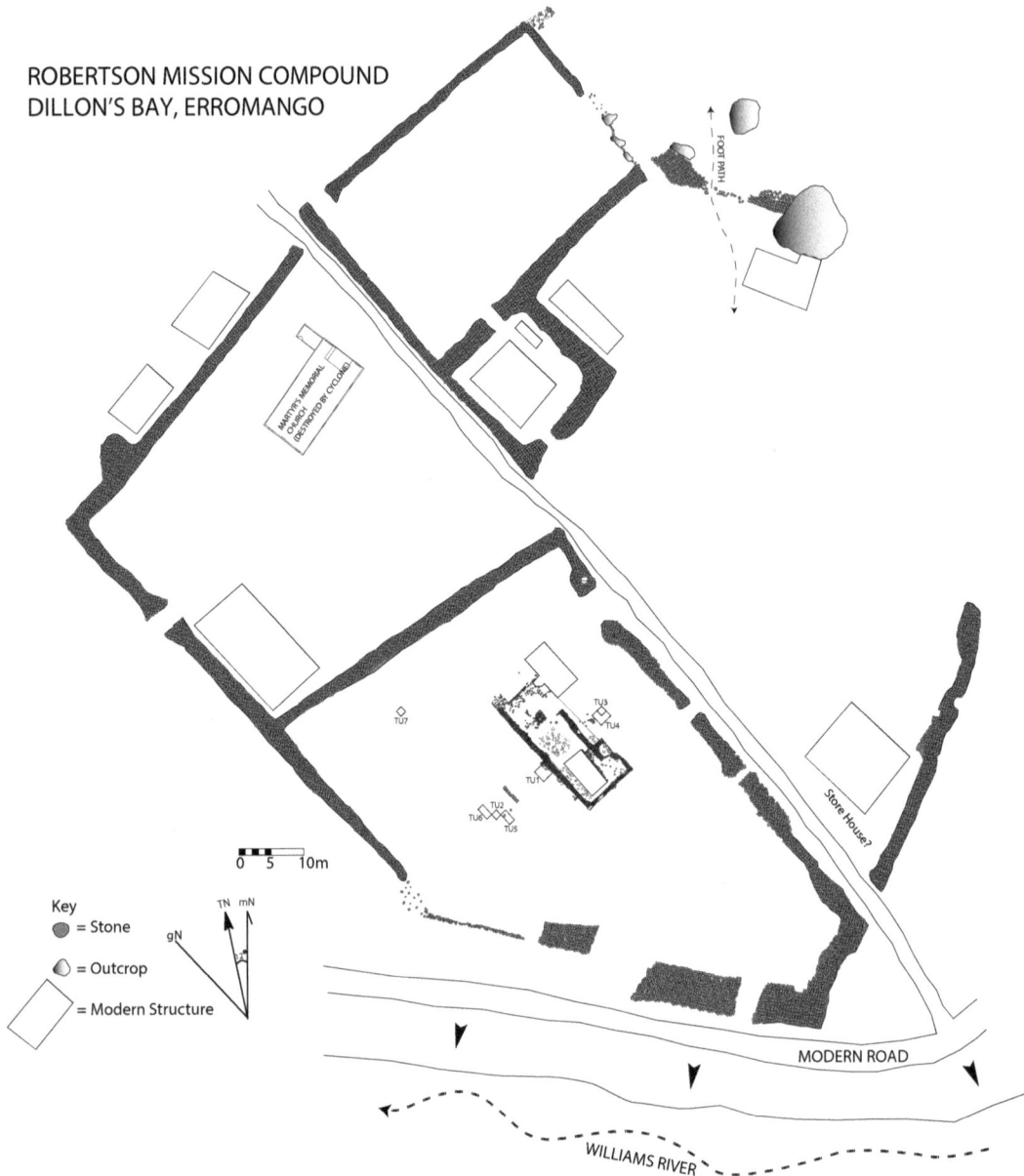

Figure 2.30 Map of stone walls in the Robertson Mission compound.
Source: James Flexner

In addition to excavating immediately next to the house, we excavated test units in the backyard area, and on the sea side (Figure 2.28). Three adjacent units (TU2/5/6) were excavated 10m west of the house foundation (Figure 2.31). The stratigraphic sequence of the southern unit (TU5) consisted of a thin topsoil layer overlying a dark brown to black sand with coral limestone pebbles, suggesting a recent pavement in the area, possibly a path leading to the house. This overlay a layer of volcanic cobbles and boulders, which in turn covered a layer of compact reddish-brown clay loam. This layer is not present to the north in the adjacent units (TU2/6). In these units, there was another layer with coral inclusions underlying the boulders (Figure 2.31).

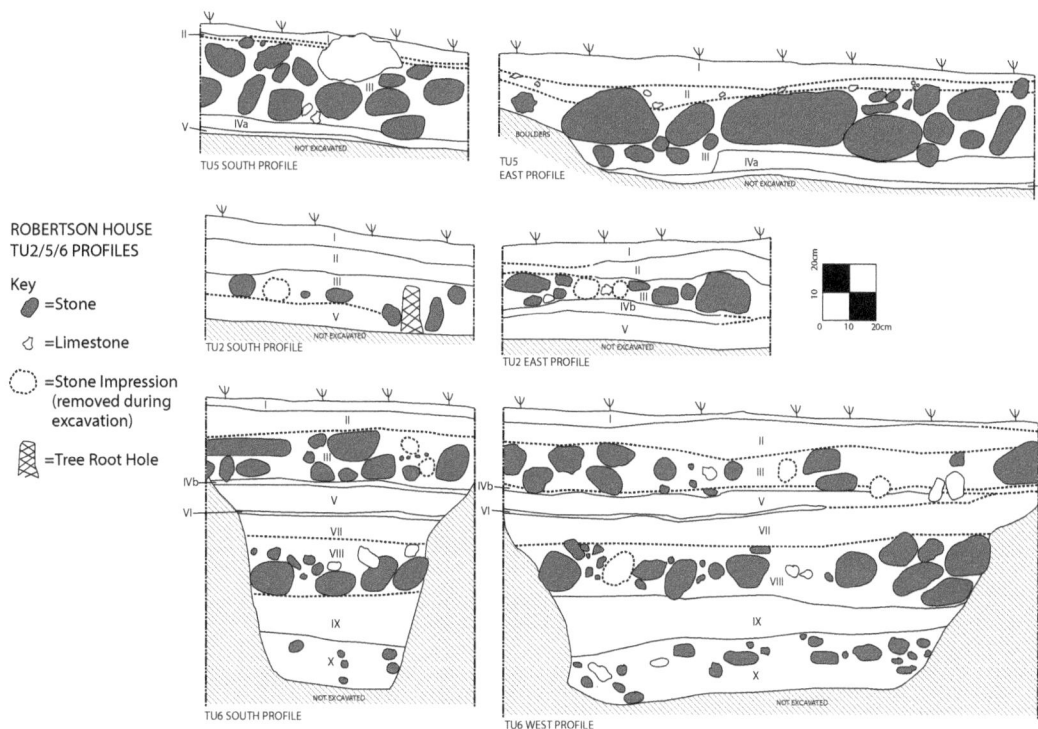

Figure 2.31 Stratigraphic profiles, TU2/5/6, Robertson House.

Source: James Flexner

The sediment underlying the archaeological deposits in TU1 was a clean black beach sand. We excavated TU6 to a much greater depth than the other units, revealing a stratigraphic sequence that alternated between deposits of sandy loam, thin lenses with coral inclusions (thought to be paving layers), and deposits of cobbles and boulders (Figure 2.31). Excavations were halted approximately 1m below the surface in a layer of very dark brown sand with cobble inclusions. The last excavated level included a piece of iron strap. It appears that the annual tropical storms that flood the river regularly deposit sediment in this area, including sometimes larger cobbles and boulders. Further, there appears to be a good deal of downward movement of materials, considering the great depth at which the metal was found (a radiocarbon sample from the same level returned a 19th-century date; see Appendix D for radiocarbon dates).

Behind Robertson House, archaeological excavations revealed significant features relating to everyday occupation of the site (Figure 2.32). Removal of the topsoil revealed two ovoid features filled with stone rubble, shells, and animal bones. Excavation revealed that the features are almost certainly earth ovens, likely dating to the later part of the Robertsons' time in Dillon's Bay. Robertson was apparently a great admirer of Erromangan cuisine, which he describes at length in his autobiography (Robertson 1902: 379–381), so it is perhaps unsurprising that some earth ovens were discovered behind his house.

ROBERTSON HOUSE, TU4 PLAN, CLOSE OF PN129

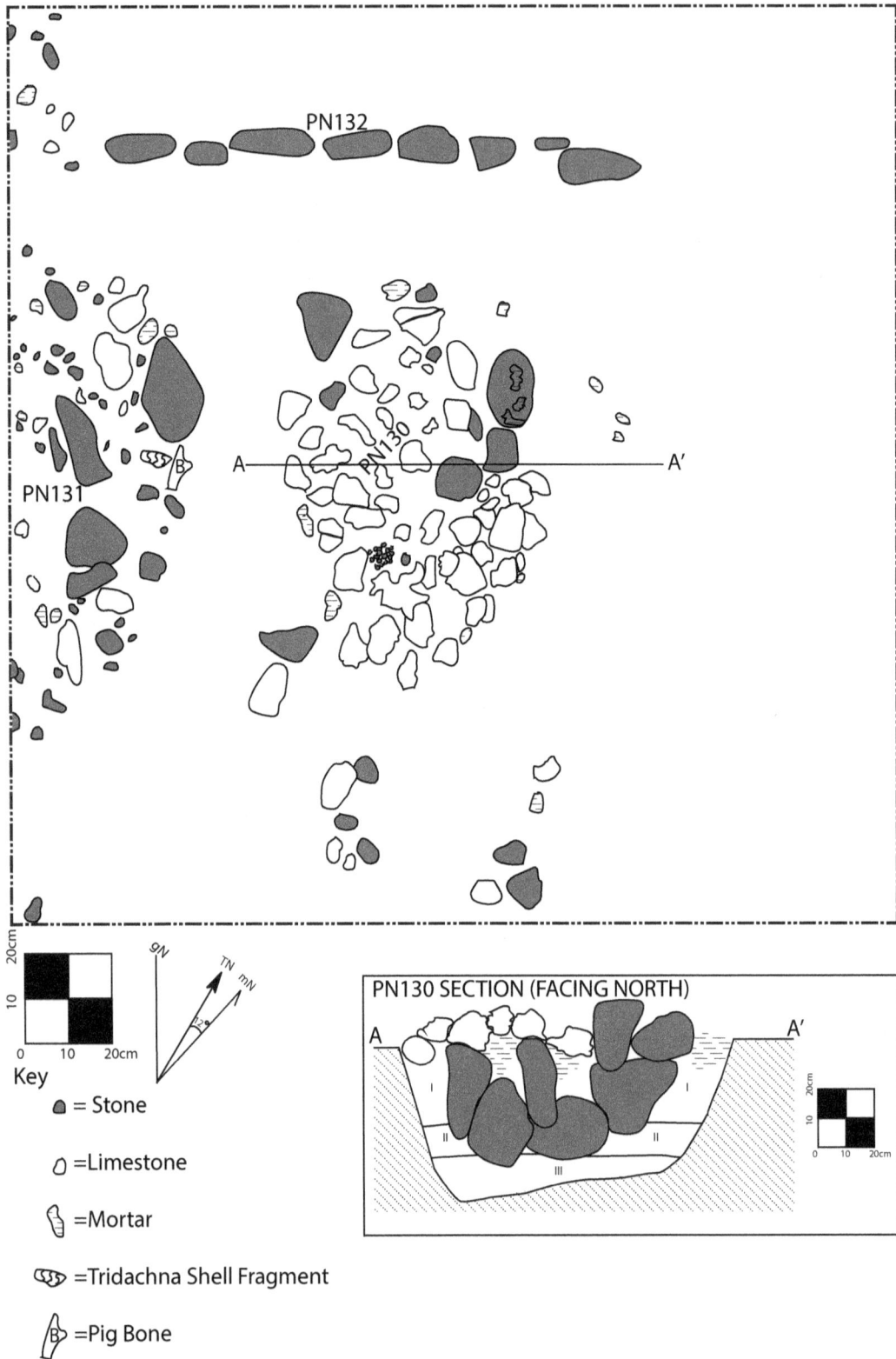

Key

◖ = Stone

◌ =Limestone

▯ =Mortar

෴ =Tridachna Shell Fragment

▱ =Pig Bone

PN130 SECTION (FACING NORTH)

Figure 2.32 Plan and cross-section of earth oven features and stone alignment, TU4, Robertson House.

Source: James Flexner

Initially, the Robertsons had trouble obtaining local foods (Robertson 1902: 208–209), but once established on the island would have included quite a lot of Melanesian ingredients and dishes in their diet. Faunal remains from the Robertson House were abundant, and again indicate heavy use of local shellfish, including *Turbo* sp., Trochidae, Conidae, Tridacna, Arcidae, and *Nerita* sp. Robertson House was also the only Erromango Mission site to yield pig bones, another indicator of the prestige the missionaries were able to achieve on the island.

The expansion of steamship voyaging in the Pacific (Steel 2011), and the regular voyages of the mission ship *Dayspring* to the New Hebrides from the 1870s onwards, would have made it easier to bring imported goods to the mission at Dillon's Bay. One result of the importance of the mission settlement to the Erromangan landscape was population aggregation, as people from villages with declining populations, especially inland, began to settle along the coast at the more populous mission stations. An unfortunate archaeological by-product of this is that many of the later missions are now large villages. What this means is that the archaeological records of these sites have been significantly impacted by contemporary activities.

Robertson House itself is partly overlain by a medical clinic built within the last 20 years. The artefacts recovered around the upper layers of the site likewise include various contemporary materials (plastic, automotive glass, glass marbles, a 1979 Nouvelles Hébrides Franc coin). Despite this, we did recover a small number of artefacts that could be definitively associated with the Robertson Mission. Three sherds of transfer-printed whiteware with a green floral motif were recovered, which represent a single vessel. In TU1, we recovered two 19th-century coins, one was an 1872 French five Centime piece, and the other was a British 'Victoria Bun' penny, though the date couldn't be read as the reverse had worn down (Figure 2.33). Three white clay tobacco pipe bowl fragments were found. Buttons, glass paste jewels, and a copper alloy thimble found around the house reflect changing habits of dress in the missionary era. The female domestic activity of sewing was an important habit cultivated among converts by missionary women.

Figure 2.33 British (left) and French (right) coins from TU1, Robertson House.
Source: James Flexner

Overall, though, surprisingly little definite 19th-century material was found in excavations around Robertson House, particularly glass artefacts. In part, this reflects a need for further extensive excavations around the site. However, sampling issues do not suffice to fully explain this pattern. It is possible that a discrete rubbish disposal area has yet to be discovered. Further, it is likely that rubbish has been dispersed over time because of various activities and other post-depositional processes in Dillon's Bay that have disturbed the archaeological deposits. Documentary evidence indicates that the Robertsons did have access to and bring in large amounts of imported material (Robertson 1902), but it appears mostly to consist of materials that would not preserve archaeologically anyway, such as cloth, flour, or wooden furniture. In addition, like other 'successful' missionaries, the Robertsons likely took much of their domestic assemblage with them when they retired from the mission field.

Despite the apparent dearth of artefacts, the Robertsons had a huge material impact on the landscape of Dillon's Bay. The Martyr's Memorial Church stood for over a century, before being destroyed in Cyclone Uma in 1987. The plaques from the church and salvageable timbers were recycled into a smaller church building that later served as a schoolhouse. The remains of the stone walls and the massive foundations of Robertson House are tangible reminders of the amount of indigenous labour used to divide the 'ordered' space of the mission from the surrounding 'disordered' Melanesian landscape (Flexner 2013: 16). After the Robertsons, Erromango was a Christian Island. Christianity, however, did not constitute a negation of *kastom*. In TU1 at Robertson House, burned fragments of a carved coconut shell armband hint at the possibility of continuity in native adornment (see also Lawson 2001), though why such an object was burned is a matter for speculation. The discussion of continuity and change in Erromangan material culture will be taken up further in Chapter 5.

3

Tanna: In the Shadow of the Volcano, 1839–1868

The most striking feature of Tanna is Mt Yasur, the active volcano rising 360m above sea level on the island's southeastern flank. Tanna is the second-largest island in TAFEA Province, covering just over 550km². It is also the most densely populated island in the province, and today is an important political and economic centre of southern Vanuatu. Rock formations on Tanna are no more than three million years old. The island is formed of three overlapping volcanic massifs, with the oldest formations in the north and eastern parts of the island, which are late Pliocene in age. Late Pleistocene formations in the southwest include Mt Tukosmeru, the highest peak on Tanna, and the most recent volcanic activity, which is ongoing, is in the southeastern part of the island. The island has been tilting to the east throughout its formation, exposing limestone terraces along the west coast of Tanna (Carney and Macfarlane 1971; Depledge 1994).

Knowledge of Tannese prehistory is very limited at this point. In part, this is because the active volcanism on the island has deeply buried many archaeological sites, especially in the southeast. More importantly, there has simply not been much archaeological fieldwork done on the island. While Lapita ceramic sites representing initial settlement almost certainly exist on the island, none have been discovered at this point. What we do know about Tannese archaeology derives primarily from fieldwork carried out by Richard and Mary Shutler in 1964 (Shutler and Shutler 1966; Shutler et al. 2002). The Shutlers worked primarily on the west coast of the island, where they excavated two rockshelters and recorded several middens and a village site. The Shutlers' work, which also extended to Erromango, Futuna, and Aneityum, resulted in the first radiocarbon dates from southern Vanuatu (Shutler 1973), though there is reason to be somewhat sceptical of these dates. A modest sample of artefacts were recovered on Tanna, both from excavations and given to the Shutlers as gifts. The gifted material included stone adzes, a fragment of a *kawas* (stone throwing club), and stone discs.

Excavations in two rockshelter sites, which the Shutlers called TaRS1 and TaRS3, recovered similar stone artefacts, as well as a variety of shell objects, including flaked *Tridacna* (giant clam), a *Conus* adze, and *Conus* beads. Human burials were uncovered in both caves, though only the TaRS1 burials were associated with grave goods. Radiocarbon dates from TaRS1 were primarily from the last 1,000 years, with a piece of wood charcoal from the deepest levels (2–2.3m below surface) dating to 2370+/-90BP (Shutler et al. 2002: 192–195). Re-analysis of the materials from these sites using modern techniques, particularly for dating, would be highly beneficial for drawing any further conclusions about these sequences. After the Shutlers, the next archaeological excavations on Tanna were carried out for this project, which included several relevant discoveries for Tannese prehistory.

European knowledge of Tanna begins, as with so many islands in the South Pacific, with Cook. After departing from Erromango in August 1774 (see Chapter 2), Cook continued south, drawn by the glow of Yasur, which was clearly visible from the sea by night. Cook and his crew spent about two weeks in Tanna, primarily in the Port Resolution area (Beaglehole, ed. 1969: 483–509; a more detailed discussion of this encounter appears below in the section on Port Resolution). Relations were mostly peaceful, and certainly more productive than on Erromango. Cook was able to exchange some things with local people, though there were clear tensions and eventually the killing of a Tannese warrior by one of the ship's marines necessitated the *Resolution*'s departure. It is from this encounter that we get the name Tanna, which in the language of the Port Resolution area simply means 'ground' or 'earth'. Johann Reinhold Forster, the ship's naturalist, had pointed to the ground assuming he would be told the name of the island, but quite reasonably, Tannese people chose to interpret his gesture literally. A local name for the island is *Ipare*, and people from neighbouring islands had names for Tanna as well, for example *Ekiamo* in Futunese (Beaglehole, ed. 1969: 489; see also Jolly 2009). Nonetheless, the name Tanna stuck through the colonial era and into the present. Such cultural misunderstandings became fairly standard in European encounters with the island.

After Cook there were fleeting contacts with explorers, such as the Russian Golovnin in 1809, or passing adventurers such as Dillon in 1825 (Adams 1984: 32–33). The rate of European contacts increased beginning in the late 1820s with the expansion of the sandalwood trade (Shineberg 1967). In the 1840s there was a sandalwood trader on Tanna named Paddon who was married to a Tannese woman, with whom he had four children. After sandalwood came the labour trade, which drew thousands of Tannese, mostly younger men, away from the island to work on plantations in Australia, Fiji, and New Caledonia (Docker 1970; Shineberg 1999). Sandalwooding and the labour trade greatly increased Tannese interest in imported goods such as metal tools and trade cloth (Bonnemaison 1994: 39–43).

Missionary contacts began with the settlement of Polynesian teachers on the island in 1839. The *Camden* stopped at Tanna before taking John Williams and James Harris on their fateful trip to Erromango. The first European missionaries were Turner and Nisbet from the London Missionary Society, who arrived at Port Resolution in 1842. They stayed for seven months, eventually departing because of native indifference and increasing local tensions. The Patons, Mathesons, and Johnstons were Presbyterian missionaries on south Tanna (Port Resolution and Kwamera) from 1858–1862, though this mission collapsed catastrophically as relationships with local people deteriorated following a series of epidemics. Long-term missionary contacts began in the 1870s in the south, though many parts of the island resisted Christian incursions of any sort well into the 20th century (Adams 1984; Liua'ana 1996; Miller 1981: 20–45, 1986: 246–425). From 1905–1925, there was a period of 'Tanna Law', when Christian courts were established and traditional activities such as kava drinking and dancing were sometimes violently repressed. If anything, this experiment with Christian theocracy in the New Hebrides served to entrench *kastom* on the island (Bonnemaison 1994; Guiart 1956).

It appears that Tanna did not suffer the same level of demographic decline from introduced diseases as occurred on neighbouring Erromango and Aneityum (Bonnemaison 1994: 44; Humphreys 1926: 1; cf. Spriggs 2007). Further research is of course needed to refine this observation. There certainly would have been some population decrease, especially after particularly virulent outbreaks of measles and dysentery from the 1840s through the 1860s (Adams 1984). However, Tanna seems to have remained relatively densely populated, and the population began to recover earlier than on neighbouring islands. Tannese people would have explained the apparent resilience of their population in contrast to those of their neighbours in magical terms, and this may relate to the longer period of resistance to missionaries and European colonisers more generally.

Ironically, that Tanna had the largest population in the southern New Hebrides made it an important administrative centre during the era of formal colonialism in the islands (Guiart 1956: 130–150). In 1887, a Joint Anglo-French Naval Commission was established in the New Hebrides, partly to protect Europeans from Melanesian 'aggressions'. More importantly, the Joint Naval Commission was meant to stabilise relationships between French settlers from New

Caledonia and British settlers from Australia. Both groups were agitating for exclusive annexation of the New Hebrides, which would almost certainly have resulted in conflict. The end result was the formation of the Anglo-French 'Condominium', which served (mostly dysfunctionally) as the colonial government from 1906 until independence in 1980. One of the main functions of the Condominium was the adjudication of land disputes, primarily among European settlers, but also where native people had reasons to complain, though in the latter case there was little the government could or would do (Bonnemaison 1994: 83–87; Jacomb 1914; Rodman 2001: 21–50; Van Trease 1987).

Tanna was an important location of resistance to colonial policies, both governmental and missionary. It likewise became an important site in the independence movement. In both cases, the strength of resistance was drawn from the strength of *kastom* on the island. Traditional beliefs and practices structured and became emblematic of Tannese attachment to *ples* (place) as they defined life on their islands in the colonial and postcolonial environment. In more recent decades, *kastom* continues to evolve on the island, with the presence of more conservative traditions existing alongside more innovative phenomena such as the John Frum 'cargo cult'. The resistance, resilience, and innovation inherent in Tannese *kastom* has in some cases been said to take its current form in part because of the excesses of the missionary era, especially in the first decades of the 1900s (see Bonnemaison 1994; Guiart 1956; Lindstrom 1982, 1993). That said, there is nothing foreign about *kastom* on Tanna, which owes its form entirely to the knowledge, traditions, and ingenuity of Tannese people.

Kastom on Tanna

Knowledge about Tannese *kastom* is a contested field, both academically and in vernacular terms. Tanna has been the most intensely studied island in southern Vanuatu, and so there is more scholarly detail to discuss. At the same time, a habit of Tannese 'secrecy', where power is derived from letting people know that one holds significant knowledge without fully divulging the details of that knowledge, contributes to both outsider and insider understandings of *kastom* (Adams 1987; Lindstrom 1982, 1990). There are enough agreed-upon ethnographic 'facts' that we can lay out a general model of Tannese *kastom* in the century or so leading up to missionary presence on the island. As always, though, this knowledge should be taken with the caveat that it represents only a rough framework to understand some of the patterns that emerged in the colonial era. It also needs to be noted that much of the early knowledge about Tannese people was filtered through a missionary lens (e.g. Gray 1892; Turner 1861: 69–94; Watt 1895), which continued to influence the work of later ethnographic observers (e.g. Humphreys 1926: 71–72). Further complicating the matter, there are five main languages on Tanna, and possibly a dozen dialects (Nehrbass 2012). *Kastom* terms vary across the different areas of the island. Here I will use the Nafé language of the Kwamera area of southwest Tanna, with references to other languages where these are commonly used in other sources or geographically relevant to the area being discussed.

As on the neighbouring islands, land divisions on Tanna were called 'canoes' (*netata* in Nafé, *niko* in Lenakel; cf. Aneityum *nelcau*, Erromango *lo*). As we saw, Erromango was divided into six *lo*, each of which had a paramount chief (see Chapter 2). Aneityum was divided into approximately 55 districts, which were distributed among seven *nelcau*, each of which likewise constituted a 'chiefdom' (Spriggs 1985, 1986). Tanna, in contrast, contained at least 116 *netata* (Figure 3.1), without any higher-level chiefs. This has led Tannese society to be described as 'atomistic' in comparison to its more hierarchical neighbours (Brunton 1979). Lack of hierarchy on Tanna should not be equated with a lack of social complexity. If anything, the heterarchical nature of Tannese chiefship increases the complexity of day-to-day social and political interactions (e.g. Guiart 1956: 107–115).

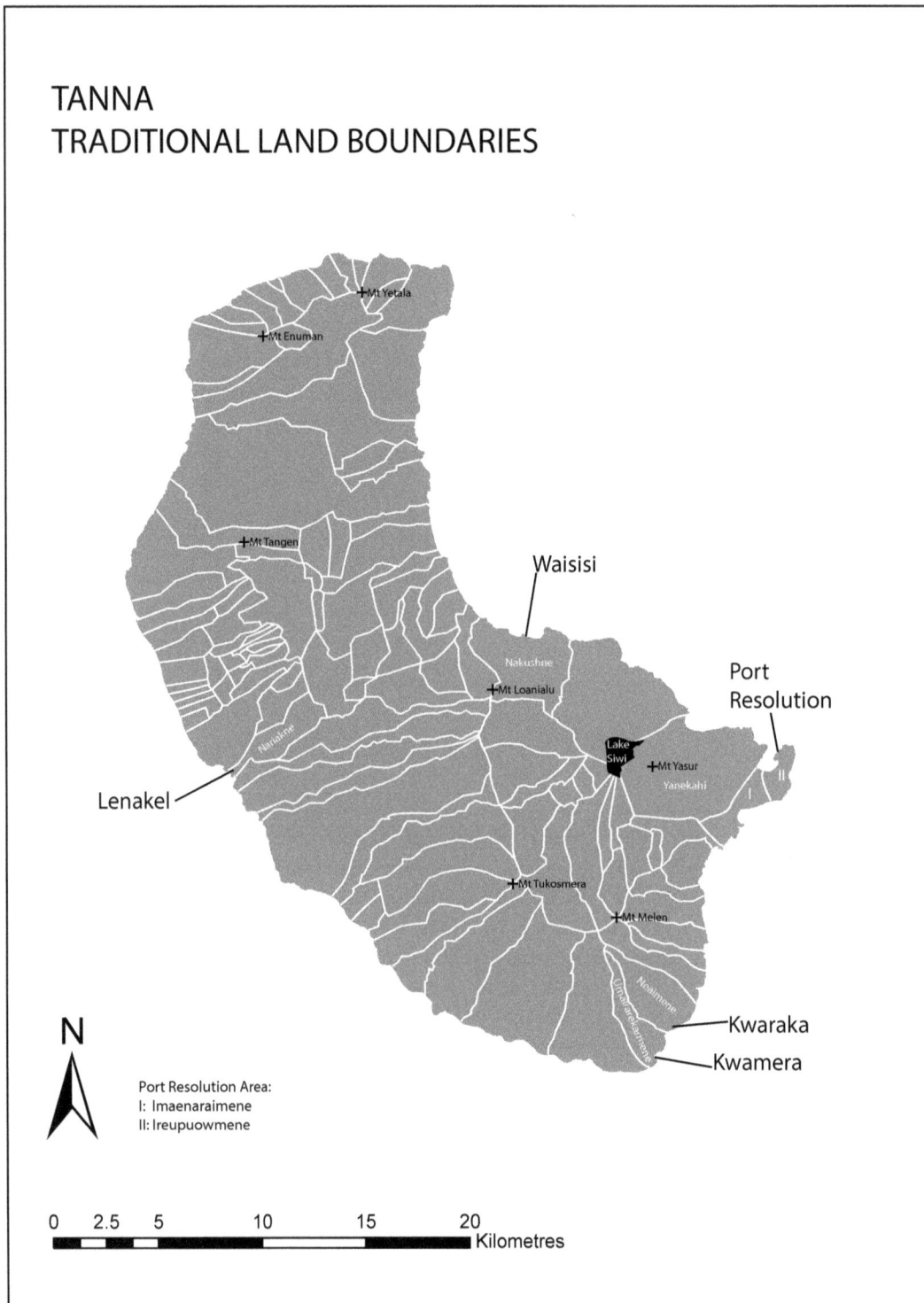

Figure 3.1 Map of *netata* (land divisions) on Tanna, including sites and locations mentioned in the text. Note that division boundaries are approximate only and meant to be for general reference.

Source: James Flexner

European visitors to the island, from Cook to early ethnographers to contemporary anthropologists, have remarked on the limited nature of chiefly power, with decision-making largely a matter of establishing consensus among groups of men who hold chiefly titles (e.g. Beaglehole, ed. 1969: 507–508; Bonnemaison 1994: 152; Humphreys 1926: 35–36). One mid-20th-century survey on the island counted 601 'chiefs' against a total population of 6,937. This comes out to one chief for every 11–12 individuals (Guiart 1956: 9). Such a profusion of chiefs, assuming that the ratio hadn't changed much for at least 200 years or so, meant any major decisions involved lengthy discussions and negotiations among chiefs from neighbouring villages and *netata*, not to mention the various ritual specialists involved. Chiefly discussions would have revolved around preparing, planting, and harvesting gardens, holding ceremonial exchanges or dances, and going to war. Consumption of kava was often a central activity surrounding these chiefly occupations.

One of the main chiefly titles was *Yeremwanu*, which belonged to men who had the right to wear a hair ornament of hawk feathers (see Chapter 5). There were other chiefs who bore the title of *Yani*, including *Yani Netata*, district chiefs (Bonnemaison 1994: 146–156; Guiart 1956: 15–17). Among this rank the *Yani en Dete* follow to some extent the role of Oceanic 'talking chiefs', being responsible for speaking at various sorts of gatherings, and playing the role more broadly of 'guardian of social well-being and local values and practices' (Douglas 1996: 243). Chiefly titles were generally inherited, though where the oldest son of a chief was considered unfit, the title could be passed on to a different individual, presumably another son (Humphreys 1926: 36). Beyond passing on certain privileges, there is evidence that chiefly titles involved to some extent the Oceanic 'Heroic I'. Those who hold a title lay claim not only to their own achievements, but those of every previous holder of that title (Lindstrom 2011).

Besides chiefs, there were various magical specialists in Tannese society. As on Erromango, magic could take on benevolent or malevolent forms. The primary goal of benevolent magic is to increase agricultural productivity, especially for yams. Yams are not only a dietary staple, but also feature in important annual exchange rituals. Magic stones, usually shaped like the crop that was to benefit from the magical activity (called *nukwei narak*), were kept and used by particular individuals to increase productivity. Similarly, beneficial magic could be used to bring rain or sunshine, summon fish, ensure the successful breeding and growth of pigs, and many other purposes (Bonnemaison 1991, 1994: 172–178; Guiart 1956: 63–66; Humphreys 1926: 71). There were also oracles called *Narumin* who were thought to have the ability to predict the future and divine the unknown (Humphreys 1926: 70).

Black magic was the domain of greatly feared sorcerers called *Tupunas*. All cases of illness and death were attributed either to the activities of *Tupunas* or malevolent ghosts called *ierehma* (*yarmis* or *yermis* in other Tanna languages). In the practice of black magic (*narak*), an item from the body, including hair, food scraps, clothing or another item, is bundled in leaves with a magic stone. If the leaves are burned, the victim perishes almost immediately, or lesser illnesses can be caused by keeping the personal effect at some distance from the malevolent stone (Bonnemaison 1994: 179–180; Guiart 1956: 69–72; Humphreys 1926: 72–73). Significantly, the magic stones of Erromango were said to come from Tanna, suggesting the practice may have spread from one island to the other (Chapter 2). Spiritual beliefs on Tanna appear to have been primarily concerned with these various types of magic and relationships to ancestral beings. Tannese people attributed the action of supernatural forces causally to the behaviours of human ritual practitioners. This is a more anthropocentric perspective when compared with neighbouring Aneityum, where spirits were treated more as autonomous beings (Douglas 1989).

There was apparently belief in a supreme being called *Kwumwesin* (Humphreys 1926: 71), but as with *Nobu* on Erromango, *Kwumwesin* appears to have made the world and then withdrew from all involvement with it. There are other important deities and legendary figures in Tannese cosmology, the most significant being *Mwatiktiki* (from the Polynesian Maui-tiki-tiki, one of the main deities whose existence can be traced linguistically to Proto-Polynesian, *Maaui*; Kirch and Green 2001: 243). *Mwatiktiki* stories in some ways parallel their Polynesian counterparts, for example in stories that say he fished the islands out of the sea. Others pertain specifically to

Mwatiktiki's arrival on Tanna, for example that he introduced pigs and 'real' kava to the island. *Tangalua* (the sea snake) is another clear Polynesian introduction that can be traced back to Proto-Polynesian (*Taangaloa*; Kirch and Green 2001: 245). There is a great deal of evidence for Polynesian influence on Tanna, particularly in the language and rituals pertaining to kava (Lindstrom 2004; Lynch 1996).

The everyday ritual of kava drinking is central to men's lives, and social life more broadly on Tanna (Bonnemaison 1994: 182; Humphreys 1926: 81–83). Men retreat each afternoon to the *imwarim* (in the language of south Tanna; *yimwayim* in west Tanna; *nakamal* in Bislama), large, cathedral-like clearings usually surrounded by large banyan trees (Figure 3.2). The kava is prepared (traditionally the root is chewed) while men discuss the events of the day. As each drinks he makes his *tamafa*, a prayer accompanied by the spitting of fine droplets of saliva and kava (Lindstrom 1980). As they become intoxicated, each man retreats to his own corner of the *imwarim* to listen to the spirits or ancestors. It has been likened to a 'daily dissolution of society', in which this retreat to 'listen' to kava contributes to the egalitarianism of Tannese people (Brunton 1979).

Figure 3.2 Kava-drinking ground near Waisisi.
Source: James Flexner

The *imwarim* were important nodes on the Tannese landscape. A traditional system of 'roads' (conceptual as much as physical) connected *imwarim* to networks of hamlets and gardens. One *imwarim* could host men from multiple hamlets, and while each man would have a 'home' place to drink kava, it was common for men to move between different kava-drinking grounds (Brunton 1989: 130–138; Lindstrom 1996). These networks would become important during the annual dance festivals, *toka* and *nao*, which served as significant exchange ceremonies. During these events, brides were exchanged, and alliances for both exchange and warfare were solidified. Significant to the structure of these exchanges were the two main rival 'moieties' on the island, *Koyometa* and *Numrukuen* (Bonnemaison 1994: 148–153; Guiart 1956: 24–27; 90–94).

Tannese gardens were enchanted spaces, powered by the magic stones that made various plants grow (Bonnemaison 1991, 1994: 173–176). The primary staple crop is yam, of which many varieties are grown, including giant 'aristocratic' yams raised specifically for exchange. Yams are sown in mounds (*takwu*) formed from holes in the ground that are then heaped with a mixture of earth, burned vegetation, ash, and magic leaves (Figure 3.3). One early observer noted *takwu* measuring 7 feet (2m) in height and 60 feet (20m) in circumference. The yams from these mounds could grow to four feet (1.5m) in length, and weigh up to 50 pounds (22kg; Turner 1861: 87). Alongside yams were grown taro, coconut, sugarcane, and a variety of gourds and fruit trees. Agricultural surplus was used to raise pigs, which were primarily important for chiefly exchanges. Competitive feasting was significant on Tanna as elsewhere in the southern New Hebrides. This may have been one of the mechanisms that further maintained the egalitarian social structure on the island, relating to a focus on quality rather than quantity of agricultural production (Spriggs 1986: 16–18).

Figure 3.3 'Yam gardens, East Tanna', Symons Collection, Australian Museum (AMS354–244).
Source: Australian Museum Archives.

The everyday ritual of kava, the annual cycles of *toka*, *nao*, and other events, such as clearing, planting gardens, and the yam harvest, structure the sense of temporality on Tanna. In the language of the Kwamera area of south Tanna, 'the word for the day after tomorrow (*neis*) is the same as the word for the day before yesterday, and the word for indefinite future (*kwumweisin*) is the same for the indefinite past' (Lindstrom 2011: 146). This suggests a 'timeless' or 'cyclical' element to time on the island. At the same time, Tannese people do recognise a sense of historical progress and rupture. This is marked by legendary events in the deeper past, such as the arrival of *Mwatiktiki*, whose footprint is located on the coast near Kwaraka; or the arrival of the canoe carrying the magic stones that resulted in the formation of *Koyometa* and *Numrukuen*. It is also marked by the reverberations of European contacts, both direct, as with the arrival of European explorers or missionaries, and more broadly, as in the 'stolen war' of *Shipimanwawa* (Bonnemaison 1994; see also Chapter 4). This type of 'historicity' (Ballard 2014) parallels in some ways the archaeological approach used here, where specific events are measured against patterns of everyday life over the long term (see also Braudel 1980).

A Tannese Village: Anuikaraka Before the Mission Era

Thus far, we have explored mission encounters in the New Hebrides from the perspective of mission houses and the surrounding landscapes. Melanesian people appear where they interacted with the mission, either in the form of evidence for local materials, exchanges, and local labour, or as named individuals in missionary accounts. Archaeological remains of Tannese village sites in the area of Anuikaraka and Kwaraka provide a significant counterpoint (Flexner et al. 2016c). These sites are located within 2km of the mission remains in the Kwamera area (Figure 3.4). The remains from this area, which span several centuries, offer an opportunity to catch glimpses of everyday life in a Tannese village before, during, and after the period of mission encounters on the island. While these sites may not be completely 'typical' for Tannese villages, they do offer a certain baseline, and exhibit patterns that would have been broadly similar at least across the southern part of the island. These sites offer an opportunity to 'span the prehistory/history divide' (Lightfoot 1995), a necessary endeavour to understand southern New Hebrides missions and Melanesian landscapes from a broader temporal as well as spatial perspective.

The archaeological landscape of Anuikaraka and Kwaraka consists of a series of stone walls, enclosures, and mounds, covering an area of roughly 400m of coastal plain, extending slightly over 100m inland from the sea (Figure 3.5). The archaeological landscape is bisected by Komaru stream. Komaru also serves as the boundary between the two *netata* in the area: Umairarekarmene to the southwest, and Neaimene to the northeast. The area of Anuikaraka and Kwaraka has been surveyed and all the surface features mapped. A limited number of features were excavated, but knowledge of site stratigraphy, function, and chronology could be greatly improved with further research. The form of surface features and the excavation work that has been done has offered valuable information about these sites, and long-term landscape archaeology on Tanna more broadly (Flexner et al. 2016c).

KWAMERA
ARCHAEOLOGICAL FEATURES

Itapua Village ●

Mwatiktiki Footprint ●

Nokwenuk   'Macmillan'
Iarisi Garden ●   ● ●Irumien
          ●Netata
                    ●Kwaraka

          ●
Enapa ●   'New Kwaraka'

● Kawimeta

N

● Imua
● Kapuku Grave

● Mission Boat Winch

● Watt Mission
● Mission Graves

0   125 250   500   750   1,000
█──█──█──────█──────█──────────█ Metres

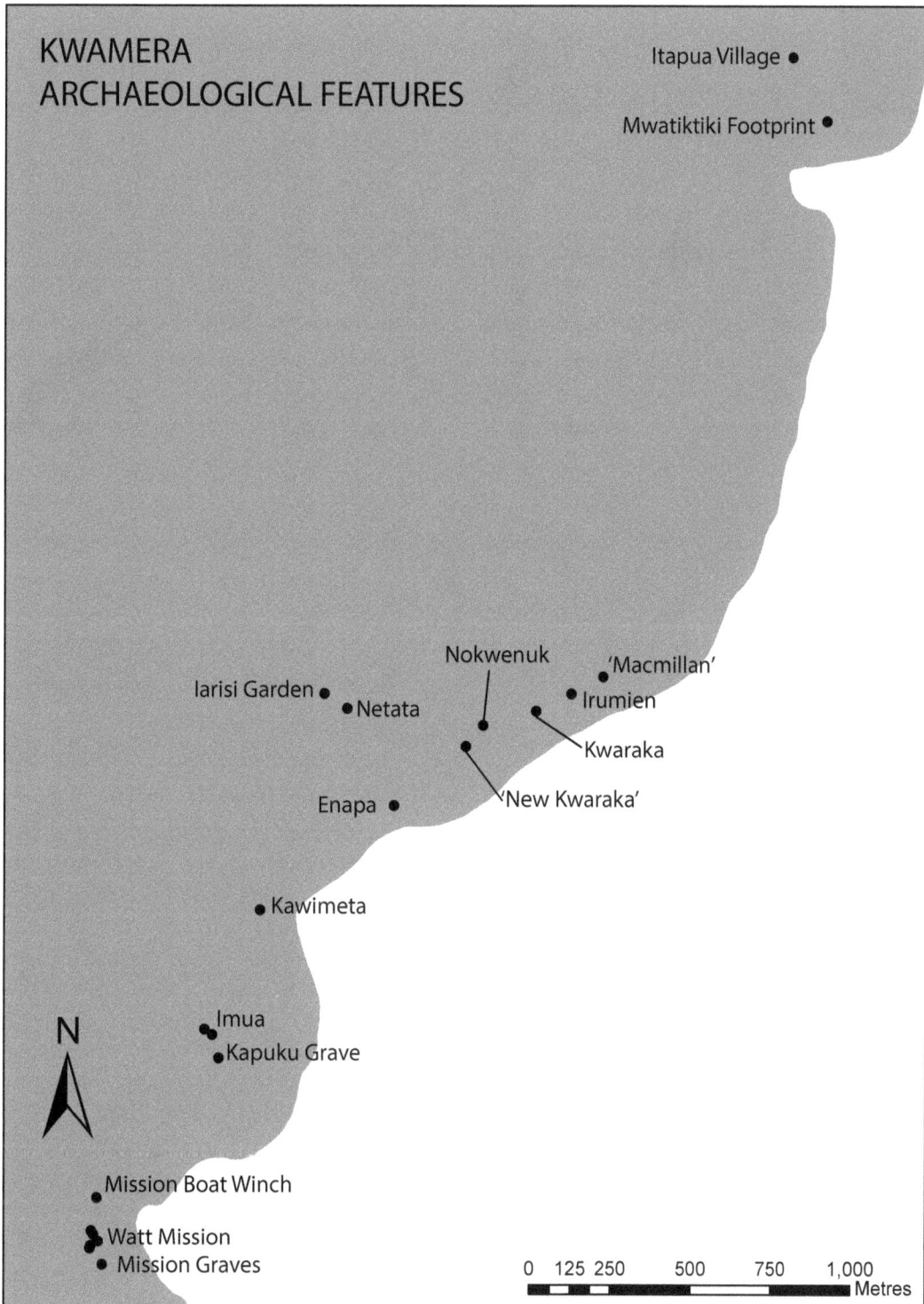

Figure 3.4 Archaeological features, Kwamera area, south Tanna.
Source: James Flexner

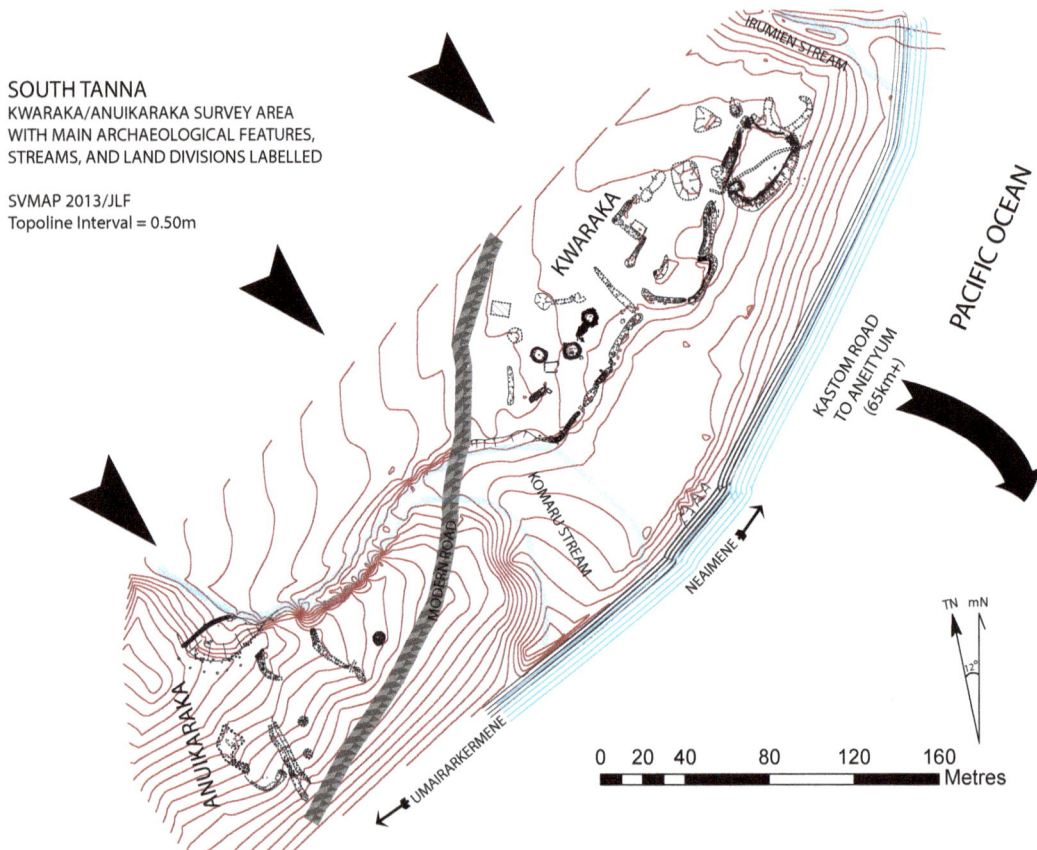

SOUTH TANNA
KWARAKA/ANUIKARAKA SURVEY AREA
WITH MAIN ARCHAEOLOGICAL FEATURES,
STREAMS, AND LAND DIVISIONS LABELLED

SVMAP 2013/JLF
Topoline Interval = 0.50m

Figure 3.5 Plan map of survey area, Kwaraka and Anuikaraka.
Source: James Flexner

For an overview of the landscape, we will start in the northeast of Kwaraka (Figure 3.6), then move southwest through to Anuikaraka. The first feature we encounter is a stone-walled enclosure, sunken slightly below the surrounding ground surface (Figure 3.7). This is the old *imwarim* (kava-drinking and dancing ground) Irumien. Within the feature there are several stones worth noting. There is a grinding stone with impressions from the processing of *natapoa* (in Bislama; scientific name *Terminalia catappa*) nuts in the eastern, seaward wall. Further south along this wall there is a row of stones embedded in the ground surface at the base of the wall. It is not known what function they have, but considering their location inside the *imwarim*, it is likely that they had some kind of ritual significance for the men who would drink their kava in this place. Further south, there is a flat stone inside of the rounded terminus of this wall, next to the southern entrance to the *imwarim*. This stone served as a refuge stone for people fleeing conflict. If the stone could be reached ahead of one's pursuers then the *imwarim* offered protection (Flexner 2014c: 15–17).

KWARAKA, TANNA

Key
◯ =Tree
□ =Test Unit
M =Mound
W =Wall
H =House
P =Path (not numbered)
G =Grave

Hachure indicates slope.

Surface stones drawn,
with exception of mounds
2, 3, and 4, which were
cleared for survey, and
Irumien, which is maintained
by the local community.

Dashed line indicates
poorly preserved or
unclear boundary.

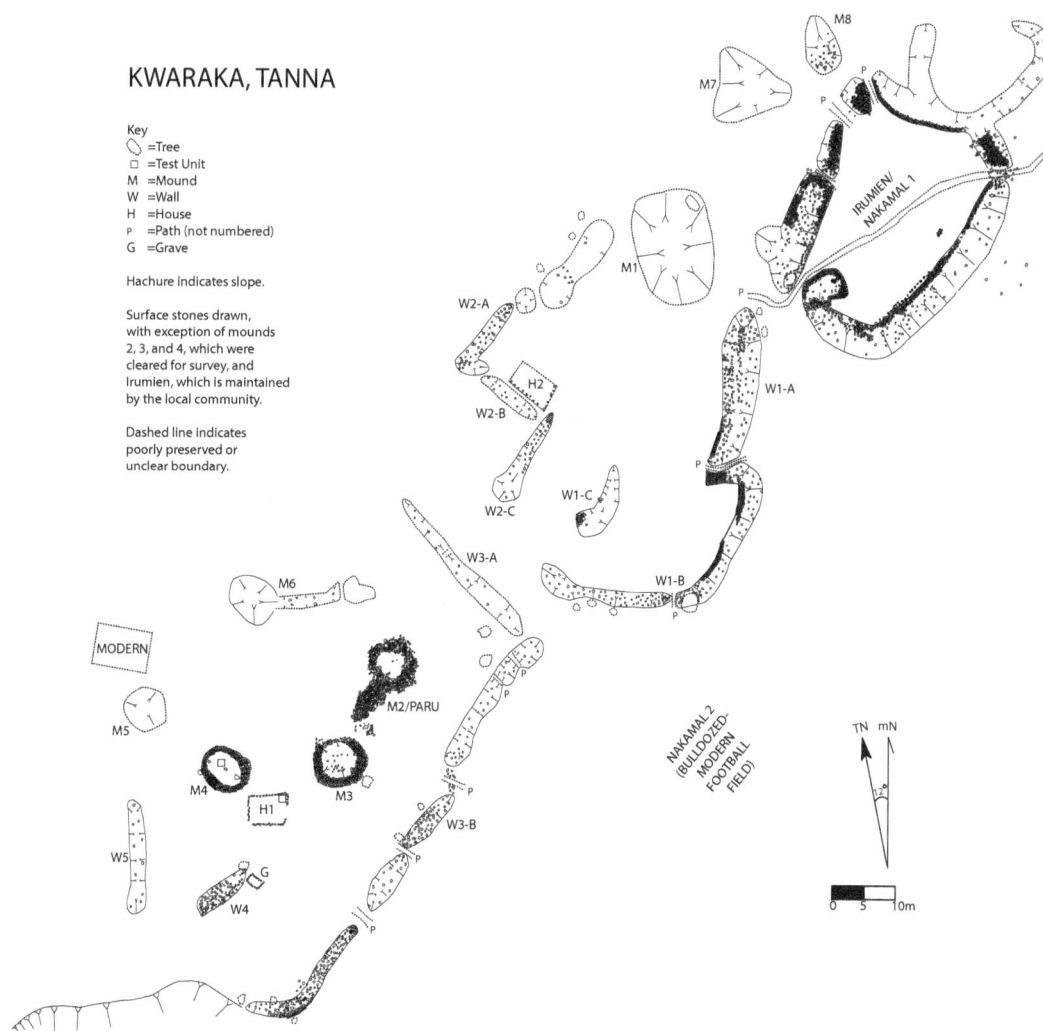

Figure 3.6 Surface features, Kwaraka.

Source: James Flexner

Continuing on from Irumien, we enter a landscape of stone walls running parallel to the seashore, and punctuated with mounds of stone and earth. The walls may have served as stormbreaks against major surges on the sea side. The easternmost set of walls (W1-B and W3-B in Figure 3.6) form a low terrace of sorts for the village. Below this, there was another *imwarim*, which was cleared to make way for a football field in recent history. The mounds are remembered locally as being built to raise houses and storage areas, as the ground surface could become extremely muddy during the rainy season (usually lasting from November until July). These features are mostly unexcavated at this point. A shovel test pit (STP17) excavated in the area of 'Wall 3' (W3-A in Figure 3.6) contained charcoal, bone, shell, glass, and metal artefacts, suggesting a midden deposit in this area (Flexner et al. 2016c). A group of three round stone-faced mounds (M2, M3, and M4) are particularly well-preserved. These become of interest in the missionary and post-missionary era at Kwaraka, and will be returned to below. Inland from Kwaraka, there is a collection of smooth yam stones (*nukwei nuk*) of fine-grained basalt (Figure 3.8). These would have provided the magic to make the yams grow in the inland gardens connected to the hamlets and *imwarim* of this area.

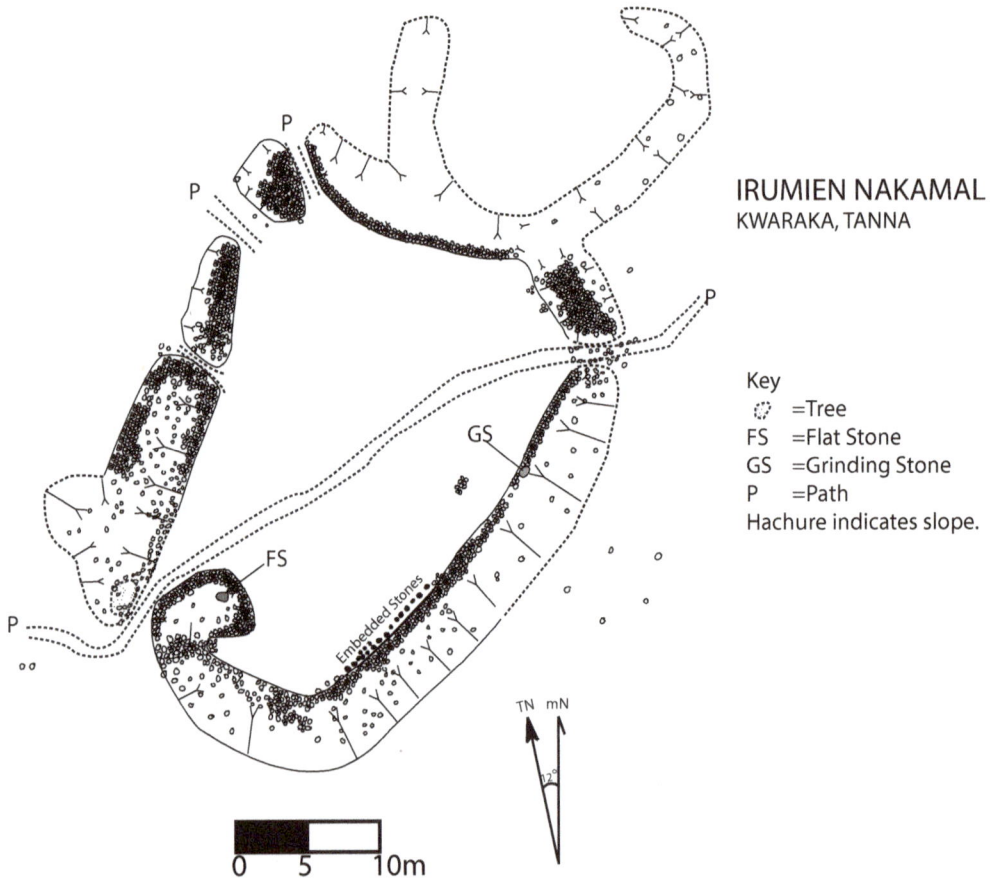

IRUMIEN NAKAMAL
KWARAKA, TANNA

Key
⊘ =Tree
FS =Flat Stone
GS =Grinding Stone
P =Path
Hachure indicates slope.

Figure 3.7 *Imwarim* (kava-drinking ground) at Irumien.
Source: James Flexner

Figure 3.8 *Nukwei nuk* (yam stones).
Source: James Flexner

Two of the well-preserved stone-faced mounds in the western part of Kwaraka (M3 and M4 in Figure 3.6) bear a striking resemblance to contact-era house mounds from Samoa (Green and Davidson, eds 1974). This raises the possibility that this kind of construction technique was introduced to Tanna either directly by Samoan teachers, or by Aneityumese who learned from the Polynesians (note once again that the Aneityumese were themselves accomplished builders in stone, see Spriggs 1981). At this point, further excavation work is needed to test this hypothesis. This site is extremely significant for the history of mission contacts in southern Vanuatu, because of its association with important oral histories, and its great archaeological potential (see Flexner 2014c: 12–18; Flexner et al. 2016c).

ANUIKARAKA, TANNA

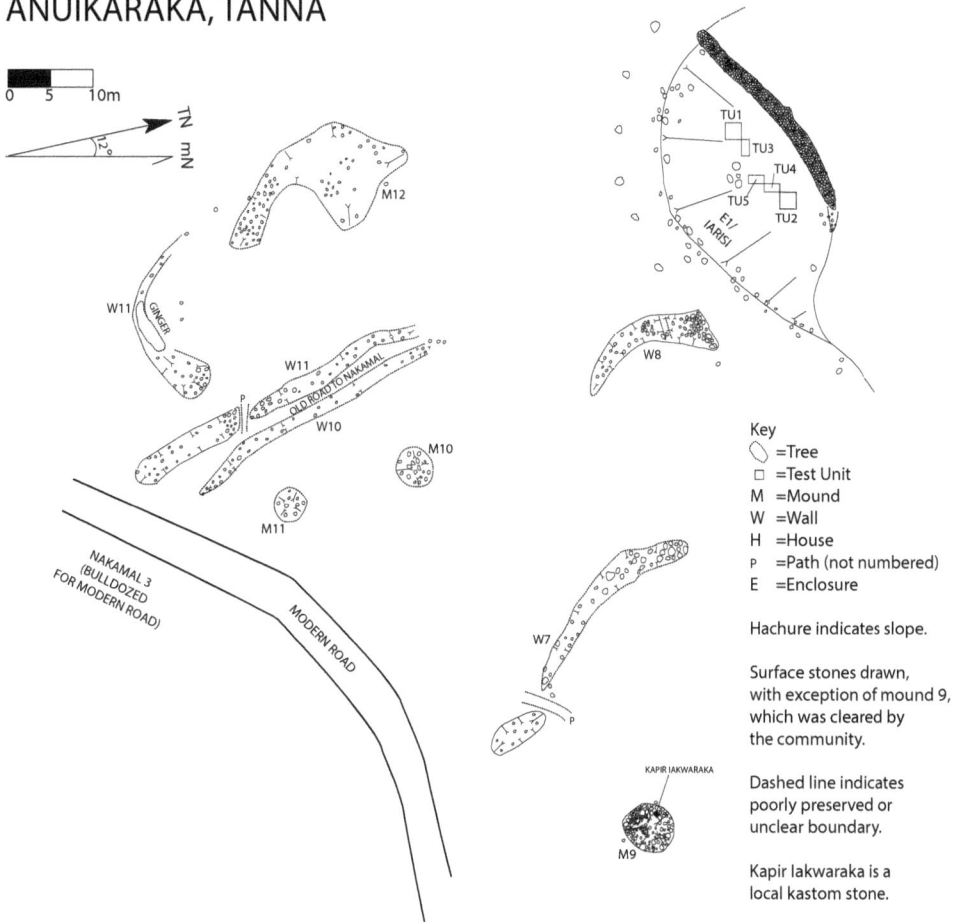

Figure 3.9 Surface features, Anuikaraka.
Source: James Flexner

Across the rocky channel of the intermittent Komaru stream (which flows during heavy rains and throughout the wet season), the features continue into Anuikaraka (Figure 3.9). The stone walls and mounds in Anuikaraka are less well-preserved than in Kwaraka. Where Kwaraka is flat, Anuikaraka is relatively steeply sloped. Further, the walls tend to run perpendicular to the seashore, directed downslope. The reason for this is unclear, though channelling rainwater downslope may offer a reason for this. At least some of the walls (W10 and W11) flanked a traditional road leading to another *imwarim*, which has also been lost to much more recent road-building activities. The enclosure in the northern area of the site (E1 in Figure 3.9) is associated with the chief Iarisi, who was an important individual in early mission history on Tanna.

Figure 3.10 Mound 9 plan and TU6 stratigraphic profile, Anuikaraka.

Source: James Flexner

One of the round, conical mounds (M9 in Figure 3.9) held a *kastom* stone on the surface, which was associated with women's magic relating to the *toka* dance. It was said to have been placed there by Iarisi to contain its power. A 1x4m trench was excavated across one side of this mound to better understand its stratigraphy and age (Figure 3.10). The mound was constructed of an undifferentiated deposit of stone cobbles, boulders, and earth. The construction fill contained several smooth, cobble-sized pieces and smaller fragments of red ochre, pig bones, *Cypraea* (cowrie) and *Turbo* shell fragments, and the distal end of a fine-grained basalt adze blade. These materials, particularly the pig bone and ochre fragments suggest a ritual deposition of some sort. Pigs were extremely significant to chiefly exchanges on Tanna, and red ochre was important as a pigment, especially as body paint. Ochre was often traded from neighbouring Aneityum Island, which was connected to this area by a major *kastom* 'road' (canoe voyaging route).

Radiocarbon dates indicate that the mound was constructed in the mid-17th or 18th century (Appendix D), almost certainly before Cook set foot on Tanna. This feature may have been constructed as part of a ritual feasting event. The remains of sacrificed pigs, food debris, and red ochre were heaped together, possibly as a way of closing a major ceremonial event or as a sacrifice to propitiate *ierehma* (ancestral beings). At this point, stone features such as this are known only from Anuikaraka and Kwaraka. In part, this reflects the lack of archaeological fieldwork overall on Tanna. However, this kind of landscape may be unique to the southern part of Tanna, which has close connections to Aneityum, an island well-known for large-scale stone construction (Spriggs 1981, 1986). Future research on Tannese settlement patterns will be needed to clarify this. Regardless, these features offer a valuable dataset for understanding at least some of the practices that existed prior to missionary arrival on Tanna. Annual cycles of agricultural production, community and island-wide ceremonies, and the daily rituals of kava at the *imwarim* are integral components of Tannese *kastom*. These practices existed for centuries before missionary arrival and, as will be seen, continued well beyond the period when missionaries were no longer active on Tanna.

Contacts in the Fish's Tail: Port Resolution

> I named the Harbour, Port Resolution after the Ship, as she was the first who ever entered it
> — James Cook, 1774 (Beaglehole, ed. 1969: 508)

The *Resolution* was not the first long-distance maritime vessel to land in Port Resolution, as Oceanic sailing canoes would have regularly visited the naturally sheltered harbour for millennia before Cook's arrival. As seen above, south Tanna had important exchange 'roads' leading to Futuna, Aniwa, and Aneityum. It may be this geographic feature, and the historical precedent set by Cook, that partly explains why so many 'contact events' took place in the Port Resolution area. The landform that created the much-desired harbour is locally called *Nipikinamu* (literally 'the fish's tail'; Figure 3.11). The Port Resolution area spans three *netata* (see Figure 3.1), a significant fact for later complications in missionary work.

Figure 3.11 View along 'the fish's tail', Port Resolution. The small outcrop on the far right of the peninsula is named 'Captain Cook'.

Source: James Flexner

Cook at Port Resolution

The *Resolution* sailed into the harbour for which it would be named on 5 August 1774. As was typical of initial encounters with Pacific Islanders during Cook's voyages, the initial moments were marked by exchange of materials, including cloth, medals, and nails for coconuts, yams, and other crops. Cook notes in his diaries that the landing party sent the following day to establish friendly relations and to collect water and wood was met by two parties of armed men (possibly representing *Koyometa* and *Numrukuen* or two of the *netata* in the area). On the second landing, there were at least 1,000 people present, and apparently this number grew with each subsequent landing. This landing was also met with an arrangement of reeds on the shore, in the middle of which were bundles of food (Beaglehole, ed. 1969: 482–484). It is possible that Cook and his crew were seen as *ierehma* (ghosts) who had returned over the sea. As such they were dangerous, and it is likely that this offering was meant to propitiate them in the hope that they would simply leave (feeding the *ierehma* is a traditional *kastom* work; Bonnemaison 1994: 178–179).

Superficially friendly relations were established through the help of an old man named Paowang, a local mediator who must have been a high-ranking chief. Among other gifts, Paowang received a pair of Tahitian dogs from Cook. Keeping to an established structure for controlling such encounters, Cook used firearms, first muskets then larger cannon, to frighten the Tannese when it appeared that they had the upper hand. The guns were never to be fired at people except as a last resort, and apparently this remained the case for the first part of this encounter. Despite his interest, Cook was generally unable to trade for clubs or other arms, though he was able to collect a few objects in the encounter (see Chapter 5). After a few days, Cook befriended a young man named 'Wha-a-gou' (a Polynesian-sounding name, suggesting possibly a visitor from Aniwa or Futuna), who was persuaded to come on board the *Resolution*. Though they won some friends among the coastal dwellers, Cook and his party were generally prevented from travelling inland. Specifically, they were not able to walk to Mt Yasur, the volcano that had drawn them to Tanna in the first place (Beaglehole, ed. 1969: 486–493). It is possible that crossing the boundary to the *netata* of Yanekahi was *tabu* for some reason. Or perhaps the idea of Cook's crew as unknown entities walking to Yasur, a highly sacred place, was simply seen as too potentially dangerous. Regardless, every attempt to reach the volcano was turned into a wild goose chase that inevitably meandered back to the small area of beach used by the crew of the *Resolution* as a landing place.

On the 19 August 1774, Cook's relationship to people in Port Resolution was tragically and irreparably damaged when a sentry shot and killed one of the local people. Even though the men (and apparently some women) of the area went about constantly armed, and occasionally made menacing gestures, there had not been a single attack during the two weeks the *Resolution* was at harbour. All it took was a single thoughtless moment by one of the ship's marines to shatter the tentative peace. The following day, Cook decided to weigh anchor and summarily departed (Beaglehole, ed. 1969: 499–500). What this encounter would have meant to Tannese people is difficult to know precisely, though it certainly left an imprint on social memory. In the 1840s, the missionary George Turner recorded an oral tradition interpreting the events, in which Cook came to Tanna to attack a *Tupunas* in the Port Resolution area, after which he departed. 'For the Tannese, the event assumed significance in terms of a different cultural framework; as it turned out in political terms, it became an instance of their control over the European' (Adams 1984: 31). Cook's presence has been sedimented into the landscape via toponyms, from the misnomer island name 'Tanna' (Jolly 2009), to a sandstone outcrop from which he is said to have made cartographic measurements (Figure 3.12).

Mission Contacts from Williams to Watt

Missionary endeavours on Tanna began with John Williams and Jacob Harris in November 1839. The earliest contacts occurred in the Port Resolution area. As elsewhere, these encounters are an integral part of the cultural landscape in Port Resolution (Figure 3.12). The most notable event that occurred involving the initial visit of the London Missionary Society (LMS) men was a Tannese chief spitting down the throat of Mr Harris (Lindstrom 1980: 228). When Williams and Harris travelled on to Erromango the following day, they left three Samoan missionaries, Mose, Lalolagi, and Salamea, at Port Resolution. They were joined in 1840 by Pomare and Vaiofaga. Shortly after the new arrivals landed, there was a major outbreak of disease, which was blamed on the foreign god of the missionaries. This was in spite of the fact that the Samoans themselves became ill during the same epidemic, and Salamea and Pomare both died in the event. The Tannese cut off contact with the mission. In 1841, two more teachers, Faleese and Apolo, joined the struggling mission, while Lalolagi returned home to Samoa (Latai forthcoming; Liuaʻana 1996: 52). The *imwarim* of Yakuperang, now referred to as 'Samoa', is likely the place where these teachers lived during their first two years on Tanna.

PORT RESOLUTION ARCHAEOLOGICAL FEATURES

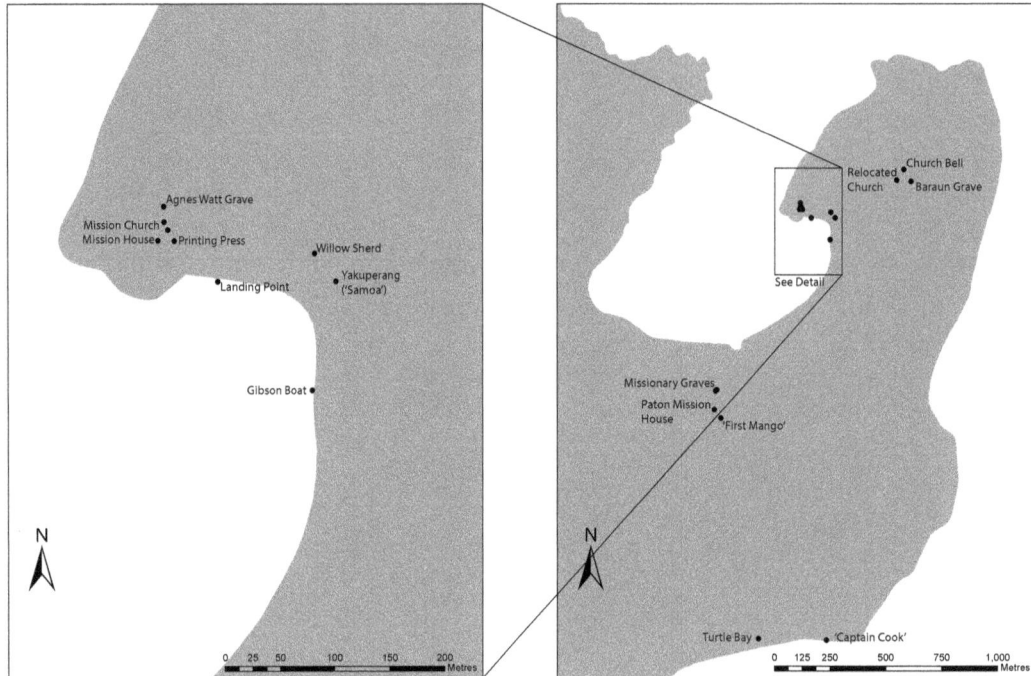

Figure 3.12 Port Resolution area site locations.
Source: James Flexner

The Scottish LMS missionaries Turner and Nisbet arrived in Port Resolution in 1842 along with the Cook Islands teacher Kapao (Liua'ana 1996: 52). Within a few days of their arrival, the area was thrown into a state of upheaval after local people were attacked, apparently without reason, by the crew of an American trading vessel. Turner and Nisbet spent roughly seven months on Tanna. Their first act was to build a 'sixty feet weather-boarded cottage' from materials they had brought on the ship (Turner 1861: 7). This may have been the first prefabricated building in the New Hebrides, and would have been one of the earliest in the region (see Flexner et al. 2015: 266–267). Theft was a great concern, both during the construction of this building and after, though Turner suggests that the practice was ubiquitous and not particularly targeted at the missionaries (Turner 1861: 8).

Almost immediately after their arrival, Turner and Nisbet witnessed a battle taking place directly on the mission ground. They endeavoured to stop the fighting, but were unable to do so. Within a few months, there appeared to be renewed interest in Christianity among local people. A printing press was set up, and a few hymns composed in the local language. Emboldened, Turner and Nisbet sought to move inland towards the volcano, but were resisted on that front. Almost inevitably, another epidemic, this time of dysentery, struck in the area. The *Tupunas* vocally blamed the missionaries and their god as the source of the outbreak. A local chief, Teman, had started as a supporter of the mission but switched sides and perished shortly thereafter. Within a few days, war was declared upon the missionaries and their remaining supporters. As the situation deteriorated, Turner and Nisbet decided to abandon the mission on Tanna. In the last act, Iāru, a chiefly supporter of the mission, asked for the gun that the missionaries had brought with them to turn the tides. The missionaries refused. Another supporter, Kuanan, had his club taken by opposing warriors in an ambush, a significant loss. After a few days of planning, the missionaries had to flee in the night on the brig *Highlander* under Captain Lucas, returning to Samoa (Turner 1861: 11–68).

One of the main challenges of early mission work on Tanna was lack of understanding of local culture. Language was a major challenge, as Polynesian terms could not be simply translated into Tannese languages. This led to a number of difficulties in attempting to explain Christian beliefs to local people, especially in translating terms for 'god', 'devil', 'spirit', and so on. Further, the missionaries inadvertently placed themselves in the middle of a conflict between the local tribes. Neraimene and Nepikinamame, eastern tribes led by Viavia, formed one side. Kaserumene and Yanekahi to the west, led by Lamias, were the other. When epidemic disease broke out, Turner and Nisbet were seen as sorcerers on the Neraimene/Nepikinamame side. By refusing a propitiatory gift from Kaserumene, Turner and Nisbet only showed that this was indeed the case (Adams 1984: 56–69).

While there would have been temporary relief at Turner and Nisbet's departure, the epidemics continued. This caused some local people to change their minds about the potency of the missionaries' god, believing that the missionaries' settlement, objects, and rituals were indeed *tabu*. Polynesian teachers returned to Tanna in 1845. The Samoans included Adamu and Iona, who fled from Aniwa, along with Ioane, Petelu, Pita, and Tagifo, from Tutuila, accompanied by their wives. Some of these missionaries were settled among the Kaserumene and Yanekahi to try to avoid the earlier mistake of apparent missionary partisanship. In 1846, the Polynesians were joined by two more Samoans, Lefau and Vasa, and three Cook Islanders, Marugatanga, Upokumanu, and Rangia. But by this point, epidemic disease had broken out again. Those Samoans who didn't succumb were accused of sorcery. Vasa was clubbed to death by Neraimene warriors. The fortuitous appearance of a whaling ship allowed the majority of the teachers to escape to Aneityum. Upokumanu, who was protected by a Yanekahi *yeremwanu* named Kapahai, appears to have stayed for a time before returning to Aneityum (Adams 1984: 70; Liua'ana 1996: 54–55).

From 1846–1853, Polynesian teachers continued to be settled at Port Resolution, with almost no success. A smallpox outbreak in 1853 finally ended the LMS endeavour at Port Resolution (Liua'ana 1996: 55–56; Miller 1978: 36–37). Archaeologically, almost nothing is known about this period, aside from the oral traditions associated with the *imwarim* Yakuperang. No archaeological excavations have been carried out at Port Resolution at this point. A brief survey recorded a number of archaeological surface features, mostly relating to later mission contacts in the area (Figure 3.12). In 1858, the Scottish Presbyterian missionary John G. Paton settled on Tanna along with the Canadian John Matheson. Paton and his wife settled at Port Resolution, while Matheson and his wife settled in the Kwamera area. Samuel Johnston, another Canadian, joined the Tanna Mission in 1860. Within two years, Johnston, John G. Paton's wife Mary, and the Patons' son died. (Adams 1984: 99–115; Miller 1981: 20–35; Paton 1907 Vol. 1; Patterson 1864). Like their LMS predecessors, the Presbyterians struggled to win converts on Tanna, owing largely to difficulties in translating Biblical concepts, and lack of understanding of Tannese *kastom*. Paton showed himself to be particularly hard-headed, and prone to making these kinds of errors (e.g. Adams 1984: 112–113). In 1862, following a series of deadly measles outbreaks, and a destructive cyclone, missionaries were again condemned as dangerous foreign sorcerers, and forced to flee the island (Adams 1984: 116–149).

The surface remains in the Port Resolution area relating to these early contacts include the grave site of Paton's first wife and child, as well as Rev. Johnston, all of whom died of illness on the island. These graves were located next to Paton's first mission house in Port Resolution. The house had been built of wattle and plaster, and apparently contained, 'A grand piano, china dinner, and silver cutlery services', typical markers of civilised domestic life (Adams 1984: 100). After these deaths, Paton chose to relocate to a more 'healthful' location up the hill (Paton 1907 Vol. 1: 128–138). The site is marked by a minor rubble scatter, and not much else, though apparently gardeners in the area occasionally find pieces of earthenware. The site would merit future test excavation. Nearby is an old mango tree said to have been the first in the area, planted by the missionaries in the late 1850s. These features all cluster on the south side of the harbour.

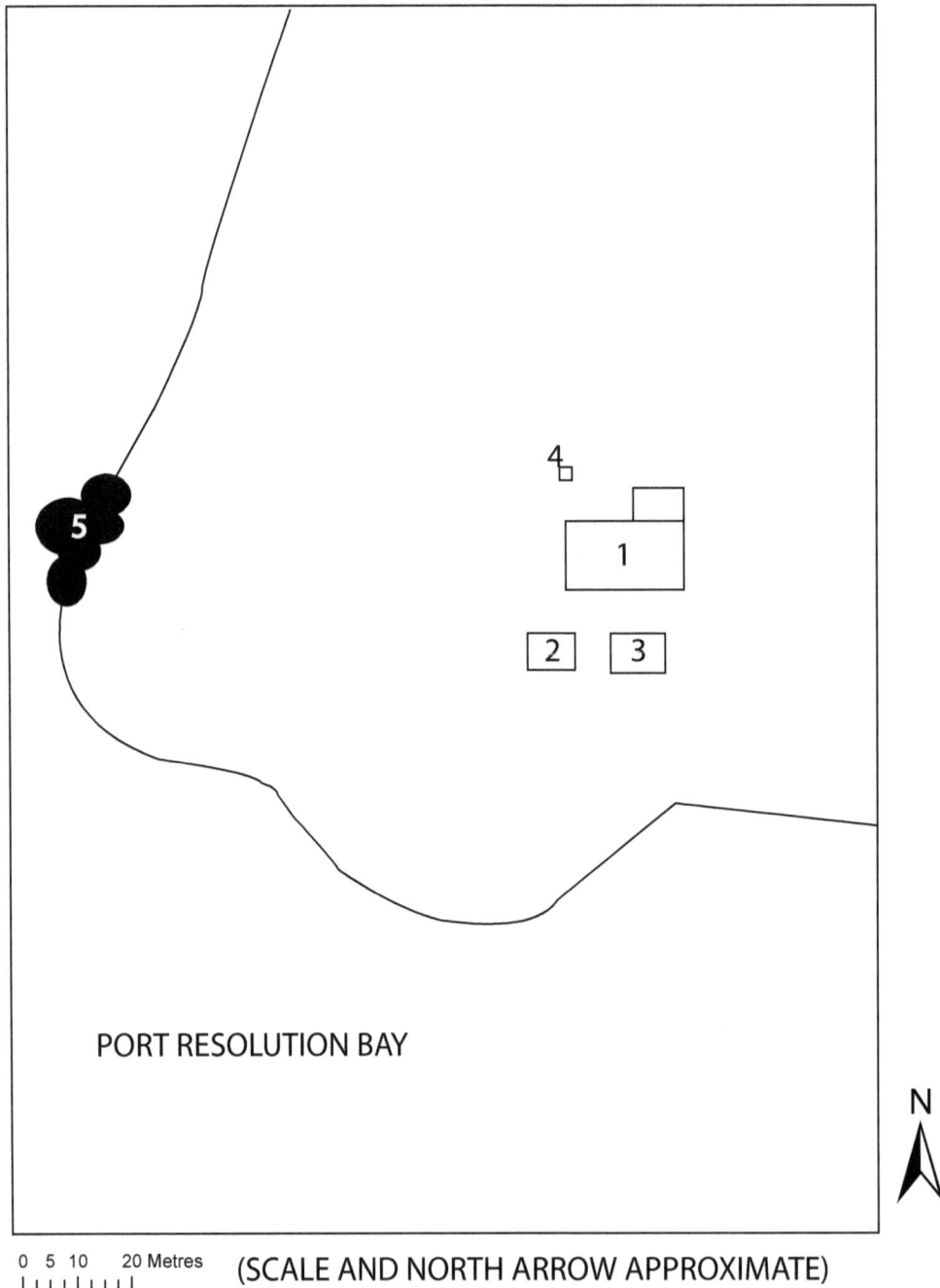

Figure 3.13 Schematic of the later mission compound at Port Resolution (1: mission church; 2: mission house; 3: printing house; 4: Agnes Watt grave; 5: boat landing). Forms and locations of features are approximate only.

Source: James Flexner

The features on the east side of the harbour relate primarily to the later missionary tenure of the Watts, Scottish missionaries supported by the New Zealand Reformed Church who were settled on Tanna in 1869 (Lindstrom 2013; Miller 1981: 38–39; Watt 1896). These later contacts will be the focus of Chapter 4, but bear brief description here as the features are presented in Figure 3.12. No clear structural remains are present at this point as the mission site is now also the location of the Port Resolution Yacht Club. The general layout of the mission could be roughly reconstructed based on local social memories (Figure 3.13). Agnes Watt died in 1894 and is buried next to the old church. Her marble headstone came from the manufacturers Bouskli and McNab of Auckland, reflecting both the New Zealand connections of the mission, and the increasing availability of heavy materials from overseas in this period. Construction activity on the site uncovered a lid from an iron ship's tank bearing the mark of 'JOHN BELLAMY BYNG ST. MILLWALL'. These kinds of tanks were often used in colonial Australia as water tanks or boilers (Pearson 1992). Presumably this would have been the case at Port Resolution as well.

Two more features are worth noting, as they relate to more recent integration of mission heritage and *kastom* in the 20th century (Flexner and Spriggs 2015). The bell from the Watts' church at Port Resolution has been placed in a tree in one of the central areas of the current village. The bell bears the inscription, 'COME UNTO ME. [ST.] PAUL'S, GLASGOW. 1890. JOHN C. WILSON & Co FOUNDERS. GL[ASGOW]' (Figure 3.14). The tree stands near the site of the church erected by the Watts in 1891 (Watt 1896: 321–324). The other feature is the grave site of early church elders, including 'BARAUN' (also sometimes spelled Braun), who was one of the teachers helping the Watts at a new station established in Ikurupu (Watt 1896: 315). The continued significance of the graves of Tannese elders reflects the importance of Melanesian integration of Christianity into local life. Local curation of artefacts from the mission period, such as the bell, shows that material from this era holds continued relevance. This is especially notable in the Port Resolution area, where local reinterpretation of modernity has taken the form of the John Frum 'cargo cult' (Lindstrom 1993; Tabani 2010).

Figure 3.14 Old mission bell in a tree, Port Resolution.
Source: James Flexner

The Mathesons at Imua

John and Mary Matheson settled in the Kwamera area in the *netata* of Umairarekarmene in 1858 as part of an effort to revitalise the Tanna Mission. Their initial house location was on the coast, where they built a three-room cottage measuring 40x15 feet (13x5m) with a view of Aneityum and easy access to fresh water (Patterson 1864: 381–382). In 1859, after recurring illnesses, the Mathesons decided to quit the mission station in Kwamera for the cooler climate of Aneityum. Presumably they also had better access to healthcare and other resources in Geddie's Mission stronghold at Anelcauhat. Eventually they spent a short time at the neighbouring mission station of Umetch, and a rainy season on Erromango (Patterson 1864: 397–445).

Having recovered, the Mathesons resumed their labours on Tanna in April 1860. The missionaries moved their house inland to higher elevation, which was thought to be less likely to cause illness (see also discussion of G. Gordon House, Chapter 2). Nonetheless, they continued to suffer to greater and lesser degrees for their remaining time on Tanna (Patterson 1864: 446–466). The Mathesons were under the protection of a local chief named Kapuku. As elsewhere on the island, there were major outbreaks of measles and dysentery, and the aforementioned cyclone in 1860. Kapuku was one of the ones who became severely ill during one of the measles outbreaks, and afterwards avoided the mission. The Mathesons insisted that only their God could cause or cure illness. Once again, the missionaries cast themselves as *Tupunas*, dangerous sorcerers. When John Matheson asked local people about their hostility, one response from the *yeremwanu* Kati was that as long as God didn't know about their heathenism, he couldn't punish them for it, so by avoiding the missionaries, they avoided illness (Adams 1984: 119–121). Eventually, the position of the missionaries became unsustainable, and with ongoing epidemics, failing health, and increasing local hostility, including the burning of the church building at Kwamera, the Mathesons were forced to flee from Tanna, along with the Patons, on 2 February 1862 (Adams 1984: 143–145; Miller 1981: 32–33; Patterson 1864: 494–498). Both of the Mathesons died of illness shortly after this, Mary a few weeks later on Aneityum and John on Maré in the Loyalty Islands of New Caledonia in June 1862.

Imua Mission Excavations

The place where the Mathesons' second house was built is called Imua, a local orthography of 'Samoa' in honour of the teachers who were settled in the area from 1854 onwards. Kapuku, who despite his avoidance remained a friend of the mission, is buried near the house site (see Figure 3.4). The remains of the mission site consist of single-course stone alignments visible on the surface (Figure 3.15). Artefacts, primarily transfer-printed refined earthenwares, were also present on the surface. The stone alignments appear to group into two 'structures', though site stratigraphy suggests that the western alignments were likely garden boundaries around which the house collapsed. Visiting the site in 1869, Agnes Watt noted that the ruins of the house, garden paths, and broken dishes were still visible on the surface, and the lemon trees the Mathesons had planted were still bearing fruit (Watt 1896: 91).

Excavations at the house (to be referred to as 'Imua Mission' below, to distinguish it from the earlier Matheson house, which has yet to be discovered) consisted of a 2x2m test unit in the eastern structure, and a 4x4m area consisting of four contiguous units in the west. The unit in the eastern structure (TU3) had a simple stratigraphic sequence, with a very dark brown topsoil layer overlying a layer containing mortar fragments and artefacts, which overlay a clay subsoil (Figure 3.16). The ceramic assemblage from TU3 appears to be somewhat distinct from the western area, suggesting functionally different use of space. Specifically, TU3 contained a chamberpot and mineral water bottle, so this part of the house may have been used for rituals relating to personal hygiene. The western excavation area showed a similar stratigraphic sequence (Figure 3.17), but the concentration of artefacts was much higher across most of the unit. Excavation of the topsoil revealed that the dense concentration of artefacts was bounded on the southwestern corner (Figure 3.18), and was not correlated with the stone alignments. For this reason we doubt that the surface stones to the west were building wall footings, though they may have supported or framed low walls or fences.

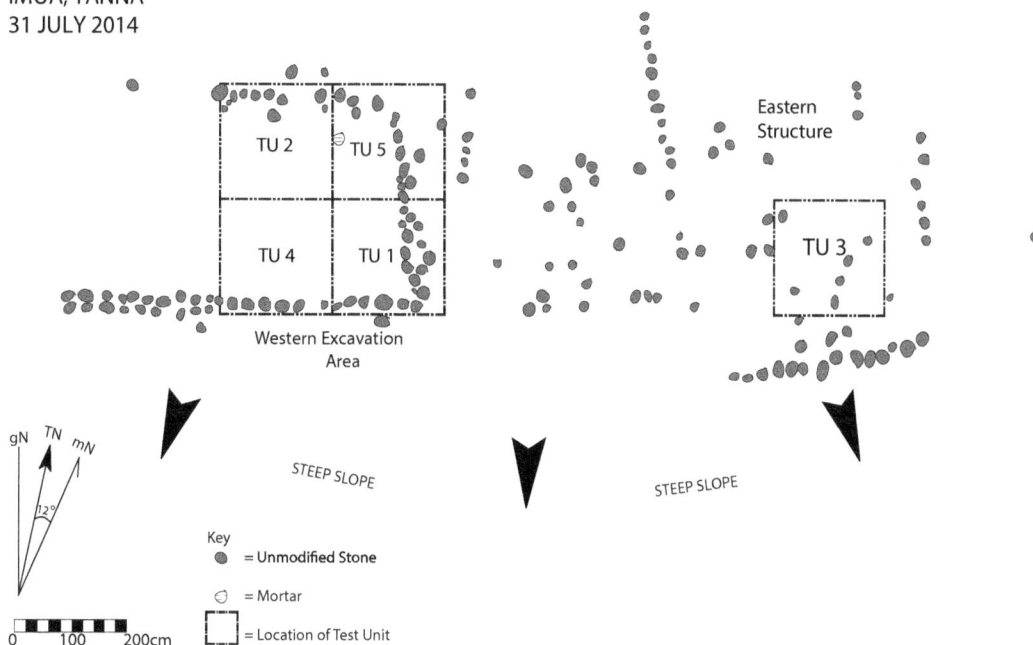

Figure 3.15 Plan of Imua Mission.

Source: James Flexner

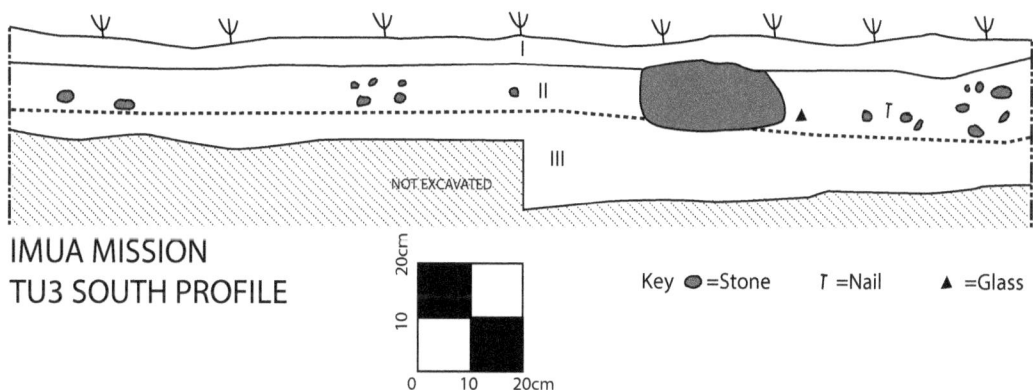

Figure 3.16 Stratigraphic profile, TU3, Imua Mission.

Source: James Flexner

IMUA MISSION WESTERN EXCAVATION AREA PROFILES

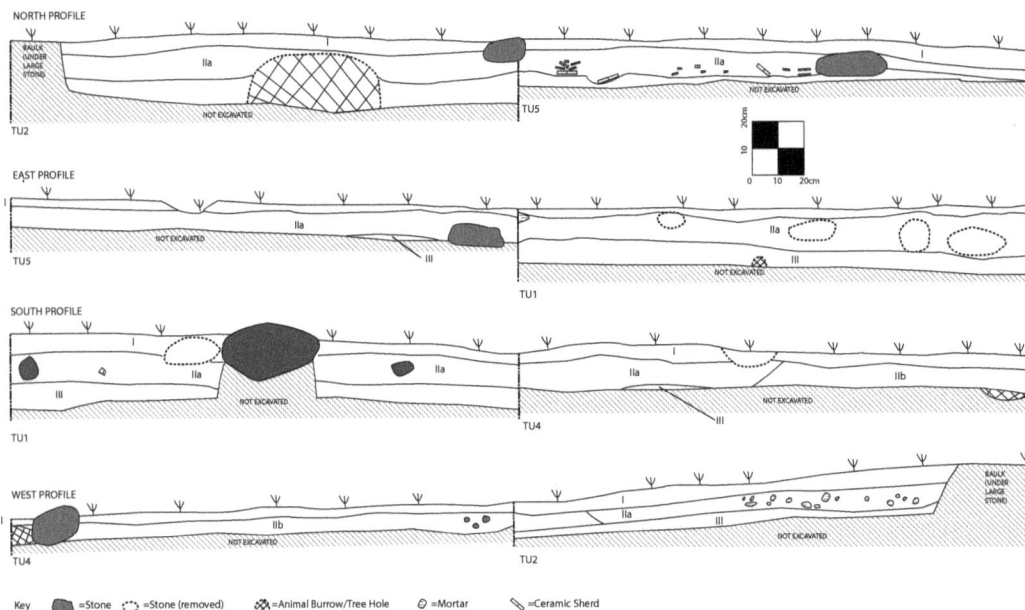

Figure 3.17 Stratigraphic profiles, TU1/2/4/5, Imua Mission.

Source: James Flexner

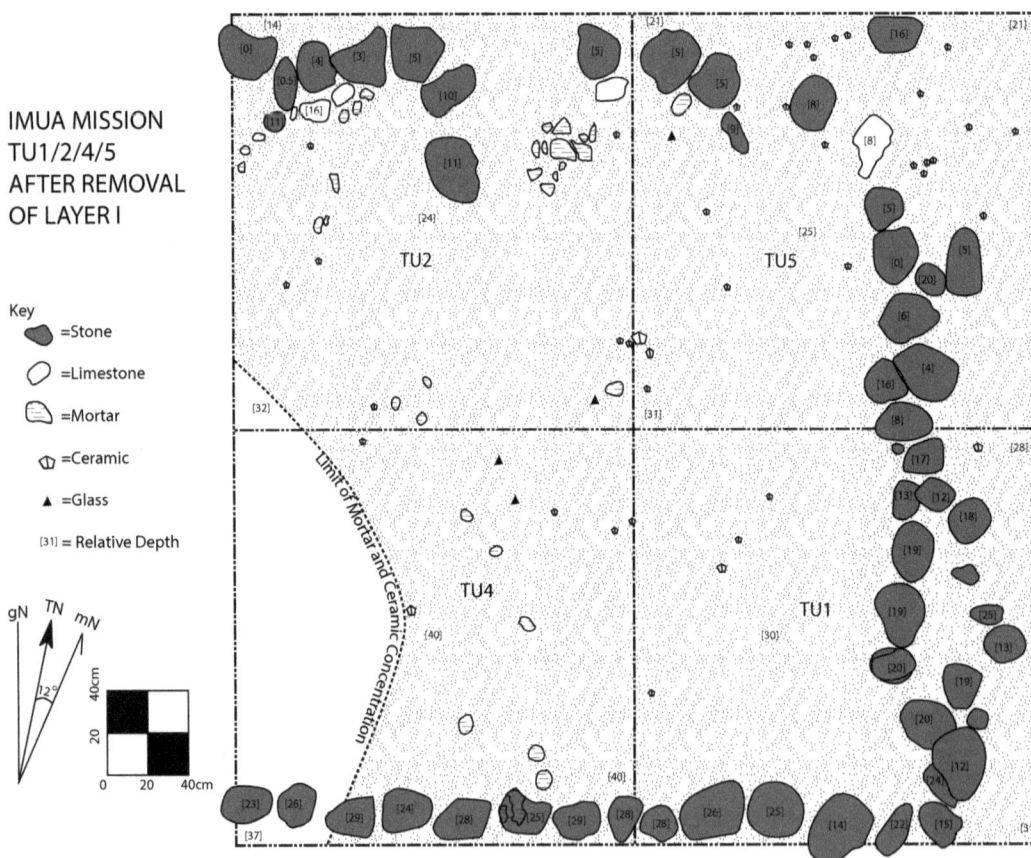

IMUA MISSION
TU1/2/4/5
AFTER REMOVAL
OF LAYER I

Key

⬤ =Stone

◯ =Limestone

⬭ =Mortar

⬠ =Ceramic

▲ =Glass

[31] = Relative Depth

Figure 3.18 Plan of western excavation area after removal of the topsoil revealed the full extent of stone alignments, and concentration of building materials and artefacts from the mission house at Imua.

Source: James Flexner

Even before the Mathesons abandoned the site, the house and other mission buildings, including a church and storehouse closer to the coast, had been badly damaged in a storm (Patterson 1864: 482). After the house was abandoned, the structure and whatever materials remained inside would have deteriorated rapidly. The deposit of artefacts and lime mortar fragments in the western excavation area at Imua Mission was the highest recovered from any site excavated for this project. This is interpreted as a 'destruction layer', which formed after the house had been abandoned. The high concentration of materials reflects in part the suddenness with which the Mathesons departed, leaving most of the household goods behind (though there is some evidence that a few valuables were placed in a boat house that a later observer found unplundered; Patterson 1864: 497–498).

In some places, ceramic sherds were stacked on top of each other, and groups of lime mortar fragments clustered together where larger sections of wall had fallen down (Figure 3.19). A 2x2m area of this deposit in the northwest (PN196, TU5) contained more ceramic artefacts than had been recovered from all of the other excavations on Tanna and Erromango mission sites combined. If anything, artefact concentration appears to *increase* towards the north and west, suggesting the house was located in this direction. There is evidence for postdepositional movement of artefacts and mortar fragments, primarily as a result of the activities of burrowing animals, including rats and crabs, as well as tree root growth. There was some vertical tilting of ceramic sherds. Stratigraphically, the stone alignments overlie some of the artefact concentration, though this is interpreted as occurring because of animal burrowing and tree roots moving things under the stones.

Figure 3.19 *In situ* concentration of lime mortar fragments and ceramic sherds, Imua.
Source: James Flexner

Future research could pinpoint the location of the house and any other buildings on the site, as well as recovering more of the very rich artefact assemblage from the site. The house was made of wattle and lime mortar, probably set directly onto compacted earth. Because of the aforementioned formation processes (Schiffer 1987) at the site, the house structure will probably appear as a concentration of mortar fragments and artefacts rather than a discrete architectural 'feature'. The stone alignments on the surface are thus more likely interpreted as garden paths or other features, though the eastern structure has not been ruled out as a possible building.

Imua Artefact Assemblage

The artefacts from Imua Mission provide an astonishing glimpse into mission life on Tanna for the brief period that the house was inhabited by the Mathesons. The amount of material recovered from the site far outweighs what was recovered from any of the other excavated mission sites from Tanna and Erromango. Lime mortar was only sampled from the site, because of limitations on how much could be brought back to the National Museum in Port Vila for analysis. Over 30kg of mortar was removed from the site and analysed. Of this, roughly 28 per cent by weight (8.5kg, N=175) had beam impressions from the wattle structure of the house (Figure 3.20). Another 7 per cent still retained the original whitewash from the wall surfaces, with 13 of these fragments coming from a single concentration within the western excavation area.

Figure 3.20 Lime mortar fragments with wattle impressions, Imua.
Source: James Flexner

Other architectural materials were abundant as well, including 827g of window glass fragments. Again this is far more than was recovered from any other site, even taking into account the slightly larger excavation area at Imua (20m² total). A total of 1,550 nails and nail fragments were recovered. The identifiable nails were primarily of the hand-wrought type (N=1422, 3.76kg), though there were also a few machine-cut nails (N=11, 16.5g), and modern round wire nails (N=30, 69g). The latter are thought to be evidence for more recent activities around the site long after its abandonment, also shown by some 20th-century glass vessels found on the surface. Of the wrought nails, roughly 16 per cent by count (N=232) showed some evidence of being bent, including 56 that are thought to have been intentionally bent into hooks (Figure 3.21).

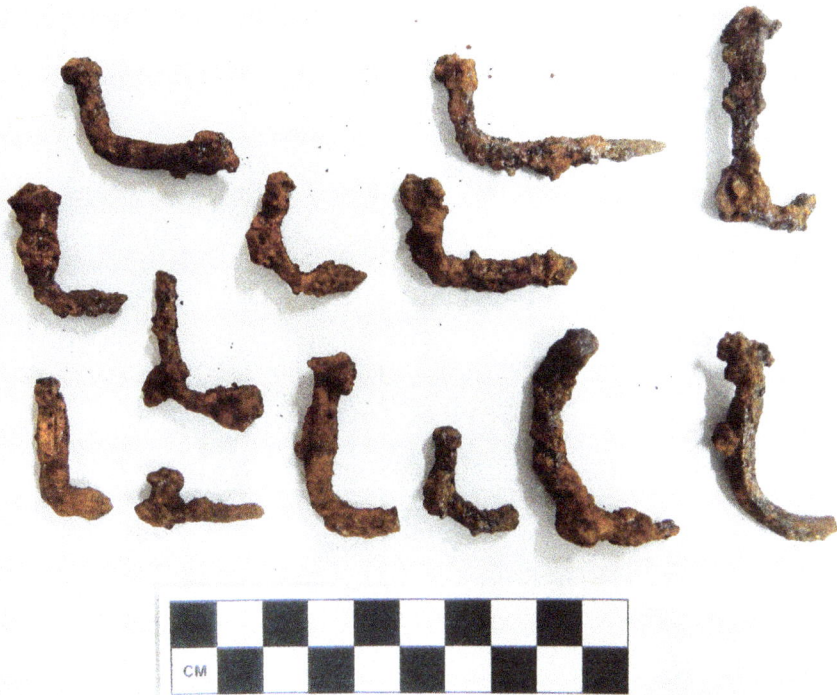

Figure 3.21 Hand-wrought iron nails, possibly bent intentionally, Imua.
Source: James Flexner

Very few glass artefacts aside from the window glass shards were recovered at Imua. Not counting the two 20th-century examples already noted, glass was limited to 13 colourless and aquamarine shards of thin-walled bottles. Notably, two of the colourless bottle fragments included embossed writing, one simply 'ON' or 'NO', and the other '… ERION …' Two conjoining sherds of an aquamarine bottle include the letters '… IC', suggesting 'TONIC'. It is certainly likely that the Mathesons would have used some kinds of medicine or tonics typical of the 19th century considering their apparent ill-health. Thus far, there is no clear evidence for alcohol consumption at Imua. As is typical, faunal remains were dominated by shellfish, including the usual taxa of *Turbo, Cypraea,* Trochidae, Conidae, *Nerita,* and Arcidae. A few taxa not found on other mission sites, including Ostreidae and *Triton* were also present. The *Triton* is intriguing, as it was used not only as a food source but for large shell trumpets (called *bubu* in Bislama). The presence of several large *Triton* fragments suggests that such a trumpet may have indeed been used to call people to meetings at the Mathesons' Mission.

Artefacts relating to personal adornment included six buttons (Figure 3.22). Four consisted of round metal alloy backings with dark blue glass paste jewels. There was also a plain copper alloy disc, which could have had a decorative covering that did not preserve, and a copper alloy shank with a mother of pearl disc. A single handmade bone button with three holes was also recovered. Missionaries attempted to maintain Victorian standards of dress in the field, while also attempting to encourage changing habits of dress among local people. Mary Matheson may have been particularly driven to cover the body as a way of suppressing its dangerous passions, especially in contrast to the nakedness of the Melanesian people who surrounded the mission (Adams 1984: 99–100). At the same time, increasingly localised frames of reference in bodily adornment are apparent in the form of a *Nerita* shell that has been perforated on one side to form a simple pendant (Figure 3.23).

Figure 3.22 Buttons from Imua (top row, from left: three iron with blue glass paste jewel, one copper alloy disc; bottom row, from left: handmade bone button with three holes, mother of pearl disc with copper alloy shank).

Source: James Flexner

Figure 3.23 *Nerita* shell pendant, Imua.

Source: James Flexner

The most impressive finds from Imua were the ceramic artefacts (Flexner and Ball 2016). Included among these was a ceramic sheep's head (Figure 3.24). This is thought to have come from a child's toy. Such artefacts are generally rare from mission sites in Australasia (Middleton 2008: 219–220). A porcelain doll was recovered from Ebenezer Mission in southeast Australia. Such artefacts were meant to habituate indigenous female children to Western standards of domesticity (Lydon 2009: 138–139). In this case, the sheep may also have related to an idealised pastoral British identity, not to mention the other obvious Biblical references to the 'Lamb of God'. It should also be noted that the Mathesons had a baby girl in 1861, though she only lived for a few months (Patterson 1864: 493–494). It is possible that this object was originally intended for the Mathesons' child, then used for native children before being left behind when the house was abandoned.

IMUA MISSION CERAMIC SHEEP'S HEAD

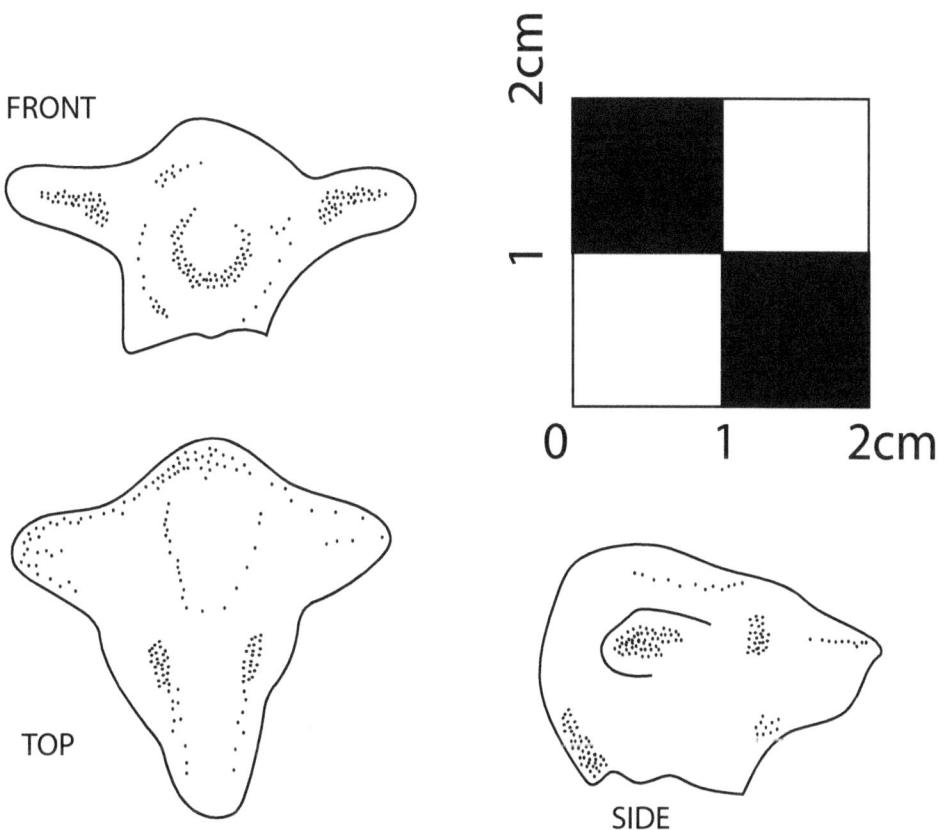

Figure 3.24 Ceramic sheep's head, Imua.
Source: James Flexner

The ceramics from Imua house likewise have a distinctly pastoral theme. A total of 2,739 sherds weighing 16.6kg were recovered from Imua. The sherds have been reconstructed to a minimum of 36 vessels (Table 3.1). Of these, 26 are of the dense, white refined earthenware generally called 'whiteware' with variations of the same blue transfer-printed design. The motifs are pastoral, featuring sheep, cattle, and castle ruins (Figure 3.25). These are arranged in a central vignette, and then elements of the design are repeated in cartouches around the rim. Two of the vessels bear the stamp 'ARCADIA', and the remaining 24 pastoral vessels bear an identical pattern or related variation. It was typical for only a small portion of vessels in a transfer-printed set to bear stamps (Samford 1997: 1). Arcadia was produced by J. & M. P. Bell & Co., a Glasgow pottery active from 1842–1928 (Brooks 2005: 69; Coysh and Henrywood 1982: 24). The pottery is a projection of idealised British pastoral landscapes (see Brooks 1999), and possibly the Scottish identity of the missionaries. John G. Paton served as a city missionary in Glasgow before departing for the New Hebrides (Adams 1984: 88–94; Paton 1907: 53–84), though Bell ceramics were common throughout Australasia so there is no reason to assume these vessels came directly with Paton.

Table 3.1 Reconstructed vessels from Imua (minimum number of vessels).

Vessel Frags.	Context	MNV Count	Short Description	Transfer Group
VF10-19	TU1/2/4/5	2	Flow Blue bowl	Flow Blue
VF8	TU1/2/4/5	1	Linear cup	Linear
VF2-7	TU1/2/4/5	2	Linear plate	Linear
VF9	TU1/2/4/5	1	Brown stoneware storage jar or jug	NA
VF41	TU1/2/4/5	1	Handled vessel, hand-painted floral motif	NA
VF35-36	TU1/2/4/5	2	Arcadia round shallow bowl	Romantic-Pastoral
VF63/64	TU1/2/4/5	1	Repeated motif, Arcadia round shallow bowl (one of these two might go with VF35)	Romantic-Pastoral
VF21-27	TU1/2/4/5	2	Large rectangular platter, Arcadia	Romantic-Pastoral
VF40, 42	TU1/2/4/5	1	Moulded rim bowl, smaller, Arcadia	Romantic-Pastoral
VF43	TU1/2/4/5	1	Pastoral storage bowl, interior (cattle/cartouche) and exterior (architecture), Arcadia	Romantic-Pastoral
VF62, 69-73	TU1/2/4/5	1	'Mezzanine'/Meat Strainer, Arcadia variant	Romantic-Pastoral
VF63-64, 66-68	TU1/2/4/5	2	Possibly fragments of the same open vessel base, repeated boat motif on non-mending sherd, also repeating motif on VF63/64. VF110 rim might go with this set. VF66 and VF68 are clearly the same pattern, though slightly overlap (so 2 vessels min). Possibly an Arcadia variant, but not definite	Romantic-Pastoral
VF65	TU1/2/4/5	1	Very blurry base with slightly different pastoral motif, again possibly Arcadia but not certain	Romantic-Pastoral
VF44-61, 75-150	TU1/2/4/5	14	Most common pastoral motif, minimum vessels based on non-repeating motif of base fragments. There are slightly sharper and slightly blurrier (blurry is represented by VF55, VF56 of the bases) versions of the pattern, more variable on the rims. Rims indicate at least three rectangular platters, at least four shallow bowls or plates, and of course there would be more of each. The round shallow bowl/plate was the more common form, so the estimate is an MNV of 10 round ones and 4 rectangular.	Romantic-Pastoral
VF1	TU1/2/4/5	1	Black 'JOHN' saucer	Scriptural
Sherd 2103	TU3	1	Selter's Mineral Water bottle, stoneware	NA
Sherd 2104	TU3	1	Undec. whiteware bowl	NA
VF37-39	TU3	1	Chinese Fountains chamberpot	Oriental

Figure 3.25 'Arcadia' transfer pattern, Imua.
Source: James Flexner

Other transfer-printed vessels from Imua include a chamberpot from TU3 with a pattern identified as 'Chinese Fountains' (Figure 3.26a), which was produced by Elkin Knight and Bridgwood in England from 1822–1846 (J. Adamson, pers. comm.; Williams and Weber 1978: 110). There were at least two plates and one cup with a linear design of blue and seafoam green (Figure 3.26b). A small, fine-moulded saucer bore the only black transfer-printed design, which consists of a geometric border and the name 'JOHN' in the middle (Figure 3.26c). This may have been part of a set of children's teawares, with the names of the gospels (Matthew, Mark, Luke, and John) printed on the saucers. These kinds of moralising children's wares were fairly common in the Victorian era (Williams and Weber 1978: 534–570). There were at least two bowls of the type known as 'Flow Blue' (Gaston 1989), bearing a transfer pattern that was intentionally over-inked so that the blue colour bled. The motifs on the Flow Blue bowls are quite similar to the Chinese Fountains pattern (Figure 3.26d).

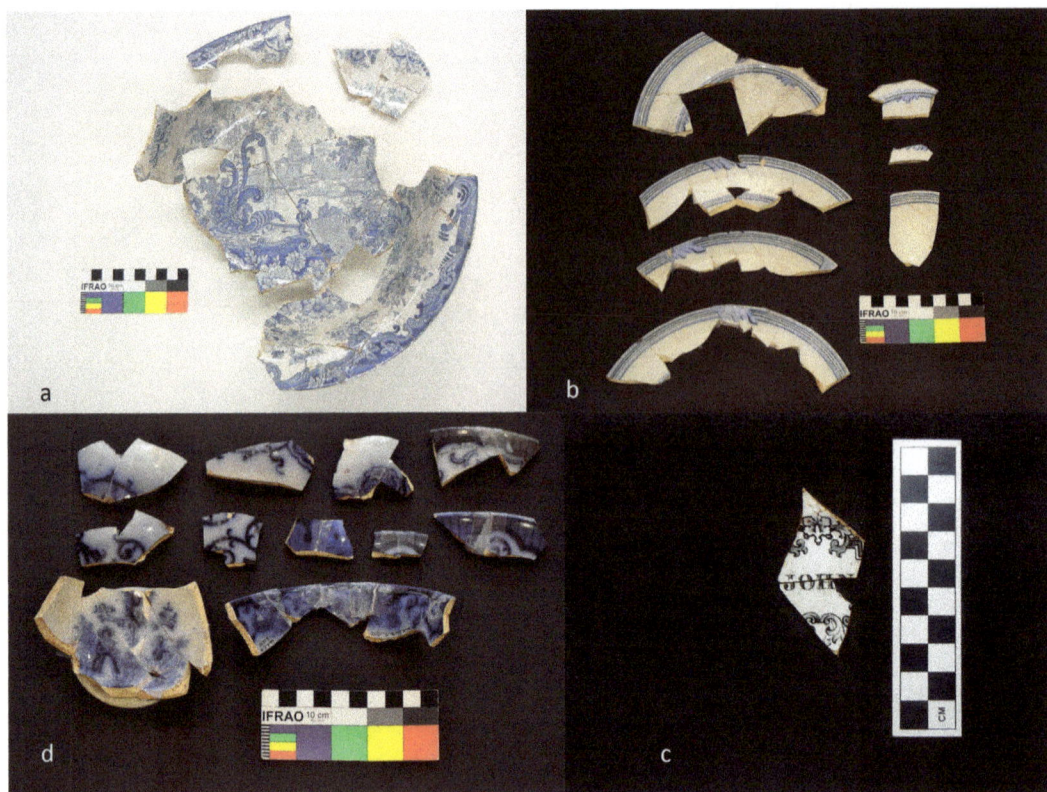

Figure 3.26 Other transfer patterns from Imua (see text for details).
Source: James Flexner

There were only three vessels that did not bear transfer printing. There was a single undecorated whiteware bowl from TU3. The remaining two vessels are utilitarian stonewares. The mouth of a brown glazed stoneware jug is represented by three sherds. None of the body of this vessel was recovered. The other stoneware vessel is a cylindrical bottle bearing a stamp on the shoulder that consists of a lion surrounded by two concentric circles, with the word 'SELTERS' within the circles. Below this the letters '[H]ERZOGTH[UM]' were stamped (Figure 3.27). This bottle contained mineral water from a famous spring in the Taunus Mountains of Germany. These were common trade items in the 1700s and 1800s (Lockhart 2010: 98). A recent find from a Polish shipwreck indicates that these bottles were sometimes refilled with alcoholic beverages (PAP 2014). Considering the ill health of which the Mathesons complained throughout their time on Tanna (Patterson 1864), it is more likely that in this case the mineral water was consumed for its medicinal properties.

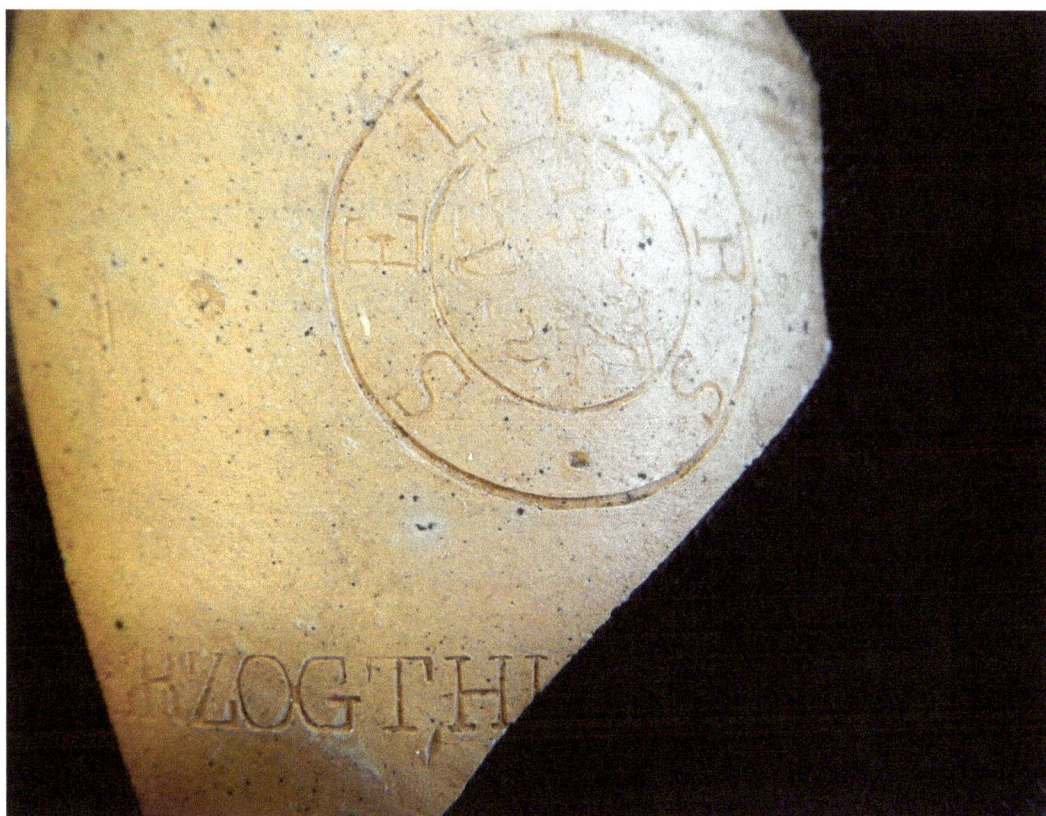

Figure 3.27 Selter's stoneware mineral water bottle from Imua.
Source: James Flexner

The vessel forms from the transfer-printed vessels consisted primarily of shallow bowl forms generally referred to as 'soup plates' (Figure 3.28; Brooks 2005: 47). There were also at least two large rectangular platters of Arcadia ware. Other vessel forms included a 'Mezzanine' or meat strainer, which was a flat vessel that would have sat on top of a platter, with holes in the body to allow the juice from meat or fish dishes to drip through (Brooks 2005: 49). These dishes were an important component of Victorian dining rituals. However, they likely were used to serve overwhelmingly local ingredients and meals. The typical British diet of bread, butter, bacon, and tea was probably replaced with *laplap* (a kind of starchy pudding made from grated tubers mixed with water and other ingredients and cooked in an earth oven), yams, and local seafood on most occasions. Overall, this remarkable assemblage of ceramics provides a glimpse into the ways that the missionaries performed a civilised Scottish Victorian identity on a daily basis, while also trying to adapt to life on Tanna. Dining rituals would have been internally important to the missionaries and any European visitors they hosted (for example, Mary Matheson was John Geddie's niece, and Geddie as well as the missionary John Inglis visited; Patterson 1864: 895). Equally important, though, these objects may have offered an opportunity to engage with potential converts as foreign 'curiosities' for Melanesian people. Arcadia ware especially may have been an expression of a nostalgic homeland that could be a reminder for their owners, and a storytelling device for cultural others.

VF2 (Linear Pattern Plate)

VF8 (Linear Pattern Cup)

VF113 (Soup Plate)

VF36 (Soup Plate)

VF24 (Rectangular Platter)

VF126 (Rectangular Platter)

IMUA
Ceramic Vessel Forms
All vessels pastoral transfer-printed
earthenware unless otherwise indicated.

VF23 (Rectangular Platter)

VF9 (Stoneware Jug)

VF62 (Mezzanine/Meat Strainer)

2cm

1cm

0   1cm   2cm

VF1 (Scriptural Saucer)

VF10 (Flow Blue Bowl)

VF14 (Flow Blue Bowl)

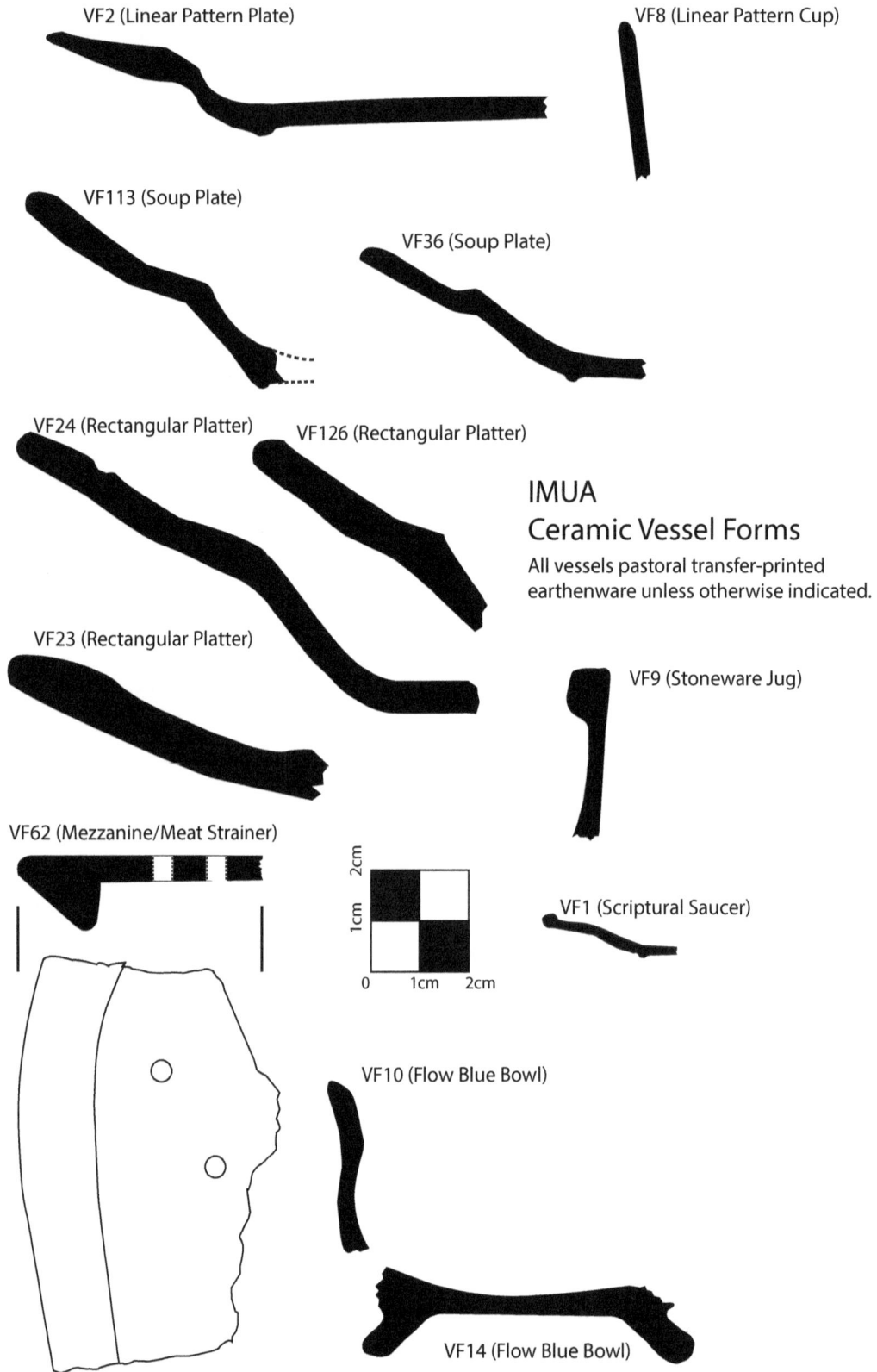

Figure 3.28 Ceramic vessel forms, vessels are whiteware with Arcadia transfer-pattern unless otherwise indicated.

Source: James Flexner

The Mission Period at Anuikaraka

There was a chief named Iarisi (also spelled Yarisi and Jarisi in various missionary sources) who was a *Yani en Dete* in the Kwaraka area in the 1850s. One of Iarisi's chiefly duties was to organise and lead canoe voyages to exchange with neighbouring Aneityum Island. The Tannese would carry grass skirts, yams, and other goods, and in exchange, would receive taro, mats, red ochre, and other items from Aneityum. When a voyage was being arranged, the men from Kwaraka would go to one of the nearby *imwarim*, where they would drink kava. While intoxicated, they would use the spirit of the kava to send a message to their counterparts on Aneityum, who would prepare for the arrival of a canoe the next day. Iarisi's canoe was named *Paru*. It was kept on a special stone mound with a ramp when not in the water (Figure 3.29).

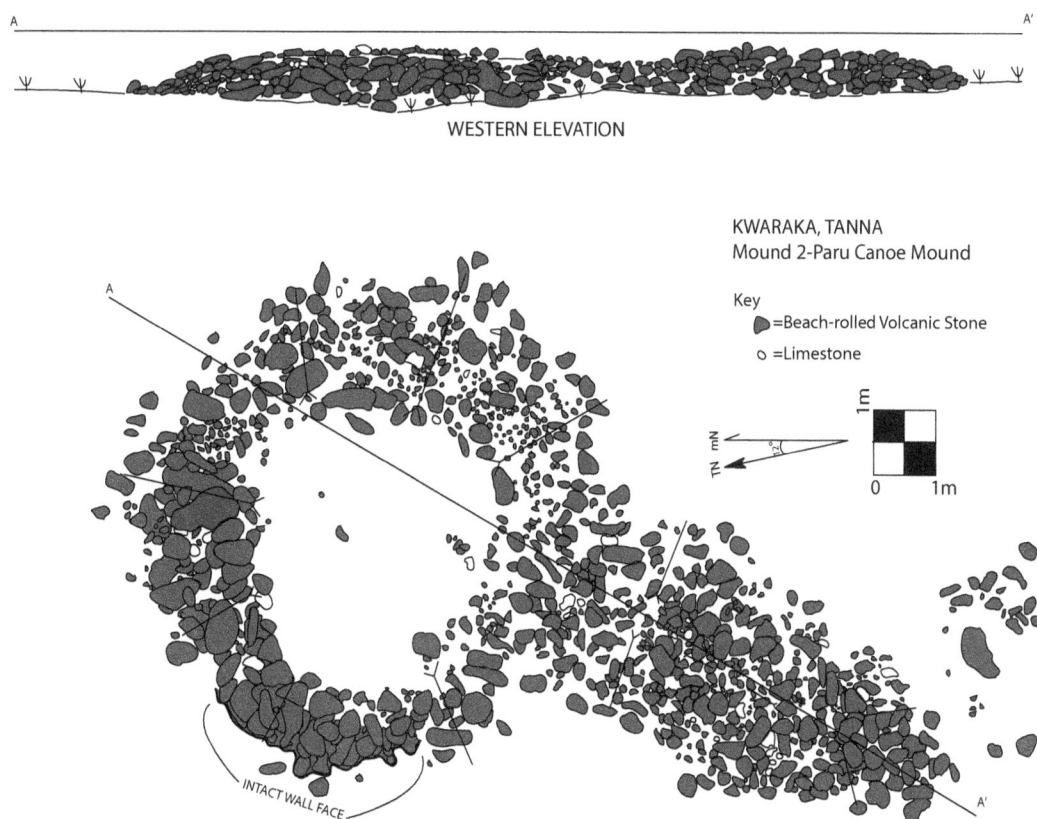

Figure 3.29 Canoe mound where *Paru* rested when not at sea, Kwaraka.

Source: James Flexner

On one of his voyages to Aneityum early in the 1850s, Iarisi met some of the Aneityumese converts to Christianity, and possibly one of the European missionaries. Of course, Iarisi would also have heard of and possibly even met the missionaries who had settled in the failed Port Resolution settlement over the course of the 1840s. This trip to Aneityum must have made a positive impression on Iarisi, who decided to open the way for Christianity to come to the Kwaraka area. Likely it was this connection that allowed for the settlement of Aneityumese teachers at Anuikaraka in 1854 (Miller 1978: 37; Murray 1863: 158; Turner 1861: 451). The missionaries assumed that Iarisi's interest in Christianity was directly related to the new material wealth accumulating among Aneityumese Christians (Gordon, ed. 1863: 127–128).

Excavations in 'New Kwaraka'

Not all of the residents in Kwaraka were so enthusiastic about the new religion that Iarisi brought with him. The epidemics that had racked the Port Resolution area had been blamed on the missionary-sorcerers, so perhaps there was fear that inviting such people to Kwaraka would only bring the same fate. Perhaps there were also worries that the missionaries were going to take away the magic stones, as had happened on Aneityum (Crook et al. 2015). The loss of *nukwei nuk*, the stones that made the yams grow, would have been nothing short of disastrous for the district. The tension between the pro- and anti-missionary factions eventually led Iarisi to take a small group of followers across Komaru stream to set up a small settlement bounded by a stone fence in Anuikaraka, remembered in oral traditions as 'New Kwaraka' (Figure 3.30). As noted above, this is just on the other side of the division between *neteta*, in Umairarekarmene.

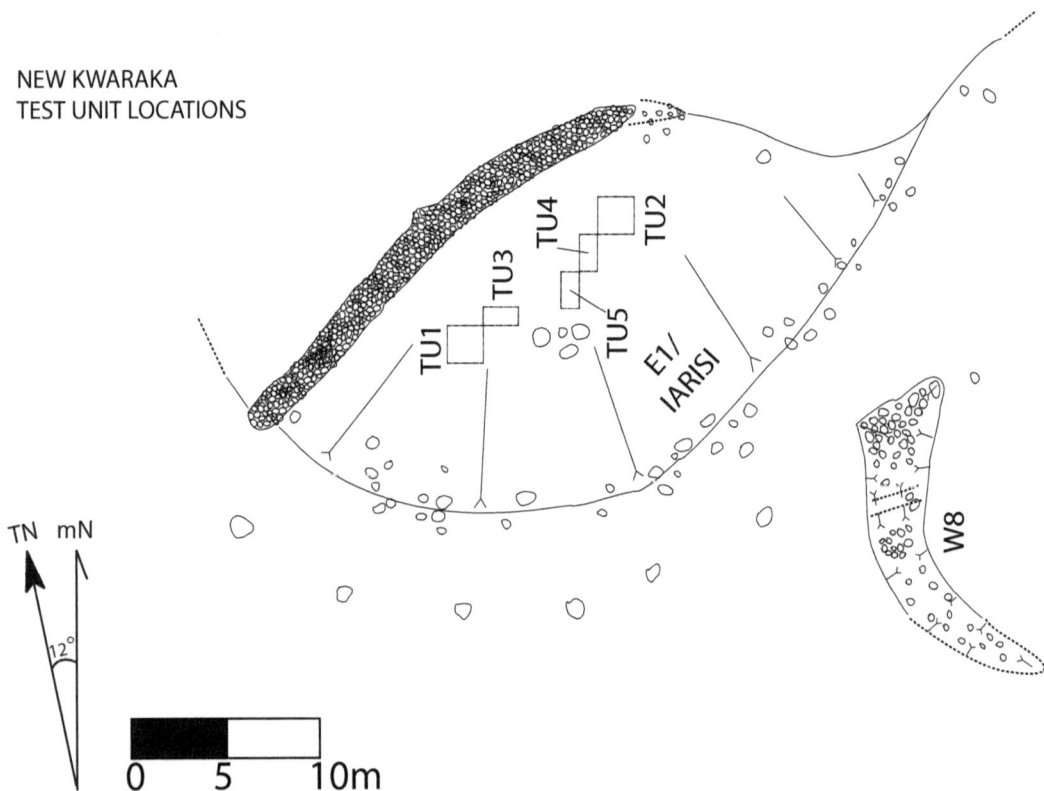

Figure 3.30 Detail plan of excavation locations in Enclosure 1 ('New Kwaraka'), Anuikaraka.
Source: James Flexner

When the first European missionaries arrived at Kwamera in 1858, they purchased land not from Iarisi, but from Kapuku and Kati, about 2km, or less than an hour's walk, to the southwest. Iarisi was remembered in friendly terms by the Mathesons as a supporter of the mission (Patterson 1864: 382). The land record from Inglis, Paton, and Copeland includes a strip of coastal plain stretching from Anuikaraka to the stream of Mimretam (Numretam), next to the current mission station in Kwamera. This massive area was exchanged for red and white calico, handkerchiefs, an axe, and some fishhooks (Vanuatu National Archives Land Record 31 S.I.1). That Iarisi was not included in the purchase suggests the missionaries were largely unaware of who the actual landowners of the area they claimed to have 'purchased' were. Land transactions from this era were generally characterised by serious misunderstanding on both sides, partly stemming from practical barriers such as language and literacy, but also more subtle issues that had to do with how 'ownership' of land was understood from a cultural perspective (Flexner 2015; Van Trease 1987).

To better understand the material conditions of Iarisi and his fellow early converts, we excavated a series of five 1x2m and 2x2m test units across the enclosure where the *Yani en Dete* was said to have moved his house in New Kwaraka (Figure 3.30). Stratigraphy across the site consisted of a thin topsoil layer, which overlay a very rocky layer in the western units (TU1, TU3, and TU5), and a sandy loam in the eastern units (TU2 and TU4). In TU2, which was partly excavated to a greater depth, there was another rocky layer underlying the sandy loam, probably evidence for periodic deposition of larger stones during flooding events from Komaru. We can't completely rule out the possibility at this point of some of the stone being architectural in TU1 and TU3, which had very dense concentration (up to 50 per cent of the sedimentary matrix) associated with high charcoal concentration. However, it appears that the sedimentary layering in the units is primarily a result of periodic flood deposits that created the terrace surrounded by the stone wall (Figure 3.31).

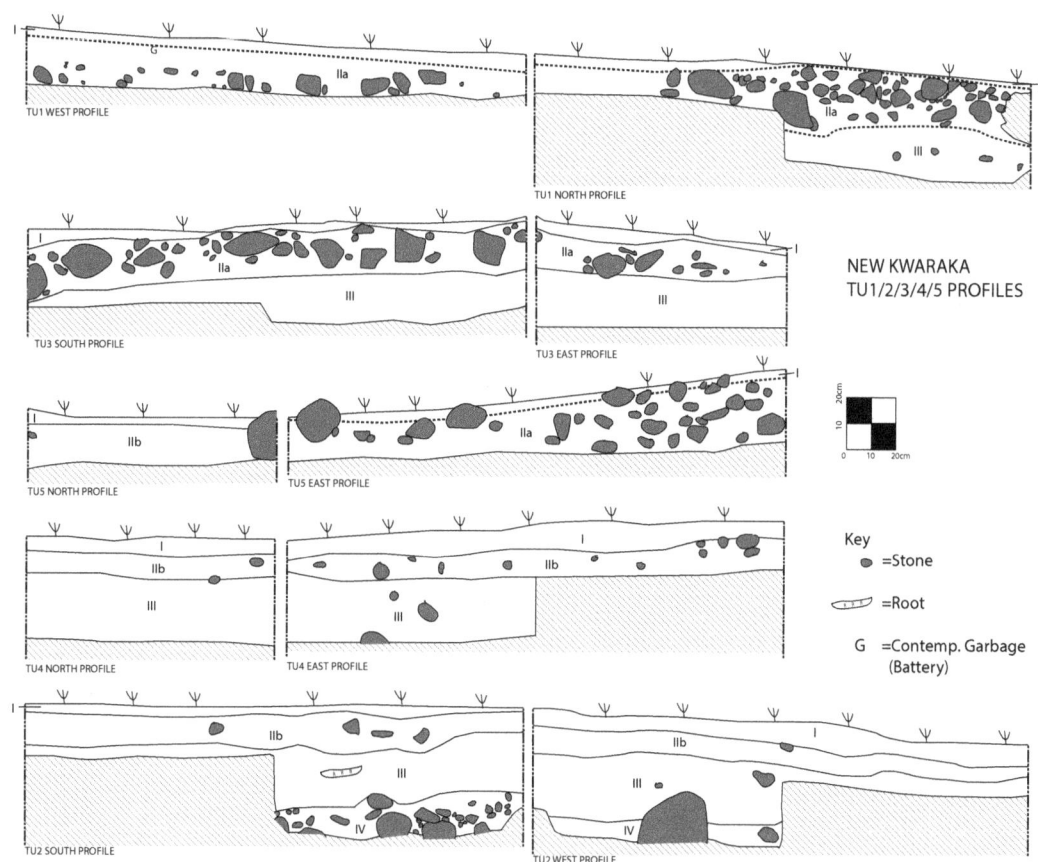

Figure 3.31 Stratigraphic profiles, TU1/2/3/4/5, Enclosure 1 ('New Kwaraka'), Anuikaraka.
Source: James Flexner

Very few artefacts were recovered from these excavations. The vast majority of collected material consisted of charcoal and burned coconut shells (N=1,239, 200.5g). A small amount of shell was found (two fragments of *Cypraea* in TU1 and seven of *Turbo* in TU3). An adze blade fragment with the distal and proximal ends missing was found in the rocky deposit of TU3. Post-contact materials were likewise fairly rare at New Kwaraka. There were unidentifiable fragments of rusted iron in the rocky layer of TU3, but only a small amount (N=102, 18g). These could have come from a single tool or metal vessel. A single piece of amber bottle glass, likely from the 20th century, emerged from TU2. The lone artefact that probably dates to the missionary era is a fragment of a clay pipe bowl from TU4, though it should be noted that clay tobacco pipes remained in use well into the 20th century on Tanna.

Overall, the archaeological remains at New Kwaraka do not indicate huge amounts of European trade goods filtering from the missions to nearby indigenous settlements. This interpretation must be qualified with the fact that periodic flooding at this site may have impacted preservation, and that many trade goods, such as cloth, would be extremely unlikely to preserve archaeologically in this environment. It is also possible that the duration of occupation at the site was brief, with Iarisi and his followers returning to Kwaraka after a few years. Even so, the evidence seems to suggest that Iarisi was not the grasping materialist he was made out to be. Shovel test pits excavated around Anuikaraka likewise did not yield any European artefacts. One possibility is that when the *Yani en Dete* did receive gifts from the missionaries, these were then re-gifted, and would have circulated across Tanna and into neighbouring islands, which would result in a low density of European artefacts on the site.

This, then, was village life on Tanna in the mid-19th century. The missionary presence was causing certain kinds of internal tensions, and even minor changes in settlement patterns. Introduced materials were filtering into local communities, but apparently in very small amounts. Alliances between local communities and loyalties among chiefly individuals shifted in response to these contacts (Adams 1984). Patterns of everyday life, though, remained largely the same. The yam gardens were still planted, men still gathered at the *imwarim* to drink kava each afternoon, *toka* and *nao* dances were held. People still relied on the yam stones for a good harvest, and feared *narak*. This was likely true both for people who were holding tight to *kastom*, and people who were apparently enthusiastic converts to the new religion. Missionaries weren't so much transforming life on Tanna, as some Tannese people were incorporating missionary things and ideas into *kastom*.

4

Expanding the Tanna Mission, 1868–1920

The dissolution of the Tanna Mission in 1862 had been a catastrophe for the Presbyterian Church. To make matters worse, John G. Paton convinced the British Navy to become involved in the mission, arguing (incorrectly, in hindsight) that he and his fellow missionaries had 'legally' purchased land in south Tanna, and were attacked without provocation by the Tannese. Sailing with the HMS *Curaçoa* under Captain Wiseman in 1865, Paton presented his complaints to people in the Port Resolution area, demanding that the responsible parties be delivered for justice. He also presented a fine of £1,000, an incredibly large sum for most people in the 1860s, and patently ridiculous as far as the Tannese were concerned. In response to indigenous rejection of Paton's claims, the crew of the *Curaçoa* bombarded the island with the aim of destroying as many houses and gardens as they could (Adams 1984: 151–161; Brenchley 1873).

While only four Tannese died in the attack, this event did little to ingratiate the Presbyterian Church to the islanders, nor indeed to European observers. In the decade following this event, Tannese people fell into a pattern of avoiding foreigners as dangerous, or attempting to use them in the context of local chiefly disputes (Adams 1984: 168–181). An attempt to reinvigorate the Port Resolution Mission under Rev. Neilson, a Scottish missionary married to one of John Geddie's daughters, was attempted in 1868 (Miller 1981: 37). The endeavour ended when it became clear that 'Like his predecessors, Neilson had become more and more enmeshed in the intricate web of intrigue and rivalry which constituted Tannese political life' (Adams 1984: 179). In 1869, the Watts were settled at Kwamera, where they would have more success. At this point, the Presbyterians still had not been able to establish a mission station north of Port Resolution.

The 1870s saw something of a turning point for the Presbyterian Mission. On Erromango, the first long-term mission was established in 1872, and lasted through the early 1900s (see Chapter 2). Apparent progress on Tanna shifted from promising starts and sudden failures to slow and steady in the closing decades of the 19th century (Miller 1986: 246–425). New stations were opened on the east coast of the island (Waisisi) and the west (Lenakel). This progress correlated with increasing investment in mission infrastructure, in the form of larger mission houses, and more functionally distinct buildings in mission stations. In part this reflects new maritime technologies, not least regular steam ships connecting major ports in Oceania (Steel 2011). By the early 1900s, the Presbyterian Church was shipping entire buildings to the New Hebrides (Flexner et al. 2015), and establishing 'model villages' for its growing numbers of converts.

At the same time, *kastom* continued to provide the structure for life on Tanna. Attempts to drive out what were perceived as the 'dangerous' elements of *kastom,* which, depending on the missionary could range from *narak* (black magic) to kava drinking and dancing, resulted in the establishment of Christian courts to enforce a Presbyterian 'Tanna Law', which reached its height from 1905–1925 (Bonnemaison 1994: 201–211). Far from purifying Tanna of its 'heathen' practices, this experiment with church policing of native practices only entrenched *kastom* in parts of the island. In others, it was driven underground, as people performed Christianity on the surface while maintaining *kastom* on a deeper level. Unease in the later part of the 20th century, from the 'cargo cult' of John Frum to the violence of the independence era, relates in part to the dialectics created in attempts to cleanse Tanna of its *kastom* (Bonnemaison 1994; Guiart 1956; Lindstrom 1993). Yet aside from a few telling, dramatic events, the resilience of *kastom* on Tanna was its everyday basis, as the patterns of the *imwarim*, *toka*, *nao*, and so on adapted and continue through the present in the face of ongoing incursion of missionaries, capitalists, and other European interlopers.

The Watts at Kwamera

William and Agnes Watt were Scottish missionaries who were brought to the New Hebrides under the aegis of the Reformed Presbyterian Church of New Zealand. They settled at Kwamera in 1869 (Figure 3.4). Among the positive signs, the Watts obtained a printing press from the Glasgow Foundry Boys in 1873, and began printing religious books in local language (Miller 1981: 38–39; Watt 1896: 150). Examples of original texts from this period survive in the present, and have important local significance, reflecting the incorporation of mission artefacts into local conceptions of heritage (see Chapter 5; Flexner and Spriggs 2015). The Watts won the first baptised Tannese converts on 4 October 1881, as two men, four women, and three children took the sacrament (Bonnemaison 1994: 198; Guiart 1956: 123). Agnes Watt died in 1894, after 25 years on the island (Lindstrom 2013; Watt 1896: 36–46). William Watt remarried, and remained on Tanna until 1910 when he retired to Australia after a long career (Miller 1981: 39).

Watt Mission Site

The Watts were active across south Tanna, and had a significant station in Port Resolution as well as at Kwamera. Like many other missionaries of the era, they itinerated between the different stations. Significantly, both Port Resolution and Kwamera featured multiple functionally distinct buildings, including a main house, church, printing house, storage buildings, and other outbuildings. I will focus on the Kwamera station here, as that is where the majority of archaeological fieldwork on the Watts' Mission sites took place. As mentioned above (see Chapter 3), the Port Resolution Mission is currently underneath the Port Resolution Yacht Club. There is potential for subsurface archaeology at the site, but at this point no excavation work has been done in the Port Resolution area. As will be seen below, the location of the Watt Mission in the contemporary village of Kwamera has likewise caused the archaeological landscape to be impacted significantly by recent activities.

Shortly after arriving at Kwamera, Agnes Watt spent extensive time describing the new mission house to her family in Scotland. This letter provides a valuable description, as well as insights into what was materially significant about the house from a missionary perspective:

> At present we have two rooms. The parlour is 19x14 ft., and has two windows, and the bedroom is 15x14 ft., also with two windows. We have no ceiling; the room is open to the rigging, which makes it nice and airy. Now, suppose you were landing here, you would see a nice house enclosed by a pretty reed fence. Coming inside that, you walk up a nice gravel walk to five snow-white steps. Ascend these and you come to our verandah with its white painted floor and a low reed railing painted green. The outside of the house is pure white, and the doors and windows are painted bright green [...] The door opens against the middle wall; and on this wall I have our largest mirror for the use of the natives, and also some coloured pictures which amuse them much. To the left is the harmonium, which also interests them greatly; and a chest, which serves as an ottoman, is under the window. Against the gable wall stands the iron sofa bed, and over it hangs the barometer.

Against the back wall stands a meat-safe, another ottoman is set under the window and a home-made chiffonier; above these hangs the clock, and on it I have some books and two kerosene lamps. In the middle of the floor stand two tables put together; and when a well cooked dinner, of chicken soup, yam, and native cabbage, with a nice plumpudding [sic], plenty of bananas, and a cup of tea with rich goat's milk, is laid out on a pure white table cloth, we are not to be pitied. I have no carpet, as so many natives come in, and I think a clean floor fresher. My bedroom is laid with mats [presumably local mats of woven dried pandanus leaf], the walls whitewashed, and the doors and windows painted light green. We have in it a wardrobe, military secretaire, and an arm-chair. On the walls are photographs of our loved ones and the R. P. [Glasgow Boys' Foundry Reformed Presbyterian?] students. Our bed is made of banana leaves with feather pillows. As there is no ceiling, I have put up four posts on the bedstead to hold up a calico roof and mosquito netting (Watt 1896: 83–84).

Note the emphasis on the 'pure white' elements of the house, from the whitewashed walls to the tablecloth. Lime mortar and whitewash at Kwamera, as elsewhere in the Pacific (Mills 2009), was an important marker of difference, contrasting missionary housing against that of the Tannese. The great variety of furniture in the house is also notable, especially as that would not normally preserve archaeologically. The inclusion of a clock is significant as it shows the introduction of a Western means of keeping time, in contrast to the way time was marked under *kastom* (Bonnemaison 1994: 56; Lindstrom 2011). Further, the presence of a barometer in the house reflects the global spread of scientific instruments, and the growing interest in meteorological phenomena at this point.

Eventually, the Watt Mission complex would grow to include a timber church, attached to the house by a covered hallway, and a number of outbuildings at the rear. These likely included a printing house for the press that arrived in 1874, and possibly other buildings such as storage shed, cookhouse, and chicken coop. Photographic evidence for the complex is extensive, including an overhead photo taken from the hillside behind the house, which shows not only the outbuildings, but also formal garden in the yard of the complex (Figure 4.1). There is a church bell hanging outside of the mission ruins, though this is remembered locally not as coming from the Watt Mission, but from one of the Aneityum Mission churches. This may in fact represent ongoing exchange of culturally significant objects between the two islands (see Chapter 3).

Outside of the immediate area of the house, there was also a winch for the mission boat landing, which was cleared away during construction of a football field (see Figure 3.4). There is a more recent church building to the southwest of the Watt Mission, and in front of this building there is a massive *Tridacna* (giant clam) shell. The shell is over 60cm in diameter, and is remembered locally as being used alternately as a baptismal font, and a bathtub for the Watts' young children. On the south side of the mission there are two graves, one of which is marked by a plain concrete slab. The other bears a marble headstone, now broken, which reads, 'In Memory of WILLIAM ALEXANDER SECOND SON OF THE REV W. GRAY WHO DIED 1st JULY 1886 AGED 9 MONTHS'. The stream Mimretam forms the southern boundary of mission land, and is significantly also the *neteta* boundary for Umairarekarmene. There is a set of mortar steps next to a spring that flows into the stream, which also dates to the mission period.

Figure 4.1 Photograph of the Watt Mission compound in the 1890s.
Source: Image courtesy Knox Archives of the Presbyterian Church of Aotearoa/New Zealand (PA-10 No. 99).

Archaeological testing at the Watt Mission was aimed at determining the extent of evidence related to 19th-century activity. We excavated a series of test units ranging from 1x1m to 2x2m across the site (Figure 4.2). As on Erromango, there is a marked increase in house size and complexity in this later mission house. The mission house remains consist of a scatter of stones, some of which retain their original mortar, particularly around the front steps. The site has been extensively robbed of stone, and also bears the scars of recent construction activities, most recently a stage built on the house foundations in 2013 for a Presbyterian Church celebration. To compare with excavations at the Robertson House at Dillon's Bay, Erromango (see Chapter 2), a 2x2m test unit (TU1) was placed alongside the front step of the building. In contrast to Robertson House, excavation of this unit revealed that the foundations of Watt House were in fact quite shallow, extending no more than 25–30cm below the current ground surface (Figure 4.3). Stratigraphy included layers relating to the 'nice gravel walk' noted above, overlying a mixed sandy deposit with cobble and boulder-sized beach rock inclusions. There was some evidence for post-depositional disturbance of these deposits, including a large animal burrow that was found to be still hollow upon excavation.

WATT MISSION
KWAMERA, TANNA
6 AUGUST 2013

Key

⚬ = Unmod. Stone

○ = Coral Stone

⋯ = Coarse Gravel

⋯ = Fine Gravel

⌐ = Coral Gravel

⊟ = Mortar

⟮⟯ = Pandanus Tree

⁄ = Hachure (indicates slope)

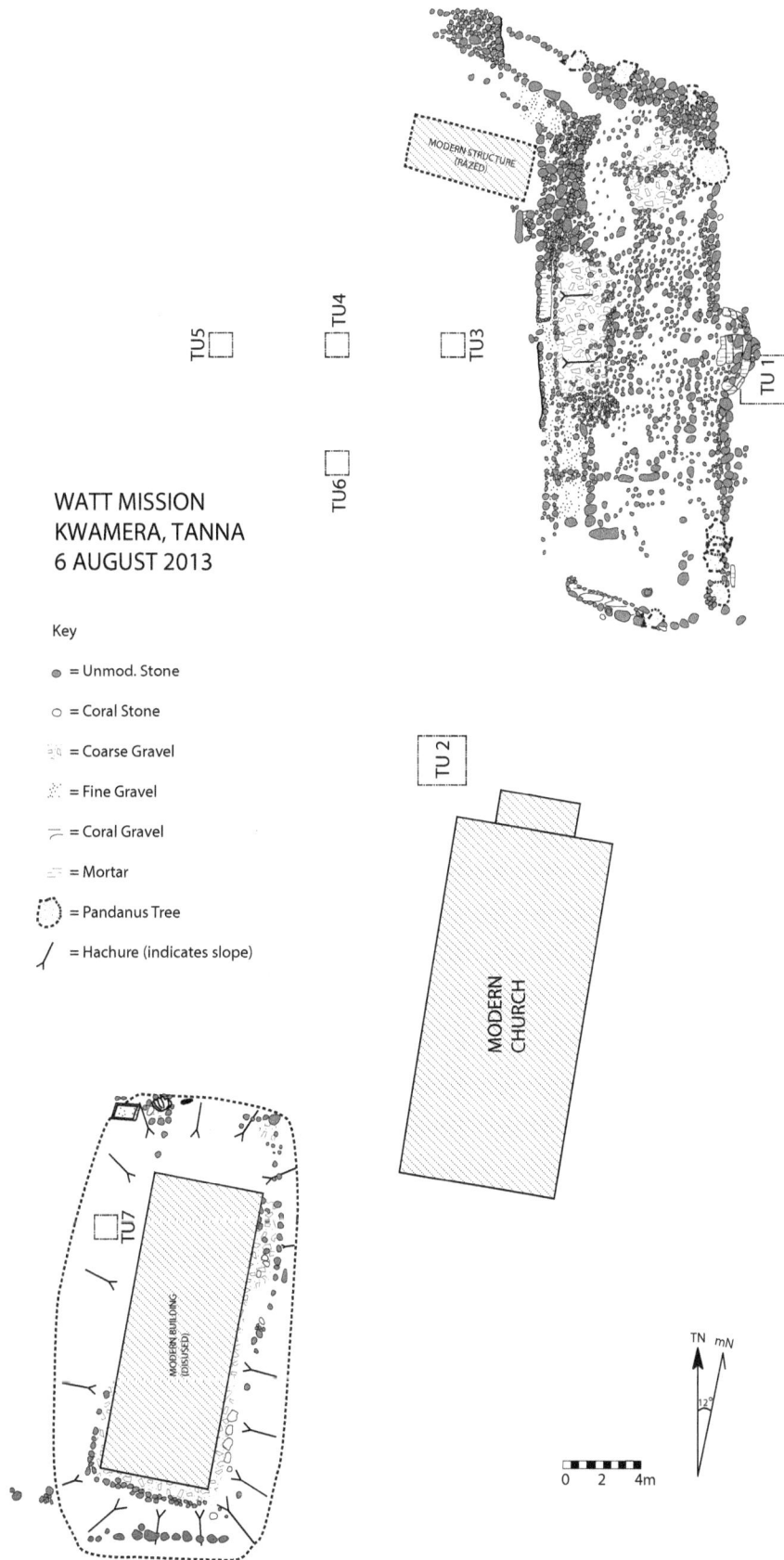

Figure 4.2 Plan of the Watt Mission area, showing test unit locations.

Source: James Flexner

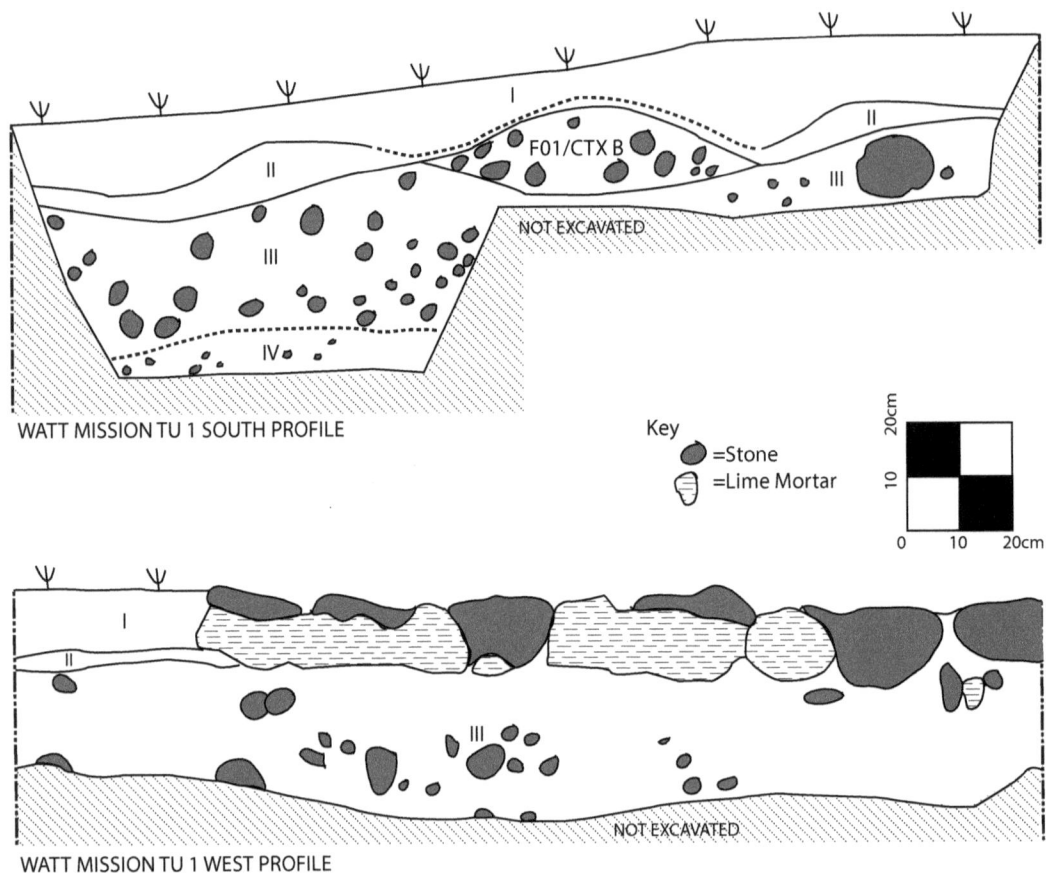

Figure 4.3 Stratigraphic profiles, TU1, Watt Mission.

Source: James Flexner

At the base of the excavations, we encountered a single human burial, with the skeleton lying on its back (sex could not be identified as the pelvis was not preserved), at about 50cm below the surface (Figure 4.4). A piece of coconut shell was collected just next to the right femur, which was among the best-preserved (and hence least likely to have been disturbed) bones of the skeleton. This sample was radiocarbon dated, and suggests that the burial dates to the 11th or 12th century (Appendix D). There were no preserved grave goods, though the burial was marked with limestone cobbles, and discoloured sediment found along with the limestone suggests there may have been some kind of bundles associated with the markers. This finding is above all interesting because it indicates that the Watts may have been settled on *tabu* ground (Flexner and Willie 2015). As noted previously, the spirits of the dead (*ierehma*) could cause illness or even death (see Chapter 3; Bonnemaison 1994: 179). While the burial may not have been remembered for a named individual in the mission period, it is reasonable to conclude that the area where the Watts built their house was probably at least associated with *ierehma*. When the Watts' young son perished, or indeed *misi pran* (a term of endearment used locally for Agnes, literally 'missionary woman'; see Lindstrom 2013) herself, Tannese people may have understood the illness and eventual death in such a way.

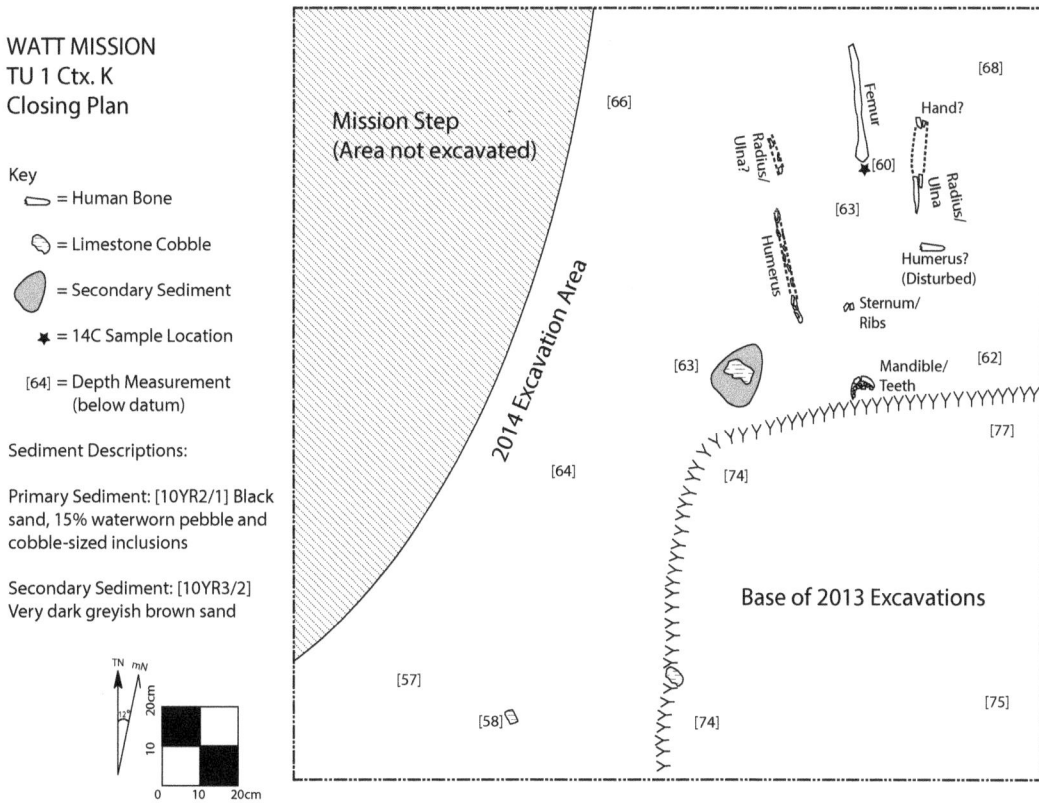

Figure 4.4 Plan of the human burial, TU1, Watt Mission.

Source: James Flexner

Excavations elsewhere around the Watt Mission site were significantly impacted by recent activities. Specifically, local people remember the area being bulldozed extensively in the late 1990s. There is a large debris pile towards the southeast of the site behind the modern church, which may have been created by this event. Excavation of a 1x1m unit in another mound to the southwest (TU7 in Figure 4.2) indicated that the area was intentionally built up, as the unit stratigraphy consisted of a thin topsoil layer overlying two rocky fill layers, with dark greyish brown sandy loam overlying black loam (Figure 4.5). The top layer contained some glass artefacts and contemporary material, including plastic. The upper rocky fill contained charcoal and faunal material, as well as a few flakes of olive bottle glass. Only charcoal was found in the lower rocky fill. While much more extensive testing would be needed, it would be worthwhile to examine whether this mound represents a contact-era feature of some sort, perhaps relating to indigenous activities, analogous to the mound features at Kwaraka and Anuikaraka (see Chapter 3).

The remaining test units (TU2, 3, 4, 5, 6) were excavated behind the Watts' main building. TU2 was a 2x2m unit that contained primarily 20th-century material, including a mortar dump, probably relating to construction of the adjacent modern church (Figure 4.6). Local people claimed to have found large amounts of clay smoking pipes, buttons, bottle glass, and ceramics in the area while constructing the current church on the site. All of these artefacts were apparently lost shortly after they were removed from the ground. Almost none of these were present in TU2. It is thus unfortunately possible that the main rubbish dump from the Watts is located under the modern church building.

Figure 4.5 Close up of excavation photograph, TU7, Watt Mission.
Source: James Flexner

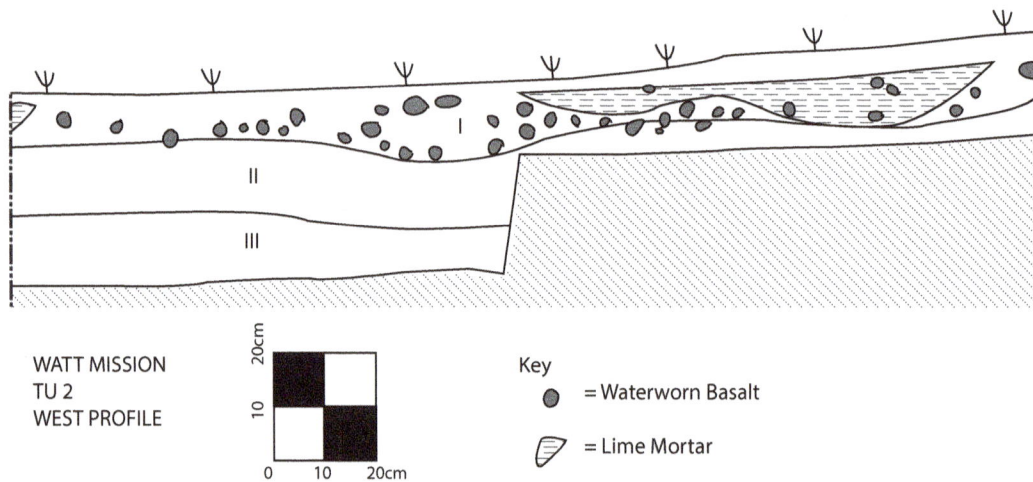

Figure 4.6 Stratigraphic profile, TU2, Watt Mission.
Source: James Flexner

Four 1x1m units were placed to test the area containing the garden and outbuildings based on photographic evidence (Figure 4.7). All of these units were to some degree disturbed by activities taking place decades after the missionary period, through to the present. There were intact layers underlying the topsoil that related to the Watt Mission, with recovered artefacts including a metal button and fragments comprising approximately half of a writing slate in TU3 (Figure 4.8). In TU4, the stratigraphy was cut by multiple postholes, which contained plastic and other contemporary materials. More extensive excavations would be necessary to understand what kind of structure these relate to. The unit that offers the highest potential for mission era structural remains is TU5, which featured a linear arrangement of stones in the center of the unit. These could be wall footings, or garden path alignments. The stratigraphic sequence of TU6 consisted of a series of rocky layers with small amounts of glass and metal artefacts, which appear to be mostly 20th century in age. As always, more extensive excavations would be revealing. These test units offer a sense of the variable stratigraphy, as well as the extent of disturbance in this area of the site.

WATT MISSION TU3/4/5/6 PROFILES

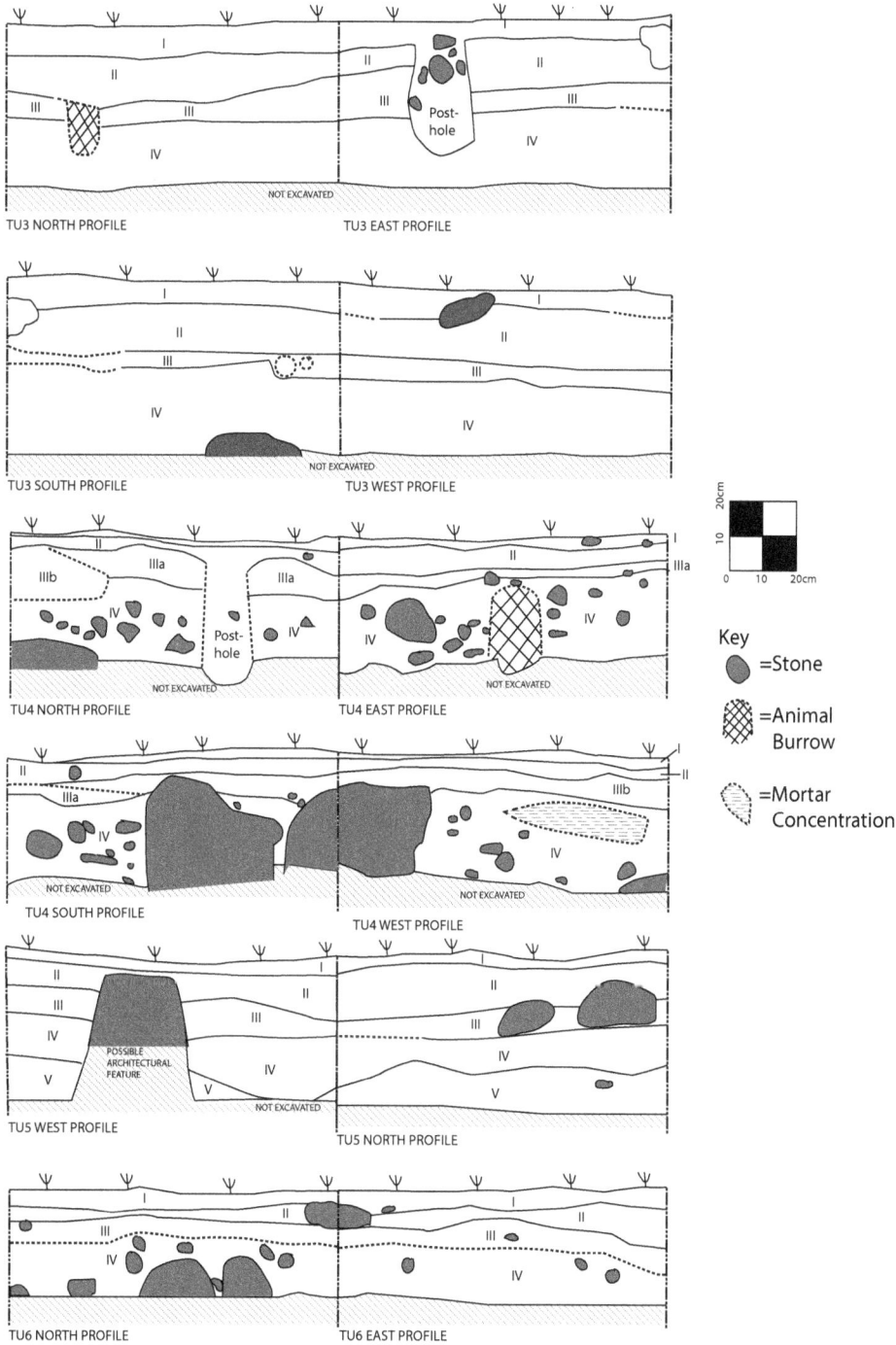

Figure 4.7 Stratigraphic profiles, TU3/4/5/6, Watt Mission.

Source: James Flexner

Figure 4.8 Writing slate fragments from TU3, Watt Mission.

Source: James Flexner

The artefact assemblage from the Watt Mission site reflects the ongoing modern activities in the area. The main Presbyterian Church in Kwamera is still on the site, and the area serves as a meeting place for various kinds of community activities for the village. Approximately 95 per cent of the identified nails were of the round wire type (N=107 out of 112 total). While a portion of these was likely used during the later stages of the Watts' time in Kwamera, artefacts certainly continued to accumulate after the missionaries left. The glass artefact assemblage is composed primarily of window glass (81.6 per cent of the assemblage by count, N=208 of 255 total glass artefacts). The remaining shards are mostly colourless bottles and other vessels, none of which could be definitively attributed to the mission period. Only eight ceramic sherds were recovered, and almost all are 20th century in age, with the possible exception of a single stoneware vessel, probably an ink jar, from TU1 (Figure 4.9). In a way, the lack of mission-period artefacts at the Watt Mission site should not be completely surprising. As noted above, the most promising area has been heavily disturbed by modern construction activities. When William Watt and his second wife Jessie Paterson retired to Australia in 1910, they probably would have taken most of their belongings with them. This is a pronounced difference from the earlier mission sites, where sudden, catastrophic abandonment contributed to the richness of mission period artefact assemblages.

Figure 4.9 Stoneware ink jar fragment, Watt Mission.
Source: James Flexner

William Gray at Waisisi

The expanding global network of Presbyterianism in the closing decades of the 1800s is reflected in a wider geographic area of origin, and international support for mission work. From the 1880s onwards, the Australian Church was increasingly involved in New Hebrides mission work, just as Australia became increasingly entangled in New Hebrides colonial politics. William Gray and his wife Elizabeth came from the Presbyterian Church of South Australia. Arriving at Waisisi (Figure 3.1) in 1881, the Grays had some success at gaining converts, though interest in the church waxed and waned. There was an outbreak of war in 1891–1892, accompanied by the usual association of the mission with *narak* (sorcery). However, when the Grays left in 1894, they had managed to create a small congregation at Waisisi and opened the way for further mission work on east Tanna under the subsequent tenure of Rev. MacMillan (Miller 1986: 260–263, 274–282). Overall, this period in the 1880s–1890s represents the major era of geographic expansion for mission work on Tanna, encapsulated in local social memories that suggest Waisisi be remembered as 'way is easy', as the Grays' successes arguably opened the way for the church in west and north Tanna.

Around Waisisi

Archaeological fieldwork in and around Waisisi was very brief, involving only one full day of survey. Fieldwork did successfully document various features relating to the Grays' Mission, and other features of local historical significance (Figure 4.10). Along the coast in the northeast of the area there is an old kava-drinking ground called 'Naburi', which was used for fishing magic, among other things. Inland from this along an intermittent stream is an old *tabu* stone called

'Temitonga' (literally 'white man'), which is said to commemorate one of the Europeans killed in the area, though the name of the individual is not remembered. Further west along the shore is an old stone altar where the dead were displayed before burial at sea, called 'Lamatetengi'. Nearby are two features relating to the *Shipimanwawa* war, 'Nitela' and 'Manuaua'. An old banyan (*nabanga* in Bislama) tree marks the *tabu* site of 'Netanu', which is associated with the consumption of turtles. Eating the head of the turtle was a special chiefly prerogative (Guiart 1956: 108).

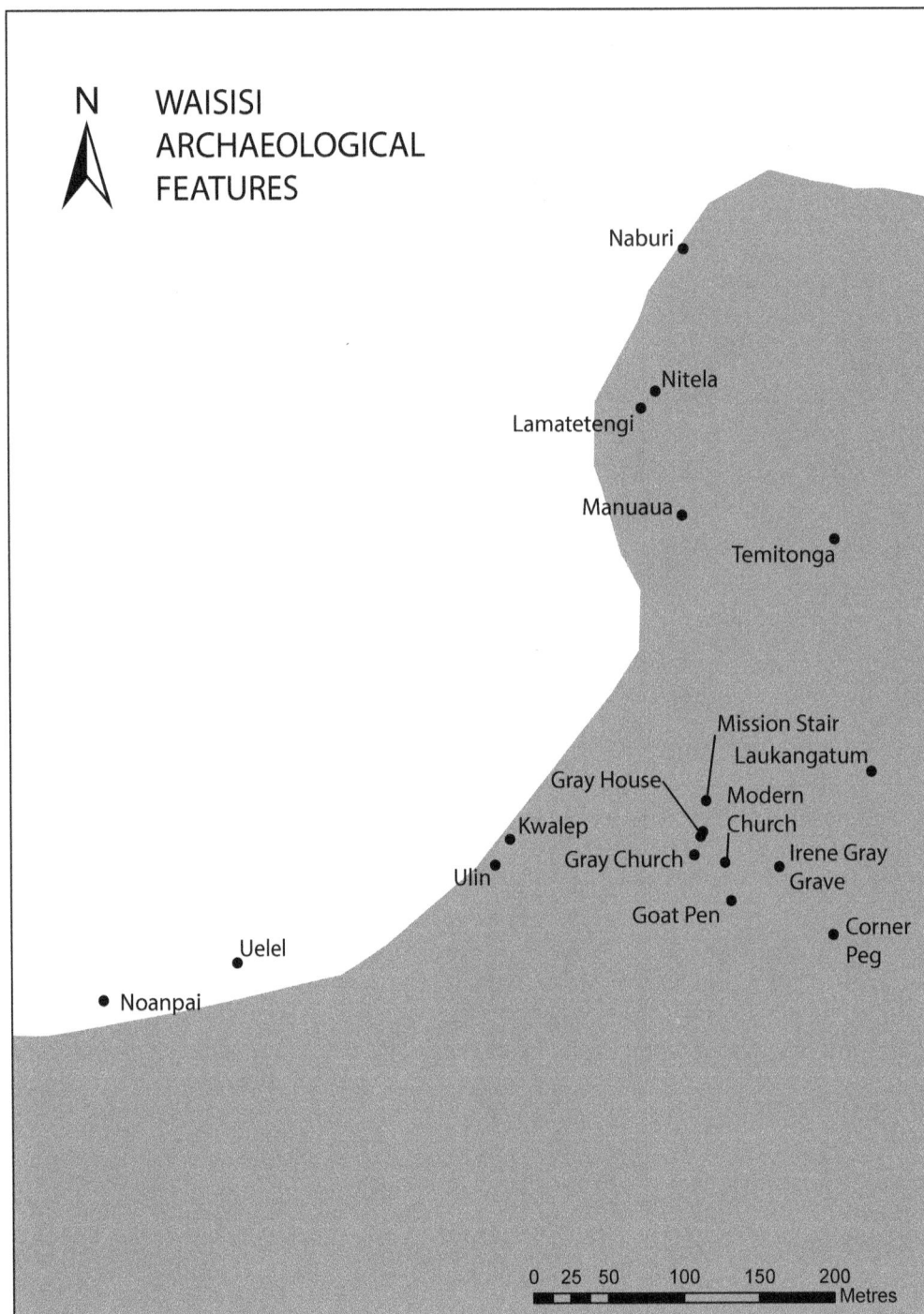

Figure 4.10 Waisisi area features.

Source: James Flexner

The Grays did not move into an empty landscape, nor was their presence on the island seen as politically neutral. Gray was in fact remarkably sensitive to, and interested in, local culture. He even produced a short ethnological treatise based on his observations during his time on Tanna (Gray 1892). When Gray arrived at Waisisi, he was welcomed at 'Kwalep', a coastal kava-drinking ground (Figure 3.2), by the chief Iopot, who made the missionary *tabu* in order to protect him. Immediately behind Kwalep is the dangerous *tabu* place 'Ulin', the shadow of which could cause illness and death. The early mission era at Waisisi from 1882–1894 was also a period of the dangerous 'stolen wars' on Tanna (Bonnemaison 1994: 165–166). There is some reason to question the extent of gun violence as documented in missionary accounts, as overemphasising the state of 'constant warfare' was a useful ideological trope to gain support for mission work (Adams 1984: 35–36). However, it does appear that at least some Tannese people were tired of the fighting and in part saw the presence of missionaries as a mitigating factor against ongoing warfare.

The *Shipimanwawa* war is an important episode in the history of the White Sands region, of which Waisisi is a part. It relates to the last major open conflict between the two traditional 'moieties', *Koyometa* and *Numrukuen* (see Chapter 3; Guiart 1956: 90–94). *Numrukuen*, the senior moiety associated with strong sorcery was identified with the merchant ship ('*Shipi*'), where people used their cleverness to produce goods and held positions with multiple powers. *Koyometa*, the 'younger brother' of the moieties, was composed of aggressive warriors and thus identified as the man-of-war ('*manwawa*'), which contained a strict order and only had one function. *Numrukuen/Shipi* were the victors in this war. However, the victory was an incomplete one, and the situation was aggravated by the introduction of firearms to the island and the meddling of foreign missionaries and government officials. The conclusion of fighting was characterised as a 'stolen war', where a peace acceptable to all parties was not reached. The tension produced by such conflict continued to structure violent events on Tanna into the 20th century (Bonnemaison 1994: 152–156, 168–169, 199–200; Guiart 1956: 92).

At Waisisi, there are several features that commemorate this conflict. Along the coast in the western part of the bay at Waisisi there is a large rock overhang named 'Uelel', remembered as a place used to ambush enemy combatants during times of war. West of Uelel was the kava-drinking ground 'Noanpai', which was used to gather forces during times of war, and is associated with Nalpini Asim, a strong war leader. Noanpai's primary links were to the hamlets of Lapiahlu and Naknasses. Closer to the coast downhill from the contemporary village of Waisisi, which is also the location of the old mission grounds, are the locations of two trees planted to mark the ending of the *Shipimanwawa* war in the area (Figure 4.10). At 'Nitela' there is a massive old *natapoa* (Bislama; *Terminalia catappa*) tree that was planted by *Shipi* (*Numrukuen*) to commemorate their victory (Figure 4.11). Roughly 80m away is the location where *Manuaua* (*Koyometa*) planted their tree to mark the peace, though this tree has been washed away during a cyclone because of its location next to an intermittent stream.

Figure 4.11 'Nitela', the large *natapoa* tree planted by *Shipi* to mark the end of the *Shipimanwawa* conflict.

Source: James Flexner

Bonnemaison (1994: 155) highlighted the unfinished nature of the *Shipimanwawa* conflict, suggesting that ongoing fighting on the island stemmed at least in part from the unstable order created by the victors. In contrast in Waisisi, some emphasis is placed on the resolution of the conflict via the planting of *natapoa* trees by the two sides. In part this may reflect the timing of fieldwork. When Bonnemaison was on Tanna in the 1980s, the wounds of violent events in the independence era may still have been quite sore for many. In contrast, after 36 years of independence, people on Tanna today may seek to emphasise unity and peace on their island. Simultaneously, the memory of peaceful resolution presented by *Nitela* and *Manuaua* may reflect the dominant *Numrukuen* version of events, masking underlying tensions still simmering below the surface. That the tree planted by *Manuaua* was wiped out in a cyclone may well be interpreted in magico-historical terms as part of the social memory of this conflict. The two trees were located by the sea, but *Shipi* has been strong, standing up through all the tropical storms of the last century or more, while *Manuaua* was blown away.

Gray Mission

After their acceptance at Waisisi, the Grays settled in up the hill from Kwalep on a series of terraces cut into the steep coastal slope. Gray assiduously documented the mission land claim in Waisisi, even providing a scale plan of the areas the mission had purchased (Figure 4.12), which is in contrast to earlier, vague and generally inappropriate land claims (Flexner 2015; Van Trease 1987). For the year 1883, Gray notes in his diary (Gray 1884):

Last December our new church was completed. It is made entirely of native material, 33 ft X 20. I have valued it at £ 8.6.0. This was a gift of the worshipping people. They were assisted to a considerable extent by all our native helps. A return present was made to the workers, chiefly of clothing. and food [sic.] This with food for a feast at the opening of the church I value at a little over three £ 3. The Sunday Schools of the Presbyterian Church of South Australia have sent us a bell. The manual labour bestowed on our premises during the last ten months both by myself and our natives has been heavy and intensive. Two houses for native helps, a large house to be used as workshop, wash-house, and store-room for timber and empty cases, a goat / house and yard, and a large new boat-house, have been built of native material. The heaviest part of the work in these cases fell to the natives. They also bore the toil of making a quantity of lime and various other works for the improvement of our premises. I had my share of work in completing and improving the Mission house and kitchen.

In 1884, he added:

During the week we completed the giving the storm rigging of our house. Four wire ropes, about 42 in. thick [?] are passed right over the house cross-wise. Both ends of each rope is fixed to posts set firmly in the ground. At one end of each rope there is a roller to tighten as / required. These will be removed when the season is over. The front verandah, which will be much exposed to a hurricane should it come, has special permanent fixings. These we put on also, and gave the whole roof an overhauling. After completing the storm rigging, which we did on Friday, I made an excursion under the floor of our house to secure some tottering posts. The joists are so near the ground that one can only move by dragging oneself along the ground. The net work of cobwebs, quantity of fine dust, and the difficulty of using tools made this a very unpleasant work. I think what I have done this time will be permanent.

Again we can see the increasing investment and elaboration of mission infrastructure, and particularly adaptations towards making the mission buildings more stormproof.

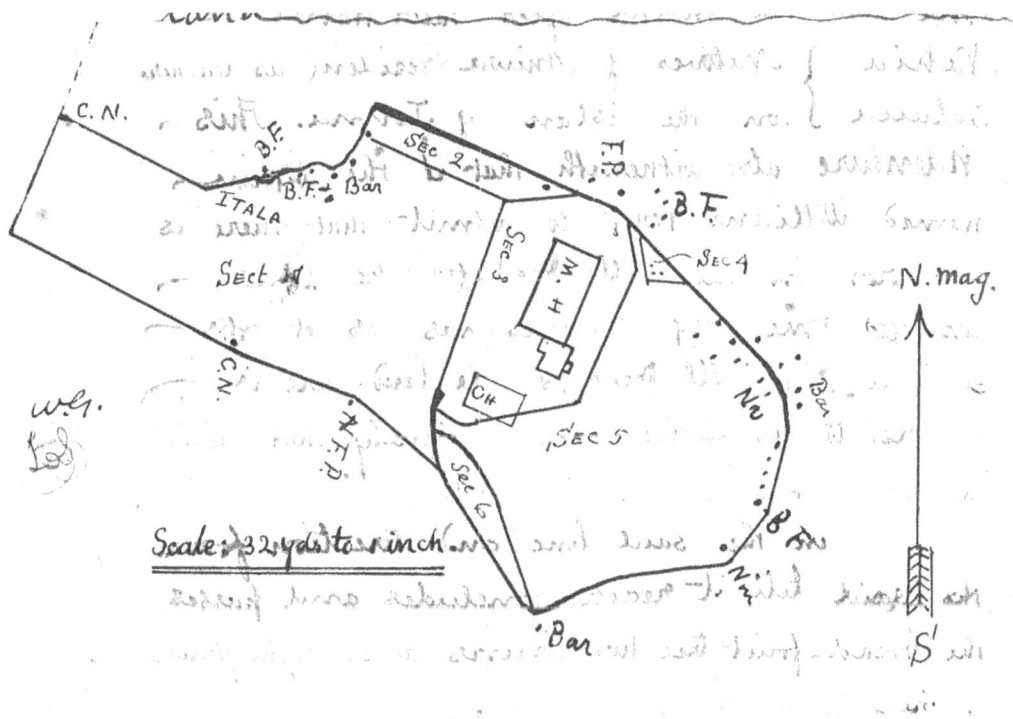

Figure 4.12 Detail of a land survey plan by William Gray of mission land in Waisisi.
Source: Image courtesy of Vanuatu National Archives (Land Record 29 S.I.4).

Archaeological work on the mission sites, and indeed any sites in the Waisisi area is made difficult by the enormous amounts of volcanic ash dumped on the area by Yasur. Nevertheless, we were able to document the surface remains relating to the mission. The original path from the sea near Kwalep to the mission house and church is still in place, and a mortar, stone, and brick stair is partly preserved in the northern part of the site (Figure 4.13). The mission house footing is represented by a line of stones, underlying a currently inhabited house, while the church is similarly only present as a remnant foundation on a clear terrace towards the south of the site. From the church, local people have curated the bronze bell, which bears an inscription that reads: 'MADE BY J WARNER & SONS FOR F. LASSETTER & Cᵒʸ LIMTED SYDNEY NSW'. Compared with the earlier bells, which were primarily from Scotland, this shows the shift in economic orientation towards Australasia. Kept in association with the bell are two massive *Triton* shell trumpets that had also been used to call people to worship (Figure 4.14). The grave of the Grays' daughter Irene is present and kept protected by local stewards. The wall of a goat pen, possibly the one described in Gray's diary, is still present towards the south (Figure 4.15). No excavations were carried out at Waisisi, and again the large amount of volcanic ash dumped there annually would make any such work a serious challenge.

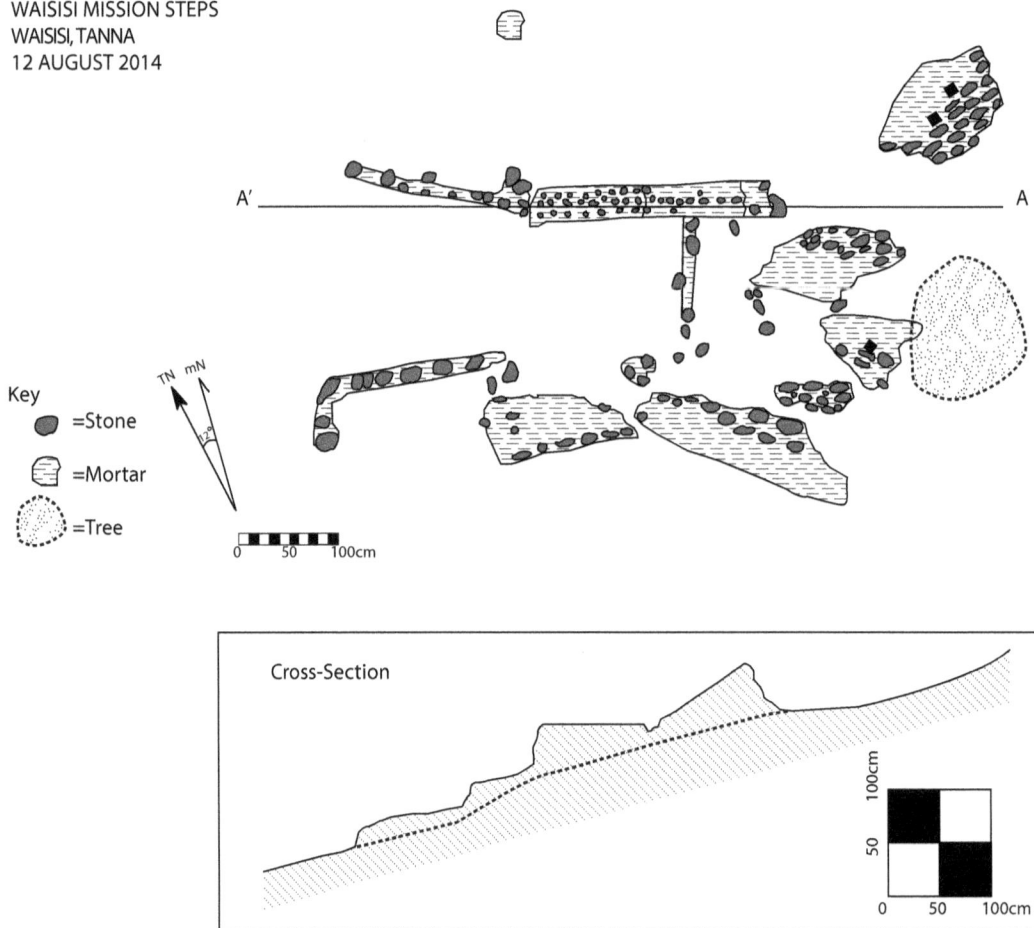

Figure 4.13 Mission steps, Waisisi.

Source: James Flexner

Figure 4.14 Mission bell (top) and *Triton* shell trumpets (bottom), Waisisi.

Source: James Flexner

WAISISI MISSION
GOAT PEN
WAISISI, TANNA
12 AUGUST 2014

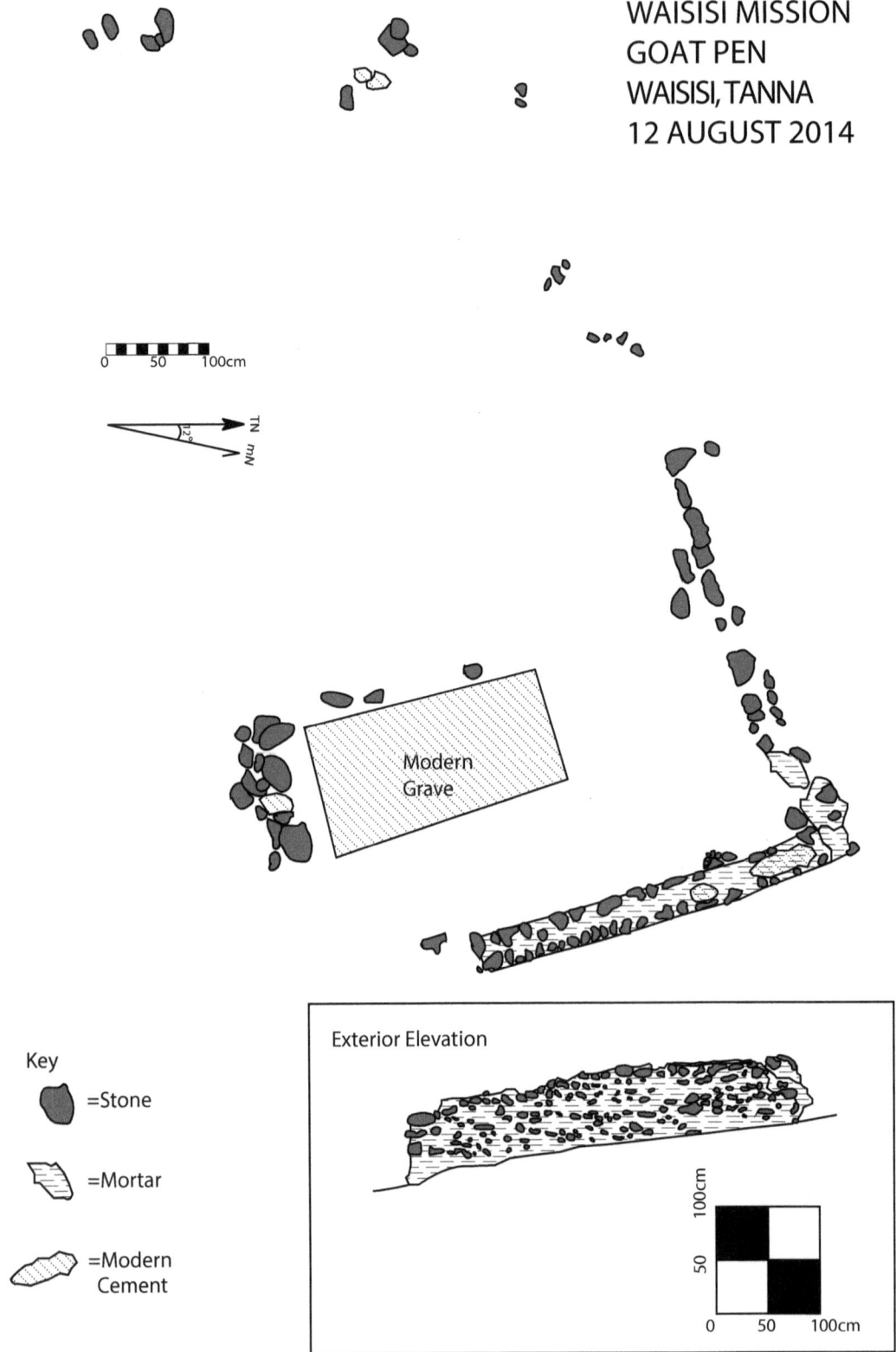

0   50   100cm

TN

12°

mN

Modern
Grave

Key

=Stone

=Mortar

=Modern
Cement

Exterior Elevation

100cm

50

0   50   100cm

Figure 4.15 Goat pen, Waisisi.

Source: James Flexner

Lenakel: The Ultimate Mission

West Tanna was one of the last areas on Tanna to undergo missionisation, and the latest mission site examined for this research project. The chiefs Lomai, Titonga, and Iavis invited Frank Paton (son of John G. Paton) to settle in the area in 1896. The younger Paton spent six years working on west Tanna (Miller 1986: 285–303; Paton 1903). According to contemporary local memories, the decision to invite the missionaries was, as at Waisisi, at least in part taken as a measure to reduce the risk of warfare in the area. Even when the missionaries were settled, there was some fighting. Mission supporters were attacked, resulting in the death of Numanian, one of the early converts (Miller 1986: 296–297). A likely cause can be found in a later testimony that suggests the area where the missionaries settled was disputed territory. A chief named Ichnain attempted to claim that the land had belonged to his people, and had recently been taken in warfare by Lomai and Iavis when the missionaries arrived. Asked to adjudicate on the matter, the missionaries naturally took the side of their loyal converts (Vanuatu National Archives Land Record S.I.22 25–26).

Paton and his colleagues settled among the Louweniu 'tribe', in the area of Lenakel. As elsewhere on Tanna, the missionaries began the work of conversion as a material process. The initial house of worship built at Lenakel was a small structure of local materials. The following year a more substantial structure was built, measuring 45x25 feet (15x8m). The opening of that church was attended by a handful of recent converts (Paton 1903: 19–21, 30, 98). By 1898 church attendance spiked with several hundred people coming to services (Miller 1986: 286). When Frank Paton left Tanna in 1902, owing to ill health, he had laid the groundwork for church expansion in Lenakel (Paton 1903). A few concrete pylons may mark the location of the early church. The grave of Lomai, who was instrumental to bringing Christianity to Lenakel, is nearby. When Lomai died in December 1916 the Lenakel Church was a massive operation, but it was appropriate that he was buried near the initial church that he had championed (Figure 4.16).

Paton was succeeded at Lenakel by Dr J. Campbell Nicholson in 1903. Working alongside fellow missionaries Watt and Macmillan, Nicholson spent 14 years on the island, and was at least partly responsible for major investments in mission infrastructure, specifically in Lenakel and more broadly on Tanna (Miller 1986: 348–406). Here we will focus on the spatial layout of the Lenakel Mission (Figure 4.17), and its global and local resonances. A prefabricated church that remained standing in the area until Cyclone Pam in 2015 perhaps best encapsulates the immense networks of material that the Presbyterian Mission in the New Hebrides could draw upon (Flexner et al. 2015, 2016a).

Figure 4.16 Grave of Lomai, Lenakel.
Source: James Flexner

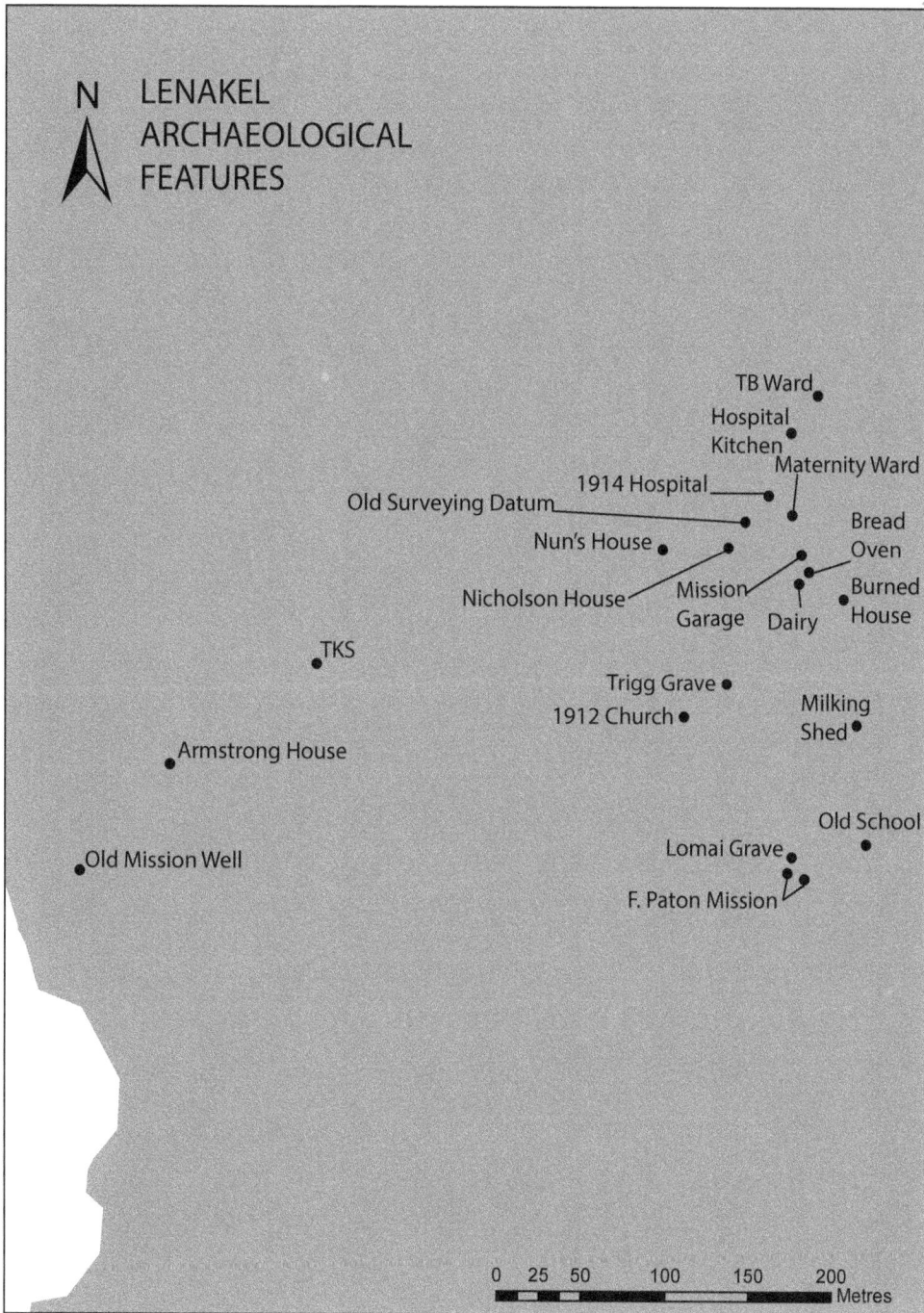

Figure 4.17 Lenakel area features.
Source: James Flexner

The 1912 Church

In April 1912, a newly built prefabricated church was opened at Lenakel (Miller 1986: 388; simply 'the 1912 Church' below). Just under a century later, the building was the subject of intensive archaeological documentation, and is now one of the most thoroughly recorded buildings in Melanesia (Flexner et al. 2015). This building was the third one to stand on the site. It rested on a massive terrace cut into the hill slope in the area (Figure 4.18). Under the direction of Lomai, Titonga, and Iavis, local labourers removed over 3,500m³ of earth using hand tools and baskets (Flexner 2014c: 18–20). Archaeological investigation of the footings at the site revealed that the church building evolved from a small rectangular structure, to a T-shaped building, and finally the cruciform plan of the 1912 Church, which incorporated the footings of the earlier buildings (Figure 4.19; Flexner et al. 2015: 269–271).

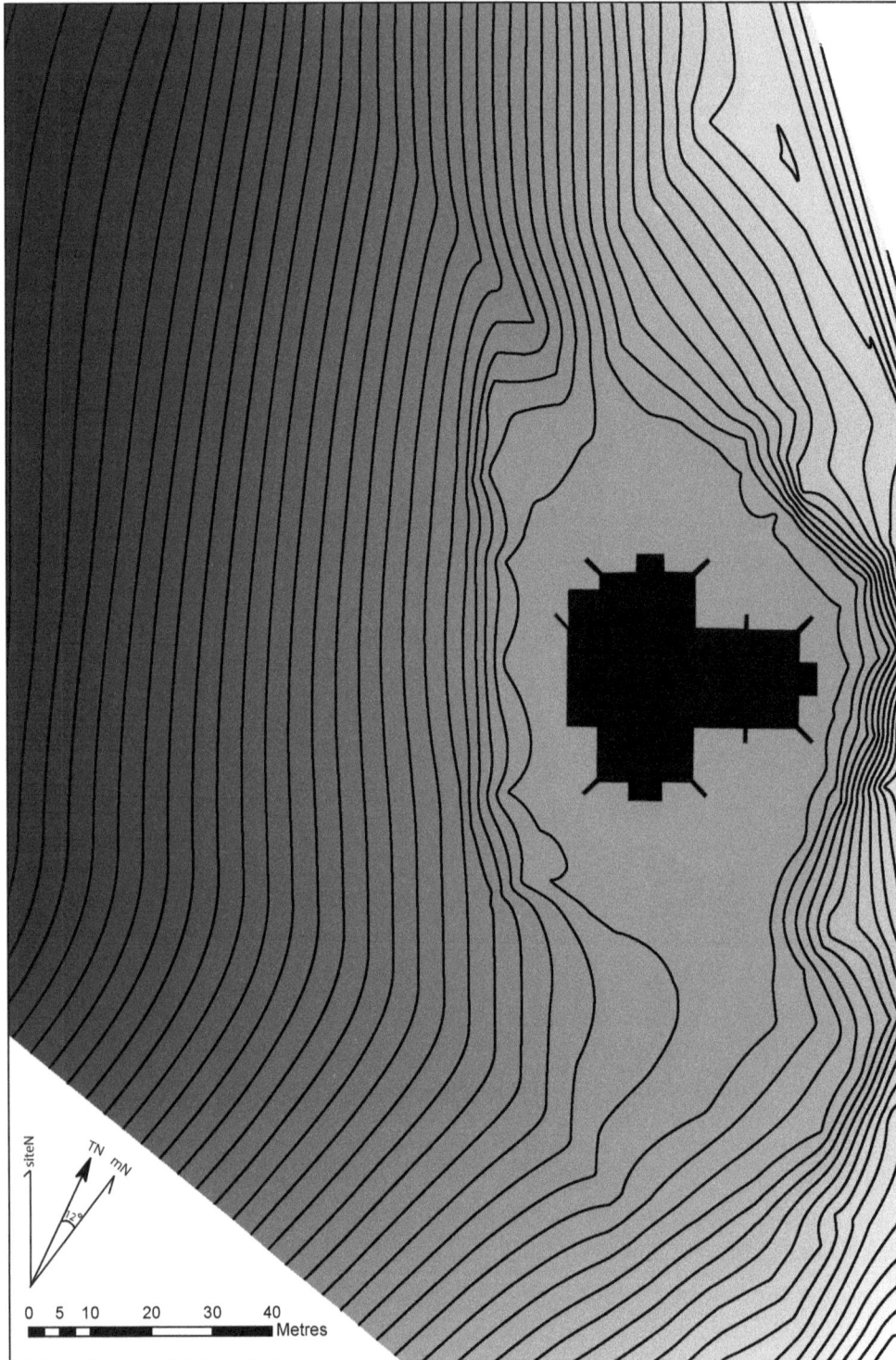

Figure 4.18 Topographic map and hillshade showing the Lenakel church on its terrace. Approximately 3,500m³ of earth were moved to make room for the church.

Source: James Flexner

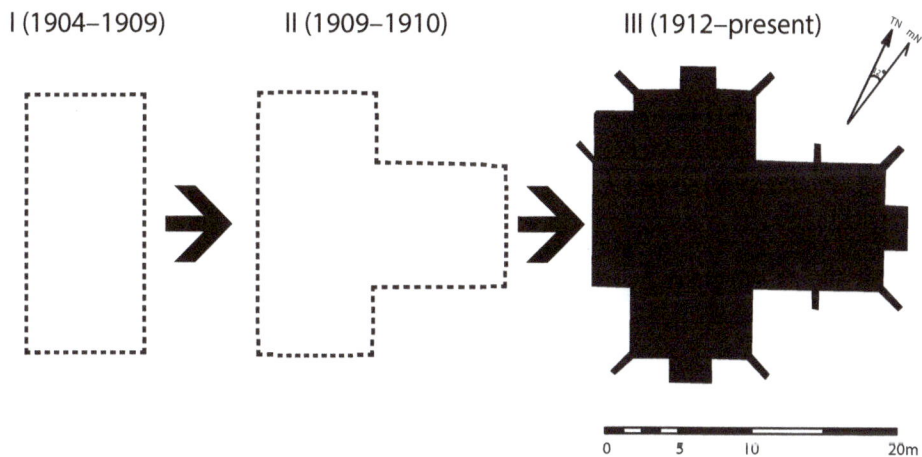

Figure 4.19 Detail of footings stratigraphy and foundation plans as they changed through time, Lenakel church.

Source: James Flexner

The 1912 Church was built from a prefabricated kit produced by the Sydney firm Saxton & Binns (later Saxton Island Homes). A 1920 catalogue suggests the building is a top of the line 'Peter' model (Rodman 2001: 131–133). Detailed examination of the church fittings, including the doors, lancet windows, altar rails, and some mouldings shows they match closely those offered in the 1910 *Saxton & Binns Illustrated Catalogue* (Saxton & Binns 1910). There is also ample evidence for local modification of the building. In the attic space, there are vertical supports for the ridge beam that are broken unevenly on the ends, and bear mortis holes (Figure 4.20). These beams appear to be top plates that were repurposed as roof supports. It is likely that they were damaged in January 1912, when during construction of the church a cyclone blew down the mostly erected building frame (John G. Paton Mission Fund 1912 Vol. 77: 13). This disaster resulted in the carpenter redesigning the roofline of the church, replacing gabled ends with hipped gablets. This was in part presumably to save on timber, but also apparently resulted in the building being more cyclone-proof. Other design modifications include a replacement of some of the glass lancet windows on the nave and transepts with swing shutters, which would have allowed for better ventilation, while also able to be shut quickly in a sudden storm (Flexner et al. 2015: 278–279).

Figure 4.20 Repurposed top-plate used as a roof support pillar, Lenakel church.
Source: Martin J. Jones

The 1912 Church was built in a Gothic style, with angled buttresses on the corners and arched lancet windows, though the modifications noted above also incorporated some 'Arts and Crafts' elements into the design (Figure 4.21). The church plan is cruciform, consisting of a nave and transepts, with a sanctuary on the end of the church facing the sea. The vestry is located to the right of the sanctuary if looking from the nave, and the pulpit also juts from the right side of the raised sanctuary. Significantly, the church is not oriented to cardinal directions, but to the local landscape, with the most sacred space facing the Pacific Ocean. These directions would have been more important in terms of Tannese forms of spatial orientation. One result of this is that the main entrance of the nave is somewhat awkwardly placed very close to the vertical cut made into the terrace on which the church sits. Further, local people indicated that unlike the Victorian Protestant norm of church attendees sitting in nuclear family groups, the sacred space of the church was divided by gender and age, with men sitting in the nave, married women in one transept, and unmarried women and older children in the other transept. This pattern of segregating church space by gender remains standard in rural areas of Vanuatu today.

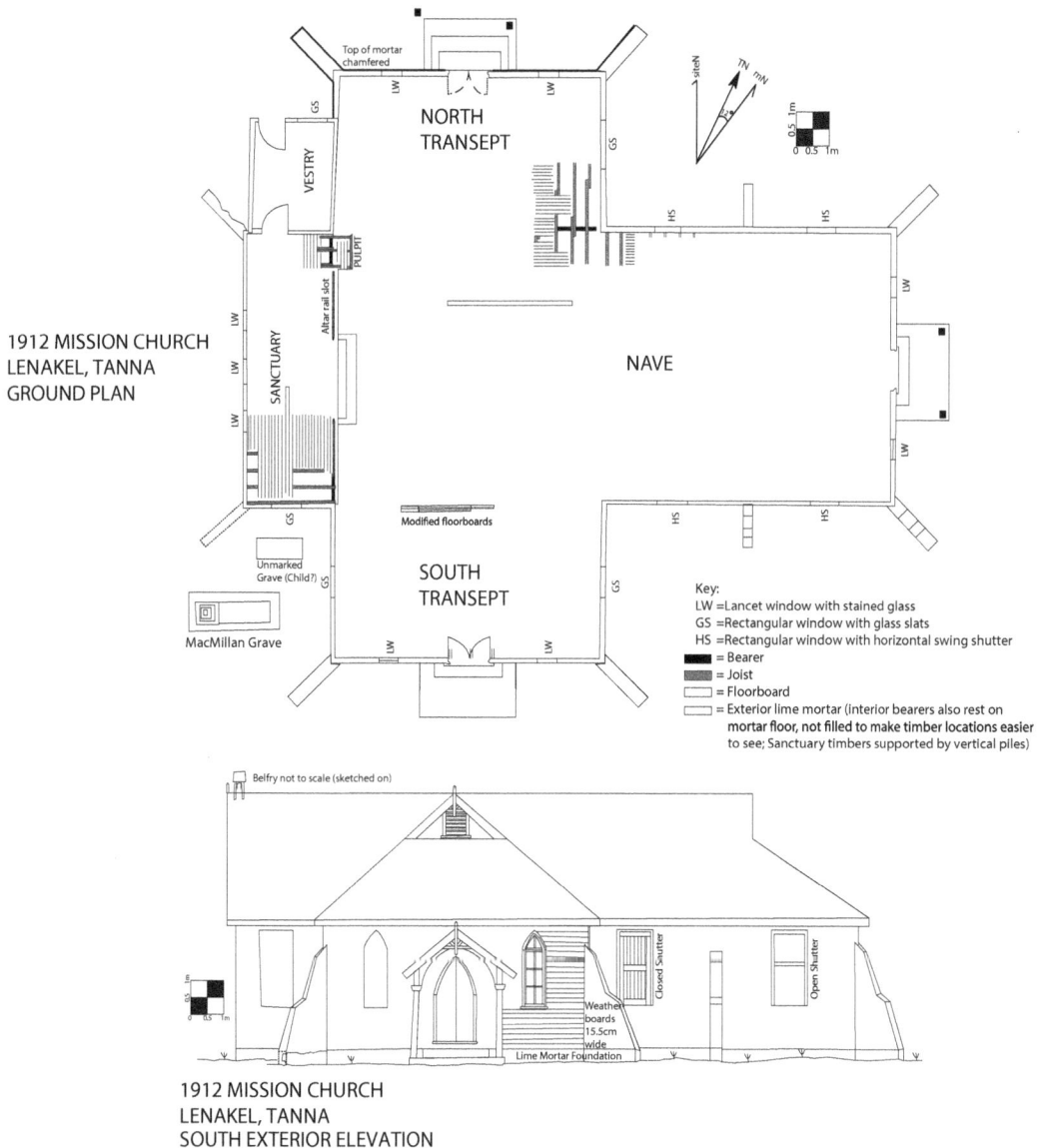

Figure 4.21 Detailed plan and elevation of the Lenakel church.
Source: James Flexner

While the 1912 Church was adapted closely to the local context, the building fabric itself reflects the global reach of capitalism during the early 20th century. Metal locks from H&T Vaughan (Wolverhampton) and corrugated roofing iron from Lysaght Orb (Bristol) reflect continued dominance of British industry in the early 20th century. Analysis of building timbers revealed wood harvested in North America, Australia, Europe, and probably New Zealand for different elements. These would have been shipped to the Saxton & Binns factory at Pyrmont, Sydney, where they would have been cut and finished, and then shipped throughout the Pacific. Different kits bore stencilled 'despatch marks' to make sure the right kit went to the right island. Several of the piles under the sanctuary, floor joists, and roof beams bear the stencil 'JCN TANNA' (JCN for J. Campbell Nicholson). Other marks include 'P' on the piles, and numbers around the doors and lancet windows, which would have guided the construction process when the kit arrived at its destination (Flexner et al. 2015: 273–278; Flexner et al. 2016a).

The 1912 Church encapsulates the entanglement between global and local forces in a period when missionary networks had an unprecedented material reach. On the one side, the church incorporates materials from throughout the entirety of the British Empire. On the other, the building was adapted to the local climate and local social ritual habits. The opening of the church was timed with the annual harvest:

> As it was time for our Harvest Thanksgiving the natives decorated the Church, and the bright colours of crotons and fruits, and the green of palms, potted in casks and cases, hid the bare unlined walls and unceiled roof. The people made strenuous efforts. Each person, young and old, brought a yam or taro, and each village brought its share of the decorations (John G. Paton Mission Fund 1912 Vol. 78: 7).

Graffiti on the 1912 Church shows that this important event continued to be marked as recently as 2000, the year that the building was ritually closed as its condition had degraded until it was no longer usable.

The site of the 1912 Church remains an important part of community identity in Lenakel. This is true despite the fact that the building was completely destroyed in the 280km/h winds of Cyclone Pam in March 2015 (Flexner et al. 2016a). For the Melanesian people who continue to include this site within the pantheon of sacred, *tabu* places, the percentage of 'original' fabric so important in Western heritage is less important than the living memories associated with the site. Some of the relics from the building, such as the church bell, are being curated by local people. At the same time, the local communities on West Tanna continue to discuss at their kava-drinking places the possibility of 'rebuilding' a church at this historically and culturally important place, reflecting the integration of mission sites into indigenous *kastom* (Flexner and Spriggs 2015). Such a project may take place in the future if the material and funding can be arranged, but it is a matter of speculation at this point.

The Globalised Mission on West Tanna

The 1912 Church was a focal point in a much wider mission landscape in Lenakel. As the Lenakel Mission grew, they established a 'model village' in the area, called 'Isini' (a local orthography of 'Sydney', the source of so much mission cargo; see Miller 1986: 361–362). The place was originally called 'Numpwanaken', which in the Lenakel area language means 'forehead'. It was both a place from which to look out (and indeed overlooks the harbour at Lenakel) and an important meeting place for the surrounding communities ('forehead' can be used to mean 'front', 'place of leadership' in Bislama). It remained so for Tannese Presbyterian converts throughout the 20th century.

To the south of the church there was a mission school. The remains of the early 20th-century school, if any survive, are buried in the contemporary schoolyard. To the north of the school, and east of the 1912 Church there is a concrete slab from a milking shed, which apparently remained in use within living memory. Continuing north, there was a cluster of mission features, including a dairy, bread oven, and later in the 20th century, a garage for maintaining the mission's vehicles. Road-building was a major undertaking for the Tanna Mission, as improved communication and ability to move materials was seen as essential to the Presbyterian Church's success (Miller 1986: 253–254). To the west of this cluster of features is the location of Dr Nicholson's house, now represented by a concrete, stone, and brick footing (Figure 4.22). The water tank support, entrance steps, and vertical concrete supports from the basement remain on the surface. Continuing west from here, there is a prefabricated 'Sisters' House', which was inhabited by the women who worked in the hospital and school through the middle of the 20th century (Figure 4.23).

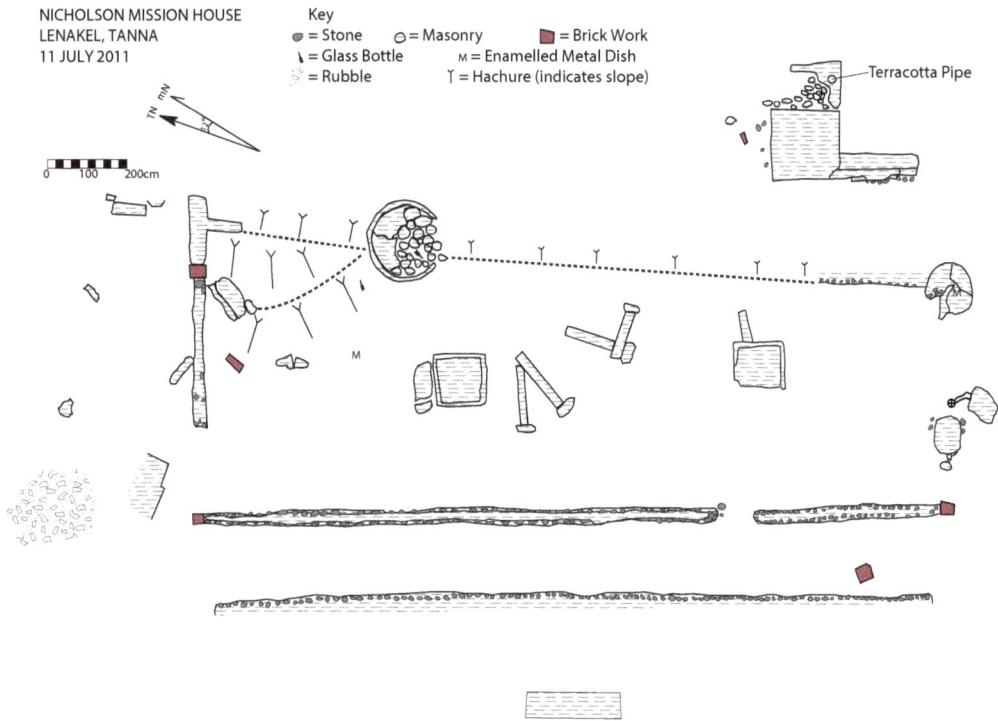

Figure 4.22 Nicholson House plan, Lenakel.
Source: James Flexner

Figure 4.23 'Nun's' house, Lenakel.
Source: Martin J. Jones

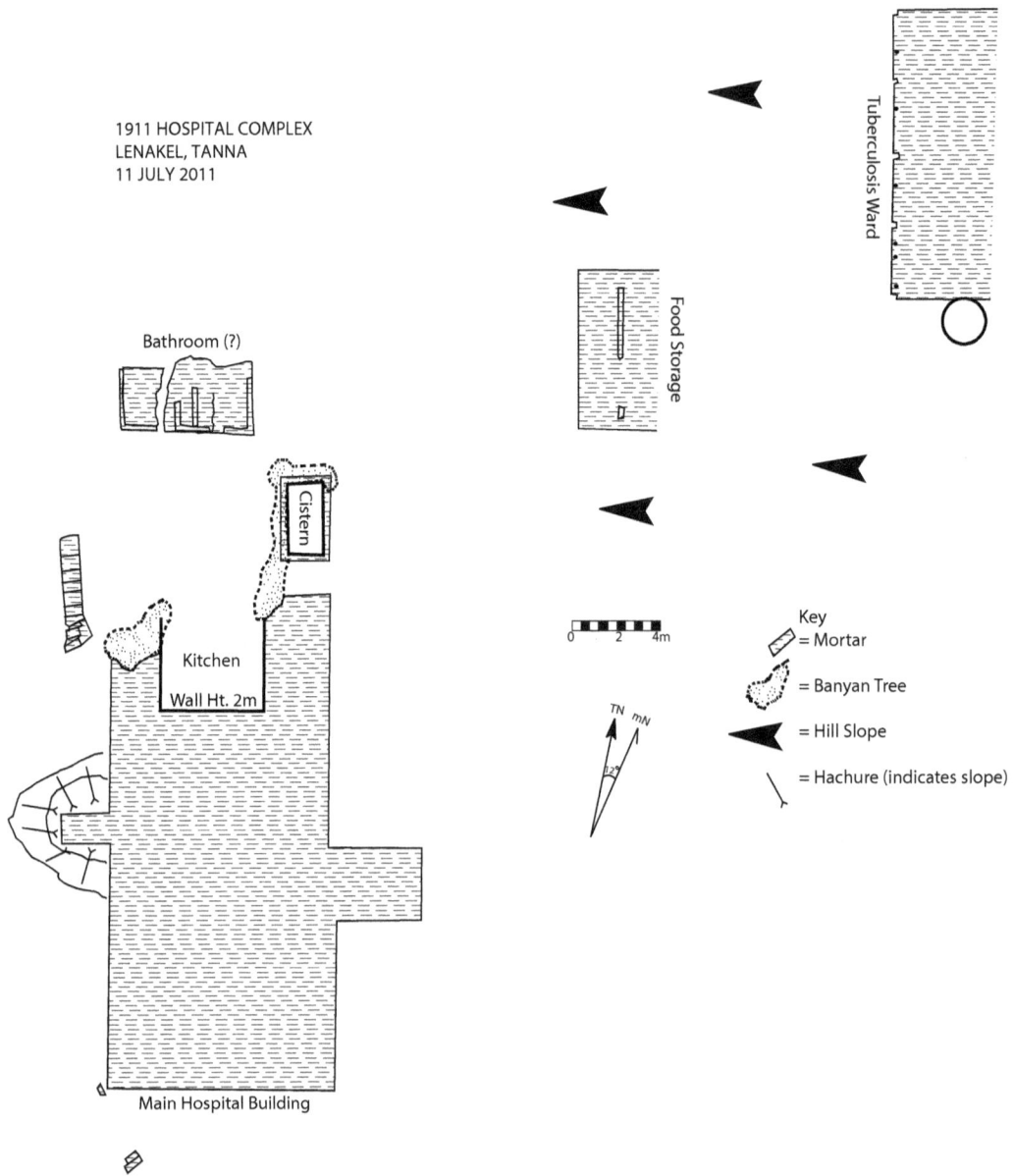

Figure 4.24 Mission hospital foundation features, Lenakel.

Source: James Flexner

Lenakel was the location of Tanna's first hospital. A commemorative plaque at the current hospital notes that there has been a hospital at Lenakel from 1903, and that in 1905 an operating room was opened by an Irishman named William Marshall. The foundation of the main hospital structure dating to 1911 (Miller 1986: 92) is still visible along with the separate foundations of the hospital's food storage pantry, and the tuberculosis ward (Figure 4.24). Across the street to the south of these features is a concrete slab that was the foundation of the hospital's maternity ward. Apparently uphill from this area was a series of grass huts with dirt floors containing the leprosy ward, but no remains were visible on the surface. Medical services were yet another of the important material benefits that the Presbyterian Church offered to the New Hebrides (Miller 1986). Early in the church, medical attention could be as much of a hindrance as anything else, as it further served to cast the missionaries as *Tupunas* (sorcerers; see Chapter 3). By the early 1900s, though, germ theory began to become widely accepted in the medical world and the technology and infrastructure improved (Risse 1999). Results improved on a scientific basis, while increasingly successful missionary healing practices continued to improve their standing in the New Hebrides from a spiritual perspective.

Village Life in Kwaraka after the Mission Period

The history of mission work on Tanna is more than simply a story of expansion, improvement, and native conversion to Christianity. Colonial religious change did not so much resolve as mask the tensions present on Tanna during the time of missionary settlement. The overextension of church power, allied with an increasingly effective colonial government, during the time of 'Tanna Law' led to consolidation of a countermovement in which *kastom* became entrenched. Elsewhere on the island, people took on the trappings of Christianity through material and ritual practices (wearing trousers, attending Sunday worship), while maintaining *kastom* at a deeper level (Bonnemaison 1994; Guiart 1956). Probably the most dramatic outcome of these unresolved contradictions are the various 'cargo cults' that emerged on Tanna. Most famous of all is the 'John Frum' movement, whose followers continue to paint themselves and march in mock military formation, to the delight of contemporary tourists (Lindstrom 1993; Tabani 2010).

But what of life elsewhere on Tanna? Here again we can turn to the archaeological landscape at Kwaraka (see Chapter 3) to understand long-term patterns of everyday life on the island. Excavations at Kwaraka were extremely limited, as the area was only accessible in 2013, when most of the time was spent mapping and digging shovel test pits around the site (Flexner 2014c: 12–18; Flexner et al. 2016c). There are two round, stone-lined mounds to the southwest of the canoe mound where *Paru* was kept in Iarisi's time (Figure 4.25). These bear superficial resemblance to contact-era house mounds from Samoa (Green and Davidson, eds 1974), which is compelling considering the presence of Samoan missionaries on Tanna (Lua'ana 1996). Whether this connection is real, however, is a matter for future research. According to local sources, the mounds were built to raise living spaces above the surrounding coastal plain, which becomes quite muddy during the annual rainy season.

On one of these mounds (M4 in Figure 3.5), a 1x1m test unit (TU1) was excavated to understand the interior construction deposits and recover any artefacts associated with construction and inhabitation of the mound. The excavation revealed a relatively simple sequence (Figure 4.26), with a shallow topsoil layer overlying an undifferentiated fill layer of earth and volcanic cobbles. This overlay the subsoil upon which the mound was constructed. The fill deposit was about 70cm deep. Thus the mound was constructed by heaping earth and stones in a circle, which were then covered in more earth that was levelled off, and the outside of the circle was lined with waterworn volcanic cobbles and boulders.

Artefacts recovered from the M4 excavation were primarily 20th century in age. The evidence generally relates to habitation of this mound long after the missionaries had left south Tanna. Considering the limited extent of the excavations, however, further research could find more evidence relating to the 19th century. In general, the artefacts came from the topsoil layer and the upper 30cm of the construction fill. The finds included a lead rifle bullet, a glass syringe, and most surprisingly, a glass lightbulb with a metal filament. The lightbulb is surprising because, before the availability of cheap solar panels, there was no reliable electricity on south Tanna. It is certainly possible that people used a diesel generator, or perhaps the lightbulb was simply a foreign 'curiosity' for its owner or a memento of a trip abroad. There was a small quantity of charcoal and burned coconut shell (5.1g total) in the lowest layer, along with two pieces of unidentified mammal bone, which date to an earlier period.

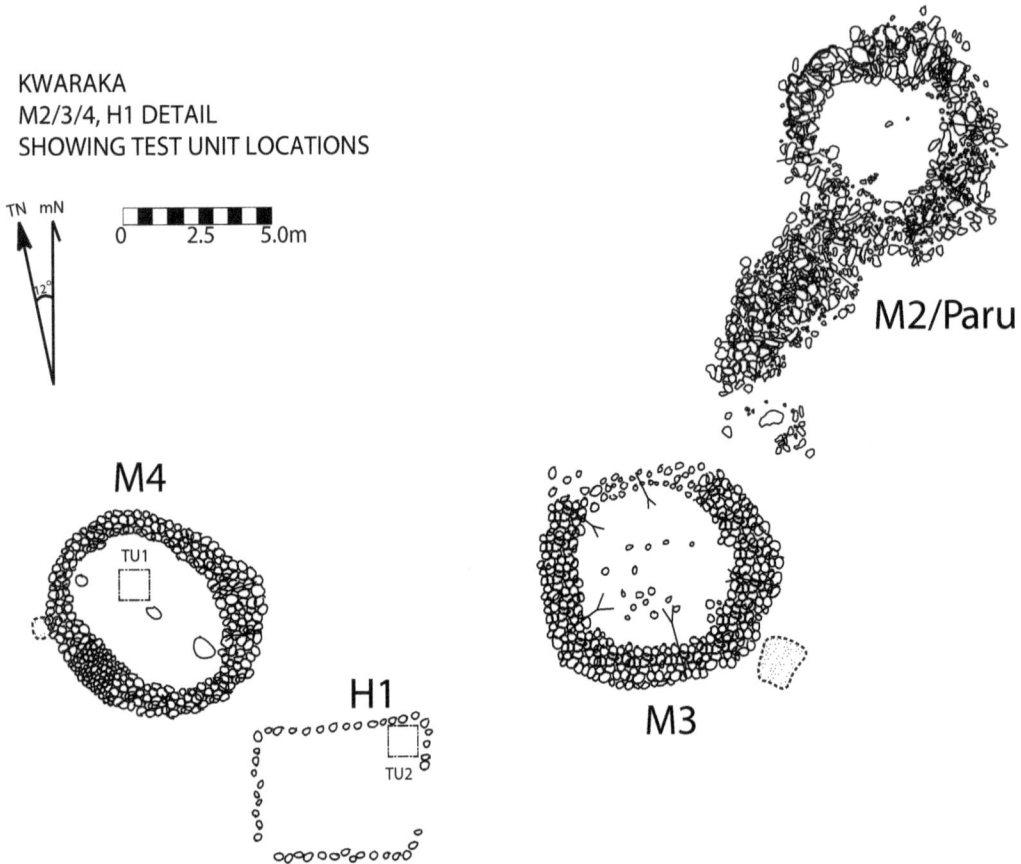

Figure 4.25 Central cluster of mounds and house alignment, Kwaraka.

Source: James Flexner

Abutting this mound to the southeast is a rectangular stone alignment that was thought to be a house footing (H1 in Figure 4.25). A 1x1m test unit (TU2) was excavated in the northeast corner of the structure. The excavation revealed a layer of rounded gravel that is interpreted as part of the interior stone paving of the house, as well as a series of small postholes (Figure 4.27). Excavation of this layer, and a 'drip line' feature within the unit recovered artefacts dating to after the 1950s. This included two blue plastic pen caps, and the torso of a toy plastic soldier figurine. What was found appears to be a traditionally constructed Tannese house, which would have consisted of a triangular cross-section wooden frame in which the slope of the roofline reached basically to the ground, covered in thatch. The artefacts in the house, however, indicate it was probably built in the 1950s or 1960s, and indeed this area was inhabited within living memory. It is notable that the recovered artefacts consist of children's toys and writing implements. As Ni-Vanuatu continue to engage with capitalism in the 21st century, most people work primarily to earn money to cover their children's school fees, and to offer them a few luxuries (candy, toys, and sporting equipment). It is a selective approach to the cash economy, which is a supplement to, rather than a replacement of, the traditional subsistence and exchange economy, though this is rapidly changing.

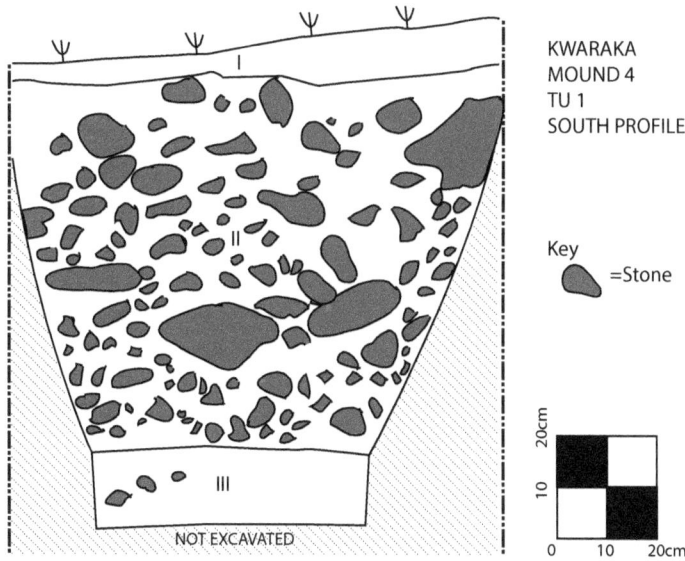

Figure 4.26 Stratigraphic profile, Mound 4, TU1, Kwaraka.
Source: James Flexner

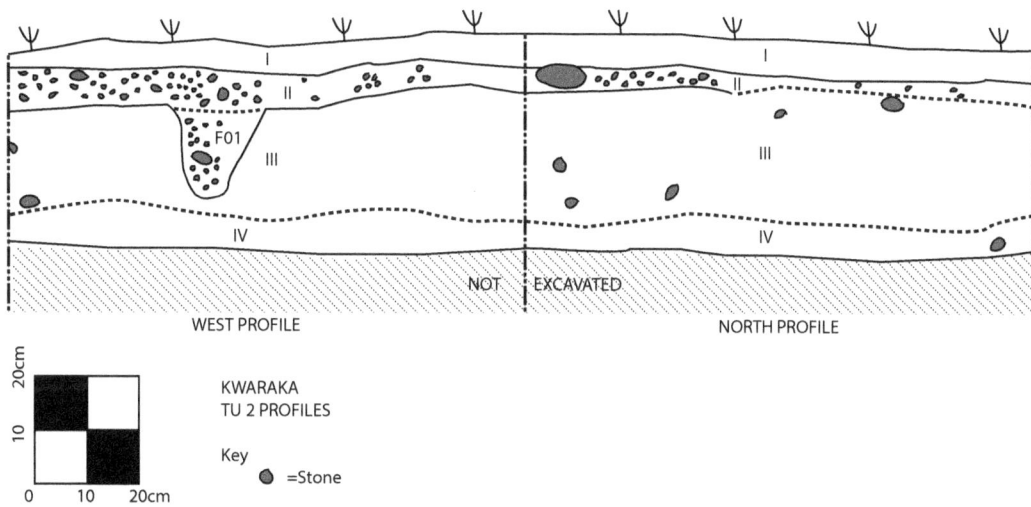

Figure 4.27 Stratigraphic profiles, House 1, TU2, Kwaraka.
Source: James Flexner

These excavations are relevant to the patterns of life on Tanna that persisted across the 20th century, through the period of most intensive colonialism on the island, the struggles for independence and stability in the 1970s and early 1980s, and on into the present. The gardens were and are powered by magic stones, which are still used throughout the island, including in former mission stations. Houses continue to be constructed using traditional materials and techniques, though supplemented with iron nails and other introduced materials. Increasingly, people strive to build '*haos blong bloks*' (cement and cinderblock houses) as a projection of wealth, though with the devastation wrought by Cyclone Pam in March 2015, alongside ongoing worries about climate change, there is a renewed interest in the more resilient and sustainable traditional architecture (Coiffier 1988: 141–151). Everyday life both in communities that held tight to *kastom*, and among those that converted, continues to be structured by the everyday rituals of afternoon kava at the *imwarim*, cycles of agricultural practice, and the annual exchanges and dances. On Tanna, *kastom* provides the framework on which the trappings of modernity are occasionally hung.

5

Museum Encounters: From the New Hebrides to the World

Missionaries were some of the first long-term European settlers among the islands of Oceania. They formed the closest social ties with local people of the early settlers, and were the keenest observers of indigenous culture during this era (Douglas 2001; Jolly and Macintyre, eds 1989). Missionaries left ethnographic observations (e.g. Gray 1892; Inglis 1854; Watt 1985) that would form the foundations for subsequent work as the first professional anthropologists entered the region at the beginning of the 20th century. In addition to observing indigenous Melanesian culture, a number of Presbyterian missionaries in the New Hebrides became avid collectors of indigenous things (Craig 2007; Lawson 1994a; Smith 1997). The trade in Oceanic 'curios' had marked European encounters from early moments of contact in the late 1700s through to the creation of a formal tourist trade in the early 1900s (Thomas 1991; Torrence 2000). Many of the objects collected during this period ended up in museum collections around the world. Much has been written concerning what museum collections reflect about colonial ideologies regarding colonised peoples (e.g. Bennett 2009; Gosden and Knowles 2001; Jacobs et al., eds 2015; Lawson 1994a). In this chapter, what missionaries or other collectors were attempting to represent in the collections will be a secondary consideration, with the focus being the context of Melanesian exchanges, and indigenous contexts of production and use.

The preceding chapters have examined missionary interactions with Melanesian people through the landscapes and sites where missionaries settled. Artefacts recovered from these sites are primarily European in origin. They represent objects brought to the New Hebrides as the missionaries sought to maintain a semblance of 'respectable' domesticity in the island environment, and to cultivate an interest in consumer goods among potential converts. Museum collections of Melanesian objects represent the other side of colonial exchanges. It is something of an irony that the majority of preserved indigenous objects from this era are to be found outside of Oceania. In excavating sites on Tanna and Erromango, we recovered hundreds of fragments of ceramic vessels, glass bottles, and iron hardware, while locally derived materials consisted almost entirely of lime mortar (a European material type made using local labour), charcoal, and shell fragments. Most indigenous objects, made of local organic materials, simply do not preserve in archaeological sites in Vanuatu. In a few cases, local people curate 19th-century objects. A friend at Dillon's Bay keeps two iron axes hafted on traditional Erromangan carved wooden club handles (Figure 5.1). The National Museum of Vanuatu likewise holds a significant but small collection of colonial-era objects from the southern islands (including objects repatriated from Western museums, such as decorated *nemasitse*, Erromangan barkcloth, from the Australian Museum; see Huffman 1996). But, to see very large assemblages of preserved 19th-century Tannese or Erromangan things, one has to travel to Europe, North America, or the European settler societies of Australia and New Zealand.

Figure 5.1 Iron hatchets hafted on carved wooden club handles, probably from the 1800s.
Curated in Dillon's Bay by Thomas Poki.

Source: James Flexner

As missionaries traded for or were gifted various kinds of objects, they sent them back to their homelands to be displayed. Some of the objects were used to demonstrate the 'warlike' nature of the people who were in need of Christian conversion. As missionaries went on furlough, they would travel to offer guest sermons at their 'home' churches as part of mission fundraising. They would bring Melanesian things with them as a material illustration of difference for European congregations whose donations were needed to support ongoing mission work. In other cases, directors of the new museums growing in various urban districts would ask missionaries to collect objects as evidence of the technology or culture of living 'Stone Age' peoples (Lawson 2005; Smith 2005). Directly or indirectly, objects from the New Hebrides wound up in Victorian museum collections, where they were displayed in a non-religious context but with the same purpose of displaying the inferior otherness of non-European peoples. Today, they represent rare or even unique examples of native craft and creativity during the colonial era.

Assemblages and Networks

Museum collections can be treated as artefact assemblages, and examined from an archaeological perspective as such. Two theoretical frameworks influence my approach to collections from the colonial New Hebrides. Assemblage theory embraces the 'the interdependence and entanglement of heterogeneous human and non-human elements into an emergent entity' (Law Pezzarossi 2014: 354). In an analysis of metal objects from a Native American basketmaker's toolkit, the artefacts consist of a set of things from a particular time and place. They also implicate a host of linked materials, activities, and relationships (Law Pezzarossi 2014; see also DeLanda 2006).

Actor–Network Theory likewise deals with webs of relationships. Objects and places as well as people are included as nodes within the networks, which are not stable entities but can shift over the course of everyday lives. Further, the connections in the networks are themselves considered as 'things' in the sense that changing or moving a connection will affect the form of the network just as much as transforming one of the nodes (in other words, there is not necessarily a hierarchical relationship between nodes and connections in the network; see Byrne et al. 2011; Latour 2005).

Archaeologists have found Actor–Network Theory to be an especially powerful tool for approaching museum collections (e.g. Byrne et al., eds 2011; Harrison et al., eds 2013). Early ethnological collections have been used to trace changes in indigenous craft production practices, materials use, form, and agency in the colonial curiosities trade, as in case studies from Papua New Guinea and Aboriginal Australia (Clarke and Torrence 2011; Harrison 2002, 2006; Torrence 2000; Torrence and Clarke 2013). In the case of missionary-derived collections, the objects can reflect the intimate connections formed between missionaries and their converts. The collection of Edith Safstrom, a female Anglican lay missionary in the Solomon Islands, illustrates, 'the gendered perspective of mission life, and the specific social relationships formed between Edith and the women and children of the mission' (Smith 2010: 207). These kinds of objects can provide data to link everyday exchanges and relationships to the larger historical processes of material change as they relate to religious transformation in Melanesia.

Missionary collections from the New Hebrides are sedimented in the museum stores in which they are held. They have made long journeys from the islands where they were made, used, exchanged within a Melanesian context, and eventually traded to Europeans, sometimes via indigenous middlemen. Starting from the objects and their contemporary context, usually located 'behind the scenes' in shelves rarely if ever seen by the public, the networks of relationships, activities, and people related to these objects can be traced into an expanding web eventually beginning with the objects' origins in the southern New Hebrides. These objects form both a 'supplement' to archaeological data, and a significant 'record' of indigenous agency in material exchanges during the mission era (Flexner 2016b). Just as previous chapters dealt with archaeological sites and the materials they contain, here I will offer a survey of museum collections, focusing on objects from the southern New Hebrides. A list of most objects analysed in the survey appears as Appendix E (some sensitive or restricted objects and some raw material or 'natural history' specimens are not included in the appendix). The discussion below covers generally each of the collections, focusing in each case on a particularly well-represented class of objects or individual objects that encapsulate aspects of religious and cultural change in the colonial New Hebrides. The goal is to expand outwards from the particular 'archaeological' context of the museum assemblages to the social lives these objects would have had in their dynamic cultural context in the islands.

A total of 856 objects from 13 museums were examined in this study (Table 5.1). While they derive from 'ethnology' or 'ethnographic' collections, the objects were treated as archaeological artefacts (Hicks 2013: 3–6). The contexts consist of collection stores rather than stratigraphic units, but the underlying premise is the same: assemblages of objects can be connected to a wider social landscape relating to their life history, from production to deposition. As with an archaeological excavation, there was a sampling strategy, which was judgemental in this case. Each of the collections below could merit an extensive analysis detailing every object. Here, the goal is to highlight representative or evocative objects to explore more deeply issues of material exchange in the New Hebrides missions. Holding to the archaeological analogy, what appears is more of a 'surface collection' of data, where deeper digging into these assemblages would certainly produce new and interesting results.

Table 5.1 Surveyed museum collections, and the islands represented therein.

Island	Auckland Museum	Australian Museum	Hunterian Museum	Museums Glasgow	National Museum of Scotland	New Brunswick Museum	Nova Scotia Museum	Otago Museum	Queensland Museum	Redpath Museum	Royal Ontario Museum	University of Aberdeen Museums	Weltmuseum	Grand Total
Ambrym					1									1
Aneityum	3	14	1	14	33		2			1		2		70
Aniwa					1									1
Anuta/Erro?	1													1
Aoba								1						1
Efate				1										1
Emae				5	1									6
Epi/Paama											1			1
Erromango	7	120	3	12	24	1	24	4	11	70	6	11	41	334
Erromango(?)		13												13
Futuna		18		13	29			3				3		66
Malakula				1	1						1	1		4
Malakula, Solomon Islands									3					3
New Caledonia	2			5	2									9
New Caledonia/New Hebrides					1									1
New Hebrides	14	4	3	36	27	67	39	3	5	46	15	15	7	281
Tanna	8	20	1	8	6	2	1	7	2			3	2	60
Tongoa				2	1									3
Grand Total	35	189	8	97	127	70	66	18	21	117	23	35	50	856

Research focused on objects from the southern New Hebrides to record things most closely associated with the early Presbyterian missions, though objects identified generically to the New Hebrides and a small sample of objects from central and northern islands were also included. In addition to Tanna and Erromango, the neighbouring islands of Futuna, Aniwa, and Aneityum were included in the survey, as were a few objects from New Caledonia. This increased the sample size and richness as more objects of different types were included. There were also regular exchanges between these southern islands, so the material culture could be expected to be somewhat mobile within this geographic range. Roughly two-thirds of the objects came from missionary collections (65.9 per cent, N=564). A small sample of non-missionary-derived collections was examined for comparative purposes (12.4 per cent, N=106), with the remaining objects having documentation that was not available or was unclear (21.7 per cent, N=186).

Table 5.2 Missionary and non-missionary components of museum collections.

Museum	Missionary	Mixed/Unknown	Non-Missionary	Grand Total
Auckland Museum	3	31	1	35
Australian Museum	126	54	9	189
Hunterian Museum	7		1	8
Museums Glasgow	79	10	8	97
National Museum of Scotland	104	9	14	127
New Brunswick Museum	23	47		70
Nova Scotia Museum	65	1		66
Otago Museum		18		18
Queensland Museum			21	21
Redpath Museum	117			117
Royal Ontario Museum	6	16	1	23
University of Aberdeen Museums	34		1	35
Weltmuseum			50	50
Grand Total	564	186	106	856

The objects are made of a variety of materials: shell, stone, wood, leaves, seeds, spider webs, as well as foreign iron and glass. They cover a variety of activities across the range of ritual and everyday life. Originally, missionary collectors believed they were salvaging fragments of a 'disappearing' native culture being reformed towards Christianity. Recently, there has been renewed interest in these kinds of collections among artists, cultural practitioners, and communities in Vanuatu seeking to revive traditional craftmaking and related practices (Carillo-Huffman et al. 2013; Craig 2003, 2007; Huffman 1996; Lawson 2001, in press). *Kastom,* as always, did not disappear so much as evolve. In a sense, despite the assumptions of missionaries and their 19th-century contemporaries, traditional objects have been preserved for the time when they might re-emerge in a new, but still traditional, context.

Canadian Collections

The Church of the Lower Provinces of British North America was the primary supporter of early mission work in the southern New Hebrides (Presbyterian Church of the Lower Provinces of British North America 1849–1873). All of the excavated sites on Erromango were inhabited by Canadian missionaries (see Chapter 2), as was the Imua Mission on Tanna (see Chapter 3). The islands of Vanuatu would be largely unfamiliar to most Canadians today. These collections represent a period when there were close connections between the two places. The Lower Provinces, particularly Nova Scotia and Prince Edward Island, sent missionaries to the New Hebrides.

The missionaries in return sent curios from the South Seas (Lawson 2005; Smith 2005). These collections tend to be among the earlier missionary collections held in Western museums. They also are generally more focused on the southern islands of Vanuatu, since that area was the focus of missionary work through the 1880s.

Nova Scotia Museum

The Nova Scotia Museum's collection of objects from the New Hebrides is almost entirely attributed to Rev. John Geddie. Geddie was born in Scotland, but his family moved to Pictou, Nova Scotia, in 1816. Geddie followed in his father's footsteps, training as a clockmaker before he was called to missionary work (Patterson 1882: 17–24). A still-working example of one of Geddie's clocks is located in the First Presbyterian Church in Pictou, which also holds a small collection of wooden clubs, combs, and beaded objects. Geddie's 'home church' also keeps a set of transfer-printed ceramic dishes of 'British Marine' pattern whiteware that had apparently been part of the household assemblage on Aneityum. Geddie, as has been mentioned, settled on Aneityum in 1848, and is generally credited with establishing a successful mission that became the stronghold for the Presbyterian Church over the course of its early history in the New Hebrides (Miller 1978: 69–104; Patterson 1882). After 15 years of mission work, Geddie's health was suffering, and it was determined that a trip home would refresh mind, body, and spirit. He arrived back in Halifax, via Australia and Britain, on 3 August 1864. The furlough was to last for almost two years, which were spent preaching in various congregations in an appeal for greater support for mission work. Geddie departed to return to Aneityum on 2 February 1866 (Patterson 1882: 466–482). The collection now held by the Nova Scotia Museum may partly derive from objects that Geddie brought with him on this visit. However, it is probable that much of the 'Geddie collection' in fact came from H.A. Robertson, a missionary on Erromango who was a much more active collector and donor of objects to Canadian museums (Lawson 1994a: 247). While I refer to the 'Geddie collection' below, it should be assumed that many if not most of the objects in fact came from Robertson.

If he did engage in assembling objects for the Nova Scotia Museum, Geddie wrote little about his collecting habits. He appears to have generally held a low opinion of indigenous material culture, particularly weapons, though plaited and woven objects are given some praise (Patterson 1882: 122). He also notes his interest in wooden and stone 'idols' (*Natmas*), which were the objects of traditional worship (Patterson 1882: 128–129). A number of the stone *Natmas* were intentionally buried, or integrated into mission architecture at Anelcauhat, the main mission station on Aneityum (Crook et al. 2015). There is one hint at Geddie's collecting habits from his biography: 'describing his departure from Aneityum, which he had found fifteen years before wholly given to idolatry, he had sought for some of the old gods to bring home, but he could find no god on the whole island but the God who had made the heavens and the earth' (Patterson 1882: 472). This is certainly hyperbole. There are two egg-shaped sacred stones of calcite from Aneityum in the Geddie collection (NS Museum 1971.90.25k, r; Figure 5.2). Geddie could have also taken one of the larger *Natmas* stones from the mission grounds, though there are none included in this collection. In addition, later missionaries were apparently able to collect sacred stones from Aneityum.

Figure 5.2 Sacred stones from Aneityum.

Source: Image courtesy Nova Scotia Museum.

There are 125 entries attributed to Geddie's collection in the catalogue of the Nova Scotia Museum. Of these, 66 were available to be analysed during the museum survey. The majority that could be attributed to a specific island (N=24) were not from Geddie's main base on Aneityum, but from Erromango, two islands to the north, which again points to Robertson as a more likely collector. Of particular interest are four examples of *navela*, Erromangan 'stone money' (NS Museum 1971.90.9, 10, 44, Z.880; Figure 5.3). *Navela* were extremely valuable exchange items on Erromango. The form was a polished stone ring or crescent-shape, usually of calcite. The largest ring-shaped *navela* could be 1.5m in diameter, weighing up to 25kg. They were not believed to have been made by people, but were attributed to a supernatural origin, sometimes originating with the creator deity *Nobu*. *Navela* could only be traded among members of the chiefly (*Fan lo*) class, and were only exchanged at significant ceremonial occasions, as during the *nevsem*. Upon the death of a chief, his *navela* could be inherited. However, sometimes *navela* were lost if a chief died suddenly, or without naming an heir. In such cases, the properties of the lost *navela* could be passed on to a lesser stone held in the chief's village. *Navela* had names and special properties. If a *navela* was found hidden in the bush, it might be recognised as a lost example to *Fan lo* who held appropriate knowledge (Humphreys 1926: 191–192; Naupa, ed. 2011: 66; Robertson 1902: 390).

Figure 5.3 *Navela* (stone money) from Erromango.
Source: Image courtesy Nova Scotia Museum.

Robertson (1902: 390) notes the difficulty he had in obtaining *navela*, which only became available to him after several decades as resident missionary on Erromango: 'I can often buy them, though, in nearly every case, I am given to understand that I am wonderfully lucky in securing such a prize.' This begs the question of how Geddie could have secured the four *navela* now held in the Nova Scotia Museum. There are three ring-shaped examples, which represent the full moon, and one crescent-shaped example, which represents the crescent moon. Both are important symbols in Erromangan cosmology. Of the ring-shaped examples, one is broken into six pieces, which raises the possibility of intentional breakage of the sacred object, though it could also have been broken during shipment to Nova Scotia. There is also a rare example made of a reddish-brown volcanic stone rather than calcite. It is possible that one of Geddie's early converts had a special connection to Erromango as part of the traditional exchange networks linking the southern islands of Vanuatu. The stones could also have derived from the Gordons, who had settled at Dillon's Bay before Geddie returned to Nova Scotia. However, it would be surprising if the Gordons had been able to acquire such significant objects considering how poorly the Gordons appear to have integrated into the local community (see Chapter 2). More likely, *navela* in the Nova Scotia Museum collections should be attributed to Robertson. Robertson (1902: 359) notes being gifted a number of *navela* as well as trading for them. Perhaps with the epidemics decimating the Erromangan population from the 1850s through the 1880s, as numbers of *Fan lo* perished, *navela* became easier to acquire. At the same time, the specific ritual where Robertson was gifted these sacred stones by a particular chief may also have been a way of entangling the missionary in local networks, granting the Erromangan chief control over foreign powers and material connections (see Chapter 6).

The other major group of Erromangan objects in the Geddie collection were wooden clubs. Of 13 wooden clubs, eight were diagnostic Erromango forms (NS Museum 1971.90.1a, b, d, g, h, j, k, i). Clubs on Erromango were of three types: the *netnivri, novwan,* and *telugohmti.* The *novwan* was a simple form that apparently had the same shape on the pommel and club head, though surviving examples of these were not found in this museum survey. The *netnivri* is a spindle-headed club. It consists of a carved hemisphere on the pommel, with a carved design on the flat end, and a club head consisting of two flat wooden discs beneath a lozenge-shaped head capped with another flat disc (Figure 5.4). The *telugohmti* or star-headed club had a similar pommel to the *netnivri,* but a head carved into eight points. The *telugohmti* was used more for display and exchanges, particularly marriage arrangements, rather than for warfare. Traditionally, the clubs were hung in the rafters of the *Siman lo* (men's house; see Chapter 2), where they acquired a dark polish from the smoke of the cooking fire (Humphreys 1926: 144, 163–164; Robertson 1902: 371–372).

ERROMANGO CLUBS
(based on museum examples)

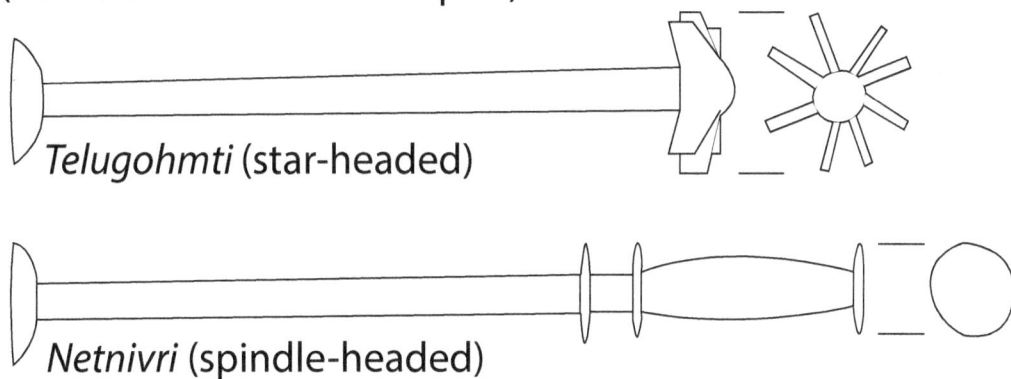

Telugohmti (star-headed)

Netnivri (spindle-headed)

Figure 5.4 The two main Erromangan club forms (above, *telugohmti* star-headed club; below, *netnivri* spindle-headed club).

Source: James Flexner

Other objects in the Geddie collection included two iron axes hafted on carved wooden club handles, a common hybrid form that emerged from the colonial era (NS Museum 1971.90.14a, b). Further evidence of remixing of European and indigenous forms are evident on a decorated piece of *nemasitse* (*tapa* or barkcloth; 1971.90.27a; Figure 5.5). This example includes images of a person on horseback, as well as a person smoking a tobacco pipe. There is also writing on the cloth, which Lawson (in press) translates as 'May God be with you' and 'For you beloved misi'. Lawson suggests this object was presented to Robertson around 1883 and later brought back with him to Canada. The collection also includes seven of the *neko* (barkcloth beaters) used in the manufacture of the cloth for which Erromango is well known (NS Museum 1971.90.4a–g; Figure 5.6). There were 14 adze blades of the plano-convex Melanesian type (NS Museum 1971.90.25a–j, l–p). These included one adze blade of light, fine-grained stone with a trapezoidal cross-section, and one rectangular adze blade of calcite, which appear to be Samoan forms (cf. Green and Davidson, eds 1969). These might have been collected during Geddie's brief stop in Samoa on the way to Aneityum (Patterson 1882: 91–105), or brought with one of the Samoan teachers working in the southern New Hebrides (Liua'ana 1996).

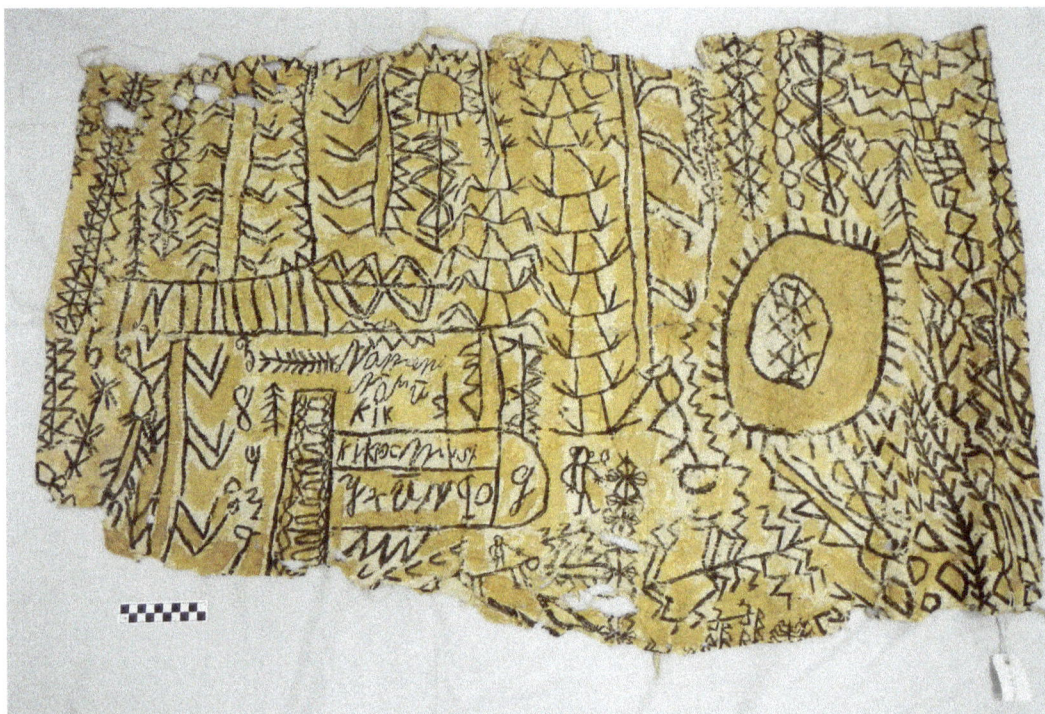

Figure 5.5 *Nemasitse* (barkcloth) with writing, man on horseback as well as traditional designs.
Source: Image courtesy Nova Scotia Museum.

Figure 5.6 *Neko* (barkcloth beaters) from Erromango.
Source: Image courtesy Nova Scotia Museum.

Redpath Museum

The collection of H.A. Robertson held at the Redpath Museum in Montreal is the most well-documented of missionary collections from the New Hebrides (Lawson 1994a, 1994b, 2001, 2005). The collection was a source of pride for the Redpath Museum, because of its rare, even unique sampling of Erromangan material culture, but also as an expression of a shift from Canada as a colonised culture to a colonising one (Lawson 1994a: 46–47, 153). A total of 117 objects from this collection were included in this survey. Robertson appears to have focused on many aspects of everyday life. He seems to have eschewed objects relating to warfare in the collection. This was despite the fact that local people were encouraged by the missionary to continue making clubs for trade (Robertson 1902: 372). Perhaps the apparently 'inferior' clubs made specifically for trade were considered below the quality of object that the missionary sought to collect for the museum. There are two Erromangan clubs in the collection, both of which are of the *netnivri* form. This is somewhat surprising considering the near ubiquity of *telugohmti* in other collections.

Where the Robertson collection truly excels is in its collection of objects relating to Erromangan adornment, specifically women's clothing (Lawson 1994a: 143–146; 2001). Men's objects include decorated bamboo combs (N=10; Redpath ACC.481.1–2, 482.1–8; Figure 5.7) and carved coconut shell armbands (N=8; Redpath ACC.484.1–7a/b). Women's adornment is represented by *nemasitse* (barkcloth, N=4; Redpath ACC.465.1–3, 466), as well as the *neko* used to make the cloth (N=3; Redpath ACC.835.1–3), and *numplat* (grass skirts, N=16; Redpath ACC.464.1–16). Clothing was one of the realms in which missionaries most forcefully sought to change indigenous habits, seeking to replace penis sheaths and grass skirts with trousers and calico dresses. Yet Robertson was something of a grudging admirer of Erromangan clothing. He describes the *numplat* as 'very pretty', and further suggests that some Erromangan male converts disliked the calico dresses introduced by the missionaries, which made their wives appear 'too slim' (Robertson 1902: 326–327, 366).

Figure 5.7 Carved bamboo combs from Erromango.
Source: Image courtesy Redpath Museum.

Decorated *nemasitse* is one of the most iconic of Erromangan things (Carillo-Huffman et al. 2013; Huffman 1996; Naupa, ed. 2011: 52–56). *Nemasitse* was traditionally a women's art. It was made with the bark of banyan, mangrove, and a few other types of tree. The bark was removed from the trees, then placed on a long, smooth log, where it was sprayed with water and pounded with the *neko*. As the bark became a soft pulp, additional strips were added, forming a continuous length of cloth that was then dried. A design could be drawn on the cloth in charcoal while damp, and the cloth could be further coloured using ground *nohorat* root. Traditional motifs included leaf shapes, the sun and crescent moon, as well as stylised birds, fishes, lizards, or flying foxes. The cloth was a highly valued exchange item, reflecting the contribution of women to the traditional economy. It was worn as a raincloak, and also commonly tied around the shoulders as a baby-carrier (Humphreys 1926: 159–160; Lawson 2001; Robertson 1902: 368–369). The human figures and writing on the Nova Scotia Museum example discussed above were clearly an incorporation of introduced ideas and motifs alongside traditional decorations (Robertson 1902: 369). By the early 20th century, production of *nemasitse* had largely declined, and the highly carved traditional *neko* had basically disappeared (Humphreys 1926: 159), though the practice was revived later on (Huffman 1996).

Numplat were the primary article of clothing for Erromangan women. They were made from leaves, usually pandanus, but also banana, young coconut, hibiscus, or the stem of *tampoli* (native cabbage). For pandanus skirts, the spines on the edges of the leaf and the fibrous centre vein were removed. A pattern was then applied by folding the leaves to produce linear designs or chewing, using the shape of the dental arcade to make a round design. The green leaves were then placed in still, shallow water to soak. After soaking, the ends of the leaves would be cut into strips using a bamboo knife, and then woven into a twine made of the silky inner bark of the *worenevau* ('bastard cotton') tree. The completed skirt could then be coloured by the application of dye, or by burying the skirt in dark mud (Humphreys 1926: 160–161; Robertson 1902: 366–367). Unmarried girls would wear a shorter, usually undecorated *numplat*, adopting the longer, elaborately decorated version after marriage (Humphreys 1926: 144). Women of the chiefly class (*Nasimnalan*) might wear as many as 20 or 30 *numplat* at once, a reflection of conspicuous wealth (Lawson 2001).

In part, the Robertson collection is an expression of missionary ambitions and ideology in relation to the simultaneous erasure and appropriation of 'heathen things' on Erromango (Lawson 1994a, 2001). At the same time, the objects were reinterpreted in a museum setting for Victorian audiences who simultaneously may have seen them as 'trophies' of colonial religious and cultural transformation, as well as relics of a dying indigenous culture. The museum setting offered those objects an artificial longevity, keeping them intact for much longer than they would have survived in their 'natural' tropical environment. In the present, these things may be reinterpreted and revived by indigenous artists and cultural practitioners (Huffman 1996; Lawson 1994b: 34–35; Naupa, ed. 2011).

Beyond this, the objects reflect the choices Erromangan people may have made about what to produce, and what to trade with the missionary. The large collection contains only a single, small example of *navela* (Redpath ACC.480), the 'great prize' that was so difficult to procure (Robertson 1902: 390). Other exchange valuables, such as *numpuri* (cowrie) were more common, and were displayed on neck ornaments (*kirikiri*; Redpath ACC474.1–5). There are other things that may reflect the unique position of the Robertsons as missionaries on Erromango over the course of four decades. There is a rare 'sorcerer's kit', consisting of a small rectangular basket that contained four 'ritual bundles' of unknown substance wrapped in leaves (Redpath ACC.471.1a–e).

There are also several lengths of carved bamboo that may have had a ritual significance (Redpath ACC.485.1–5), and even more personal, the traditional plaited hair of a young Tannese man (Redpath ACC.1354/572).

Royal Ontario Museum

The New Hebrides missionary collection of the Royal Ontario Museum (ROM) is associated with the activities of Rev. Joseph Annand (Smith 1997, 2005). Annand and his wife arrived to take up missionary positions in the New Hebrides, beginning with Iririki in 1873. They would relocate several times: to Aneityum in 1877, and the south of Espiritu Santo Island in 1887. Eventually, Annand was appointed director of the Teacher's Training Institute in 1894, retiring home to Nova Scotia in 1913 (Miller 1981: 86–87; Miller 1985: 243–244). While Annand was not directly present on Tanna or Erromango, he did spend a decade on neighbouring Aneityum. His role as head of the Teacher's Training Institute likely also offered him contacts with students from throughout the New Hebrides. There is evidence for an internal network of curiosities exchanges among missionaries, as in 1892 Annand mentions 'putting up spears for Mrs. Watt [of Tanna] and Mrs. Robertson [of Erromango]' (quoted in Smith 2005: 268).

Annand's collection is of interest because it derives from a close relationship the missionary had with David Boyle, who was curator of the Toronto Normal School's ethnological museum. The collection later transferred with Boyle to the Royal Ontario Museum of Archaeology, now the ROM. Annand was influenced by the Victorian practice of natural science collecting, while Boyle was seeking to expand the geographical scope of his collection to include objects relating to 'primitive peoples' throughout the world (Smith 1997: 96–98; Smith 2005: 262–263). The ROM currently holds over 100 objects collected by Annand for Boyle. Because of limited time and the scope of this survey, 30 of these objects were selected for analysis. Half of these (N=15) were identified generically to the New Hebrides, and a further 13 objects were attributed to Erromango. One object was the result of later 20th-century collecting activity by ROM curators, with six objects definitely attributed to Annand, and the remaining 16 probably relating to missionary collecting, though the documentation was somewhat unclear. The examined objects included hafted adzes, one with a stone blade (ROM HB.2052), one from Malakula with a *Tridacna* shell blade (ROM HB.139), and a *Tridacna* 'chisel' (ROM HB.141), which may have been used for wood carving.

The Erromango objects included two *numplat* (grass skirts), including one of the shorter examples worn by unmarried girls (ROM HB.109). There were two examples of *nemasitse* (decorated barkcloth). One, which was definitely attributed to Annand, bears the ubiquitous leaf motif used on various kinds of Erromangan objects (ROM NS.15155). There was a bow (ROM NS.27602) and eight arrows (ROM NS.27614, 27615, 27617 27622), which were probably associated. They derive from the Toronto Normal School collection of Boyle, and thus were almost certainly sent to Toronto by Annand. It is interesting to note Annand's association with the Robertsons, who were his contemporaries on Erromango. There is no direct evidence, but it is likely that at least some of these objects were exchanged between the missionaries from different islands before being sent to North America. Also notable in relation to these objects is Boyle's request for objects relating to female activities, which 'Annand did not deem ... feasible, as, in his view, the life of the female native was not distinguishable from that of the male' (Smith 1997: 106). *Nemasitse* and *numplat* were pretty clearly gendered as a 'female' object on Erromango, just as club, bow, and arrow could be generally deemed 'male'. Perhaps Annand's reluctance came from a belief that the objects would be misrepresented in the museum setting.

New Brunswick Museum

The New Hebrides collection of the New Brunswick Museum derives primarily from the activities of Ewen McAfee, a lay missionary who came to South West Bay, Malekula, with his wife in 1907 as assistants to Joseph Annand (Miller 1989: 486). After the Annands retired to Canada, the McAfees stayed on at Malekula as traders until 1919. Given their association with Annand, it is not surprising that the McAfees took up collecting, and being from Saint John, New Brunswick was a natural destination for their curiosities. This is a large and significant assemblage of New Hebrides objects that warrants additional analysis on its own. For this survey, I focused on objects identifiable to the southern islands of Vanuatu, which are less well represented than the northern and central islands closer to where the McAfees had settled. In addition to the McAfee collection, the New Brunswick Museum holds artefacts attributed to H.A. Robertson, which came to the museum via Pine Hill Divinity Hall and the Maritime Conference of the United Church of Canada (Kirkpatrick 2009). Robertson, as noted above, was an enthusiastic collector who provided large numbers of objects to Canadian museums (Lawson 1994a).

Seventy objects from the New Hebrides were analysed as part of the survey, of which 67 were identified generically, two were attributed to Tanna, and one to Erromango. Included in the collection are many examples of objects relating to personal adornment. There is one of the nearly ubiquitous *numplat* (grass skirt) found in missionary collections (NB Museum 19031). Most notable are some of the necklaces and pendants from the Maritime Conference acquisition (Figure 5.8). A necklace of polished boar's tooth beads (NB Museum 2009.11.3) was associated with a tag that read: 'Necklace of boars' teeth. These belonged to several generations of chiefs on Aneityum.' Similar objects are known from archaeological excavations of chiefly burials on Aneityum, suggesting the practice is of some antiquity (Spriggs 1997: 212, 218). There are also five large beads (NB Museum 2009.11.6), three of which are definitely made of ground sperm whale (*Physeter microcephalus*) teeth. The other two are either ancient teeth that were collected and ground, or possibly *Tridacna* shell or reef limestone drilled and polished into an analogous form, which is seen in other collections (see Australian Museum below). Whale's tooth ornaments likewise would have been prestige valuables. As noted for the Tannese by Turner (1861: 80), 'there is nothing of which a chief is fonder for a necklace than three large whale's teeth, on three separate strings, and dangling horizontally on his breast'.

Four cowrie shells suspended on a thick cord of vegetable fibre (NB Museum 2009.11.5) represent a necklace supposedly related to one of Erromango's missionary martyrdoms. They were part of a display case from the Maritime Conference, with a label that read: 'The tag attached to this relic was torn. What remains reads as follows: "Santo Shell beads. These were taken from the neck of the murderer of …" We believe this refers to the murderer of Rev. George Gordon.' Tales of murderers and cannibals in the South Seas should be read with a high degree of scepticism, as they were often exaggerated or fabricated to titillate Western audiences (Thomas 1991: 162–167; see also Obeyesekere 2005). It is interesting to note that, despite their attribution to Santo, cowrie (*numpuri*) shells were important exchange valuables on Erromango. The fact that this object came from Robertson, who later claimed to have converted the son of one involved in missionary deaths on Erromango (Robertson 1902: 322–324), thus also renders the story feasible, if unlikely. That the missionary sought to assert this necklace came from the murderer of one of his predecessors is significant in light of treatment of indigenous objects as trophies won during the conversion process, regardless of the story's truth.

Figure 5.8 Necklaces of shell, pig tusk, and whale's tooth from southern Vanuatu (2009.11.2: shell necklace with glass beads; 2009.11.3: necklace of pig's tusk beads, Aneityum; 2009.11.4: polished cone shell tops; 2009.11.5: cowrie shells on fibre cord; 2009.11.6: whale's tooth and whale's tooth-shaped pendants).

Source: New Brunswick Museum-Musée du Nouveau-Brunswick, www.nbm-mnb.ca.

Scottish Collections

Scotland was the spiritual as well as ancestral home for the Presbyterian missionaries who travelled to the New Hebrides. As mentioned earlier, even though the Canadian Church provided the primary source of missionaries and support in the early years, the missionaries would have identified closely with Scotland. Over time, the Scottish Kirk was increasingly involved in the New Hebrides missions. As with the Canadian collections, Scottish museum assemblages of objects from the New Hebrides were sent 'home' by missionaries seeking to provide tangible evidence of their successes, and scientific information for an interested public.

National Museum of Scotland

The missionary collections of New Hebrides objects in the National Museum of Scotland (NMS) in Edinburgh as well as Museums Glasgow are primarily from James Hay Lawrie. Lawrie arrived on Aneityum in 1879, and presided over the mission there as it was transferred from the Canadian Church to the Free Church of Scotland. The population of the island continued to decrease, and by 1895 it was determined that a single missionary would suffice for Aneityum and Futuna. Lawrie left Aneityum in 1892, owing in part to his wife's ill health. He returned to Aneityum in 1894 while Gunn, the resident missionary for Futuna, was on furlough in Scotland. Lawrie was the last full-time resident missionary on Aneityum. He later worked for the Presbyterian Church in New South Wales (Miller 1986: 134–146). Of 224 objects at NMS and Museums Glasgow examined for this survey, 183 are definitely from Lawrie's collections. A further 19 objects are not well documented, but may have originated with the missionary.

Unlike many of his contemporaries, Lawrie did not leave behind a published diary or autobiography, though he did keep up regular correspondence with the home church (Free Church of Scotland 1889–1894). We know little about his motivations or interests in collecting, though we can assume they were similar to the other missionaries who engaged in this activity. It is clear from the size and scope of his collections that he accumulated large amounts of material culture, covering all areas of daily life. A total of 127 objects was examined from the NMS collection. In addition to finished objects, Lawrie collected raw materials of various kinds, as well as tools relating to everyday life. For example, he collected a box full of quartz drill bits (NMS A.1895.413.22a), eight basically unmodified limpet shells used as scrapers for root crops and breadfruit (NMS A.1895.413.21), and a large piece of branch coral (NMS A.1895.413.37) that could have been used to manufacture a throwing club. Lawrie also collected models of things that would have been too big to ship to Scotland, including several canoe models (NMS A.1895.413.2, 4) and a model of an Aneityumese house (NMS A.1895.413.1).

Reflecting his geographic location, Lawrie's collections are primarily focused on the southern islands. A total of 126 objects from the missionary collections in NMS and Glasgow could be attributed to the islands of Tanna, Erromango, Futuna, Aniwa, or Aneityum (Table 5.3). The NMS collection has the largest concentration of objects from Aneityum (N=33) and Futuna (N=29) of any of the collections examined for this survey. Included among these objects are things that likely held immense personal value for their owners, suggesting that Lawrie had forged close relationships with his trading partners. There are two rooster feather hair ornaments from Aneityum, similar to the ones still made on neighbouring Tanna today to be worn for dances and other ceremonies (NMS A.1895.413.76, 78). More impressive, Lawrie was able to collect a *kweriya*, or hawk's feather ornament, from Tanna (NMS A.1895.413.75). Hawk's feathers were the privilege of certain high-ranking members of the chiefly order of *Yeremwanu* (Bonnemaison 1994: 146–148; Guiart 1956: 83–85). The *kweriya* would have been a treasured gift indeed, perhaps coming to Lawrie via the established mission station on south Tanna, which had close traditional connections to north Aneityum (see Chapter 3), where Lawrie was initially stationed.

Lawrie collected other significant objects in relation to *kastom*. There is a fish-shaped magic stone from Aneityum (NMS A.1889.527), a wooden kava bowl that would have been important for chiefly rituals on Aneityum (NMS A.1889.563), and a *navela* (stone money) from Erromango (NMS A.1895.413.104). The collection also includes a variety of pendants and other objects of personal adornment, including the ubiquitous combs and coconut shell armbands. There is a child's pendant made of a crustacean claw (NMS A.1895.413.48), one of the only missionary-collected objects attributed specifically to Melanesian childhood. There are seven greenstone pendants in the NMS collection, one of which is attributed to Aneityum (NMS A.1889.580a). Greenstone pendants were traditional exchange items from New Caledonia (Aubert de la Rüe 1938). New Caledonia was closely connected to southern Vanuatu via maritime exchange routes. Tanna and Aneityum particularly had close ties to the Loyalty Islands (Dubois 1996; Spriggs 1997: 219–220). Connections from southern Vanuatu to the west are also represented in cord spear-throwers or 'doigtier' (NMS A.1895.413.30, 31) that had a common form between the Loyalty Islands, Tanna, and Aneityum. While it is unknown whether these things were directly exchanged, they certainly could represent common ancestry or sharing of technology between these islands (Etheridge 1899).

Table 5.3 Southern Vanuatu objects in the Lawrie collections in National Museum of Scotland and Museums Glasgow.

Object Name	Aneityum	Aniwa	Erromango	Futuna	Tanna	Grand Total
Adze, stone	4					4
Bamboo					1	1
Basket	2	1		5		8
Belt	1					1
Blindfold	1					1
Box				1		1
Canoe Model	2			1		3
Carved Bamboo			4			4
Club			4		2	6
Coconut Shell Armband				7		7
Comb	1		1			2
Coral	1					1
Doigtier/Spear Thrower	2					2
Drill Bit	1					1
Earring				1	1	2
Feather Ornament	2				3	5
Fish Gouge	2					2
Flute	1					1
Greenstone Pendant	2					2
Hair					1	1
Headrest			1			1
House Model	1					1
Kava Bowl	2					2
Magic Stone	2					2
Neck Rest	2					2
Necklace	2					2
Pearl Shell				2		2
Pearl Shell Ornament				19		19
Pendant	1					1
Quiver/Arrows			1			1
Shell Armlet				1		1
Shell Ornament					1	1
Shell Scraper	8					8
Skirt	3		6		1	10
Sleeping Mat	1					1
Sling	1					1
Stone Money			1			1
Tapa			4			4
Tapa Beater			2			2
Throwing Club				1	3	4
Tortoise Shell				1		1
Whale's Tooth Pendant				3		3
Wooden Tool	1					1
Grand Total	46	1	24	42	13	126

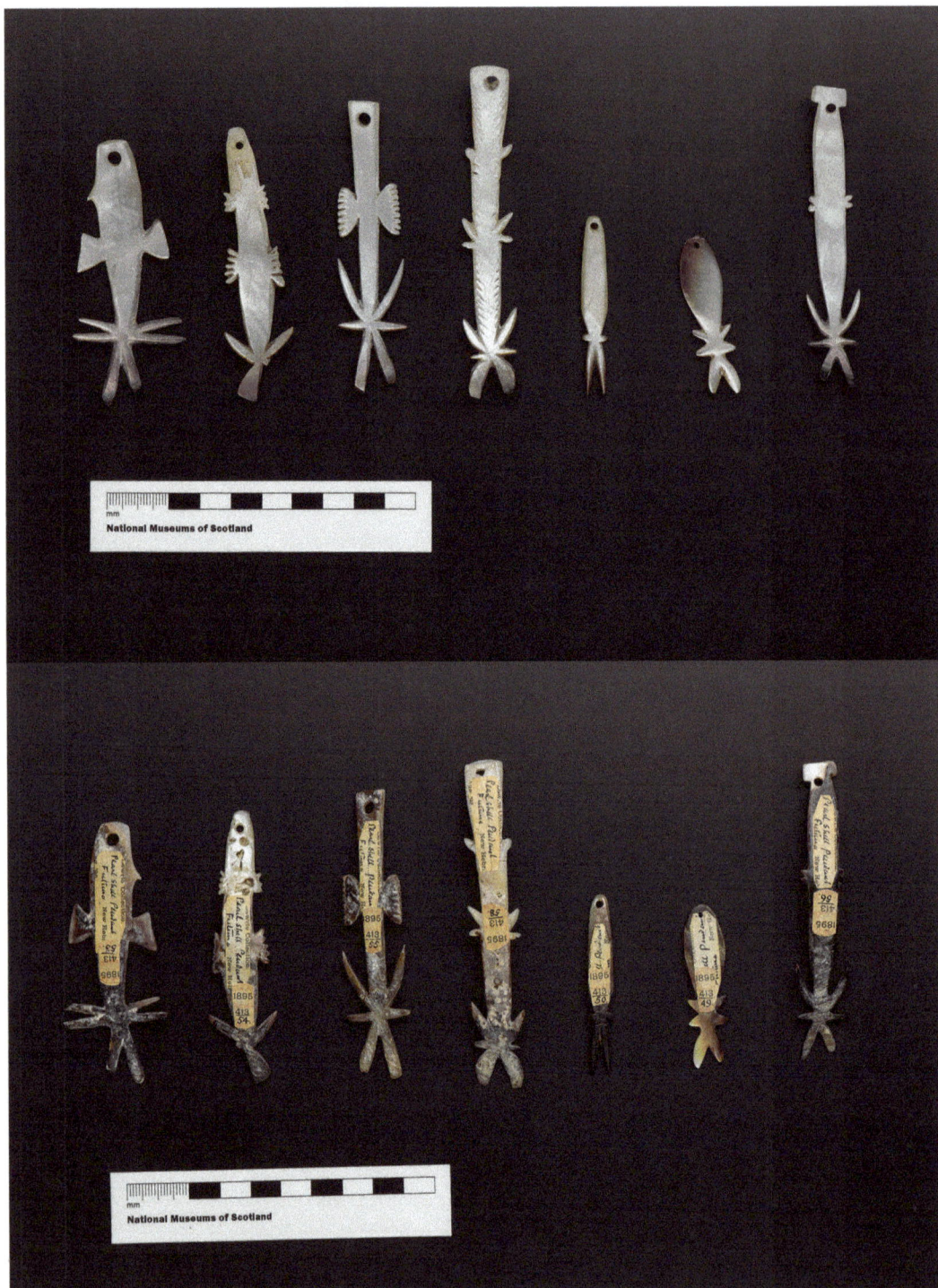

Figure 5.9 Pearl shell pendants.

Source: Image courtesy National Museum of Scotland.

The collection also includes cut and polished pearl shell pendants with forms representing antlion larvae, lizards, and flying foxes (Figure 5.9). Of the 20 examples in the NMS collection, 19 are attributed to Futuna (NMS A.1889.576, A.1895.413.49, 50, 53, 54, 55, 56, 58, 61, A.1924.806). Pearl shell pendants were a widespread form as well. The style was even reproduced in the Torres Strait after a Tannese man shipwrecked on Mer taught it to some of the local islanders (Haddon 1912: 45). Some of the items of adornment represent the incorporation of foreign materials into traditional forms, as with a tortoise shell ear ornament from Futuna with two hoops made from bent iron nails attached to the shell (NMS A.1895.413.71). There are three whale's tooth pendants from Futuna in the Lawrie collection (NMS 1895.413.45, 45a, 47), as well as a necklace with four such pendants and *Conus* shell rings from Aneityum (NMS A.1889.575). These would have been important prestige valuables in their indigenous context.

Museums Glasgow

Museums Glasgow also holds a large assemblage of objects originally collected by Lawrie in the 1880s and 1890s while he was stationed on Aneityum. As at NMS, they have southern Vanuatu pendants of greenstone (Museums Glasgow 1897.143.bx, by), pearl shell (Museums Glasgow 1897.143.bo.1–3), and whale's tooth (Museums Glasgow 1897.143.bz, ca, cb, cc). As Cook observed on Tanna in 1774:

> Both sex wear ornaments, such as braclets, Earings, necklaces and Amulets; the braclets are schiefly worn by the men and made of Sea Shells and others of Cocoa nut shells, Amulets is a nother Ornament worn by the Men, those of most Value are made of a greenish stone; the green stone of New zeland was valued by them for this purpose. Necklaces were chiefly worn by the women and made mostly of shells; Ear Rings were worn in common, those Valued most were made of Tortoise shell, some of our people got this shell at the Friendly isla[n]ds [Tonga] and brought it here to a good market it being of more value to these people than any thing we had besides … (Beaglehole, ed. 1969: 505–506, spelling as in original).

In keeping with Lawrie's habit of also acquiring examples of raw material, these pendants are accompanied by two large pearl shells that have been partly cut for pendant blanks (Museums Glasgow A.1897.143.bp1, 2), and a large piece of tortoise shell (Museums Glasgow 1897.143.bb). The assemblage of raw materials and tools further includes three stones 'used for scraping [polishing] bows' (Museums Glasgow 1897.143.ak.1–3), and a dried piece of kava root (Museums Glasgow 1897.143.ao).

The Museums Glasgow assemblage of Lawrie objects contains other items that do not appear in the NMS collections. For example, there is a long club or staff of hard wood with a triangular projection at the top, which is probably a traditional dance club from Aneityum (Museums Glasgow 1897.143.e). Both NMS and Museums Glasgow included Erromangan items of adornment, including *nemasitse* (barkcloth) and *numplat* (grass skirts). Museums Glasgow examples also included a skirt from Aneityum that alternated light strips of pandanus with darker strips, possibly young tree fern branches (Museums Glasgow 1897.143.ds). There was also a skirt made entirely of this darker material (Museums Glasgow 1897.143.du), which was described as a mourning dress.

The collection includes some significant objects from Tanna, some of which derive from non-missionary donations, though their origins are not known from the existing documentation. These include a 1924 accession from 'Miss A.M. Dougan' and a 1945 accession from Mrs McGavin. A fairly unique object included in the Museums Glasgow collection comes not from Lawrie, but McGavin, who donated a 'witchdoctor's purse', which consists of a conical bag of matted spiderwebs (A.1945.16a; similar objects are held in the Auckland Museum). This would have belonged to a *Tupunas* and may have been an object of some fear and power in its time. Generally, such objects have been associated exclusively with missionary collections (Flexner 2016b), and further research into how this object wound up in the Museums Glasgow collections might be informative in this regard. The later date may indicate changing patterns of Melanesian exchange with outsiders over the course of colonial history (Torrence and Clarke 2013).

There are two strands of human hair that has been plaited in the traditional fashion, one from Lawrie and one from Dougan (Museums Glasgow 1897.143.cp, 1924.48ah). Tannese men's hairstyle was an object of much admiration and interest among European observers, including missionaries. As one of the early ethnographers on Tanna observed:

> The native method of hair-dressing is remarkable. A curved wooden frame is used for supporting the neck of the victim, who lies on the ground on his back while the hair-dresser does his work. Beginning at the forehead, strands of hair are plaited with a twine made of fibre from the inner bark of a certain tree. The hair is pulled so tight that a headache lasting for several days often results from a dressing. The whole process is a lengthy one, for, as the hair grows, additional strands of fibre are added. Colour is now seldom used, but in earlier days these wisps would be coloured red or black. When the work is finished, all the plaits are drawn back from the forehead and a band is passed over the head from ear to ear, to hold the dressed hair in place (Humphreys 1926: 38–39).

In the 1840s, Turner (1861: 78) counted over 700 such plaits on a young man's head. This collection includes an example of the 'curved wooden frame' used for the plaiting process (Museums Glasgow 1897.143ac). These plaits are associated today with young men's preparations for major dance ceremonies on Tanna, especially the *toka* dance (see Chapter 3). Widows were also said to have worn locks of their deceased husbands' hair around their necks (Humphreys 1926: 90). Combined with the mourning skirt noted above, perhaps Lawrie attempted to collect objects related to all aspects of daily life, including those that involved mediating relationships with the dead.

Hunterian Museum, Glasgow

The Hunterian Museum holds two significant missionary collections: those of George Turner, who spent a brief time on Tanna and occasionally visited the New Hebrides afterwards (Turner 1861); and those of Agnes and William Watt, who lived on Tanna from 1869 (Watt 1896). The collection was being relocated at the time of survey, so only a handful of objects could be observed. Included in the objects from the Turner collection was a polished cylindrical basalt *kawas* or throwing club (Hunterian E.432). Turner (1861: 81) noted, 'It is about the length of an ordinary counting-house ruler, only twice as thick, and that they throw with deadly precision when their victim is within twenty yards of them'. Also included is a wooden 'canoe model', which is perhaps better described as a canoe-shaped kava bowl, from Aneityum (Hunterian E.406). The original inscription from Turner's time, written directly on the canoe in pencil and now illegible, apparently indicated that the canoe was said to have belonged to Aichirai and Nepatimepeke, the gods who had pulled Aneityum from the sea. Turner also collected two pipes, which were long, thin pieces of dark bamboo, apparently used for smoking tobacco (Hunterian E.383, 383.1). The bamboo is identified as 'native to New Caledonia' in the catalogue notes, so may indicate the close connections between that island group and southern Vanuatu.

The Hunterian holds five clubs donated by Agnes Watt in 1894 (Hunterian E.548.1–5). As noted above, the Annands and Watts occasionally swapped native curios (Smith 2005: 268). Three of the Watt clubs are Erromangan in style, one the star-headed *telugohmti* and two of the spindle-headed *netnivri* form. The other two clubs are 'spurred clubs' from Fiji. It is not totally clear how these could have ended up in the Watts possession to be donated to the Hunterian Museum, and without further documentary research the possibilities are too broad to merit speculation. The missionary collections of the Hunterian Museum are likely to offer other interesting data, and certainly deserve further research.

University of Aberdeen Museums

The missionary collections in the University of Aberdeen Museums derive primarily from two missionary collectors. Rev. F. G. Bowie was based in Tongoa at the Teachers Training Institute, succeeding Rev. Joseph Annand, who was likewise a keen collector. Bowie's missionary career, which focused on south Santo, lasted from 1896 until 1933. He headed the Teacher's Training Institute for the last 20 years of his career (Miller 1985: 264–272). The other component of the collection comes from Rev. Ross, who was based in New South Wales, but had close connections to the New Hebrides Mission. Ross bequeathed his collection of New Hebrides and Australian objects to the Aberdeen Museum in 1900 (Daily Free Press 1900). The objects were part of the collection of Museum of Marischal College, which has since been absorbed into the University of Aberdeen Museums.

Objects from the Bowie collection come primarily from Espiritu Santo and Malekula, the islands near his base at Tongoa. However, there were 19 objects from the southern New Hebrides, covering Aneityum (N=2), Erromango (N=11), Futuna (N=3), and Tanna (N=2). In addition, there were 15 objects identified generically to the New Hebrides. Included among the latter group was a set of coconut shell armbands (Aberdeen ABDUA.65409–65411) from the Ross collection, which would have been typical of the southern islands. The Futuna objects consist of three pearl shell ornaments from the Bowie collection (Aberdeen ABDUA.65413–65415). The collection also includes two Tannese-style star-headed clubs (Aberdeen ABDUA.3016, 3017), which are much more robust, and not so intricately carved as the Erromangan *telugohmti* (see e.g. Adams 1998: 35). Presumably the Tanna clubs were used more often for actual combat than the Erromangan versions, which appear to have been more for display and ceremonial functions. There were also two examples of *telugohmti* (star-headed clubs; Aberdeen ABDUA.3015, 3022) and six *netnivri* (spindle-headed clubs, Aberdeen ABDUA.3010–3014, 3082).

One of the more unusual finds in this collection is a shark's tooth dagger attributed to Erromango (Figure 5.10; Aberdeen ABDUA.39214). There are two labels associated with this object. The more detailed, and presumably older, one reads 'Shark's Tooth Kn[ife] from South Sea Islan[ds]. (?Erromanga) Presented Mrs Lawrence'. The object is quite clearly of the type produced in Kiribati in Micronesia (cf. British Museum Oc1895.-.697, Oc1921.0221.80). It is possible that we are looking at a simple error where the object was mislabelled either by the collector or as it entered and moved around museum stores over the years. Given the specificity of the attribution, though, there may be more to this (there are plenty of objects generically labelled 'South Seas', 'Polynesia', 'New Hebrides', or similar, but most objects attributed to a particular island are given that attribution for a reason). That said, even the old label indicates ambiguity about the origin of this object, so perhaps it was a case of overenthusiastic (and incorrect) attribution by a collector or museum employee.

There are several alternative possibilities that relate to the increasing mobility of Pacific Islanders over the course of the 1800s and early 1900s. During this time, people from throughout Oceania worked on ships' crews, and they moved around between different islands as labourers, often going to Fiji, Queensland (Australia), or New Caledonia to work on sugar plantations, mines, and other capitalist enterprises as part of the labour trade (Docker 1970; Moore 1992; Shineberg 1999). Both Kiribati and Erromango were part of these networks linking islands throughout the region in new ways during the colonial era. With this in mind, perhaps this dagger was given to an Erromangan labourer who had worked with an I-Kiribati on a plantation, brought it back to the island, and later traded it to Mrs Lawrence herself, or someone who gave it to her (Mrs Lawrence may have been the wife of Captain W.H. Lawrence who had been involved with the labour trade and other colonial endeavours in the Pacific). Alternatively, the object was produced by an Erromangan person in Kiribati style. Or perhaps, an I-Kiribati happened to be on Erromango at the time this object was exchanged with a European, and left its Oceanic context to become part of the global curiosities trade. Further documentary research would be needed to narrow down the list of possibilities. Regardless, these sorts of 'out of place' artefacts are important indicators of the increasing mobility of Pacific Islanders in the colonial era (Flexner 2016a).

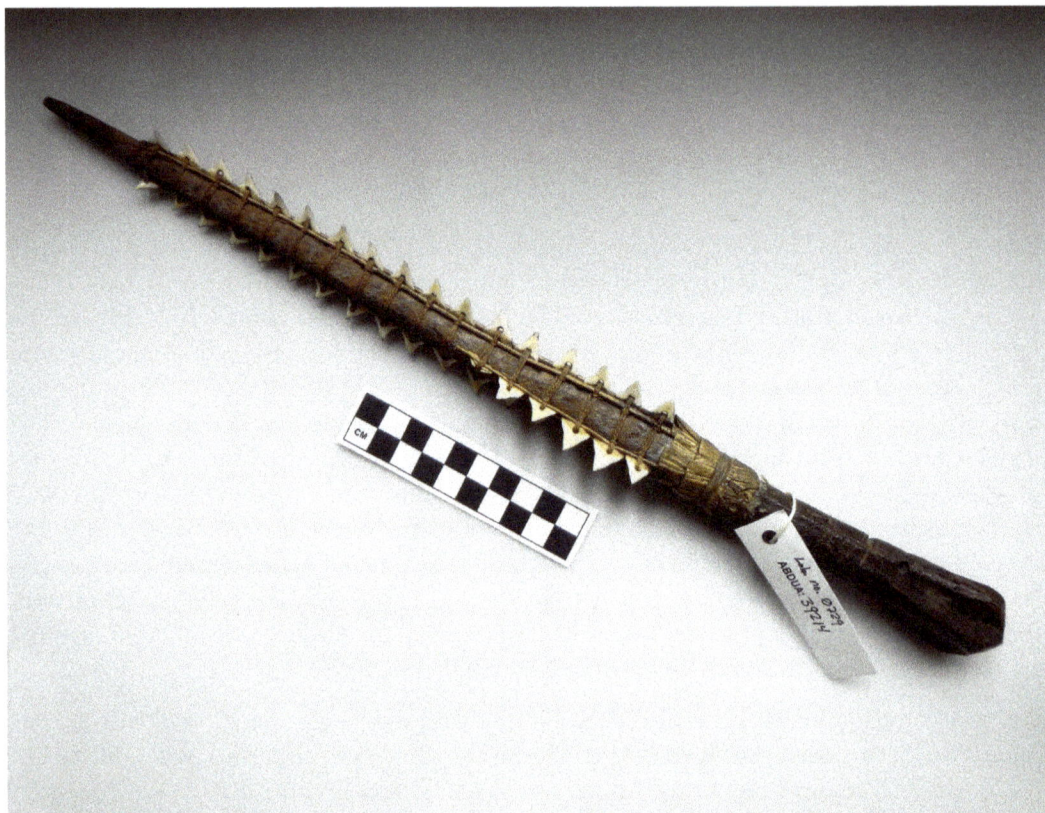

Figure 5.10 Shark's tooth dagger, said to be from Erromango but the form is typical of Kiribati.
Source: Image courtesy University of Aberdeen Museums.

Australasian Collections

Australia and New Zealand were important to Presbyterian mission endeavours in the New Hebrides. Australia especially served as a location where missionaries went on furlough, or as a stopping-off point on the way to and from the New Hebrides. It also served as a source of materials for the mission. Increasingly from the 1880s onwards, New Zealand and Australian churches directly supported mission work, including sending missionaries to the field in the New Hebrides. A result of these processes is accumulation of Vanuatu objects collected by missionaries in collections in the Australasian British settler societies of Australia and New Zealand. The missionary William Gray who worked on Tanna (see Chapter 4) was originally from South Australia, and provided a large number of objects now in the South Australian Museum, though these were not examined as part of this project (see Craig 2007).

Auckland War Memorial Museum

The Auckland Museum's missionary collections primarily derive not from the Presbyterian Mission, as in the other cases discussed here, but from the Anglican Melanesian Mission. The Melanesian Mission worked on an alternative model based on bringing Melanesian students to a central location to learn habits of prayer, bible reading, and other 'useful arts'. The mission was initially located at Mission Bay (Kohimarama) in New Zealand, near Auckland. Later the mission relocated to Norfolk Island (see Armstrong 1900; Hilliard 1978; Ross 1983). One of the Melanesian Mission buildings at Mission Bay (Figure 5.11) served as a museum displaying a collection of objects from the islands where the missionaries were active, including New Guinea, the Solomon Islands, northern Vanuatu, and the Torres Strait. This collection was later transferred to the Auckland Museum. A small sample of objects from the Auckland Museum (total N=35) is discussed here, including non-mission parts of the Auckland collection with objects from the southern New Hebrides.

Figure 5.11 Melanesian Mission building at Kohimarama/Mission Bay, formerly used as a museum displaying objects collected by the missionaries.

Source: James Flexner

The Anglican and Presbyterian missions in the New Hebrides enjoyed a close and amicable relationship, sharing supplies, information, and perhaps most importantly, ships (Miller 1978: 142–146). It is thus unsurprising that there are some objects from the southern New Hebrides in the Melanesian Mission collections, such as a *netnivri* (spindle-headed club; Auckland 25249/MEL.11). Other historical collections in the Auckland Museum include the W.O. Oldman collection and a collection of objects from James Edge Partington, who published a significant ethnological catalogue of Pacific objects with Charles Heape from 1890–1895 (Edge Partington and Heape 1969). Edge Partington also contributed a significant collection to the British Museum. The Oldman collection includes a coconut shell armband from Tanna (Auckland 31503/O.697), and a *netnivri* (Auckland 31829/O.585).

The Auckland Edge Partington collection includes a number of rare objects, among them an extremely rare *navela* (Erromangan stone money) from a non-missionary source (Auckland 14930/EP.Q53). There are also two cone-shaped bags of matted spider webs (Auckland 14363/EP.Q2, 14936/EP.Q64). These were originally listed as 'widow's caps', but this was probably a sensationalistic fabrication. Early missionaries did remark on the practice of widow strangulation on Tanna, which was said to have been imported from Aneityum (e.g. Turner 1861: 93–94). However, Turner never actually witnessed the practice, so claims about the commonness of the practice are likely exaggerated, and at any rate, there is no mention at all of the use of 'caps'. It is worth noting that a similar object in the Museums Glasgow collections is described as a sorcerer's bag. These objects may similarly have had some kind of magical or ritual function.

Other Edge Partington objects from southern Vanuatu include an adze blade from Aneityum (Auckland 14945/EP.Q93), a tapa beater (Auckland 14994/EP.Q134), barkcloth attributed to Aneityum (Auckland 14915/EP.Q37), and arrows from Erromango (Auckland 14902.1–7/EP.Q17–23). While not directly from the New Hebrides, two greenstone adzes from New Caledonia (Auckland 15039.1–2/EP.R103–104) are significant in relation to the labour trade. The collection notes indicate the adzes were used as a form of currency to entice people from the New Hebrides to work in New Caledonia. It is likely that at least some of the greenstone pendants on Tanna came about as a result of this type of exchange (see also Aubert de la Rüe 1938: 258–259).

While Edge Partington was a private collector who travelled widely in the South Pacific, it is also quite possible he was in contact with missionaries who may have been a source of curiosities. Further, it is likely that missionary activities contributed to the ease of acquiring objects. For example, Robertson notes that only Christian converts would part with *navela*, and even then only at a great price (Robertson 1902: 390). He also apparently encouraged Erromangan people to continue making clubs to trade (Robertson 1902: 372). Regarding greenstone pendants, Aubert de la Rüe (1938: 250) noted, 'Les indigènes évangelisés de côte n'ont pas le droit de les porter' ('Indigenous converts from the coast don't have the right to wear them'). Many pendants were likely given up for this reason, such as those mentioned above in the Lawrie collection. Even if missionaries were not directly involved in the curiosities exchange, their activities in some cases would have shaped the nature of those exchanges because of changing habits and perceptions of trade with Europeans among native converts.

The library of the Auckland Museum holds a significant object from the Presbyterian New Hebrides mission: a copy of an 1881 printing of Acts of Apostles in the Kwamera language (Figure 5.12). The book was printed at the Glasgow Foundry Boys Society Press, which arrived on Tanna from Scotland in 1873 (Watt 1896: 150). The production of such an object on Tanna may have taken on a localised meaning, as some Melanesians appear to have believed that missionaries worshipped the book itself as a magical object, rather than the words within the book. Printing of Biblical texts in local language also hybridised the concepts contained in the words, as Tannese words for concepts like 'spirit', 'lord', and so on provided indigenous signifiers for Christian concepts (Adams 1984: 112–113). Other such texts survive in libraries in New Zealand and Australia, and offer important records both of religious translation, and indigenous languages as practiced in the 19th century.

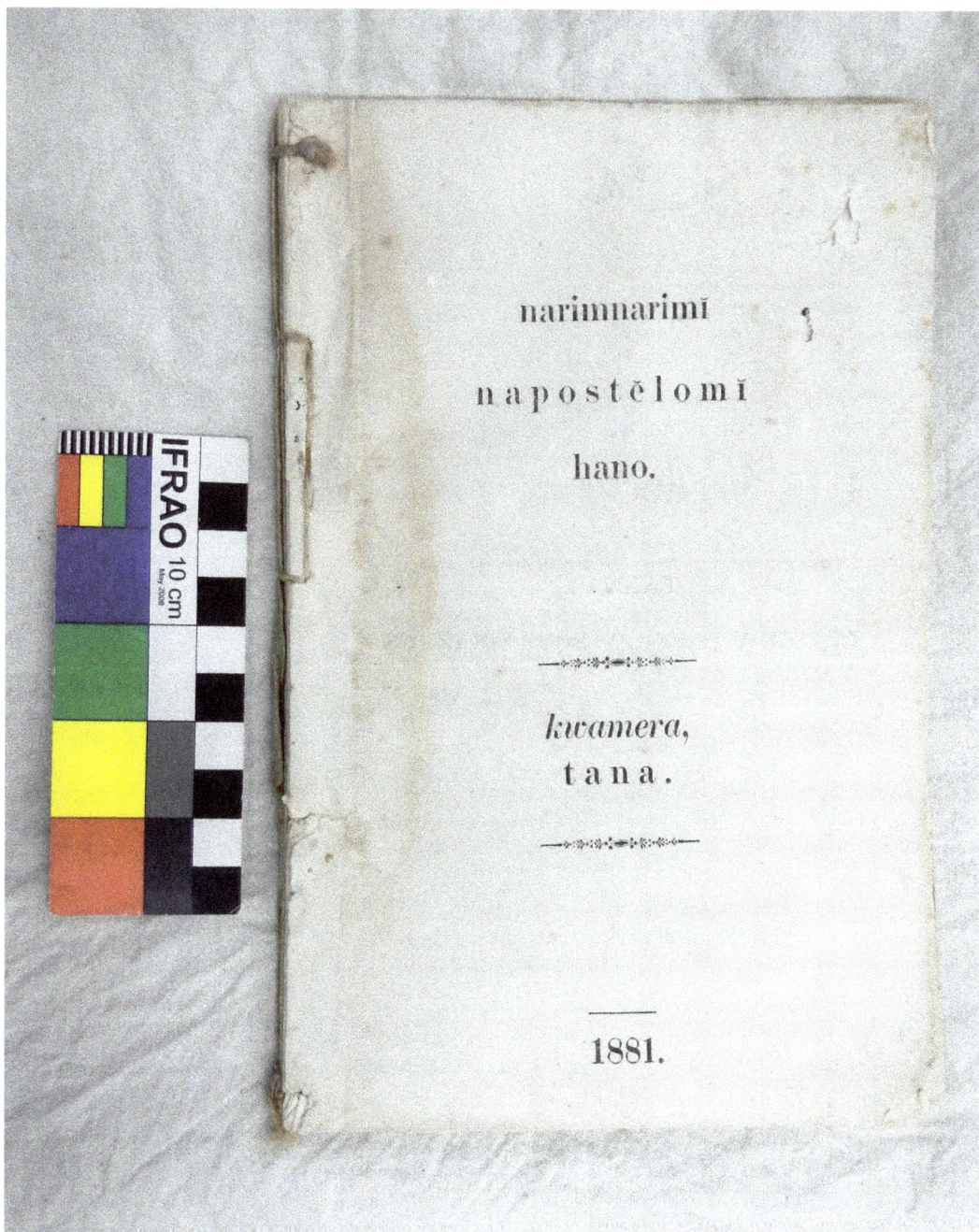

Figure 5.12 Acts of Apostles in the Kwamera language, printed at the Glasgow Foundry Boys Society Press on Tanna by William Gray in 1881.

Source: Image courtesy Auckland War Memorial Museum.

Otago Museum

As at the Hunterian, the Otago Museum's collections were in the course of being relocated at the time of survey, so only a limited number of objects could be examined (N=18). Dunedin, where the Otago Museum is located, was the home of several Presbyterian missionaries, including Peter Smaill, Oscar Michelson, and William Milne, who served in the New Hebrides (Miller 1987: 127–131, 344–353, 385–404; Miller 1989: 19–26). Milne and Smaill contributed a small amount of material to the museum, largely from the central and northern islands of Vanuatu.

At this time not enough documentary evidence has been collected in relation to the other objects in the collection to determine a definite source. However, for the southern Vanuatu materials, I would suggest that the objects derive from someone with close ties to the islands, as the assemblage includes many sacred or otherwise culturally significant things.

Within the sample, 15 objects were from the southern islands, covering Tanna (N=7), Erromango (N=5), and Futuna (N=3). Objects from Tanna include a highly polished greenstone pendant suspended on a piece of red trade cloth (Otago D35.1440), a set of pan pipes (Otago D92.82), and a pearl shell pendant of the antlion larva form (Otago D57.151). There are two coconut shell armbands, one from Tanna (Otago D57.158) and the other attributed generically to the New Hebrides, but probably from Tanna or Erromango (Otago D24.2026). Tools are represented by two coral abraders from Futuna (Otago D23.885, D24.1836). The Erromango objects included one example of a *telugohmti* (club; Otago D25.1314), and a remarkable four *navela* (stone money; Otago D21.214, D24.1798, D25.326, D65.1297), including examples of both the ring-shaped and crescent forms. There is also a 'sacred stone' attributed to Futuna (D24.2614), which appears to be a fragment of a Tanna-style *kawas* (basalt throwing club). It should be noted that generally throwing clubs from Futuna were made of coral, while basalt *kawas* were more common on Tanna. It is possible this object was exchanged, and may have been related to some part of a story relating to warfare or warriors when it was broken and brought to Futuna. A similar fragment was collected from the surface on Futuna in the 1960s by the Shutlers during their archaeological survey of the island (Shutler et al. 2002: 196). A stone from Tanna (Otago D57.153) is listed in the catalogue as a 'death stone'. The form is similar to stone throwing clubs illustrated in Speiser (1966[1923]: Plate 59).

Australian Museum

The Australian Museum, Sydney, has a large and significant collection of southern New Hebrides objects. Major portions of the collection derive from H.A. Robertson and J.H. Lawrie, complementing these missionaries' collections in Canada and Scotland. The objects from Robertson were registered over a 20-year period from 1897–1917. Earlier accessions may have been portions of larger shipments, with some of the objects going to Montreal. Lawrie sold both objects and photographs to the museum in 1922, and his connection to the Australian Museum makes sense considering his mission work and residence in New South Wales. There is also a smaller collection of objects from Captain Braithwaite, longtime captain of the Presbyterian mission ship *Dayspring*. Among the objects Braithwaite donated were five 'coral gods' from Futuna, which would have been great prizes collected by the captain of the mission ship. As noted above, though, that mission agents were able to attain such sacred items (assuming they were traded voluntarily) was not so much an expression of 'Christian triumph', as of Melanesians entrapping outsiders into local exchange networks, or possibly gaining distance from objects that had become spiritually dangerous for various reasons. Among the non-missionary donors with objects represented in the collection is Sutherland Sinclair, an early secretary of the Australian Museum who kept up correspondence with Robertson (Etheridge 1917; Lawson 1994a: 52). This reflects the professional relationships formed via engagement of missionaries with ethnological pursuits.

Like the other museums with collections from Robertson and Lawrie, the southern islands were represented by large numbers of objects, including 120 objects from Erromango, 14 from Aneityum, 18 from Futuna, and 20 from Tanna. The Australian Museum holds an impressive assemblage of decorated Erromangan *nemasitse* (tapa or barkcloth). Australian Museum curators have been instrumental in processes of repatriation and renewal of this important cultural practice and art form, and engaging with creator communities more generally, particularly Erromangans (Carillo-Huffman et al. 2013; Christidis et al. 2009; Huffman 1996). Other forms of Erromangan material culture represented widely in other collections, including examples of *neko* (barkcloth beaters), *netnivri* and *telugohmti* clubs, *numplat* (grass skirt), carved coconut shell armbands, and *navela* (stone money). The collection also has a few examples of greenstone (Australian Museum E.27023, 27024) and pearl shell (Australian Museum E.27038–27040) pendants from Futuna. Other adornment items significant to the region are whale's tooth pendant necklaces, with one example each from Erromango (Australian Museum E.27036) and Aneityum (Australian Museum E.27037). The museum holds a large collection of throwing clubs, made from both coral and coarse-grained basalt.

One of the ways that the Australian Museum's early missionary collections differ is in the large amount of tools and raw materials, particularly in Robertson's Erromango collections. Such things do occur elsewhere in the Lawrie collections, and they are not entirely absent from the Redpath Museum assemblage of Robertson objects (for example, there is a small bag of red clay, 'eaten by the Erromangans as children'; Redpath Acc.1366). A similar red clay sample, described as yam root encrustations, and also said to have been 'eaten by the natives' was sent to the Australian Museum (E.22603) in a bottle still bearing the label for 'STEPHEN'S GLOUCESTERSHIRE PICKLES'. Overall, though, tools and raw material samples do not appear in such high numbers at the Redpath as they do in the Australian Museum. Perhaps they were not considered valuable enough to ship over such a long distance. Stone adze blades were ubiquitous in museum collections, but the Australian Museum has the largest number specifically attributed to Erromango (N=10). Other tools include bamboo drills, two with bits made from split pig canines (Australian Museum E.6138, 6140), and the other with a bit made of quartzite (Australian Museum E.6143). Also included were basically unmodified shell scrapers used for cleaning tubers and other crops (e.g. Australian Museum E.7407–7409). Similar examples were collected by Lawrie.

Among the various raw materials Robertson collected, there were samples of wood from the *worenevau* ('bastard cotton') tree, which was used as a construction material for Erromangan houses as well as twine, and the bark used for *nemasitse* (Australian Museum E.12405.001–002); and *mori* ('acacia') used in fence posts as well as bows (Australian Museum E.17585, 22591.001–002). There were also numerous seeds, presumably presented to the museum as natural history specimens. Included among these items that span the 'nature/culture' boundary are a large number of candlenuts, which were used as a source of light in Erromangan houses. These appear both individually (Australian Museum E.12409.001–008), and in 'strings' now held on metal skewers (Australian Museum E.7431–7440). The collection includes stone samples of calcite as a raw material for *navela* (Australian Museum E.7449–7464, 7844–7845). That Robertson sent such a large number of basically identical stone samples to the Australian Museum suggests he may have thought they would be distributed more widely. The other stone sample was said to be of the kind of stone used in axe production (Australian Museum E.7420). However, the coarse-grained basalt sample is markedly different from the adze blades, and would not be ideal tool material, suggesting Robertson had limited understanding of the local lithic technology (which, indeed, was probably largely disappearing as iron tools became ubiquitous by the end of the 1800s).

Rare objects in the Australian Museum New Hebrides collections include a men's barkcloth belt from Tanna (Australian Museum E.43430), which came from a non-missionary collector, Mrs E.A. Freeman, in 1934. There are also several magic stones from Tanna, including a yam stone, also from a relatively later non-missionary collector. The presence of potentially ritually significant objects in non-missionary collections after the 1930s inverts the pattern seen in 19th-century collections, where only missionaries had access to sacred things. This perhaps reflects changing patterns in indigenous exchange habits, where objects that had once been withheld from outsiders became strategic in creating ties as the nature of colonial relationships in the New Hebrides changed over the course of the 20th century (for a comparative study from New Guinea see Torrence and Clarke 2013). This takes us somewhat beyond the scope of this project, but would be an interesting line of inquiry for future research.

Non-Missionary and Unexamined Collections

A number of collections were not included in this survey due to constraints in time and funding. Missionary William Gray, who was stationed at Waisisi (see Chapter 4), donated a large collection of objects to the South Australian Museum, which included a significant assemblage of southern Vanuatu materials (Craig 2007). The ethnographer Felix Speiser carried out one of the first major ethnographic surveys in the New Hebrides (Speiser 1996[1923]). Speiser collected a large number of objects himself, which are primarily held at the Museum für Volkerkunde in Basel. Speiser also purchased objects for the museum, including a collection from Aubert de la Rüe (Kaufmann 1996: 306), the French geologist who first published a detailed account of Tannese greenstone pendants (Aubert de la Rüe 1938). These and other important early New Hebrides collections, such as that of the Musée du Quai Branly in Paris, would doubtless provide additional valuable data, and may be included in future research.

Weltmuseum

I was able to include two museums with Vanuatu materials that derive exclusively from non-missionary sources in the survey. The Weltmuseum in Vienna holds two significant collections. The first consists of objects collected by Johann Reinhold Forster during the second expedition of Captain Cook. The expedition spent several weeks at Port Resolution (see Chapter 3; Beaglehole, ed. 1969: 482–509). The Weltmuseum holds a wooden headrest of the type used in the process of men's hairdressing on Tanna (Weltmuseum 000008; Figure 5.13; Humphreys 1926: 38–39) and a set of pan pipes (Weltmuseum 000001). Pan pipes generated some interest among 19th-century scholars because of the possible relationship between shared musical traditions and prehistoric migrations (O'Reilly and D'Albe 1893).

More significant for this study is a collection of objects from the voyage of the SMS *Fasana*, a ship of the Austro-Hungarian Navy, which stopped at Umpongkor (Dillon's Bay), Erromango, in 1889 (Von Jedina 1891). There are at least 41 objects from Erromango in this collection, including 27 arrows and four bows. The bow (*nefane*) was traditionally made from a section of trunk from a *mori* (or *moré*) tree. The wood was split with an axe, and then polished and shaped using a pig's tusk. The bowstring (*nelas*) was made from the inner part of the hibiscus bark. Arrows (*nagesau*) were made of a shaft of straight cane with a hardwood tip, which could be barbed or not. The arrows were not fletched, but had a fine cord of coconut husk wrapped around each end of the shaft (Robertson 1902: 370–371). The *Fasana* collection also included wooden clubs of the *netnivri* (spindle-headed; Weltmuseum 041639, 041660) and *telugohmti* (star-headed; Weltmuseum 041640) forms. There are also three *numplat* (grass skirts; Weltmuseum 041643, 041645, 041646). Considering the date and location, the crew of the *Fasana* almost certainly would have interacted with Rev. Robertson, and these objects may have been examples that were produced specifically for trade by local people at Dillon's Bay, encouraged by the missionary (Robertson 1902: 372). Also included in the *Fasana* collection is a dance girdle with a wooden back support and strings of beads on the front, which is attributed to Erromango but of a form traditional on Espiritu Santo (Edge Partington 1969 Vol. 2: 76).

Figure 5.13 Polished wooden headrest, Tanna. (Weltmuseum; Inv. Nr. 8, Neckrest, Island of Tanna, New Hebrides, Vanuatu, Coll. James Cook [1774], Weltmuseum Wien 1806 [former: Museum für Völkerkunde, Wien, 1806]. Polished wood [the root of a tree, mangrove ?]. Measurements: L. 28.5 cm, W. 12.5 cm, H. 17 cm.)
Source: Gabriele Weiss, Weltmuseum.

Queensland Museum

The Queensland Museum holds the other non-missionary collection examined as part of this survey. Many of the Vanuatu objects in the collection were donated by a Dr Marks in 1920, who served as a physician for South Sea Islanders working on Queensland sugar plantations. Other early donors included L.H. Maynard (accessioned 1912), Mrs H. Seaton (accessioned 1909), and the 'Home Department', Brisbane (accessioned 1914). The collections included 11 clubs, nine of which were attributed to Erromango and two to Tanna. These included examples of both *netnivri* (e.g. Queensland E1049), and *telugohmti* (Queensland E6984). However, there are several examples attributed to an island that doesn't match the traditional club forms. One of the 'Tanna' clubs appears to be a form attributed to Tanna, Efate, and possibly Ambrym (Queensland E.5772; Speiser 1996[1923]: Plates 57–60), while an Erromango club is a form typical of Efate (Queensland E.5589). There is also a club attributed to Erromango that is the more robust Tannese form (Queensland E.1059).

These could be interpreted as simple errors in attribution, especially where objects were obtained indirectly. However, we should also consider the increasing mobility of Pacific Islanders over the course of the 19th century because of opportunities on whaling ships, labour traders, and so on. Especially in multicultural contexts like plantations, where people from many islands were in the same place, we might expect islanders to trade objects among themselves, or even learn new styles. This could further explain why objects that are stylistically 'typical' of one island were attributed to another. There were of course already traditional routes linking Tanna to Erromango, and Erromango to Efate, but where more far-flung connections are possible, it is likely these emerged from new forms of labour migration over the course of the late 1800s and early 1900s.

Where missionary collections are informative for understanding the extended social networks of Melanesian objects created through exchange, non-missionary collections provide an interesting comparative perspective. First, sacred objects such as stone money or other magic stones are basically absent from 19th-century non-missionary collections. Much more common are the arrows, clubs, and other objects that could generally be made quickly and cheaply for exchange with visiting Europeans. The commonness of these objects can be interpreted as an indication of attempts to demonstrate the 'warlike' qualities of Pacific peoples. However, it is also likely that in many cases, this was all that was being offered to European visitors who didn't have close connections to local communities (Thomas 1991: 138, 165). A lack of familiarity might also explain the number of 'mis-attributed' objects in the non-missionary collections. As mentioned above, though, the possibility of wider indigenous movements of people as well as things during the colonial era should not be ruled out to explain this phenomenon (Flexner 2016a).

6

Material Patterns and Colonial Religious Change

The places and objects discussed in the preceding chapters reflect a material process by which Christianity became Melanesian in the first nine decades of missionary endeavours on Tanna and Erromango. Inverting the narrative of native conversion and culture change typical of missionary accounts, I read these materials as showing the ways that Christianity was integrated into indigenous *kastom* in the New Hebrides. This is not a simple matter of 'revisionist' history, but the result of a critical reading of material facts in the form of archaeological data from Melanesian landscapes, limited stratigraphic excavations across a range of sites, and artefacts recovered both in the field and in museum contexts. It is about using archaeological data to replace colonial myths with a more realistic portrayal of Oceanic cross-cultural encounters (see also Flexner 2014a: 76).

The story is about Melanesians, and about new kinds of social and material networks that emerged out of relationships with European missionaries. Missionaries had their own identities and ambitions in regard to these encounters, which were almost always undermined in some way by the local context. In one sense, the mission was a success. As mentioned before, Vanuatu is a largely Christian country, in which the Presbyterian Church remains one of the central institutions (Flexner and Spriggs 2015: 187). The form of Melanesian Christianity in Vanuatu, on the other hand, emerges from a historical context in which local people resisted and transformed the foreign religion into something that could fit into existing, and adaptable, forms relating to *kastom*. Missionaries also had to compromise and adapt to the local situation. Transformations of missionary habits reflect the realities of geographic remoteness from Europe, living in a tropical environment, and finding a way in the Melanesian social world in which they settled.

Throughout the process of religious change in colonial Tanna and Erromango, there was conflict, and there was violence on both sides. Missionaries could be killed or driven away, especially early on, as happened repeatedly on Erromango (Gordon, ed. 1863; Robertson 1902) and Tanna (Adams 1984; Patterson 1864; Turner 1861). Missionaries used their foreign connections to carry out military action against intransigent islanders, as happened with the *Curaçoa* affair (Adams 1984: 150–167). Later missionaries on Tanna, overconfident in their successes, tried to violently repress *kastom*, a move that only succeeded in further entrenching Melanesian beliefs and practices (Bonnemaison 1994: 201–256).

> Tanna's Christian kingdom collapsed in one blow, without the use of violence or any subversive plan. The new John Frum myth and the power of dreams were enough to shatter it. Nearly all Presbyterian model villages – carefully laid out around a central lawn where church, school, and bell were in proximity – became empty (Bonnemaison 1994: 226; see also Guiart 1956: 163).

Yet in their own ways, many people came back to the church on Tanna. On the island, Sundays (and for Seventh Day Adventists and Mormons, Saturdays) are days of worship in many villages. Hymns are sung, scripture read, and sermons given. But as the sun begins to set, men still retire to the *imwarim* to listen to the kava. The *toka* dance still records the year's events and prepares for the next year. Magic stones still make the yams grow, even in ostensibly Christian villages. While 20th-century resistance was less dramatic on Erromango, *kastom* found a way, and today the island is seeing something of a renaissance represented by ongoing work by Vanuatu Kaljoral Senta fieldworkers and the Erromango Cultural Association (Christidis et al. 2009; Naupa, ed. 2011). Here too the pattern is not a 'pure' return to traditional life, but a synthesis of Christian and Melanesian beliefs and practices. This should not be seen as an unresolved dialectic, but a successful negotiation of colonialism. Melanesian people managed to integrate the formidable god of the missionaries into their universe without surrendering *kastom*'s core substance. The archaeological argument is that material things made this compromise possible.

Material Patterns in the New Hebrides Missions

Archaeological research on mission encounters on Tanna and Erromango revealed a number of patterns relating to everyday life and the material aspects of religious conversion. Missionaries moved into densely settled island landscapes that contained gardens, villages, and ceremonial structures. Physical settlement was linked to a symbolically rich world of places, stories, and spirits. These landscapes continued to evolve through the colonial era and into the present. Missionary sites and stories became a part of the pantheon of *kastom* space. Where mission stations were established, mission houses were an important locus of interaction. Mission houses reflect the performance of civilised Christianity by the mission family, as well as the necessity of adapting to the local context. They also show fleeting evidence for exchanges of labour, materials, and ideas between Melanesians and missionaries. The things exchanged were objects of fascination, speculation, desire, and derision on both sides. These phenomena provide a critical lens for understanding the material underpinnings of the missionary project, and the Melanesian incorporation of Christianity into *kastom*.

Landscapes of Conversion

Mission sites on Tanna and Erromango were embedded in Melanesian landscapes. Early explorers' accounts indicate that the islands were densely populated. For example, Cook records seeing over 1,000 people in a single gathering at Port Resolution in 1774 (Beaglehole, ed. 1969: 482–484). Over time, however, the population of the islands decreased dramatically because of introduced diseases. Particularly virulent outbreaks of measles, influenza, and cholera were noted in missionary accounts (e.g. Gordon, ed. 1863: 175; Turner 1861: 29–31). In some cases, as with the measles outbreak of 1860 on Tanna, there were not enough healthy people to bury the dead. Because missionaries had already identified themselves as having a special relationship to a particularly powerful spirit that caused illness, they were soon chased from the island (Adams 1984: 116–133). As populations continued declining in the closing decades of the 1800s, there was decreasing local resistance to missionary presence, as people aggregated in coastal settlements. Demography does appear to have played a role in the higher rates of conversion by the end of the 1800s. Further archaeological research, however, would be needed to refine our knowledge about the nature of demographic decline during the colonial era (Spriggs 1997: 235, 253–254, 2007).

Missionaries did not choose directly where to settle, but were limited to places that local chiefs allocated for them. Often, they were placed in perilous positions by being located on the boundaries between land divisions, as was the case for James Gordon at Potnuma, or on contested ground, as happened with John G. Paton at Port Resolution. This led to conflict, and in some cases the failure of mission settlements. Missionaries settled in a place that was populated not just by Melanesian people, but a host of spirits, ancestors, and other supernatural beings. Often these were materialised in trees, stones, and springs (e.g. Bonnemaison 1994: 176–178). In dismissing local 'superstitions', missionaries misunderstood the ways physical hazards, such as tropical disease, might be linked to place-based spiritual dangers. In many cases, mission stations were located on *tabu* ground. This was probably the case for the Watts at Kwamera, whose house was located on a burial ground that may have been inhabited by dangerous *ierehma* (spirits; Flexner and Willie 2015). Among Melanesian people, illness or death within the missionary family would have been interpreted in spiritual terms, a sign of the power of local spirits over the foreign god.

At the same time, missionaries worked to organise social space into a pattern that worked with their own cosmology. Land was cleared to make room for mission houses, church buildings, and other infrastructure. Cutting trees likely infringed on local usufruct rights, something about which the missionaries were probably unaware, but which would have furthered tensions with local people (Adams 1984: 60). In missionary terms, they were constructing an 'ordered' landscape in contrast to the 'disordered' space of the surrounding indigenous landscape. At Dillon's Bay, the missionary family had local converts build a massive complex of walls to demarcate this division. Local forms of spatial organisation, as with the networks of gardens, hamlets, and *imwarim* on Tanna, or the villages and *Siman lo* of Erromango, were generally dismissed as a native chaos if they were recognised at all (Robertson 1902: 375–376; Turner 1861: 84–85).

Over time, missionaries could access materials more effectively. Mission houses grew in size and elaboration (Table 6.1). More and more buildings were added to the mission infrastructure. Church services moved from simple outdoor ceremonies, to buildings of local materials, to imported kits using prefabricated materials from throughout the British Empire (Flexner et al. 2015a; Robertson 1902: 321–326). This increasing complexity of mission settlements correlates with increasing numbers of converts. Eventually the missionaries sought to shape local settlement patterns, building 'model villages' for Melanesian Christians. This is not a simple causal relationship of 'more stuff, more conversion', but a reflection of the feedback loops produced by the increasing influence of the Presbyterian Church on local affairs, and its increasing affluence because of connections to global trade networks. Yet the landscapes of Tanna and Erromango retained their Melanesian character. Archaeological evidence from Kwaraka and Anuikaraka shows continuity in the construction of stone structures in a village inhabited over at least four centuries. The networks of *imwarim*, hamlets, and gardens on Tanna, and the villages with their *Siman lo* on Erromango, remain today, often in the same villages that once aggregated around the mission.

Table 6.1 Increase in area from early (G. Gordon, J. Gordon, Imua) to later (Robertson, Watt) mission houses.

Site Name	Location	Date Range	Estimated House Size (m)*	Estimated House Size (ft)*
George Gordon House	Dillon's Bay, Erromango	1856–1861	8 x 5**	25 x 15**
Imua Mission	Imua, Tanna	1858–1862	6 x 4**	19 x 13**
James Gordon House	Potnuma, Erromango	1868–1872	10 x 5	32 x 16
Robertson House	Dillon's Bay, Erromango	1872–1900s	21.5 x 7	69 x 22
Watt House	Kwamera, Tanna	1869–1900s	18 x 8	58 x 25

* Rounded to the nearest foot or metre

** House size estimated only, further excavations needed

Domestic Dilemmas

Mission houses were one of the primary loci of interaction between missionaries and Melanesians. Household archaeology was identified early on as a fieldwork priority for this reason (Flexner 2013: 16–20). These houses had to be multipurpose spaces. They were to provide a safe and 'civilised' space for the mission family. Whitewashed lime mortar, window glass, and European furniture and domestic goods were necessary markers of difference when compared with native thatched houses and material culture. At the same time, the mission house was to serve as an exemplar to which potential converts were to aspire (if not actually to achieve). Despite concerns about theft or even violence, missionaries encouraged local people to explore parts of the house, and set things out specifically to incite their interest (Patterson 1864: 257; Robertson 1902: 193; Watt 1896: 81–82).

Part of the intended transformation of local domestic life by the missionaries had to do with the gendering of labour in Melanesian and Christian societies. Presbyterian missionaries in the southern New Hebrides were shocked by the labour conditions of native women not because of the amount of work they did, but because that work was seen as gendered inappropriately (Jolly 1992). The manual labour of gardening was seen as especially unfit for wives and mothers. It wasn't so much a matter of releasing native women from hours of hard work (though there is some evidence that missionary presence did reduce this; see Spriggs 1993), but that the drudgery had to be moved inside the home, which was the domain of properly feminine endeavours. Missionary women would have modelled this behaviour for their potential converts (Lindstrom 2013; Watt 1896).

Ironically, we know more archaeologically about the domestic assemblages of earlier mission houses than the larger, more elaborate stations. The early mission houses on Tanna and Erromango were abandoned suddenly when missionaries were killed or chased away. As a result, many of the domestic goods remain within and immediately around the house structure. At Imua, it appears that almost the entire household assemblage was left behind, including an almost complete set of transfer-printed tablewares. James Gordon House on Erromango similarly has a rich domestic assemblage. The ruins of post-1870s mission houses, in contrast, tend to be located within contemporary villages, and have thus been disturbed by ongoing 20th-century activities. In addition, the later houses were less likely to be abandoned suddenly. Missionaries who retired after a long career in the field likely took much of their household assemblage with them, aside from a few gifts left to friends on the island. With the later missions, a lack of consumer things in the archaeological record reflects the formation processes associated with planned departure, rather than sudden abandonment of the mission house, combined with ongoing inhabitation of the surrounding Melanesian village.

There is some scope for interpreting variability across these domestic assemblages. One common thread reflected in the faunal remains is missionary reliance on local marine resources, especially shellfish, as a source of protein. Missionaries would also have been heavily reliant on local vegetable produce as a supplement to imported flour and rice, if not a staple (Robertson 1902: 376–380; Watt 1896: 84). Another is the use of locally produced lime mortar as an architectural material. Whitewashed lime mortar was an important marker of civilised housing in contrast to local traditions (see also Mills 2009). Both of these indicate that local resources and labour were an integral part of mission life. Documentary evidence further indicates reliance on local girls as domestic servants (Robertson 1902: 189–193; Watt 1896: 80–81). Artefacts such as tobacco pipes and slate pencils, fairly ubiquitous on these sites (Table 6.2), reflect exchanges with local people. Pencils reflect exchanges of ideas and the technology of literacy, which was critical in Presbyterian conceptions of proper Christianity. In Protestant ideology, converts had to be able to read the Bible. Pipes were more of a trade good. There are many other materials, such as trade cloth, that do not preserve archaeologically but were nonetheless important to the process of material exchange.

Table 6.2 'Small finds', including indigenous and European trade items.

Object Name	G. Gordon House	Imua Mission	J. Gordon House	Kwaraka	New Kwaraka	Robertson Mission	Watt Mission	Grand Total
Abrader	2					2	1	5
Adze					2			2
Bottle Stopper			1					1
Ochre							1	1
Pendant							1	1
Pipebowl	1			1	1	2		5
Pipestem	1			2			2	5
Red Crystal							5	5
Slate Pencil	4	3	16				3	26
Grand Total	8	3	17	3	3	4	13	51

Domestic assemblages may reflect a certain degree of consumer choice among missionary families. Transfer prints at the early mission houses show distinctive motifs. George Gordon House yielded more 'Oriental' wares featuring pagodas and bamboo, James Gordon House yielded the 'Classical' Minerva pattern, while Imua yielded a remarkable assemblage of the 'Romantic-Pastoral' Arcadia pattern. The nature of 'choice' here must be understood with the caveat that domestic goods may have been donated to the mission cause. However, the extent to which the ceramic assemblages are internally consistent within each site, rather than being standardised across the sites, likely indicates that the missionaries could to some extent decide what kinds of household items to take with them. With the different kinds of transfer prints, missionaries may have had particular moralising ends in mind, as with the associations of Minerva with wisdom, or Arcadia with the pastoral paradise.

There is some evidence that mission houses took on increasingly localised material references. European ceramics were used to serve yams, island cabbage, fish, and shellfish gathered from reefs and beaches. Native 'curiosities' adorned walls and shelves around the house, with the red-slipped Ambae pottery at Potnuma providing a key archaeological example. Converts as well as missionaries likely mixed Western clothing with local shell necklaces, as suggested by the *Nerita* shell pendant from Imua. Domestic space in the New Hebrides was permeable. Missionaries simultaneously asserted their otherness in relation to Melanesian people through their houses, and filled the house with reminders that they were indeed far from their homeland (see also Rodman 2001).

Matter and Spirit

As missionaries exchanged objects with Tannese and Erromangan people, they were creating relationships that were more than simply economic (Adams 1984: 59). Missionaries were to greater and lesser degrees aware of this, especially considering the extent to which material and spiritual change were seen as linked. In Presbyterian as much as Melanesian cosmology, it would have been recognised that matter/spirit was a false dichotomy. Persons (or 'souls') lived at the confluence of the two elements. There was some extent to which personhood was 'dividual', attached to the things that people used, kept, and exchanged (Strathern 1990), on both sides of missionary encounters in the New Hebrides. Dividuality could extend into the spiritual realm as well. The spiritual world could to some extent be controlled by ritual action, though there was variability in belief about the extent to which spirits engaged in human affairs of their own accord (Douglas 1989).

On Tanna, '[f]lows of words, labour, goods, and substances built persons and personal character for the Watts and for the Tannese alike' (Lindstrom 2013: 259). Chiefship on Tanna involved to some degree the 'Heroic I' (Lindstrom 2011), in which achievements could be passed down across generations among people with shared names and titles. Thus personhood was also dividual historically. The Tannese also appear to have seen proper ritual knowledge and action by specialists as determining outcomes in relationships with the supernatural world, with definite ramifications for the human world (Douglas 1989: 12–13, 39). Magic stones made the yams grow. Others in the possession of *narak* sorcerers caused illness and death. Contact with *ierehma* (spirits) could be dangerous, even fatal (Bonnemaison 1994: 172–182; Humphreys 1926: 70–73). A similar situation existed on Erromango. *Natemas* spirits had to be propitiated with offerings. Magical specialists called *neteme sokowar* controlled the forces of the natural world, especially wind and rain. *Natemas evai* (magic stones) also caused illness and death (Humphreys 1926: 167–177; Robertson 1902: 389, 400–401).

Spiritual and social relationships were mediated through feasts, exchanges, and rituals. As missionaries entered the scene, they became entangled in the networks produced by these systems. At times, missionaries misunderstood the nature of what people were offering. Turner and Nisbet declined a propitiatory gift of a pig, shocked that they had been identified with sorcery (Adams 1984: 68; Douglas 1989: 15). This was despite the fact that they had insisted their god was the source of the new illnesses on Tanna. In declining the gift, Turner and Nisbet broke from the expected pattern, showing they had no interest in being propitiated. Tannese people had no option but to chase them away after that. Where missionary-sorcerers were killed or fled suddenly, their things were left behind. There may have been some worry that the *natemas* or *ierehma* of departed missionaries had a potentially dangerous presence in their objects. At Dillon's Bay, the mission house was burned some time after the Gordons were killed. At Imua, the mission house appears to have been left to decay naturally, and documentary evidence shows that missionary things placed in the boathouse downhill from the site were likewise avoided (Patterson 1864: 497–498).

For many Tannese and Erromangan people, the consumer items left behind by the missionaries may also simply have been uninteresting. Ceramic dishes were heavy, breakable, unwieldy, and not particularly functional for cooking or serving local cuisine. If bamboo or shell knives were more common than volcanic glass, as appears to have been the case, then bottle glass would not provide a useful analogue. Light and resilient bottles of bamboo would have been more desirable as water containers than fragile and heavy glass. Metal tools, cloth, and tobacco smoking paraphernalia were desirable, and were traded with the missionaries. Archaeologically, these things appear in remarkably low density in the surrounding settlements, at least on south Tanna. While further research is needed, the initial suggestion is that foreign objects were exchanged as much within indigenous networks as between missionaries and Melanesians, especially considering the increasing availability of trade goods through the sandalwood and labour trades. For some people, trading directly with a missionary may have been seen as a risky bargain, because of the possibility of wider spiritual ramifications from interacting with the foreign sorcerers.

New forms of exchange, such as the capitalist pattern of goods for labour, would have been interpreted in *kastom* as a mechanism for producing relationships rather than a simple payment where one category was traded for an equivalent amount from another. Missionaries saw any signs of apparent shifts towards a capitalist mindset in positive terms. Speaking of native converts' labour patterns, Robertson (1902: 388) enthusiastically declares: 'Remembering what thieves and beggars they [Erromangans] were when they were heathens, we are often amazed as well as encouraged and delighted at the wonderful change that has come over them in this, one of the highest and best tests of a good man.' The equation of being a good wage labourer with being a good man is telling when it comes to the missionary's perspective, but what of local perceptions of these exchanges? The cash economy did not replace feasts such as the *nisekar*. The last traditional *nevsem* was recorded in 1920, and the practice was revived in the 1990s (Naupa, ed. 2011: 24–26). Initial interactions with missionaries, interpreted as 'theft', were probably structured more by expectations of material exchanges as a prelude to forming social relationships. As Melanesians adapted and learned more about the foreigners, cash exchanges were possibly seen as a different form of ritual to pacify the missionaries and further draw them into local networks.

Where missionaries acquired local things, they interpreted them as 'curios' from the exotic Melanesians. Melanesians had their own reasons for engaging in this kind of trade (Flexner 2016b; see also Clarke and Torrence 2011; Torrence and Clarke 2013). Objects such as arrows, clubs (assuming they didn't hold any special value for the owner), combs, and grass skirts may have offered a means of acquiring valued things or social prestige with a minimum of spiritual danger. More sacred objects, such as *navela* (stone money) or magic stones may have been gifted as a means of diffusing their power. As populations collapsed, there may not have been an appropriate heir for some very powerful objects. But having the object present without an owner could have been socially and spiritually dangerous. These objects may also have offered a means of securing particularly close ties with powerful foreigners. Returning again to the idea that objects inhabited nodes in extensive social networks along with the people to whom they were connected, the context of a global exchange would have amplified connections between Melanesians and Europeans.

In a telling episode, Robertson (1902: 359–360) was gifted a number of sacred objects by a *Fan lo* (chief) from Port Narvin:

> When I visited [Noroseki] then in his large *siman-lo*, I saw that there was to be quite a ceremony. In the presence of two hundred of his people, the old chief laid down on the ground before me, one by one, all his idols or sacred stones, including the one he treasured most – a beautiful *navilah* called Nanepintaru, which is a woman's name […] One of these stones had a very small *numpelat* or 'skirt' tied to it; another, again, had a charm in the shape of a pierced shell. [… E]very now and again, while walking up and down between his relics, telling me the names and histories of one after another of them, he would stop, and, turning to those around us, plead with them to "take the word" which was then doing so much for so many on Erromango.

Robertson of course interpreted this ritual in terms of sincere conversion, but there is a more nuanced interpretation that could be made of the event. Rather than simply giving up his idols, perhaps in offering them to the missionary, Noroseki was using these objects to further incorporate Robertson, and the god he represented, into the Erromangan universe. Robertson couldn't actually become a member of the *Fan lo* class, that is, he couldn't 'become Erromangan', but he could become incorporated into Erromango to the extent that the foreign god would be legible and thus controllable for Erromangan people.

Melanesians would have understood the relationship between material and spiritual worlds, though not in the capitalist terms embraced by the missionaries (see Weber 2002[1905]). Material exchanges expanded the networks of social relationships that could be called upon to organise connections with the spiritual world, which in turn had impacts on the physical world. The god of the missionaries showed itself to be dangerous. One way of neutralising this danger was to entrap the newcomers who had the greatest influence over this entity within a web of local obligations and social connections. Objects offered a means of organising society such that foreign things, people, and spirits could be subsumed within the framework of *kastom*. *Kastom* was transformed through these interactions, but it remained the overarching social ecology organising everyday life through the medium of Melanesian people's actions.

Future Research Potential

While the findings of this project are significant, the results should be seen as a preliminary step. For Vanuatu, and to some extent Island Melanesia more broadly, historical archaeology is still in something of an 'exploratory' phase (Flexner et al. 2016b). Within the context of mission encounters and colonial archaeology, any of the sites discussed in this book would benefit from further investigation. Other aspects of southern Vanuatu's colonial archaeology merit future research, particularly the environmental and social impacts of the sandalwood and labour trades. The labour trade would be particularly interesting for reconnecting Melanesia with Australian South Sea Islander communities. Archaeologists are beginning to explore evidence for Melanesians in Queensland (Barker and Lamb 2011; Hayes 2002). There is an opportunity to follow Melanesians from their starting points in the islands, to Queensland, Fiji, or New Caledonia, and 'home' again in this kind of research.

On Tanna and Erromango, there is also great potential for research examining the overall histories of settlement, interaction, and landscape change from initial Lapita settlement through the colonial era (see Shutler et al. 2002; Spriggs 1986). Erromango is better known than Tanna in archaeological perspective (see Chapter 2, Chapter 3). Even on Erromango, archaeological research is primarily focused on a few coastal areas, with the interior of the island basically unknown. On Tanna, even less fieldwork has been done. In both cases, fundamental archaeological surveys are needed, along with detailed recording and excavation of a broader sample of sites. Among other things, modelling long-term settlement patterns on Tanna and Erromango would provide a better understanding of the demographic changes that took place in the colonial era (Spriggs 1997: 235, 253–254, 2007).

Returning to mission archaeology, there are two streams of research that might be informative. One would be to expand the study of Presbyterian mission sites north into Vanuatu's central and northern islands. This would serve to continue to track material changes through time, especially in the later part of mission history from the 1890s through World War II. It would also allow for some comparative study of how missionary encounters were experienced in areas with different languages and *kastom* on other islands. The other research field that could be opened is the study of Vanuatu's other Christian sects. Anglican and Catholic missions were both active in the 19th century. The Anglicans worked closely with the Presbyterians, but it would be worth studying the ways a more centralised model of mission work, in which Melanesians were taken to the mission schools in New Zealand and later Norfolk Island (Hilliard 1978; Ross 1983), played out when converts returned home. Catholic missions followed yet another model, based also on a difference in beliefs, and examination of their materialisation of the work of conversion could offer a fascinating contrast with the Protestant missions. Some of the 'marginal' churches, such as the Seventh Day Adventists, settled their first missionaries nearly 100 years ago, and these sites are worth documenting archaeologically.

There is immense potential for historical archaeology to expand throughout Vanuatu. On Tanna and Erromango, there is also a significant opportunity for fieldwork to further expand our knowledge about cultural transformations well before the missionaries arrived. While this project has contributed in a small way to broadening our understanding of colonial encounters in Island Melanesia, and an even smaller way to expanding our knowledge of pre-contact Tanna and Erromango, there is clearly much more work to be done. To add a note of urgency, Vanuatu's colonial architectural heritage remains imperilled because of natural disasters, ongoing neglect, and capitalist economic development (Flexner et al. 2016a; Rodman 2001). Archaeological recording of standing buildings from the 19th and early 20th century should be a continuing priority for research in partnership with the Vanuatu Cultural Centre.

Archaeology of Conversion Revisited

Hayden (2003: 392–393) argues for an 'ecological' perspective on Christian conversion, in which the material and social opportunities afforded to converts shaped the religion's ability to take hold and spread, especially in the context of the terminal Roman Empire. There is certainly some degree of truth to this model, in which religious change is driven by factors that favour more stable patterns of subsistence, material wealth, and social cohesion. Social instability seems to offer some explanation for religious transformation as well, often with a material basis. In some cases, the ability of certain Islamist groups to expand and sometimes dominate local politics has been connected to their ability to efficiently control access to food, water, and other materials in comparison with government or other authorities, though often using violent methods to achieve this end (e.g. Eng and Martinez 2014).

However, in colonial settings that had already coherent systems for maintaining social, ecological, and supernatural wellbeing, the question remains as to why people would transform their practices or adopt new beliefs. The case study of missions on Tanna and Erromango may be instructive in this regard. Initially, attempts at settling missionaries on these islands were simply rebuffed by local people. Over time, as populations declined, in some cases whole villages were wiped out, and local subsistence as well as social systems began to break down. Melanesian magicians simply could not protect their people from foreign illnesses. Chiefs died, and titles could not be passed on. Simultaneously, the material wealth of the missionaries appeared to increase, surely a reflection of their access to an effective magical mode of production (Appadurai 1986: 52). Melanesians began congregating in the coastal mission settlements. The missionaries overreached, however, in their attempts to purify the islands of heathenism. The result was a counter-reaction, in which people fled back to *kastom* in order to escape the dissolution of their society. Having never disappeared, *kastom* came back to the forefront. It was not, however, a 'pure' return to the original order, but a compromise order that incorporated aspects of the new colonial systems into the overarching Melanesian one.

It is easy with hindsight to interpret missionary endeavours in the 1800s in terms of cultural ignorance. We might wonder at the missionaries recklessly casting themselves as dangerous sorcerers, or building mission houses on contested or spiritually dangerous ground. However, missionaries did not have the benefit of 120-plus years of ethnographic and ethnohistoric knowledge available to the contemporary researcher. How could anything but cultural misunderstanding result from such encounters? In many cases, the missionaries themselves were the authors of some of the first ethnographic works on the islands where they settled (e.g. Gray 1892; Inglis 1854; Watt 1895). It is also true that in contemporary terms, certain events such as the shelling of Tanna by the HMS *Curaçoa* at the insistence of John G. Paton could be seen as criminal. The goal here, however, is not to judge historical actors for our edification as holders of superior knowledge. Rather, we need to understand such historical events and data in the terms in which they were experienced, and to use that knowledge to understand patterns apparent in the present.

In writing a materialist historical archaeology of missions, I am not aiming to take anything away from the faith of the missionaries. We have to assume that their beliefs were sincere and their convictions drove them to the furthest ends of the Earth. At the same time, an archaeological perspective on these encounters reveals the material underpinnings of the conversion process. Without access to global trading and voyaging networks, mass-produced consumer goods, and the wealth produced by the industrial revolution, mission work could not have taken the form outlined in the preceding chapters. Presbyterian missionaries in the New Hebrides could not have survived or won converts using 'faith alone'. The things they brought with them had to be interesting enough to local people, and their presence seen by local chiefs especially as beneficial enough for them to be tolerated. Without the material things exchanged in mission encounters, there would be no Christianity in the New Hebrides. Often, this did not happen, and missionaries were chased away or killed. In many cases, these events tell us as much about social relationships among islanders as they do about relationships between islanders and missionaries (see also Adams 1984).

The story of religious change continues in Island Melanesia (e.g. Montgomery 2004; Tomlinson and McDougall, eds 2012). While foreign Presbyterian missionaries largely departed after the Second World War, missionaries from other sects, notably the Seventh Day Adventists and Church of Latter Day Saints (Mormons), as well as smaller evangelical churches, continue to be active in the region. The material inequalities created by European colonialism and global capitalism are expressed in patterns of mission work in the present. This is why Australian and American Evangelical missionaries remain active in Vanuatu, even though the country was 86 per cent Christian as of the most recent census (compare with 76 per cent Christian in the US and a mere 61 per cent in Australia; see Australian Bureau of Statistics 2012; US Census Bureau 2012; Vanuatu National Statistics Office 2009). It is still easier (read, economically more efficient and socially more feasible) for global missionary work to take place where the missionaries have much greater access to material wealth than their would-be converts. This is not to say that the spiritual dimension is irrelevant to missionary work, but that the material basis for processes of religious change shapes the patterns in which such work takes place.

Changing and Staying the Same

As noted above, religious change remains an ongoing process. If anything, the influence of the major world religions on global events is increasing despite secularist expectations to the contrary (Fowles 2013: 2–4). Archaeologists have recently renewed interests in the study of long-term religious change (e.g. Fowles 2013; Hayden 2003; Shaw 2013b). The spread of the 'world religions' of Christianity, Islam (e.g. Carvajal 2013; Insoll 1999, 2003), and Buddhism (e.g. Shaw 2013a) may be of particular relevance as they continue to shape the worldviews of billions of people. Archaeological studies of the spread of Christianity cover its expansion in Europe during the 'middle ages' (e.g. Älkäs and Salmi 2013; Andrén 2013; Jonuks and Kurisoo 2009; Lund 2013; Sawicki et al. 2015), as well as continuing transformations in the postmedieval period (e.g. Atzback 2015; Graves 2009; Petts 2011). An even richer archaeological literature of Christian expansion exists in the colonial context (e.g. Crossland 2006; Hiscock 2013; Lightfoot 2005; Lydon 2009; Lydon and Ash 2010; Middleton 2003, 2007, 2008; Morrison et al. 2015; Panich and Schneider, eds 2014; Smith 2014; Smith et al. 2012; Wingfield 2013).

In each case, the question of how and why people change some aspect of their relationship to the supernatural world inevitably leads to a broader discussion of the connections between religious belief, environment, the material, and the social. Ultimately, any such model will be contingent upon the specific society being analysed. As Fowles (2013) points out, there is no analysis of religious change that can completely separate 'religion' as a category from the wider ecology of connections that links the world of spirits, ancestors, and deities to the world of everyday life, material things, and interpersonal relationships. Different societies will have different ways of explaining their understanding of such networks. In Pueblo society, the shorthand is 'doings'. In Melanesia, I would suggest '*kastom*' suffices to cover this web of relationships that connects ecosystems, human activities, objects, and spirits, of which the Christian God is one. What archaeology offers is a methodology for using material evidence to understand how and why these networks change through time.

Bibliography

Adams, Ron. 1984. *In the Land of Strangers: A Century of European Contact with Tanna, 1774–1874*. Canberra: The Australian National University.

Adams, Ron. 1987. Homo Anthropologicus and Man-Tanna: Jean Guiart and the anthropological attempt to understand the Tannese. *Journal of Pacific History* 22 (1):3–14.

Adams, Ron. 1998. *Framing the Native: Rev. James Hay Lawrie's Vanuatu Photographs, 1891–1894*. Port Vila: Vanuatu National Museum.

Äikäs, Tiina, and Anna-Kaisa Salmi. 2013. 'The sieidi is a better altar/the noaidi drum's a purer church bell': long-term changes and syncretism at Sámi offering sites. *World Archaeology* 45 (1):64–82.

American Sunday School Union. 1844. *The Martyr Missionary of Erromanga; Or the Life of John Williams, who was Murdered and Eaten by the Savages in one of the South Sea Islands*. Philadelphia: American Sunday School Union.

Andrén, Anders. 1998. *Between Artifacts and Texts: Historical Archaeology in Global Perspective*. New York: Plenum Press.

Andrén, Anders. 2013. The significance of places: the Christianization of Scandinavia from a spatial point of view. *World Archaeology* 45 (1):27–45.

Appadurai, Arjun. 1986. Introduction: commodities and the politics of value. In *The Social Life of Things: Commodities in Cultural Perspective*, edited by Arjun Appadurai, 3–63. Cambridge: Cambridge University Press.

Arendt, Beatrix. 2010. Caribou to cod: Moravian missionary influence on Inuit subsistence strategies. *Historical Archaeology* no. 44 (3):81–101.

Arens, William. 1980. *The Man-Eating Myth: Anthropology and Anthropophagy*. Oxford: Oxford University Press.

Armstrong, E.S. 1900. *The History of the Melanesian Mission*. New York: E.P. Dutton & Co.

Ash, Jeremy, Lousie Manas, and David Bosun. 2010. Lining the path: a seascape perspective of two Torres Strait Missions, Northeast Australia. *International Journal of Historical Archaeology* 14 (1):56–85.

Atzback, Rainer. 2015. Between representation and eternity: the archaeology of praying in Late Medieval and Post-Medieval times. *European Journal of Archaeology*. doi: 10.1179/1461957115Y.0000000006.

Aubert de la Rüe, E. 1938. Sur la nature et l'origine probable des pierres portées en pendentifs à l'île Tanna (Nouvelles Hébrides). *L'Anthropologie* 48:249–260.

Australian Bureau of Statistics (2012) Reflecting a nation: Stories from the 2011 Census, 2012–2013. Available at: www.abs.gov.au/ausstats/abs@.nsf/lookup/2071.0main+features902012-2013 (accessed 21 December 2014).

Ballard, Chris. 2014. Oceanic historicities. *The Contemporary Pacific* 26 (1):96–124.

Barker, Bryce, and Lara Lamb. 2011. Archaeological evidence for South Sea Islander traditional ritual practice at Wunjunga, Ayr, Central Queensland Coast. *Australian Archaeology* 73:69–72.

Barker, Francis, Peter Hulme, and Margaret Iversen. 1998. *Cannibalism and the Colonial World.* Cambridge: Cambridge University Press.

Barker, John. 2012. Secondary conversion and the anthropology of Christianity in Melanesia. *Archives des Sciences Sociales de Religion* 157 (1):67–87.

Beaglehole, J.C. (editor). 1969. *The Journals of Captain James Cook on His Voyages of Discovery: The Voyage of the Resolution and Adventure 1772–1775.* Cambridge: The Hakluyt Society.

Beaudry, Mary C. (editor). 1988. *Documentary Archaeology in the New World.* Cambridge: Cambridge University Press.

Beck, Wendy, and Margaret Somerville. 2005. Conversations between disciplines: historical archaeology and oral history at Yarrawarra. *World Archaeology* 37 (3):468–483.

Bedford, Stuart. 2006. *Pieces of the Vanuatu Puzzle: Archaeology of the North, South, and Center.* Canberra: ANU Press.

Bell, J.A., and H. Geismar. 2009. Materialising Oceania: new ethnographies of things in Melanesia and Polynesia. *Australian Journal of Anthropology* 20:3–27.

Bennett, Tony. 2009. Museum, field, colony: colonial governmentality and the circulation of reference. *Journal of Cultural Economy* 2 (1):99–116.

Birmingham, Judy, and D.N. Jeans. 1983. The Swiss Family Robinson and the archaeology of colonisations. *Australian Historical Archaeology* 1:3–14.

Bonnemaison, Joël. 1991. Magic gardens in Tanna. *Pacific Studies* 14 (4):71–89.

Bonnemaison, Joël. 1994. *The Tree and the Canoe: History and Ethnogeography of Tanna.* Honolulu: University of Hawaii Press.

Braudel, Fernand. 1980. *On History.* Chicago: University of Chicago Press.

Brenchley, Julius L. 1873. *Jottings During the Cruise of H.M.S. 'Curaçoa' among the South Sea Islands in 1865.* London: Longmans, Green, and Co.

Brooks, Alisdair M. 1999. Building Jerusalem: transfer-printed finewares and the creation of British identity. In *The Familiar Past? Archaeologies of Later Historical Britain*, edited by Sarah Tarlow and Susan West, 51–65. London: Routledge.

Brooks, Alisdair M. 2005. *An Archaeological Guide to British Ceramics in Australia, 1788–1901.* Sydney: Australasian Society for Historical Archaeology.

Brunton, Ron. 1979. Kava and the daily dissolution of society on Tanna, New Hebrides. *Mankind* 12 (2):93–103.

Brunton, Ron. 1989. *The Abandoned Narcotic: Kava and Cultural Instability in Melanesia.* Cambridge: Cambridge University Press.

Byrne, Sarah, Anne Clarke, Rodney Harrison, and Robin Torrence (editors). 2011. *Unpacking the Collection: Networks of Material and Social Agency in the Museum.* New York: Springer.

Byrne, Sarah, Anne Clarke, Rodney Harrison, and Robin Torrence. 2011. Networks, agents and objects: frameworks for unpacking museum collections. In *Unpacking the Collection: Networks of Material and Social Agency in the Museum*, edited by Sarah Byrne, Anne Clarke, Rodney Harrison and Robin Torrence, 3–26. New York: Springer.

Capell, Arthur. 1958. *The Culture and Language of Futuna and Aniwa, New Hebrides*. Sydney: University of Sydney.

Card, Jeb C. (editor). 2013. *The Archaeology of Hybrid Material Culture*. Carbondale: Center for Archaeological Investigations.

Carney, J.N., and A. Macfarlane. 1971. *Geology of Tanna, Aneityum, Futuna, and Aniwa*. Port Vila: New Hebrides Geological Survey.

Carrillo-Huffman, Yvonne, Jerry Taki Umunduru, and Kirk Huffman. 2013. Erromango *nemas*: indigenous knowledge, engagement and the role of museums in cultural reactivation. In *Made in Oceania: Tapa-Art and Social Landscapes*, edited by Peter Mesenhöller and Oliver Lueb, 176–197. Koln: Köln, Rautenstrauch-Joest-Museum.

Carney, J.N., and A. Macfarlane. 1971. *Geology of Tanna, Aneityum, Futuna, and Aniwa*. Port Vila: New Hebrides Geological Survey.

Carvajal, José C. 2013. Islamicization or Islamicizations? Expansion of Islam and social practice in the Vega of Granada (south-east Spain). *World Archaeology* 45 (1):109–123.

Chenoweth, John M. 2009. Social identity, material culture, and the archaeology of religion: Quaker practices in context. *Journal of Social Archaeology* 9 (3):319–340.

Chenoweth, John M. 2012. Quakerism and the lack of things in the early modern. In *Modern Materials: The Proceedings of CHAT Oxford, 2009*, edited by Brent Fortenberry and Laura McAtackney, 73–84. Oxford: Archaeopress.

Choi, Hyaeweol, and Margaret Jolly (editors). 2014. *Divine Domesticities: Christian Paradoxes in Asia and the Pacific*. Canberra: ANU Press.

Christidis, Leslie, Vinod Daniel, Paul Monaghan, Yvonne Carrillo-Huffman, and Kirk Huffman. 2009. Engaging with creator communities: the way forward for museums. *International Journal of the Inclusive Museum* 1 (2):1–6.

Clarke, Anne, and Robin Torrence. 2011. Archaeology and the collection: tracing material relationships in colonial Papua from 1875 to 1925. *Journal of Australian Studies* 35 (4):433–448.

Coiffier, Christian. 1988. *Traditional Architecture in Vanuatu*. Suva: University of the South Pacific.

Colley, H., and R.P. Ash. 1971. *The Geology of Erromango*. New Hebrides: The British Service.

Copeland, Joseph. 1878. *Lecture on the New Hebrides Islands, the New Hebrides Natives, and the New Hebrides Mission*. Dunedin. Mills, Dick & Co.

Coysh, A.W., and R.K. Henrywood. 1982. *Dictionary of Blue and White Printed Pottery 1780–1880*. Vol. 2. Woodbridge: Antique Collector's Club.

Craig, Barry. 2003. Repaint the drum. *Records of the South Australian Museum* 36 (2):115–133.

Craig, Barry. 2007. To 'paddle our own canoe': The Rev William Gray Collection in the South Australian Museum. In *Re-presenting Pacific Art*, edited by K. Stevenson and V.-L. Webb, 6–27. Adelaide: Crawford House Publishing.

Crook, Dijana, Stuart Bedford, Matthew Spriggs, and Matiu Prebble. 2015. Waste Not, Want Not. Mission Era Appropriation of Sacred Stones in Aneityum, Vanuatu: An Ethnographic Approach to the Archaeological Record. Poster presented at 8th Lapita Conference. Port Vila, Vanuatu.

Crossland, Zoe. 2006. Landscape and mission in Madagascar and Wales in the early 19th century: 'sowing the seeds of knowledge'. *Landscapes* 7 (1):93–121.

Cusick, James G. (editor). 1998. *Studies in Culture Contact: Interaction, Culture Change, and Archaeology*. Carbondale, Illinois: Center for Archaeological Investigations.

Daily Free Press. 1900. Aberdeen University, the Ross Anthropological Collection. *Daily Free Press*, 10 May 1900.

Dalley, Cameo, and Paul Memmott. 2010. Domains and the intercultural: understanding Aboriginal and missionary engagement at the Mornington Island Mission, Gulf of Carpentaria, Australia from 1914 to 1942. *International Journal of Historical Archaeology* 14:112–135.

David, Bruno, Lara Lamb, Jean-Jacques Delannoy, Frank Pivoru, Cassandra Rowe, Max Pivoru, Tony Frank, Nick Frank, Andrew Fairbairn, and Ruth Pivoru. 2012. Poromoi tamu and the case of the drowning village: history, lost Places and the stories we tell. *International Journal of Historical Archaeology* 16 (2):319–345.

Deetz, James. 1996. *In Small Things Forgotten: An Archaeology of Early American Life*. New York: Anchor Books/Doubleday.

DeLanda, Manuel. 2006. *A New Philosophy of Society: Assemblage Theory and Social Complexity*. London: Continuum.

Depledge, Derrick. 1994. *Hydrogeological Report: The Water Resources of Isangel and Lenakel, Tanna*. Port Vila: Government of Vanuatu Department of Geology, Mines, and Water Resources.

Dickinson, William R. 2014. Petrographic Report WRD 311: Petrographic Comparison of Sand Tempers in Prehistoric Potsherds from Ambae (Aoba) and Temper in Sherd SVMAP 118 from Erromango.

Dieringer, Ernie, and Bev Dieringer. 2001. *White Ironstone China: Plate Identification Guide 1840–1890*. Atglen, PA: Schiffer Publishing.

Docker, Edward W. 1970. *The Blackbirders: The Recruiting of South Seas Labour for Queensland, 1863–1907*. Sydney: Angus and Robertson.

Douglas, Brownwen. 1989. Autonomous and controlled spirits: traditional ritual and early interpretations of Christianity on Tanna, Aneityum and the Isle of Pines in comparative perspective. *Journal of the Polynesian Society* 98 (1):7–48.

Douglas, Brownwen. 1996. *Across the Great Divide: Journeys in History and Anthropology*. Amsterdam: Harwood Academic Press.

Douglas, Brownwen. 2001. Encounters with the enemy? Academic readings of missionary narratives on Melanesians. *Comparative Studies in Society and History* 43 (1):37–64.

Dubois, Marie-Joseph. 1996. Vanuatu seen from Maré. In *Arts of Vanuatu*, edited by Joël Bonnemaison, Christian Kaufmann, Kirk Huffman and Darrell Tryon, 79–82. Honolulu: University of Hawaii Press.

Edge-Partington, James, and Charles Heape. 1969 [1933–1934]. *An Album of the Weapons, Tools, Ornaments, Articles of Dress of the Natives of the Pacific Islands*. 2 vols. London: The Holland Press.

Eng, Brent, and Jose Ciro Martinez. 2014. Starvation, submission, and survival: the Syrian war through the prism of food. *Middle East Report* 273. Available at: www.merip.org/mer/mer273/starvation-submission-survival.

Etheridge, Robert. 1899. The spear-becket or 'doigtier' of New Caledonia, the New Hebrides, and other Pacific islands. *Proceedings of the Linnaean Society of New South Wales* 24 (2):271–282.

Etheridge, Robert. 1917. Obituary – Sutherland Sinclair. *Records of the Australian Museum* 11 (10):227–230.

Flexner, James L. 2013. Mission archaeology in Vanuatu: preliminary findings, problems, and prospects. *Australasian Historical Archaeology* 31:14–24.

Flexner, James L. 2014a. Historical archaeology, contact, and colonialism in Oceania. *Journal of Archaeological Research* 22 (1):43–87.

Flexner, James L. 2014b. The historical archaeology of states and non-states: anarchist perspectives from Hawai'i and Vanuatu. *Journal of Pacific Archaeology* 5 (2):81–97.

Flexner, James L. 2014c. Mapping local perspectives in the historical archaeology of Vanuatu mission landscapes. *Asian Perspectives* 53 (1):2–28.

Flexner, James L. 2015. 'With the consent of the tribe': marking lands on Tanna and Erromango, New Hebrides. Paper presented at Material Encounters, National Library of Australia, Canberra, February 4.

Flexner, James L. 2016a. Archaeology and ethnographic collections: disentangling context, provenance, and provenience in Vanuatu assemblages. *Museum Worlds*: 167–180.

Flexner, James L. 2016b. Ethnology collections as supplements and records: hat museums contribute to historical archaeology of the New Hebrides (Vanuatu). *World Archaeology*. doi: 10.1080/00438243.2016.1195769.

Flexner, James L., and Andrew Ball. 2016. Sherds of paradise: domestic archaeology and ceramic artefacts from a Protestant mission in the South Pacific. *European Journal of Archaeology*. doi. DOI: 10.1080/14619571.2016.1147319.

Flexner, James L., and Matthew Spriggs. 2015. Mission sites as Indigenous heritage in Vanuatu. *Journal of Social Archaeology* 15 (2):184–209.

Flexner, James L. and Matthew Spriggs. In press. When early modern colonialism comes late: historical archaeology in Vanuatu. In *Historical and Archaeological Perspectives on Early Modern Colonialism in Asia and the Pacific*, edited by Maria Cruz-Berrocal and Chengwa Tseng. Tallahassee: University of Florida Press.

Flexner, James L., and Edson Willie. 2015. Under the mission steps: an 800 year-old human burial from south Tanna, Vanuatu. *Journal of Pacific Archaeology* 6 (2):49–55.

Flexner, James L., Martin J. Jones, and Philip D. Evans. 2015. 'Because it is a Holy House of God': buildings archaeology, globalization, and community heritage in a Tanna church. *International Journal of Historical Archaeology* 19 (2):262–288.

Flexner, James L., Martin J. Jones, and Philip D. Evans. 2016a. Destruction of the 1912 Lenakel Church (Tanna, Vanuatu) and thoughts for the future of the site. *International Journal of Historical Archaeology* 20(2): 463–469.

Flexner, James L., Matthew Spriggs, Stuart Bedford, and Marcelin Abong. 2016b. Beginning historical archaeology in Vanuatu: recent projects on the archaeology of Spanish, French, and Anglophone colonialism. In *Archaeology of Spanish Colonialism*, edited by Sandra Monton-Subias, Maria Cruz-Berrocal, and Carmen Ruiz-Martinez, 205–227. New York: Springer.

Flexner, James L., Edson Willie, Andrew Z. Lorey, Helen Alderson, Robert Williams, and Samson Ieru. 2016c. Iarisi's domain: historical archaeology of a Melanesian village, Tanna Island, Vanuatu. *Journal of Island and Coastal Archaeology* 11(1): 26–49.

Foucault, Michel. 1988. *Madness and Civilization: A History of Insanity in the Age of Reason*. New York: Vintage Books.

Fowles, Severin. 2013. *An Archaeology of Doings: Secularism and the Study of Pueblo Religion*. Santa Fe: SAR Press.

Frazer, James G. 1922. *The Golden Bough: A Study in Magic and Religion*. London: MacMillan Press.

Free Church of Scotland. 1889–1894. Unpublished Correspondence Folios. Edinburgh: National Library of Scotland, MS7755, 7756, 7774, 7775.

Gaston, Mary Frank. 1983. *The Collector's Encyclopedia of Flow Blue China*. Paducah, Kentucky: Collector Books.

Gilbert, Pamela K. 2004. *Mapping the Victorian Social Body*. Albany: State University of New York Press.

Godden, Geoffrey A. 1991. *Encyclopaedia of British Pottery and Porcelain Marks*. London: Barrie & Jenkins.

Goldman, Laurence R. (editor). 1999. *The Anthropology of Cannibalism*. London: Bergin and Garvey.

Gordon, James (editor). 1863. *The Last Martyrs of Eromanga, being a Memoir of the Rev. George N. Gordon, and Ellen Catherine Powell, his Wife*. Halifax: MacNab and Shafer.

Gosden, Chris. 2004. *Archaeology and Colonialism: Cultural Contact from 5000 BC to the Present*. Cambridge: Cambridge University Press.

Gosden, Chris, and Chantal Knowles. 2001. *Collecting Colonialism: Material Culture and Colonial Change*. Oxford: Berg.

Graves, C. Pamela. 2009. Building a New Jerusalem: the meaning of a group of merchant houses in Seventeenth-Century Newcastle upon Tyne, England. *International Journal of Historical Archaeology* 13:385–408.

Gray, William. 1884. Report from Mission Station, Weasisi, Tanna, 1883–1884. Unpublished Manuscript. Dunedin: Hocken Library. Manuscript No. 10047.

Gray, William. 1892. *Notes on the Tannese*. Hobart: Australian Association for the Advancement of Science.

Green, Roger C. 1991. Near and Remote Oceania: disestablishing 'Melanesia' in Culture History. In *Man and a Half: Essays in Pacific Anthropology and Ethnobiology in Honour of Ralph Bulmer*, edited by Andrew Pawley, 481–592. Auckland: The Polynesian Society.

Green, Roger C., and Janet Davidson. 1969. Description and classification of Samoan adzes. In *Archaeology in Western Samoa, Volume I*, edited by Roger C. Green and Janet Davidson, 21–33. Auckland: Auckland Institute and Museum.

Green, Roger C., and Janet Davidson (editors). 1974. *Archaeology in Western Samoa Volume II*. Auckland: Auckland Institute and Museum.

Guiart, Jean. 1956. *Un Siècle et Demi de Contacts Culturels à Tanna*. Paris: Musée de l'Homme.

Gunn, William. 1914. *The Gospel in Futuna, with Chapters on the Islands of the New Hebrides, the People, their Customs, Religious Beliefs, etc.* London: Hodder and Stoughton.

Haddon, Alfred Cort. 1912. Personal ornaments and clothing. In *Reports of the Cambridge Anthropological Expedition to the Torres Straits Volume IV: Arts and Crafts*, edited by Alfred Cort Haddon, 33–62. Cambridge: Cambridge University Press.

Hall, Martin. 2000. *Archaeology and the Modern World: Colonial Transcripts in South Africa and the Chesapeake*. London: Routledge.

Harrington, Jean Carl. 1955. Archaeology as an auxiliary science to American history. *American Anthropologist* 57 (6):1121–1130.

Harrison, Rodney. 2002. Archaeology and the colonial encounter: Kimberley spear points, cultural identity and masculinity in the north of Australia. *Journal of Social Archaeology* 2 (3):352–377.

Harrison, Rodney. 2006. An artefact of colonial desire? Kimberley points and the technologies of enchantment. *Current Anthropology* 47 (1):63–88.

Harrison, Rodney, Sarah Byrne, and Anne Clarke (editors). 2013. *Reassembling the Collection: Ethnographic Museums and Indigenous Agency*. Santa Fe: School for Advanced Research Press.

Hayden, Brian. 2003. *Shamans, Sorcerers, and Saints: A Prehistory of Religion*. Washington DC: Smithsonian Institution Press.

Hayes, Lincoln. 2002. The tangible link: historical archaeology and the cultural heritage of the Australian South Sea Islanders. *Australasian Historical Archaeology* 20:77–82.

Hicks, Dan. 2013. Characterizing the world archaeology collections of the Pitt Rivers Museum. In *World Archaeology at the Pitt Rivers Museum: A Characterization*, edited by Dan Hicks and Alice Stevenson, 1–15. Oxford: Archaeopress.

Hilliard, David. 1978. *God's Gentlemen: A History of the Melanesian Mission 1849–1942*. St. Lucia: University of Queensland Press.

Hiscock, Peter. 2013. Beyond the Dreamtime: archaeology and explorations of religious change in Australia. *World Archaeology* 45 (1):124–136.

Huffman, Kirk. 1996. The 'decorated cloth' from the 'island of good yams': barkcloth in Vanuatu, with special reference to Erromango. In *Arts of Vanuatu*, edited by Joël Bonnemaison, Kirk Huffman, Christian Kaufmann and Darrell Tryon, 129–140. Honolulu: University of Hawaii Press.

Humphreys, Clarence Blake. 1926. *The Southern New Hebrides: An Ethnological Record*. Cambridge: Cambridge University Press.

Inglis, John. 1854. A missionary tour in the New Hebrides. *Journal of the Ethnological Society of London* 3:53–85.

Insoll, Timothy. 1999. *The Archaeology of Islam*. Oxford: Blackwell.

Insoll, Timothy. 2003. *The Archaeology of Islam in Sub-Saharan Africa*. Cambridge: Cambridge University Press.

Ireland, Tracy. 2010. From Mission to Maynggu Ganai: the Wellington Valley convict station and mission site. *International Journal of Historical Archaeology* 14 (1):136–155.

Jacobs, Karen, Chantal Knowles, and Chris Wingfield (editors). 2015. *Trophies, Relics and Curios? Missionary Heritage from Africa and the Pacific*. Leiden: Sidestone Press.

Jacomb, Edward. 1914. *France and England in the New Hebrides*. Melbourne: George Robertson.

John G. Paton Mission Fund. 1912. *Quarterly Jottings from the New Hebrides*. Southend: John G. Paton Mission Fund.

Jolly, Margaret. 1992. 'To save the girls for brighter and better lives': Presbyterian missions and women in the south of Vanuatu: 1848–1870. *The Journal of Pacific History* 26 (1):27–48.

Jolly, Margaret. 1994. Kastom as Commodity: The Land Dive as Indigenous Rite and Tourist Spectacle in Vanuatu. In *Culture, Kastom, Tradition: Cultural Policy in Melanesia*, edited by Lamont Lindstrom and Geoffrey M. White, 131–146. Suva: Institute of Pacific Studies.

Jolly, Margaret. 2009. The sediment of voyages: remembering Quirós, Bougainville and Cook in Vanuatu. In *Oceanic Encounters: Exchange, Desire, Violence*, edited by Margaret Jolly, Serge Tcherkézoff and Darrell Tryon, 57–111. Canberra: ANU Press.

Jolly, Margaret, and Martha Macintyre (editors). 1989. *Family and Gender in the Pacific: Domestic Contradictions and the Colonial Impact*. Cambridge: Cambridge University Press.

Jones, Martin. 2013. Geddie House, Aneityum – Interim Report on Archaeological Recording of the Standing Structure, 2012. Unpublished Report. Submitted to Vanuatu Cultural Centre, Port Vila.

Jonuks, Tõnno, and Tulli Kurisoo. 2009. To be or not to be … a Christian: some new perspectives on understanding the Christianisation of Estonia. *Electronic Journal of Folklore* 55:70–98.

Kaufmann, Christian. 1996. The Felix Speiser collection. In *Arts of Vanuatu*, edited by Joël Bonnemaison, Kirk Huffman, Christian Kaufmann and Darrell Tryon, 305–306. Honolulu: University of Hawaii Press.

Kay, John (editor). 1872. *The Slave Trade in the New Hebrides: Being Papers Read at the Annual Meeting of the New Hebrides Mission, Held at Aniwa, July 1871*. Edinburgh: Edmonston and Douglas.

Keane, Webb. 2007. *Christian Moderns: Freedom and Fetish in the Mission Encounter*. Berkeley: University of California Press.

Kirch, Patrick V. 1992. *Anahulu: The Anthropology of History in the Kingdom of Hawaii. Volume 2. The Archaeology of History*. Chicago: University of Chicago Press.

Kirch, Patrick V., and Roger C. Green. 2001. *Hawaiki, Ancestral Polynesia: An Essay in Historical Anthropology*. Cambridge: Cambridge University Press.

Kirkpatrick, Andrea. 2009. Acquisition Proposal: Maritime Conference of the United Church of Canada. New Brunswick Museum. Unpublished manuscript. Saint John: New Brunswick Museum.

Latai, Latu. 2016. The Covenant Keepers: A History of Samoan (LMS) Missionary Wives in the Western Pacific from 1839 to 1979. Unpublished PhD Thesis. Canberra: The Australian National University.

Latour, Bruno. 1987. *Science in Action: How to Follow Scientists and Engineers through Society*. Milton Keynes: Open University Press.

Latour, Bruno. 1993. *We Have Never Been Modern*. Cambridge: Harvard University Press.

Latour, Bruno. 2005. *Reassembling the Social: An Introduction to Actor-Network Theory*. Oxford: Oxford University Press.

Law Pezzarossi, Heather. 2014. Assembling Indigeneity: rethinking innovation, tradition and indigenous materiality in a 19th century native toolkit. *Journal of Social Archaeology* 14 (3):340–360.

Lawrence, Susan, and Martin Davies. 2011. *An Archaeology of Australia since 1788*. New York: Springer.

Lawson, Barbara. 1994a. *Collected Curios: Missionary Tales from the South Seas*. Montreal: McGill University Press.

Lawson, Barbara. 1994b. Missionization, material culture collecting, and nineteenth-century representations in the New Hebrides (Vanuatu). *Museum Anthropology* 18 (1):21–38.

Lawson, Barbara. 2001. 'Clothed and in their right mind': women's dress on Erromango, Vanuatu. *Pacific Arts* 23/24:69–86.

Lawson, Barbara. 2005. Collecting cultures: Canadian missionaries, Pacific Islanders, and museums. In *Canadian Missionaries, Indigenous Peoples: Representing Religion at Home and Abroad*, edited by Alvyn J. Austin and Jamie S. Scott, 235–261. Toronto: University of Toronto Press.

Lawson, Barbara. In press. Tracking Erromango barkcloth. In *Tapa from Southeast Asia to Polynesia*, edited by Michel Charleux. Papeete: Amis de la Musée de Tahiti et des Îles.

Lightfoot, Kent G. 1995. Culture contact studies: redefining the relationship between prehistoric and historical archaeology. *American Antiquity* 60 (2):199–217.

Lightfoot, Kent G. 2005. *Indians, Missionaries, and Merchants: The Legacy of Colonial Encounters on the California Frontiers*. Berkeley: University of California Press.

Lindstrom, Lamont. 1980. Spitting on Tanna. *Oceania* 50 (3):228–234.

Lindstrom, Lamont. 1982. Leftamap Kastom: the political history of tradition on Tanna, Vanuatu. *Mankind* 13 (4):316–329.

Lindstrom, Lamont. 1990. *Knowledge and Power in a South Pacific Society*. Washington DC: Smithsonian Institution Press.

Lindstrom, Lamont. 1993. *Cargo Cult: Stange Stories of Desire from Melanesia and Beyond*. Honolulu: University of Hawaii Press.

Lindstrom, Lamont. 1996. Arts of language and space, south-east Tanna. In *Arts of Vanuatu*, edited by Joël Bonnemaison, Christian Kaufmann, Kirk Huffman and Darrell Tryon, 123–128. Honolulu: University of Hawaii Press.

Lindstrom, Lamont. 2004. History, folklore, traditional and current uses of kava. In *Kava: From Ethnology to Pharmacology*, edited by Yadhu N. Singh, 10–28. London: Taylor and Francis.

Lindstrom, Lamont. 2011. Naming and memory on Tanna, Vanuatu. In *Changing Contexts, Shifting Meanings: Transformations of Cultural Traditions in Oceania*, edited by Elfriede Hermann, 141–156. Honolulu: University of Hawaii Press.

Lindstrom, Lamont. 2013. Agnes C. P. Watt and Melanesian personhood. *Journal of Pacific History* 48 (3):243–266.

Liua'ana, Featuna'i. 1996. Errand of mercy: Samoan missionaries to Southern Vanuatu, 1839–60. In *The Covenant Makers: Islander Missionaries in the Pacific*, edited by Doug Munro and Andrew Thornley, 41–79. Suva, Fiji: Pacific Theological Seminary and the Institute of Pacific Studies at the University of the South Pacific.

Lockhart, Bill. 2010. *Bottles on the Border: The History and Bottles of the Soft Drink Industry in El Paso, Texas, 1881–2000*. Available at: www.sha.org/bottle/links.htm: Society for Historical Archaeology Glass Bottle Identification and Information Website.

Lubcke, Antje. 2009. The Photograph Albums of the New Zealand Presbyterian Mission to the New Hebrides. Unpublished MA Thesis, History. Dunedin: University of Otago.

Lucas, Gavin. 2001. *Critical Approaches to Fieldwork: Contemporary and Historical Archaeological Practice*. London: Routledge.

Lund, Julie. 2013. Fragments of a conversion: handling bodies and objects in pagan and Christian Scandinavia ad 800–1100. *World Archaeology* 45 (1):46–63.

Lydon, Jane. 2009. *Fantastic Dreaming: The Archaeology of an Aboriginal Mission*. Lanham, Maryland: Altamira Press.

Lydon, Jane, and Jeremy Ash. 2010. The archaeology of missions in Australasia: introduction. *International Journal of Historical Archaeology* 14:1–14.

Lydon, Jane, and Alan Burns. 2010. Memories of the past, visions of the future: changing views of Ebenezer Mission, Victoria, Australia. *International Journal of Historical Archaeology* 14 (1):39–55.

Lynch, John. 1996. Kava-drinking in southern Vanuatu: Melanesian drinkers, Polynesian roots. *Journal of the Polynesian Society* 105 (1):27–40.

Majewski, Teresita, and Michael J. O'Brien. 1987. The use and misuse of Nineteenth-Century English and American ceramics in archaeological analysis. *Advances in Archaeological Method and Theory* 11:97–209.

Mauss, Marcel. 1990 [1954]. *The Gift: The Form and Reason for Exchange in Archaic Societies*. Translated by W.D. Halls. London: Routledge.

Mayer, Carol E., Anna Naupa, and Vanessa Warri. 2013. *No Longer Captives of the Past: The Story of a Reconciliation on Erromango*. Vancouver: University of British Columbia Museum of Anthropology.

McArthur, Norma. 1981. *New Hebrides Population 1840–1967: A Re-interpretation*. Noumea: South Pacific Commission.

McNiven, Ian J., and Lynette Russell. 2005. *Appropriated Pasts: Indigenous Peoples and the Colonial Culture of Archaeology*. Lanham, Maryland: Altamira.

Middleton, Angela. 2003. Maori and European landscapes at Te Puna, Bay of Islands, New Zealand, 1805–1850. *Archaeology in Oceania* 38:110–124.

Middleton, Angela. 2006. Mission station as trading post: the economy of the Church Missionary Society. *New Zealand Journal of Archaeology* 28:51–81.

Middleton, Angela. 2007. Silent voices, hidden lives: archaeology, class and gender in the CMS Missions, Bay of Islands, New Zealand, 1814–1845. *International Journal of Historical Archaeology* 11 (1):1–31.

Middleton, Angela. 2008. *Te Puna – A New Zealand Mission Station: Historical Archaeology in New Zealand*. New York: Springer.

Middleton, Angela. 2010. Missionization in New Zealand and Australia: A Comparison. *International Journal of Historical Archaeology* 14:170–187.

Miller, J. Graham. 1978. *Live: A History of Church Planting in the New Hebrides, Book 1: A History of Church Planting in the New Hebrides to 1880*. Committees on Christian Education and Overseas Missions, General Assembly of the Presbyterian Church of Australia.

Miller, J. Graham. 1981. *Live: A History of Church Planting in the New Hebrides, Book 2: The Growth of the Church to 1880*. Sydney: Committees on Christian Education and Overseas Missions, General Assembly of the Presbyterian Church of Australia.

Miller, J. Graham. 1985. *Live: A History of Church Planting in Vanuatu, Book 3*. Lawson: Mission Publications of Australia.

Miller, J. Graham. 1986. *Live: A History of Church Planting in the New Hebrides, Book 4: 1881–1920*. Port Vila: The Presbyterian Church of Vanuatu.

Miller, J. Graham. 1987. *Live: A History of Church Planting in the Republic of Vanuatu, Book 5, The Central Islands, Efate to Epi from 1881–1920*. Lawson: Mission Publications of Australia.

Miller, J. Graham. 1989. *Live: A History of Church Planting in the Republic of Vanuatu, Book 6, the Northern Islands, 1881–1948*. Lawson: Mission Publications of Australia.

Mills, Peter R. 2002. *Hawai'i's Russian Adventure: A New Look at Old History*. Honolulu: University of Hawaii Press.

Mills, Peter R. 2009. Folk housing in the middle of the Pacific: architectural lime, creolized ideologies, and expressions of power in Nineteenth-Century Hawaii. In *The Materiality of Individuality*, edited by Carolyn L. White, 75–91. New York: Springer.

Montgomery, Charles. 2004. *The Shark God: Encounters with Ghosts and Ancestors in Melanesia*. Chicago: University of Chicago Press.

Moore, Clive. 1992. Revising the revisionists: the historiography of immigrant Melanesians in Australia. *Pacific Studies* 15 (2):61–86.

Morley, Steven. 2016. Historical UK inflation rates and calculator. Available at: inflation.stephenmorley.org/ (last accessed 15 April 2016).

Morrison, Michael, Darlene McNaughton, and Justin Shiner. 2010. Mission-based Indigenous production at the Weipa Presbyterian Mission, Western Cape York Peninsula (1932–66). *International Journal of Historical Archaeology* 14 (1):86–111.

Morrison, Michael, Darlene McNaughton, and Claire Keating. 2015. 'Their God is their belly': Moravian missionaries at the Weipa Mission (1898–1932), Cape York Peninsula. *Archaeology in Oceania* 50:85–104.

Murray, A.W. 1863. *Missions in Western Polynesia*. London: John Snow.

Murray, Tim (editor). 2004. *The Archaeology of Contact in Settler Societies*. Cambridge: Cambridge University Press.

Naupa, Anna (editor). 2011. *Nompi en Ovoteme Erromango (Kastom and Culture of Erromango)*. Port Vila: Erromango Cultural Association.

Nehrbass, Kenneth. 2012. A comprehensive comparison of lexemes in the major languages of Tanna, Vanuatu. In: SIL E-Books 34, SIL International.

Obeyesekere, Gananath. 2005. *Cannibal Talk: The Man-Eating Myth and Human Sacrifice in the South Seas*. Berkeley: University of California Press.

Olivier, Laurent. 2011. *The Dark Abyss of Time: Archaeology and Memory*. Translated by Arthur Greenspan. Lanham, Maryland: Altamira Press.

O'Reilly, J.P., and Fournier D'Albe. 1893. On a pandean pipe from Tanna, New Hebrides. *Proceedings of the Royal Irish Academy* 3:511–515.

Palmer, George. 1871. *Kidnapping in the South Seas, Being a Narrative of a Three Months' Cruise of H. M. Ship Rosario*. Edinburgh: Edmonston and Douglas.

Panich, Lee. 2013. Archaeologies of persistence: reconsidering the legacies of colonialism in Native North America. *American Antiquity* 78 (1):105–122.

Panich, Lee, and Tsim Schneider (editors). 2014. *Indigenous Landscapes and Spanish Missions: New Perspectives from Archaeology and Ethnohistory*. Tuscon: University of Arizona Press.

PAP (Science and Scholarship in Poland). 2014. 200-Year-Old Bottle Recovered from the Bof the Gulf of Gdańsk Contained Alcohol. Available at: scienceinpoland.pap.pl/en/news/news,401439,200-year-old-bottle-recovered-from-the-bottom-of-the-gulf-of-gdansk-contained-alcohol.html.

Paton, Frank Hume Lyall. 1903. *Lomai of Lenakel: A Hero of the New Hebrides. A Fresh Chapter in the Triumph of the Gospel*. London: Hodder and Stoughton.

Paton, John G. 1907. *John G. Paton, Missionary to the New Hebrides*. 2 vols. New York: Fleming H. Revell Company.

Patterson, George. 1864. *Memoirs of the Rev. S. F. Johnston, the Rev. J. W. Matheson, and Mrs. Mary Johnston Matheson, Missionaries on Tanna, with Selections from their Diaries and Correspondence, and Notices of the New Hebrides, their Inhabitants, and Mission Work among them*. Philadelphia: W.S. and A. Martien.

Patterson, George. 1882. *Missionary Life Among the Cannibals: The Life of John Geddie, D.D., First Missionary to the New Hebrides; With a History of the Nova Scotia Presbyterian Mission on that Group*. Toronto: James Campbell & Son.

Pearson, Michael. 1992. From ship to the bush: Ship tanks in Australia. *Australasian Historical Archaeology* 10:24–29.

Petts, David. 2011. Landscapes of belief: Non-conformist mission in the north Pennines. *International Journal of Historical Archaeology* no. 15 (3):461–480.

Poovey, Mary. 1995. *Making a Social Body: British Cultural Formation, 1830–1864*. Chicago: University of Chicago Press.

Presbyterian Church of the Lower Provinces of British North America. 1849–1873. *The Home and Foreign Record of the Presbyterian Church of the Lower Provinces of British North America*. Halifax: James Barnes.

Ramenofsky, Ann F. 1998. Evolutionary theory and the Native American record of artifact replacement. In *Studies in Culture Contact: Interaction, Culture Change, and Archaeology*, edited by James G. Cusick, 77–101. Carbondale: Center for Archaeological Investigations.

Risse, Guenter B. 1999. *Mending Bodies, Saving Souls: A History of Hospitals*. Oxford: Oxford University Press.

Robertson, Hugh Angus. 1902. *Erromanga: The Martyr Isle*. Toronto: The Westminster Company.

Rodman, Margaret C. 1992. Empowering place: multilocality and multivocality. *American Anthropologist* 94 (3):640–656.

Rodman, Margaret C. 2001. *Houses Far from Home: British Colonial Space in the New Hebrides*. Honolulu: University of Hawaii Press.

Ross, R.M. 1983. *Melanesians at Mission Bay: A History of the Melanesian Mission in Auckland*. Wellington: New Zealand Historic Places Trust.

Rubertone, Patricia. 2000. The historical archaeology of Native Americans. *Annual Review of Anthropology* 29:425–446.

Sahlins, Marshall. 2004. *Apologies to Thucydides: Understanding History as Culture and Vice Versa*. Chicago: University of Chicago Press.

Samford, Patricia. 1997. Response to a market: dating English under-glaze transfer-printed wares. *Historical Archaeology* 31 (2):1–30.

Sawicki, Zbigniew, Aleksander Pluskowski, Alexander Brown, Monika Badura, Daniel Makowiecki, Lisa-Marie Shillito, Mirasława Zabilska-Kunek, and Krish Seetah. 2015. Survival at the frontier of holy war: Political expansion, crusading, environmental exploitation and the Medieval colonizing settlement at Biała Góra, North Poland. *European Journal of Archaeology* 18 (2):282–311.

Saxton and Binns. 1910. *The Saxton and Binns Illustrated Catalogue*. Sydney: Saxton and Binns.

Schiffer, Michael B. 1987. *Formation Processes of the Archaeological Record*. Albuquerque: University of New Mexico Press.

Shaw, Julia. 2013a. Archaeologies of Buddhist propagation in ancient India: 'ritual' and 'practical' models of religious change. *World Archaeology* 45 (1):83–108.

Shaw, Julia. 2013b. Archaeology of religious change: introduction. *World Archaeology* 45 (1):1–11.

Shineberg, Dorothy. 1967. *They Came for Sandalwood: A Study of the Sandalwood Trade in the South-West Pacific 1830–1865*. Melbourne: Melbourne University Press.

Shineberg, Dorothy. 1999. *The People Trade: Pacific Island Labourers and New Caledonia, 1865–1930*. Honolulu: University of Hawaii Press.

Shutler, Mary E., and Richard Shutler. 1966. A preliminary report of archaeological explorations in the southern New Hebrides. *Asian Perspectives* 9 (1):157–166.

Shutler, Mary E., Richard Shutler, and Stuart Bedford. 2002. Further detail on the archaeological explorations in the Southern New Hebrides, 1963–1964. In *Fifty Years in the Field: Essays in Honour and Celebration of Richard Shutler Jr's Archaeological Career*, edited by Stuart Bedford, Christophe Sand and David V. Burley, 189–205. Auckland: New Zealand Archaeological Association.

Shutler, Richard. 1973. New Hebrides radiocarbon dates, 1968. *Asian Perspectives* 14:84–87.

Silliman, Stephen W. 2005. Culture contact or colonialism? Challenges in the archaeology of Native North America. *American Antiquity* 70 (1):55–74.

Silliman, Stephen W. 2009. Change and continuity, practice and memory: Native American persistence in colonial New England. *American Antiquity* 74 (2):211–230.

Silliman, Stephen W. 2014. A requiem for hybridity? the problem with Frankensteins, purées,and mules. *Journal of Social Archaeology* 15 (3):277–298.

Smith, Arthur M. 1997. Missionary as collector: the role of the Reverend Joseph Annand. *Acadiensis* XXVI (2):96–111.

Smith, Arthur M. 2005. 'Curios' from a strange land: the Oceania collections of the Reverend Joseph Annand. In *Canadian Missionaries, Indigenous Peoples: Representing Religion at Home and Abroad*, edited by Alvyn J. Austin and Jamie S. Scott, 262–278. Toronto: University of Toronto Press.

Smith, Diana M. 2010. 'We Wia Ragai': missionary collection and synergetic assemblages in the Solomon Islands 1920–1942. *International Journal of Historical Archaeology* 14:188–208.

Smith, Ian W.G. 2014. Schooling on the missionary frontier: the Hohi Mission Station, New Zealand. *International Journal of Historical Archaeology* 18 (4):612–628.

Smith, Ian W.G., Angela Middleton, Jessie Garland, and Naomi Woods. 2012. *Archaeology of the Hohi Mission Station, Volume I: The 2012 Excavations*. Dunedin: University of Otago Studies in Archaeology.

Smith, Ian W.G., Angela Middleton, Jessie Garland, and Tristan Russell. 2014. *Excavations at the Hohi Mission Station Volume II: The 2013 Excavations*. Dunedin: University of Otago Studies in Archaeology.

South, Stanley. 1978. Pattern recognition in historical archaeology. *American Antiquity* 43:223–230.

Speiser, Felix. 1922. Decadence and preservation in the New Hebrides. In *Depopulation in Melanesia*, edited by W.H.R. Rivers, 25–61. Cambridge: Cambridge University Press.

Speiser, Felix. 1996 [1923]. *Ethnology of Vanuatu*. Honolulu: University of Hawaii Press.

Spriggs, Matthew. 1981. Vegetable Kingdoms: Taro Irrigation and Pacific Prehistory. Unpublished PhD Thesis. Canberra: Australian National University.

Spriggs, Matthew. 1985. 'A School in Every District': the cultural geography of conversion on Aneityum, Southern Vanuatu. *Journal of Pacific History* 20 (1):23–41.

Spriggs, Matthew. 1986. Landscape, land use, and political transformation in southern Melanesia. In *Island Societies: Archaeological Approaches to Evolution and Transformation*, edited by Patrick V. Kirch, 6–19. Cambridge: University of Cambridge Press.

Spriggs, Matthew. 1993. Quantifying women's oppression in prehistory: the Aneityum (Vanuatu) case. In *Women in Archaeology: A Feminist Critique*, edited by Hilary du Cros and Laurajane Smith, 143–150. Canberra: The Australian National University.

Spriggs, Matthew. 1997. *The Island Melanesians*. Oxford: Blackwell.

Spriggs, Matthew. 1999. Pacific archaeologies: contested ground in the construction of Pacific history. *Journal of Pacific History* 34 (1):109–121.

Spriggs, Matthew. 2007. Population in a vegetable kingdom: Aneityum Island (Vanuatu) at European contact in 1830. In *The Growth and Collapse of Pacific Island Societies: Archaeological and Demographic Perspectives*, edited by Patrick V. Kirch and Jean–Louis Rallu, 278–305. Honolulu: University of Hawaii Press.

Spriggs, Matthew, and Stephen Wickler. 1989. Archaeological research on Erromango: recent data on southern Melanesian prehistory. *Bulletin of the Indo-Pacific Prehistory Association* 9:68–91.

Steel, Frances. 2011. *Oceania Under Steam: Sea Transport and the Cultures of Colonialism, c.1870–1914*. Manchester: Manchester University Press.

Strathern, Marilyn. 1990. *The Gender of the Gift: Problems with Women and Problems with Society in Melanesia*. Berkeley: University of California Press.

Sutton, Mary-Jean. 2003. Re-examining total institutions: a case study from Queensland. *Archaeology in Oceania* 38:78–88.

Symonds, James. 2003. An imperial people? Highland Scots, emigration, and the British colonial world. In *Archaeologies of the British: Explorations of Identity in Great Britain and its Colonies 1600–1945*, edited by Susan Lawrence, 138–155. London: Routledge.

Tabani, Marc. 2010. The carnival of custom: Land dives, millenarian parades, and other spectacular ritualizations in Vanuatu. *Oceania* 80 (3):309–328.

Taylor, John. 2010. The troubled histories of a Stranger God: Religious crossing, sacred power, and Anglican colonialism in Vanuatu. *Comparative Studies in Society and History* 52 (2):418–446.

Taylor, John. 2016. Two baskets worn at once: Christianity, sorcery and sacred power in Vanuatu. In *Conflicts and Convergences: Critical Perspectives on Christianity in Australia and the Pacific*, edited by Fiona Magowan and Carolyn Schwarz. Leiden: Brill Publishers, forthcoming.

Thomas, Nicholas. 1991. *Entangled Objects: Exchange, Material Culture, and Colonialism in the Pacific*. Cambridge, Massachusetts.: Harvard University Press.

Tomlinson, Matt, and Debra McDougall (editors). 2012. *Christian Politics in Oceania*. New York: Berghahn Books.

Torrence, Robin. 2000. Just another trader? An archaeological perspective on European barter with Admiralty Islanders, Papua New Guinea. In *The Archaeology of Difference: Negotiating Cross-Cultural Engagements in Oceania*, edited by Robin Torrence and Anne Clarke, 104–141. London: Routledge.

Torrence, Robin, and Anne Clarke (editors). 2000. *The Archaeology of Difference: Negotiating Cross-Cultural Engagements in Oceania*. London: Routledge.

Torrence, Robin, and Anne Clarke. 2013. Creative colonialism: Locating indigenous strategies in ethnographic museum collections. In *Reassembling the Collection: Ethnographic Museums and Indigenous Agency*, edited by Rodney Harrison, Sarah Byrne and Anne Clarke, 171–195. Santa Fe: School for Advanced Research Press.

Turner, George. 1861. *Nineteen Years in Polynesia: Missionary Life, Travels, and Researches in the Islands of the Pacific*. London: John Snow.

US Census Bureau. 2012. Self described religious identification of adult population. Table 75. www2.census.gov/library/publications/2011/compendia/statab/131ed/tables/pop.pdf (accessed 1 December 2016).

Van Trease, Howard. 1987. *The Politics of Land in Vanuatu*. Suva: University of the South Pacific Press.

Vance, Michael. 2005. A brief history of organized Scottishness in Canada. In *Transatlantic Scots*, edited by Celeste Ray, 96–119. Tuscaloosa: University of Alabama Press.

Vance, Michael E. 2011. From Cape Breton to Vancouver Island: Studying the Scots in Canada. *Immigrants and Minorities: Historical Studies in Ethnicity, Migration and Diaspora* 29 (2):175–194.

Vanuatu National Archives. Unpublished land records, Southern Islands (S.I.) series. Port Vila: National Archive of Vanuatu.

Vanuatu National Statistics Office. 2009. *2009 National Population and Housing Census*. Port Vila: Vanuatu National Statistics Office.

Von Jedina, Leopold. 1891. *An Asiens Küsten und Fürstenhöfen, Tagebuchblätter von der Reise Sr. Maj. Schiffes 'Fasana' und über den Aufenthalt an asiatischen Höfen in den Jahren 1887, 1888 und 1889*. Vienna: E. Hölzel.

Watt, Agnes C.P. 1896. *Twenty-Five Years' Mission Life on Tanna, New Hebrides*. Paisley: J. and R. Parlane.

Watt, William. 1895. Cannibalism as practised on Tanna, New Hebrides. *Journal of the Polynesian Society* 4 (4):226–230.

Weber, Max. 2002 [1905]. *The Protestant Ethic and the Spirit of Capitalism*. New York: Penguin Classics. Original edition, 1905.

Williams, Petra, and Marguerite Weber. 1978. *Staffordshire: Romantic Transfer Patterns*. Jeffersontown, Kentucky: Fountain House East.

Wilson, Meredith. 1999. Bringing the art inside: A preliminary analysis of black linear rock-art from limestone caves in Erromango, Vanuatu. *Oceania* 70:87–97.

Wilson, Meredith. 2002. Picturing Pacific Prehistory: The Rock-Art of Vanuatu in a Western Pacific Context. Unpublished PhD Thesis. Canberra: Australian National University.

Wingfield, Chris. 2013. Reassembling the London Missionary Society collection: experiments with symmetrical anthropology and the archaeological sensibility. In *Reassembling the Collection: Ethnographic Museums and Indigenous Agency*, edited by Rodney Harrison, Sarah Byrne and Anne Clarke, 61–87. Santa Fe: School for Advanced Research Press.

Appendices

Appendix A: Archaeological sites and features

Site/Feature Name	Location	Description
Robertson Mission		
Robertson Church	Dillon's Bay, Erromango	Standing mission church in Dillon's Bay.
Robertson House	Dillon's Bay, Erromango	Stone foundation from Robertson Mission house.
Chief Mete House	Dillon's Bay, Erromango	Lime mortar footing for a 19th-century structure under modern house.
Store House	Dillon's Bay, Erromango	Lime mortar footing from the store house in Robertson Mission.
Mission Walls	Dillon's Bay, Erromango	Stone walls surrounding Robertson Mission.
Dillon's Bay Memorial		
Nokiyangauwi	Dillon's Bay, Erromango	Memorial enclosure for missionaries killed on Erromango.
John Williams Event Landscape		
Williams' Body Laid Out	Dillon's Bay, Erromango	Place where Williams' body was taken after he was killed.
Limestone Staircase	Dillon's Bay, Erromango	Lime mortar staircase next to Williams' River.
Martyr Stone	Dillon's Bay, Erromango	Stone marked with small depressions for head, feet, and hands of Williams.
Dividing Stone	Dillon's Bay, Erromango	Stone where Williams' body was divided and sent around Erro.
Williams' Skull	Dillon's Bay, Erromango	Coconut palm where they buried Williams' skull.
George Gordon Mission		
Guard House	Dillon's Bay, Erromango	Guard house for the Gordon Mission to Dillon's Bay.
Gordon House	Dillon's Bay, Erromango	George and Ellen Gordon Mission house.
Vedavil Stream	Dillon's Bay, Erromango	Nearest water source for Gordon Mission in Dillon's Bay.
Gordon's Footprint	Dillon's Bay, Erromango	Stone where Gordon put his foot while bleeding to death.
Wash Basin	Dillon's Bay, Erromango	Stone where Gordon's murderers washed the blood from their hands.
James Gordon Mission		
James Gordon Church	Potnuma, Erromango	Lime mortar foundations from James Gordon Mission church.
James Gordon House	Potnuma, Erromango	Remains of foundation for James Gordon Mission house.
Blood Stone	Potnuma, Erromango	Upright stone marking where Gordon's blood ran after he was killed.
James Gordon Tomb	Potnuma, Erromango	Turtle-shaped lime mortar enclosure with a a concrete slab grave inside.
Pontal 2/ER 19		
Bomtal	Port Narvin, Erromango	Petroglyph field with cupules counting the battles of Sou Sou.
Malap 2/ER 23		
Malap	Port Narvin, Erromango	Petroglyph field with culture contact motifs.
Netngonavon/Navon/ER 24		
Netngonavon	Port Narvin, Erromango	Rockshelter with rock art inside near Port Narvin.
Port Narvin 'Shipwreck'		
Neilson Anchor	Port Narvin, Erromango	Anchor reported to be from a mission ship sunk by local people.
North of Potnuma		
Potnepko	Eastern Erromango	Tube in the limestone used to store sacrificial victims to close the road.
Potnepko 2	Eastern Erromango	Blowhole where people would place the dead.
Vetemanu's Footprints	Eastern Erromango	Footprints of a legendary figure who was the son of a great chief from Efate.
Ntue	Eastern Erromango	Place where Nialnowre had her pig enclosure, which was the first one.

Site/Feature Name	Location	Description
Sipiempu	Eastern Erromango	White sand beach where Novlu spotted Nerimpau, then caught and killed him.
Nipmilamli	Eastern Erromango	*Tabu* site, a tree where Nerimpau's head was put after his death.
Potmosi	Eastern Erromango	Village site inland. Beach was place where Nerimpau's body was displayed.
Nduwe	Eastern Erromango	Large boulder with pecked bird egg-shaped impressions.
Velumap Cave		
Velumap Cave	Eastern Erromango	Cave used for storing sandalwood before shipping.
Cook's Bay Mission		
Cook's Bay Mission Site	Eastern Erromango	Stone remains of the Cook's Bay Mission.
Lenakel Mission		
Old Mission Well	Lenakel, Tanna	Stone alignment possibly related to first mission well in Lenakel.
1912 Church	Lenakel, Tanna	Historic church building in Lenakel.
Trigg Grave	Lenakel, Tanna	Graves uphill from 1912 Church.
Second Church	Lenakel, Tanna	Location of earlier church, only concrete corner footings with metal brackets remain.
Grave of Lomai	Lenakel, Tanna	Grave with a limestone headstone and concrete slab where Lomai is buried.
Second School	Lenakel, Tanna	No surface remains, but local informants noted as location of old school.
Milking Shed	Lenakel, Tanna	Concrete slab used in recent memory for milking cows.
Nun's House	Lenakel, Tanna	Standing wooden house on concrete piers.
Lenakel Mission Hospital		
1911 Hospital	Lenakel, Tanna	Remains of old hospital consisting of a large concrete slab and some walls.
Hospital Pantry	Lenakel, Tanna	Concrete slab with row of cinder blocks in the middle.
TB Ward	Lenakel, Tanna	Concrete slab with beam slots on downhill side, water tank on southern end.
Laundry and Bread Oven	Lenakel, Tanna	Old features possibly related to hospital.
Maternity Ward	Lenakel, Tanna	Concrete slab where the maternity ward for the hospital was located.
Nicholson House	Lenakel, Tanna	Remains of Dr Nicholson's house.
Surveyor's Datum	Lenakel, Tanna	Old surveyor's datum, a small pipe in a concrete cylinder.
Inland Paton Mission		
John Paton Mission	Port Resolution, Tanna	Not many surface remains, but apparently first place Paton settled in the area.
First Mango	Port Resolution, Tanna	Apparently first mango trees, which came with missionaries in the 1800s.
Relocated Paton Grave	Port Resolution, Tanna	Graves of John Paton's wife and son, as well as Johnston.
Main Port Resolution Mission		
Gibson Ship	Port Resolution, Tanna	Shipwreck on the beach from a 1960s mission boat.
Yakuperang	Port Resolution, Tanna	First *nakamal* where missionaries arrived.
Relocated Church	Port Resolution, Tanna	After first church destroyed in a storm, it was moved here, though no remains today.
Church Bell	Port Resolution, Tanna	Old brass bell from 1890 placed in a tree.
Elders' Graves	Port Resolution, Tanna	Graves from the first church elders in Port Resolution.
Mission Church	Port Resolution, Tanna	Located under current yacht club, which follows old mission church footprint.
Mission Printers	Port Resolution, Tanna	Under yacht club bungalow, but apparently where old printing press was located.

Site/Feature Name	Location	Description
Mission House	Port Resolution, Tanna	Under yacht club bungalow, but apparently where old mission house was located.
Mission Landing	Port Resolution, Tanna	Landing used by missionaries for Port Resolution Mission near current yacht club.
Watt Grave	Port Resolution, Tanna	Grave of Agnes Watt (described at length in introduction to '25 Years Mission Life').
Captain Cook		
Captain Cook	Port Resolution, Tanna	Outcrop where Cook stood to take surveying measurements.
Watt Mission		
Kwamera Mission Graves	Kwamera, Tanna	Two graves, one of which has a headstone in memory of Rev. Gray's son.
Watt Mission	Kwamera, Tanna	Mission house and church complex built by the Watts.
Old Bell	Kwamera, Tanna	Place where bell used to call people to worship used to hang.
Mission Launch	Kwamera, Tanna	Former location with a winch to pull in the mission launch.
Kwaraka		
Kwaraka	Kwaraka, Tanna	Stone walls in area where Yeni Yarisi brough gospel to south Tanna.
New Kwaraka	Kwaraka, Tanna	Stone enclosure where people took gospel from old Kwaraka.
Nokwenuk	Kwaraka, Tanna	*Kastom* stone of the yam god.
Netata	Kwaraka, Tanna	Stone shaped like a ship, symbolic of Kwaraka.
Iarisi Garden	Kwaraka, Tanna	Iarisi's garden, now visible as a single stone mound from clearing the soil.
Miscelaneous Kwamera Features		
Mark Mellon	Kwamera, Tanna	Big tree named for a surveyor who worked on south Tanna.
Imua	Kwamera, Tanna	Hill where Paton and Matheison first settled in south Tanna.
Enapa	Kwamera, Tanna	No surface remains, but local informants noted as location of a trading post.
Irumien		
Irumien	Kwaraka, Tanna	Large, well preserved historic *nakamal* with stone walls.
Waisisi Mission		
Gray Church	Waisisi, Tanna	Place where Gray's original church was located (now only marked by foundation stones).
Gray Mission Path/Stair	Waisisi, Tanna	Old path connecting the church to the mission house and sea, ruined mortar stairs remain.
Gray House	Waisisi, Tanna	Remains of Gray's house.
Goat Pen	Waisisi, Tanna	Stone goat pen built by a later missionary (Ken Calvert), includes recent grave.
Irene Gray Grave	Waisisi, Tanna	Grave of the Grays' daughter.
Corner Peg	Waisisi, Tanna	Upright stone marking the boundary of mission lands erected by Gray.
Shipi-Manwawa		
Nitela	Waisisi, Tanna	Natapoa tree planted by 'Shipi' at the end of the Shipi-Manwawa war.
Manwawa	Waisisi, Tanna	Natapoa tree planted by 'Manwawa' at the end of the Shipi-Manwawa war (no longer standing).
Uelel	Waisisi, Tanna	Stones where people hid during wartime.
Noanpai	Waisisi, Tanna	Sea side *nakamal* of Nalpini Asim, a war chief. Now underwater, moved inland.
Waisisi *Kastom* Sites		
Temitonga	Waisisi, Tanna	*Tabu* stone where a white man was killed in the colonial era.
Naburi	Waisisi, Tanna	Old *nakamal* remembered as a place for fishing magic.

Site/Feature Name	Location	Description
Lamatetengi	Waisisi, Tanna	Stone altar ('chair') where the spirits of the dead would rest before joining the ancestors.
Kasali	Waisisi, Tanna	*Kastom* stone.
Ulin	Waisisi, Tanna	Small hillock next to Kwalep Nakamal, had the power to cause illness.
Kwalep	Waisisi, Tanna	*Nakamal* where William Gray was accepted in 1882.
Sakutu	Waisisi, Tanna	Burial ground on the other side of Kwalep village.
Netanu	Waisisi, Tanna	Relates to the turtle. Very sacred, marked with the skulls of sacrificed turtles and pigs.

Appendix B: Excavated contexts and brief descriptions

Site/Area	Layer/Feature	Munsell Colour	Sediment Texture	Brief Interpretation
G. Gordon House				
TU1/2/3	I	[10YR2/2] Very Dark Brown	Sandy Loam	Topsoil layer accumulated since site abandonment.
TU1/2/3	II	[7.5YR3/2] Dark Brown	Clay Loam	Occupation layer abutting stone retaining wall.
TU1/2/3	III	[7.5YR3/2] Dark Brown	Sandy Clay (80%), Limestone Pebbles (20%)	Transition to clay subsoil with underlying uplifted reef limestone (bedrock) inclusions.
TU4	I	SEE NOTES	Sandy Loam	Topsoil/shallow superficial occupation deposit.
TU4	II	SEE NOTES	Clay	Subsoil.
TU5	I	SEE NOTES	Loam	Topsoil.
TU5	IIa	SEE NOTES	Clay Loam, Compact	Main occupation layer (inside house).
TU5	IIb	SEE NOTES	Silty Clay, Compact	Occupation layer (outside house).
TU5	IIIa	SEE NOTES	Silty Clay Loam (85%), Limestone Pebbles (10%), Charcoal (5%)	Possible construction fill from the terrace on which the site was built. Cross-bedded with other LyIII/LyIV deposits.
TU5	IIIb	SEE NOTES	Clay	Possible construction fill from the terrace on which the site was built.
TU5	IVa	SEE NOTES	Silty Clay	Possible construction fill from the terrace on which the site was built.
TU5	IVb	SEE NOTES	Clay, Compact	Possible construction fill from the terrace on which the site was built.
TU5	V	SEE NOTES	Clay Loam	Subsoil underlying construction fill deposits.
TU6	I	SEE NOTES	Loam	Topsoil/occupation deposit.
TU6	F01 (PN17)	SEE NOTES	Loam (20%), Limestone and Volcanic Cobbles (80%)	Linear stone feature, possibly a former wall footing.
TU6	II	SEE NOTES	Clay, Compact	Subsoil.
TU7	I	SEE NOTES	Loam	Topsoil/shallow superficial occupation deposit.
TU7	II	SEE NOTES	Clay	Subsoil.

Site/Area	Layer/Feature	Munsell Colour	Sediment Texture	Brief Interpretation
J. Gordon House				
TU1	I	[10YR3/2] Very Dark Greyish Brown	Silty Clay (90%), Limestone and Volcanic Cobbles (10%)	Occupation deposit, abuts base of lime mortar wall footings.
TU1	II	[7.5YR2.5/2] Very Dark Brown	Clay	Subsoil; disturbed by animal burrowing (crabs).
TU2	I	[10YR2/2] Very Dark Brown	Silty Clay Loam (90%), Limestone and Volcanic Cobbles and Pebbles (10%)	Occupation deposit, abuts base of lime mortar wall footings.
TU2	II	[10YR3/2] Very Dark Greyish Brown	Silty Clay	Subsoil; disturbed by animal burrowing (crabs).
TU3	I	[10YR2/2] Very Dark Brown	Silty Clay	Occupation deposit.
TU3	II	[10YR3/2] Very Dark Greyish Brown	Silty Clay	Subsoil.
Robertson House				
TU1	I	[7.5YR2.5/1] Black	Sandy Loam (40%), Waterworn Pebbles (60%)	Topsoil.
TU1	F01	[7.5YR2.5/1] Black	Loam	Planting Feature.
TU1	IIa	[7.5YR2.5/1] Black	Sand (20%), Coral Fragments (80%)	Paving Layer.
TU1	IIb	[7.5YR2.5/1] Black	Sandy Loam (90%), Waterworn Pebbles (10%)	Paving Layer.
TU1	IIIa	[7.5YR2.5/1] Black	Sandy Loam	Fill (flood deposit?)
TU1	IIIb	[7.5YR4/4] Brown	Sandy Loam, Compact	Paving Layer.
TU1	IVa	[7.5YR2.5/1] Black	Sand (40%), Waterworn Cobbles (60%)	Paving Layer.
TU1	IVb	[7.5YR2.5/1] Black	Sandy Loam (10%), Coral Fragments (90%)	Paving Layer.
TU1	V	[7.5YR3/2] Dark Brown	Sandy Loam (30%), Waterworn Cobbles (60%)	Lowest paving layer; abuts lime mortar wall footing/buried step. Overlies construction fill.
TU1	VI	[7.5YR2.5/1] Black	Sand (30%), Waterworn Cobbles and Boulders (70%)	Construction fill relating to the house foundation, base of the layer corresponds to the lowest level of the footings.
TU1	VII	[7.5YR2.5/1] Black	Sand	Beach sand underlying the house, no artefacts or inclusions.
TU2/5/6	I	SEE NOTES	Sandy Loam	Topsoil.

Site/Area	Layer/Feature	Munsell Colour	Sediment Texture	Brief Interpretation
TU2/5/6	II	SEE NOTES	Sandy Loam (80%), Coral and Pebbles (20%)	Paving layer from the path leading to the house.
TU2/5/6	III	SEE NOTES	Sandy Loam (40%), Large Cobbles and Small Boulders (40%)	Construction fill underlying the path, or flood deposit (?).
TU5	IVa	SEE NOTES	Sand, Compact	Compact layer of reddish sand (cf. TU1 LyIIIb), possible pavement layer.
TU2/6	IVb	SEE NOTES	Sandy Loam (50%), Coral Fragments (50%)	Possible lenses of coral pavement.
TU2/5/6	V	SEE NOTES	Sand	Beach sand deposit.
TU6	VI	SEE NOTES	Sand (40%), Coral Fragments (60%)	Coral lens.
TU6	VII	SEE NOTES	Sand	Beach sand deposit.
TU6	VIII	SEE NOTES	Sand (70%), Waterworn Cobbles (30%)	Possible flood/storm surge deposit.
TU6	IX	SEE NOTES	Sand	Beach sand deposit.
TU6	X	SEE NOTES	Sand (75%), Pebbles and Small Cobbles (25%)	Possible flood/storm surge deposit.
TU3/4	I	SEE NOTES	Sandy Loam	Topsoil/recent sedimentary deposition.
TU3/4	F01 (PN130)	SEE NOTES	Sandy Loam (30%), Volcanic and Limestone Cobbles (65%), Mortar Fragments (5%)	Possible earth oven. Rounded pit feature filled with cobbles and rubbish.
TU3/4	F02 (PN131)	SEE NOTES	Sandy Loam (50%), Volcanic and Limestone Cobbles (50%)	Possible earth oven. Rounded pit feature filled with cobbles and rubbish, including large amounts of faunal material.
TU3/4	II	SEE NOTES	Clay Loam, Compact	Paving layer (cf. TU1 LyIIIb; TU5 LyIVa). Cut by earth oven/pit features.
TU3/4	III	SEE NOTES	Sandy Loam	Sedimentary deposit underlying the red clay loam (not excavated).
Anuikaraka				
TU1/2/3/4/5	I	[10YR2/2] Very Dark Brown	Loam	Topsoil.
TU1/3/5	IIa	[7.5YR2.5/2] Very Dark Brown	Loam (60%), Volcanic Cobbles and Pebbles (40%)	Rocky layer, probably a flood deposit from the nearby intermittent stream though there is a slight possibility this is a stone paving or levelling fill.
TU2/4	IIb	[10YR3/3] Dark Brown	Loam (95%), Pebbles (5%)	Much less rocky sediment closer to the stream, some shell and charcoal. Possibly accumulated from habitation/slope wash?

Site/Area	Layer/Feature	Munsell Colour	Sediment Texture	Brief Interpretation
TU1/2/3/4	III	[10YR3/3] Dark Brown	Loam	Subsoil layer?
TU2	IV	[7.5YR2/3] Very Dark Brown	Sand (85%), Pebbles and Cobbles (15%)	Rocky layer, probably a flood deposit.
TU6	I	[10YR2/2] Very Dark Brown	Loam (30%), Pebbles, Cobbles, and Boulders (70%)	Construction fill of the mound feature, high concentration of artefacts including shell, bone, charcoal, large cobbles of red ochre.
TU6	II	[10YR2/1] Black	Loam	Sediment underlying the mound; ground surface from before the mound was constructed.
TU6	III	[10YR2/1-2/2] Very Dark Brown	Loam (80%), Pebbles (20%)	Slightly lighter subsoil mottled in places with LyII, no cultural materials found.
Imua Mission				
TU1/2/4/5	I	[10YR2/2] Very Dark Brown	Loam	Topsoil. Sediment overlying the stone features.
TU1/2/4/5	F01 (PN193/194/203/204)	--	Small Boulders	Stone alignment, probably a garden path or fence footing, abuts/overlies abandonment layer (bioturbation-animal burrows)
TU1/2/4/5	IIa	[7.5YR2.5/2] Very Dark Brown	Loam (60%), Pebble-sized Lime Mortar (40%)	Destruction/abandonment layer from the house. Contains the bulk of cultural materials. Materials from this layer were disturbed by animal burrows.
TU4	IIb	[10YR3/2] Very Dark Greyish Brown	Loam	Abuts LyIIa, but lacks cultural materials, probably contemporaneous level but outside the area of the house.
TU1/2/4/5	III	[10YR3/3] Dark Brown	Clay Loam	Compact sediments underlying LyII. Subsoil.
TU3	I	[10YR2/2] Very Dark Brown	Loam	Topsoil.
TU3	II	[7.5YR2.5/2] Very Dark Brown	Clay Loam (90%), Pebble-sized Lime Mortar (10%)	Occupation layer from the house, includes mortar, ceramics, etc., but much lower concentration than TU1/2/4/5.
TU3	III	[7.5YR2.5/3] Very Dark Brown	Clay, Compact	Subsoil.
Watt Mission				
TU1	I	[10YR3/2] Very Dark Greyish Brown	Sandy Loam (60%), Small Pebbles (40%)	Topsoil/paving deposit, abuts the base of the building footings.
TU1	II	[10YR3/2] Very Dark Greyish Brown	Sandy Loam	Sediment underlying the building. Possibly a levelling fill, or the extant beach sand upon which the mission building was constructed.
TU1	III	[10YR2/1] Black	Sand (75%), Waterworn Pebbles and Cobbles (25%)	Beach terrace fill, predates the mission (bioturbation-animal burrows).

Site/Area	Layer/Feature	Munsell Colour	Sediment Texture	Brief Interpretation
TU1	IV	[10YR2/2] Very Dark Brown	Sand (95%) Waterowrn Pebbles (5%)	Deposit in which the human burial was discovered (excavation halted; burial uncovered but left in situ).
TU2	I	[10YR3/2] Very Dark Greyish Brown	Sandy Loam (80%), Pebbles (20%)	Topsoil and later 20th-century disturbance from construction of the nearby church.
TU2	II	[7.5YR3/1] Very Dark Grey	Sand	Possible mission-period deposit, with a small concentration of 19th-century material.
TU2	III	[7.5YR3/1] Very Dark Grey	Sand	Subsoil.
TU3	I	[10YR2/1-2/2] Very Dark Brown	Loamy Sand (90%), Pebbles (10%)	Topsoil.
TU3	F01 (PN226)	[10YR2/2] Very Dark Brown	Loam (70%), Pebbles and Cobbles (30%)	Later 20th-century (post-mission) posthole.
TU3	II	[7.5YR2.5/2]	Loamy Sand (97%), Pebbles (3%)	Fill layer. Later 20th century (post-mission).
TU3	III	[10YR2/1-2/2] Very Dark Brown	Loamy Sand (75%), Pebbles and Coral Fragments (25%)	Fill layer, possibly mission-era/19th century.
TU3	IV	[10YR2/1] Black	Sand (98%), Pebbles and Cobbles (2%)	Subsoil.
TU4	I	[10YR2/2] Very Dark Brown	Sandy Loam	Topsoil.
TU4	II	[10YR3/2] Very Dark Greyish Brown	Sandy Loam (85%), Coral Fragments (15%)	Fill or paving layer. Later 20th century (post-mission).
TU4	F01 (PN220)	[10YR3/2] Very Dark Greyish Brown	Sandy Loam (90%), Coral Fragments and Pebbles (10%)	Later 20th-century (post-mission) posthole.
TU4	IIIa	[7.5YR3/2] Dark Brown	Sandy Loam	Fill deposit.
TU4	IIIb	[7.5YR3/2] Dark Brown	Sandy Loam with Limestone Flecks	Fill deposit.
TU4	IV	[10YR2/1] Black	Sandy Loam (70%), Small Pebbles to Large Cobbles (30%)	Fill deposit. Overlies a deposit with fewer stone inclusions (not excavated).
TU5	I	[10YR2/2] Very Dark Brown	Loam	Topsoil.
TU5	II	[10YR3/6] Dark Yellowish Brown	Clay Loam	Fill deposit.
TU5	F01 (PN240)	--	Small Boulders	Possible stone alignment (wall footing?).
TU5	III	[10YR2/2] Very Dark Brown	Loam (80%), Mortar Fragments (20%)	Abuts the stone feature, mortar may relate to this.
TU5	IV	[10YR3/3] Dark Brown	Loam	Fill deposit.
TU5	V	[10YR2/2] Very Dark Brown	Loam	Fill deposit, probably transitioning to subsoil.

Site/Area	Layer/Feature	Munsell Colour	Sediment Texture	Brief Interpretation
TU6	I	[10YR2/2] Very Dark Brown	Loam	Topsoil.
TU6	II	[10YR2/2] Very Dark Brown	Loam (85%), Pebbles and Coral Fragments (15%)	Fill deposit.
TU6	III	[10YR2/2] Very Dark Brown	Clay Loam, Compact (90%), Pebbles (10%)	Fill deposit.
TU6	IV	[10YR2/1-2/2] Very Dark Brown	Sandy Loam (95%), Cobbles and Pebbles (5%)	Fill deposit. Overlies slightly darker, looser deposit (possibly the beach terrace sediment, cf. TU1 LyIII).
Kwaraka				
TU1	I	[10YR2/1] Black	Loam	Sediment overlying the construction fill of the mound.
TU1	II	[10YR2/2] Very Dark Brown	Sandy Loam (50%), Large Pebbles and Cobbles (50%)	Loose, rocky construction fill, contains some 19th/20th-century material in the top 30cm of the deposit, which probably have drifted down post-deposition from LyI; lower levels contained charcoal and faunal materials.
TU1	III	[10YR2/1] Black	Sandy Loam	Sediment from the surface upon which the mound was built.
TU2	I	[10YR3/3] Dark Brown	Sandy Loam	Topsoil.
TU2	II	[10YR2/1] Black	Sandy Loam (85%), Pebbles (15%)	Occupation/paving layer from the house, which is mid-20th century or later based on artefacts (plastic pen caps, etc.).
TU2	F01 (PN65)	[10YR2/1] Black	Sand (60%), Pebbles (40%)	Drip line with three associated small (5-10cm diameter) postholes from mid-20th-century house.
TU2	III	[10YR2/1] Black	Sandy Loam	Fill deposit containing some 20th-century material.
TU2	IV	[10YR2/2] Very Dark Brown	Sandy Loam	Slightly lighter sediment, contains charcoal and faunal materials only (predates the house).

Appendix C: Summary artefact tables, Erromango and Tanna sites

Erromango Summary Artefact Table (NISP)

	G. Gordon House	J. Gordon House	Robertson Mission	Undam	Grand Total
Alloy	**2**	**1**	**6**		**9**
Bar	2				2
Bullet			1		1
Button		1	4		5
Coin			1		1

	G. Gordon House	J. Gordon House	Robertson Mission	Undam	Grand Total
Aluminum			16		16
Fragment			2		2
Pull tab			5		5
Screen			1		1
Washer			8		8
Architectural stone	1				1
Architectural stone	1				1
Basalt flake	1		2	13	16
Basalt flake	1		2	13	16
Bird bone			1		1
Gallus(?)			1		1
Bone			16		16
Unid. bone			16		16
Brass			1		1
Shotgun shell			1		1
Brick	113		1		114
Brick	113		1		114
Bronze			2		2
Coin			2		2
Carbon rod			4		4
Carbon rod			4		4
Ceramic	2		4		6
Button			1		1
Pipebowl	1		3		4
Pipestem	1				1
Charcoal	317	501	446	70	1334
Bulk	281	166	432	69	948
Coconut shell	12	119	11	1	143
Tiny/crushed	0		0		0
Twig/branch	24		3		27
Twigs/branches		216			216
Coarse EW		12	1	3	16
Unid.		12	1	3	16
Coconut shell			3		3
Armband			3		3
Copper	1		7		8
Earring			1		1
Nail			2		2
Sewing pin			2		2
Strap	1				1
Tack			1		1
Wire			1		1

	G. Gordon House	J. Gordon House	Robertson Mission	Undam	Grand Total
Copper alloy	**1**	**3**	**11**		**15**
Bullet			1		1
Cap			1		1
Eyehook			1		1
Peg			1		1
Pipe			3		3
Safety pin			2		2
Sheet	1				1
Shell			1		1
Strap		3			3
Tack			1		1
Coral	**6**		**1**		**7**
Coral	4		1		5
Fragment	2				2
Crystal			**1**		**1**
Gem			1		1
Fire-cracked rock	**10**	**37**	**61**	**14**	**122**
Fire-cracked rock	10	37	61	14	122
Fish bone			**6**		**6**
Unid. fish bone			5		5
Elasmobranchii			1		1
Fish scale			**1**		**1**
Unid. fish scale			1		1
Garbage			**10**		**10**
Garbage			10		10
Glass	**258**	**648**	**279**		**1185**
Bead			1		1
Bottle	86	143	89		318
Bottle stopper		1			1
Bottle/jar			1		1
Drinking glass		1			1
Flake	3	2	8		13
Jar		3			3
Lightbulb			1		1
Marble			2		2
Mirror			7		2
Paste jewel			1		1
Plate			1		1
Unid.	116	36			152
Vessel	10	223	17		250
Vial		46	1		47
Window	43	193	155		391

	G. Gordon House	J. Gordon House	Robertson Mission	Undam	Grand Total
Iron	**232**	**204**	**650**		**1086**
Button		2			2
Clothespin spring			1		1
Cut nail		5	10		15
Finish nail			10		10
Fragment	44	8	237		289
Grate			1		1
Hinge	1				1
Hook		1			1
Key			1		1
Nail	52	41	156		249
Rod			1		1
Round wire nail	2	15	154		171
Screw			18		18
Staple			1		1
Strap			1		1
Tack			9		9
Vessel	22	62			84
Washer			3		3
Wrought nail	111	70	47		228
Lead	**3**	**1**	**1**		**5**
Piece		1			1
Sheet	1				1
Solder			1		1
Strap	2				2
Limestone	**1**	**3**	**4**	**4**	**12**
Limestone	1	3	4	4	12
Lithic flake, unid.			**1**		**1**
Lithic flake, unid.			1		1
Mammal bone			**54**		**54**
Unid. mammal bone			6		6
Sus scrofa			4		4
Sus(?)			44		44
Mammal tooth			**3**		**3**
Ovis/Capra(?)			1		1
Phocidae(?)			1		1
Sus scrofa			1		1
Metal			**1**		**1**
Thimble			1		1
Mineral			**4**		**4**
Clay			4		4

	G. Gordon House	J. Gordon House	Robertson Mission	Undam	Grand Total
Mortar	624	176	1403		2203
Mortar frag.	624	176	1403		2203
Nut shell			1		1
Nut shell			1		1
Other			1		1
Graphite			1		1
Plastic			21		21
Bead			1		1
Comb			3		3
Plastic			17		17
Porcelain	1	16	5		22
Closed vessel	1	4			5
Measuring cup		1			1
Open vessel			4		4
Teacup			1		1
Unid.		11			11
Pumice			20		20
Pumice			20		20
Red ochre	3		2		5
Red ochre	3		2		5
Red stone		1	3		4
Red stone		1	3		4
Refined EW	15	71	9		95
Bowl		5			5
Closed vessel		6			6
Jar		4			4
Open vessel	3	31	2		36
Plate		6	2		8
Platter		1			1
Unid.	12	18	5		35
Rubber			1		1
Sandal			1		1
Sea urchin spine	6		14	3	23
Abrader	2		2		4
Fragment	4		12	3	19
Sheetrock			7		7
Sheetrock			7		7
Shell	27	51	1215	14	1307
Unid. Shell	8	1	1		10
Arciidae	1		77		78
Bead	1				1
Button	1				1

	G. Gordon House	J. Gordon House	Robertson Mission	Undam	Grand Total
Cardiidae		1	3		4
Cerithiidae	2	1	62		65
Chiton			22		22
Conidae	2		294	1	297
Crustacean			2		2
Cymatiidae			16		16
Cypraea			105		105
Gafrarium			7		7
Limpet			5		5
Mitridae			1		1
Muricidae	1		40		41
Nacellidae			6		6
Nerita		10	142		152
Nerita sp.	1				1
Polymesoda			1		1
Spondylydae			16		16
Strombidae			25		25
Terebra				3	3
Tridachna sp.	1				1
Tridacna			29		29
Trochidae	2	1	118		121
Turbo	1	30	125		156
Turbo (operculum)			30		30
Turbo sp.	2				2
Unid.	4	7	86	10	107
Veneridae			2		2
Slate			**1**		**1**
Slate			1		1
Stone	**4**	**18**	**2**		**24**
Chip			1		1
Curl			1		1
Slate pencil	4	17			21
Unid.		1			1
Stone and metal			**1**		**1**
Stone and metal			1		1
Stoneware	**21**	**10**			**31**
Closed vessel	5	5			10
Jar	1	2			3
Lid		2			2
Unid.	15	1			16
Terra Cotta			**5**		**5**
Flowerpot			5		5

	G. Gordon House	J. Gordon House	Robertson Mission	Undam	Grand Total
Tin			1		1
Foil			1		1
Waterworn stone	2				2
Waterworn stone	2				2
Grand Total	1651	1753	4310	121	7835

Tanna Summary Artefact Table (NISP)

Row Labels	1912 Church	Imua Mission	Kwaraka	New Kwaraka	Watt Mission	Grand Total
Alloy	3	1			6	10
Button		1			3	4
Coin	3				3	6
Aluminum					6	6
Fragment					2	2
Plate					1	1
Washer					3	3
Basalt core		1				1
Basalt core		1				1
Basalt flake		29	6		1	36
Basalt flake		29	6		1	36
Bone		1	9		65	75
Unid. bone			9		19	28
Button		1				1
Chelonioidea(?)					1	1
Gallus(?)					2	2
Pteropus(?)					1	1
Unid.					42	42
Brass					1	1
Button					1	1
Ceramic		1	4	1	2	8
Figurine		1				1
Pipebowl			2	1		3
Pipestem			2		2	4
Charcoal		81	446	1978	508	3013
Bulk		45	326	648	480	1499
Bulk (Point Prov.)				7		7
Coconut shell		25	120		22	167
Coconut shells				1207		1207
Crushed		0		0		0
Nut shell (burned)					1	1
Point prov				15		15
Point prov charcoal					3	3
Twig/branch					2	2
Twigs/branches		11		99		110
Twigs/branches (Point prov.)				2		2

Row Labels	1912 Church	Imua Mission	Kwaraka	New Kwaraka	Watt Mission	Grand Total
Coarse EW					2	2
Unid.					2	2
Composite		3				3
Button		3				3
Copper	1					1
Coin	1					1
Copper alloy		4	2		2	8
Fragment			2			2
Nail					1	1
Nub		1				1
Strap		3				3
Tube					1	1
Coral		1			2	3
Coral		1			2	3
Crustacean		2				2
Unid. Crustacean		2				2
Fire-cracked rock		9	6		53	68
Fire-cracked rock		9	6		53	68
Fish bone			2		1	3
Unid. fish bone			2		1	3
Fish tooth					1	1
Tetraodontidae(?)					1	1
Foam					1	1
Foam					1	1
Garbage			1		3	4
Garbage			1		3	4
Gill plate					1	1
Unid. gill plate					1	1
Glass	6	738	105	1	257	1107
Bead			2			2
Bottle		13	19	1	11	44
Bottle/jar		2				2
Button		1			1	2
Drinking glass	1					1
Flake			36		15	51
Marble	2				1	3
Other					1	1
Shotglass					5	5
Syringe			4			4
Vessel			30		15	45
Window	3	722	14		208	947
Glass and metal			1		1	2
Clasp					1	1
Lightbulb			1			1
Gum					1	1
Unid.					1	1

Row Labels	1912 Church	Imua Mission	Kwaraka	New Kwaraka	Watt Mission	Grand Total
Human tooth			2			2
Homo sapiens			2			2
Iron	1	1641	640	102	2026	4410
Ball					1	1
Block					1	1
Box					19	19
Button					1	1
Cut nail		11	2		3	16
Eyelet			1		1	2
Finish nail					2	2
Fragment		56	611	102	1797	2566
Large fragment			1			1
Lock					1	1
Nail		87	10		81	178
Plate		1				1
Round wire nail		30	15		107	152
Screw	1				8	9
Spiral nail					1	1
Spring					1	1
Vessel		34				34
Wrought nail		1422			2	1424
Lead			1			1
Ammunition, rifle bullet			1			1
Mammal bone		5	107	34	9	155
Unid. mammal bone		5	64		5	74
Bos(?)			1		2	3
Sus scrofa			1		1	2
Sus(?)			41	34	1	76
Mammal bone/tooth			2			2
Sus scrofa			2			2
Mammal tooth			26	12	2	40
Unid. mammal tooth			6			6
Canis(?)					1	1
Capra(?)			2			2
Sus scrofa			18	12		30
Sus(?)					1	1
Metal					2	2
Fragment					1	1
Safety Pin					1	1
Mineral					1	1
Ochre					1	1
Mortar	9	1628			943	2580
Mortar frag.	9	1628			943	2580
Nut shell					1	1
Nut shell					1	1

Row Labels	1912 Church	Imua Mission	Kwaraka	New Kwaraka	Watt Mission	Grand Total
Plastic	1		9		18	28
Button	1				2	3
Figurine			1			1
Fragment					2	2
Pen			1			1
Pen cap			2			2
Plastic			5		11	16
Plate					1	1
Rope					1	1
Toothbrush					1	1
Porcelain					2	2
Closed vessel					2	2
Pumice					1	1
Pumice					1	1
Red ochre		3		76		79
Red ochre		3		76		79
Refined EW		2735			2	2737
Bowl		11				11
Chamberpot		50				50
Knob					1	1
Open vessel		381			1	382
Other		2				2
Plate		2				2
Strainer		9				9
Unid.		2280				2280
Sea urchin spine		29			20	49
Abrader					1	1
Fragment		29			19	48
Seed				2		2
Seed				2		2
Shell	2	569	161	103	1383	2218
Unid. Shell					2	2
Arcidae		19				19
Arciidae			6		178	184
Buccinidae			2			2
Cerithiidae		140	1		61	202
Chiton			1		12	13
Conidae		18	5		160	183
Conidae(?)	1					1
Conus		28				28
Cowrie		3				3
Crustacean		1			4	5
Cymatiidae					3	3
Cymattidae		10				10
Cypraea		24	3	3	135	165
Gafrarium		49			2	51

Row Labels	1912 Church	Imua Mission	Kwaraka	New Kwaraka	Watt Mission	Grand Total
Limpet		33			50	83
Muricidae		2	4		18	24
Nerita		28	3		55	86
Olividae		1				1
Ostreidae		9				9
Pectinidae					2	2
Pendant		1				1
Polymesoda		13				13
Pulmonadae		10			167	177
Spondylydae			1		46	47
Strombidae		4	1		6	11
Tonnidae			1			1
Tridacna					2	2
Triton		59				59
Trochidae		36	17		126	179
Turbo		20	53	97	166	336
Turbo (operculum)			18		37	55
Unid.	1	61	45	3	151	261
Stainless					1	1
Straight pin					1	1
Stone		3		2	16	21
Adze				2		2
Pendant					1	1
Red crystal					6	6
Slate pencil		3			3	6
Tool					1	1
Volcanic rock					5	5
Stoneware		4			2	6
Bottle		1				1
Jar					1	1
Open vessel		1				1
Unid.		2				2
Vessel					1	1
Wood	25					25
Wood	25					25
Writing slate		15			34	49
Writing slate		15			34	49
Grand Total	48	7503	1524	2317	5377	16769

Appendix D: Radiocarbon dates

BETA Sample No.	Deposit	calAD(68%)	calAD(95%)	Conventional 14C Age
389338	TN/KW New Kwaraka Mound 9/TU6 Construction Fill	1665–1805	1655–post-1950	210 +/-30BP
389339	TN/KW New Kwaraka Mound 9/TU6 Base of Excavations (120cmbs)	1510–1645	1500–1655	330 +/-30BP
389340	TN/KW Watt Mission Burial Context	1155–1215	1055–1225	910 +/-30 BP
389341	ER/DB Robertson House TU6 Base of Excavations	1700–post-1950	1680–post-1950	130 +/-30 BP

Appendix E: Museum objects sorted by museum and island

Note: Island names in bold, objects from each island follow below. Because of page size limitations, list is composed of two sections: Section 1 covers (alphabetically) the museums from Auckland to Nova Scotia; Section 2 covers (alphabetically) the museums from Otago to Weltmuseum and the Grand Total.

Section 1: Auckland Museum-Nova Scotia Museum

Island	Auckland Museum	Australian Museum	Hunterian Museum	Museums Glasgow	National Museum of Scotland	New Brunswick Museum	Nova Scotia Museum
Ambrym					1		
Arrow					1		
Aneityum	3	14	1	14	33		2
Adze, stone	1			1	3		
Basket				2			
Bead		1					
Belt					1		
Blindfold					1		
Canoe model			1	1	1		
Club		1					
Comb	1				1		
Coral					1		
Dance club		1					
Doigtier/spear thrower					2		
Drill bit					1		
Feather ornament					2		
Fish gouge					2		
Flute				1			
Greenstone pendant				1	1		
Head scratcher		1					
House model					1		
Kava bowl				1	1		
Love charm		1					
Magic stone				1	1		
Neck rest				1	1		

Island	Auckland Museum	Australian Museum	Hunterian Museum	Museums Glasgow	National Museum of Scotland	New Brunswick Museum	Nova Scotia Museum
Necklace				1	2		
Pendant					1		
Sacred stone							2
Shell scraper					8		
Skirt				3			
Sleeping mat					1		
Sling					1		
Slit gong		1					
Stone axe		1					
Tapa	1						
Whale's tooth pendant		7					
Wooden tool					1		
Aniwa					**1**		
Basket					1		
Anuta/Erro?	**1**						
Comb	1						
Efate				**1**			
Canoe model				1			
Emae				**5**	**1**		
Fan					1		
Shell ornament				5			
Erromango	**7**	**120**	**3**	**12**	**24**	**1**	**24**
Costume piece							
Adze, shell		2					
Adze, stone		10					
Apron							
Arrow	4						
Basalt		1					
Basket and bundles, magic							
Belt							
Bow							
Candlenut		19					
Carved bamboo		1			4		
Club	1	32	3	4	9		9
Coconut shell armband		2					
Comb		1		1			
Coral charm		1					
Dagger							
Digging stick		1					
Drill		2					
Fish palate charm		12					
Hatchet		1			1		
Headrest				1			
Magic stone		2					

Island	Auckland Museum	Australian Museum	Hunterian Museum	Museums Glasgow	National Museum of Scotland	New Brunswick Museum	Nova Scotia Museum
Necklace		1					
Quartzite		1					
Quiver							
Quiver/arrows					1		
Red ochre		1					
Sacred stone							
Scraper		1					
Sinker		1					
Skirt		4		4	3	1	
Sleeping mat							
Slit gong		1					
Stone money	1	13			1		4
Tapa	1	6		2	2		4
Tapa beater		2			3		7
Throwing club		1					
Whale's tooth necklace		1					
Erromango(?)		**13**					
Miniature pot		13					
Futuna		**18**		**13**	**29**		
Abrader							
Basket				4	1		
Box				1			
Canoe model					1		
Club		1					
Coconut shell armband		4		4	3		
Coral gods		5					
Ear plug		1					
Earring					1		
Greenstone pendant		2					
Pearl shell				2			
Pearl shell ornament		3			19		
Sacred stone							
Shell armlet				1			
Throwing club		2			1		
Tortoise shell				1			
Whale's tooth pendant					3		
Malakula				**1**	**1**		
Adze, shell							
Figurine							
Pearl shell ornament					1		
Shell ornament				1			
New Caledonia	**2**			**5**	**2**		
Adze, greenstone	2						
Doigtier/spear thrower					2		
Necklace				1			
Pearl shell ornament				4			

Island	Auckland Museum	Australian Museum	Hunterian Museum	Museums Glasgow	National Museum of Scotland	New Brunswick Museum	Nova Scotia Museum
New Caledonia/New Hebrides					1		
Adze, greenstone					1		
New Hebrides	**14**	**4**	**3**	**36**	**27**	**67**	**39**
Adze				1			
Adze, limestone							1
Adze, shell					3	10	
Adze, stone		1			2	6	14
Armguard					1		
Arrow						18	
Axe handle		1					
Bamboo				1			
Basket	1						
Bead	1						
Belt							
Boomerang							
Bow						5	
Canoe model							1
Carved bamboo							1
Chisel							
Club	5			3	1		3
Coconut shell armband							
Comb	1				8	10	
Cord							1
Dance club				1			
Ear plug				1			
Ear spool				1		2	
Earring				4			
Fan							
Fishhook				1		2	
Flute				1			
Greenstone							1
Greenstone pendant				1	6		
Hair							
Hat, Western							
Hatchet							2
Headrest							2
Kava bowl							1
Kava root				1			
Lasso		1					
Musical instrument						2	
Neck rest							
Necklace	1			1	1	4	
Paddle				1			
Pan pipes				1	1		

Island	Auckland Museum	Australian Museum	Hunterian Museum	Museums Glasgow	National Museum of Scotland	New Brunswick Museum	Nova Scotia Museum
Pearl shell ornament				3			
Pig tusk						1	
Pipe			2				
Pottery							
Pudding knife							6
Sacred stone							
Sandalwood				1			
Scraper	2						
Shell ornament							2
Shell trumpet				1			
Skirt				3		1	
Sleeping mat				1			
Spear							4
Spiderweb cone	2					1	
Spiderweb purse				1			
Stone tool				3	4		
Tapa							
Tapa beater	1						
Throwing club		2					
Whale's tooth pendant				4		5	
Yam knife							
Tanna	**8**	**20**	**1**	**8**	**6**	**2**	**1**
'Death stone'							
Adze, shell		1					
Adze, stone	1						
Arrow	1					1	
Bamboo				1			
Bamboo 'churn'							
Belt		1					
Bow						1	
Bracelet	1						
Club	2	2		1	1		1
Coconut shell armband							
Earring		2		1			
Feather ornament				2	1		
Greenstone pendant							
Hair				2			
Necklace	1	1					
Pan pipes							
Pearl shell ornament	1						
Polished stone							
Seed pod		4					
Shell money		1					
Shell ornament					1		
Skirt		1			1		

Island	Auckland Museum	Australian Museum	Hunterian Museum	Museums Glasgow	National Museum of Scotland	New Brunswick Museum	Nova Scotia Museum
Slaying stone		1					
Stone 'adze'	1						
Stone axe							
Throwing club		5	1	1	2		
Yam stone		1					
Tongoa				2	1		
Adze, stone				1			
Breastplate				1			
Canoe model					1		
Grand Total (each museum)	35	189	8	97	127	70	66

Section 2: Otago Museum-Grand Total (all museums)

Island	Otago Museum	Queensland Museum	Redpath Museum	Royal Ontario Museum	University of Aberdeen Museums	Welt-museum	Grand Total (all museums)
Ambrym							1
Arrow							1
Aneityum			1		2		70
Adze, stone							5
Basket			1				3
Bead							1
Belt					1		2
Blindfold							1
Canoe model							3
Club							1
Comb							2
Coral							1
Dance club							1
Doigtier/spear thrower							2
Drill Bit							1
Feather ornament							2
Fish gouge							2
Flute							1
Greenstone pendant							2
Head scratcher							1
House model							1
Kava bowl							2
Love charm							1
Magic stone							2
Neck rest							2
Necklace							3
Pendant							1
Sacred stone							2

Island	Otago Museum	Queensland Museum	Redpath Museum	Royal Ontario Museum	University of Aberdeen Museums	Welt-museum	Grand Total (all museums)
Shell scraper							8
Skirt					1		4
Sleeping mat							1
Sling							1
Slit gong							1
Stone axe							1
Tapa							1
Whale's tooth pendant							7
Wooden tool							1
Aniwa							**1**
Basket							1
Anuta/Erro?							**1**
Comb							1
Aoba	**1**						**1**
Kava bowl	1						1
Efate							**1**
Canoe model							1
Emae							**6**
Fan							1
Shell ornament							5
Epi/Paama				**1**			**1**
Club				1			1
Erromango	**4**	**11**	**70**	**6**	**11**	**41**	**334**
'Costume piece'						1	1
Adze, shell							2
Adze, stone							10
Apron						3	3
Arrow			38	1		27	70
Basalt							1
Basket and bundles, magic			5				5
Belt						2	2
Bow				1	1	4	6
Candlenut							19
Carved bamboo							5
Club	1	9	2		8	3	81
Coconut shell armband							2
Comb							2
Coral charm							1
Dagger					1		1
Digging stick							1
Drill							2
Fish palate charm							12
Hatchet					1		3
Headrest							1

Island	Otago Museum	Queensland Museum	Redpath Museum	Royal Ontario Museum	University of Aberdeen Museums	Welt-museum	Grand Total (all museums)
Magic stone							2
Necklace							1
Quartzite							1
Quiver			1				1
Quiver/arrows							1
Red ochre							1
Sacred stone	1						1
Scraper							1
Sinker							1
Skirt		1	16	2			31
Sleeping mat						1	1
Slit gong							1
Stone money	2		1				22
Tapa		1	4	2			22
Tapa beater			3				15
Throwing club							1
Whale's tooth necklace							1
Erromango(?)							**13**
Miniature pot							13
Futuna	**3**				**3**		**66**
Abrader	2						2
Basket							5
Box							1
Canoe model							1
Club							1
Coconut shell armband							11
Coral gods							5
Ear plug							1
Earring							1
Greenstone pendant							2
Pearl shell							2
Pearl shell ornament					3		25
Sacred stone	1						1
Shell armlet							1
Throwing club							3
Tortoise shell							1
Whale's tooth pendant							3
Malakula				**1**	**1**		**4**
Adze, shell				1			1
Figurine					1		1
Pearl shell ornament							1
Shell ornament							1
Malakula, Solomon Is.		**3**					**3**
Ear spool		3					3

Island	Otago Museum	Queensland Museum	Redpath Museum	Royal Ontario Museum	University of Aberdeen Museums	Welt-museum	Grand Total (all museums)
New Caledonia							**9**
Adze, greenstone							2
Doigtier/spear thrower							2
Necklace							1
Pearl shell ornament							4
New Caledonia/New Hebrides							**1**
Adze, greenstone							1
New Hebrides	**3**	**5**	**46**	**15**	**15**	**7**	**281**
Adze					5		6
Adze, limestone							1
Adze, shell			2	3			18
Adze, stone			8	1			32
Armguard							1
Arrow							18
Axe handle							1
Bamboo							1
Basket			1		1	1	4
Bead				2			3
Belt				1			1
Boomerang					4		4
Bow							5
Canoe model							1
Carved bamboo		2	5				8
Chisel				1			1
Club				6	1	1	20
Coconut shell armband	1		8		3		12
Comb			10			2	31
Cord							1
Dance club							1
Ear plug							1
Ear spool							3
Earring							4
Fan			1				1
Fishhook							3
Flute		1		1			3
Greenstone							1
Greenstone pendant							7
Hair			2				2
Hat, Western			1				1
Hatchet	1						3
Headrest							2
Kava bowl							1
Kava root							1
Lasso							1

Island	Otago Museum	Queensland Museum	Redpath Museum	Royal Ontario Museum	University of Aberdeen Museums	Weltmuseum	Grand Total (all museums)
Musical instrument							2
Neck rest						1	1
Necklace			5				12
Paddle							1
Pan pipes						1	3
Pearl shell ornament							3
Pig tusk							1
Pipe							2
Pottery			1				1
Pudding knife			1				7
Sacred stone	1		1				2
Sandalwood							1
Scraper							2
Shell ornament							2
Shell trumpet							1
Skirt							4
Sleeping mat							1
Spear						1	5
Spiderweb cone							3
Spiderweb purse							1
Stone tool							7
Tapa		2					2
Tapa beater							1
Throwing club							2
Whale's tooth pendant							9
Yam knife					1		1
Tanna	**7**	**2**			**3**	**2**	**60**
'Death stone'	1						1
Adze, shell							1
Adze, stone							1
Arrow							2
Bamboo							1
Bamboo 'churn'	1						1
Belt							1
Bow						1	2
Bracelet							1
Club		2			2		11
Coconut shell armband	1						1
Earring							3
Feather ornament							3
Greenstone pendant	1						1
Hair							2
Necklace							2
Pan pipes	1						1
Pearl shell ornament	1						2

Island	Otago Museum	Queensland Museum	Redpath Museum	Royal Ontario Museum	University of Aberdeen Museums	Welt-museum	Grand Total (all museums)
Polished stone	1						1
Seed pod							4
Shell money							1
Shell ornament							1
Skirt							2
Slaying stone							1
Stone 'adze'							1
Stone axe						1	1
Throwing club					1		10
Yam stone							1
Tongoa							**3**
Adze, stone							1
Breastplate							1
Canoe model							1
Grand Total (each museum)	18	21	117	23	35	50	**Total Assemblage: 856**